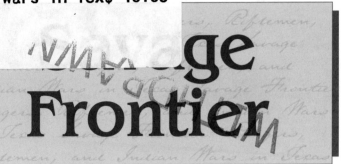

Frontier

Rangers, Riflemen, and
Indian Wars in Texas

Volume I
1835-1837

Stephen L. Moore

D1379519

Republic of Texas Press
Plano, Texas

Library of Congress Cataloging-in-Publication Data

Moore, Stephen L.
  Savage frontier : rangers, riflemen, and Indian wars in Texas /
  Stephen L. Moore.
    p. cm.
  Includes bibliographical references and index.
    ISBN 1-55622-928-3
    1. Indians of North America—Wars—Texas. 2. Indians of North
  America—Texas—Government relations. 3. Texas Rangers—History. 4.
  Frontier and pioneer life--Texas--History. 5. Texas—Politics and
  government—1836-1846. I. Title.
  E78.T4 M675 2002
  976.4--dc21   2002000480

Republic of Texas Press is an imprint of Wordware Publishing, Inc.
No part of this book may be reproduced in any form or by
any means without permission in writing from
Wordware Publishing, Inc.

Printed in the United States of America

ISBN 1-55622-928-3
10 9 8 7 6 5 4 3 2 1
0202

All inquiries for volume purchases of this book should be addressed to
Wordware Publishing, Inc., at 2320 Los Rios Boulevard, Plano, Texas 75074.
Telephone inquiries may be made by calling:

(972) 423-0090

Table of Contents

Volume 1

Prologue

The Indians of the prairies have no local habitations, and, therefore, we can not hope to conquer them by any number of troops . . .
Everything will be gained by peace, but nothing will be gained by war.

President Sam Houston's address to First Congress of Texas, May 5, 1837.

As long as we continue to exhibit our mercy without showing our strength, so long will the Indians continue to bloody the tomahawk.

President Mirabeau B. Lamar's inaugural address to Third Congress of Texas, December 9, 1838.

President Houston's message before the First Congress of the Republic of Texas stressed that the government should pursue a conciliatory policy towards the Indians to help prevent depredations on Texas settlers. His successor, President Lamar, adopted a far less tolerant Indian policy upon taking leadership of Texas and its frontier forces.

From the first rangers employed by Stephen F. Austin in 1823, settlers of Texas had been subjected to Indian hostilities from the earliest days of colonization. Militia districts and periodic ranging companies were employed during the next decade to protect the settlements, largely from attacks by hostile coastal Karankawas.

The year 1835 was significant in that it saw a whole new level of fighting between the whites and native Indians. Depredations became more frequent, but more importantly, the settlers became more organized to offensively take the fight to the Indians. The Texas Rangers were formally and legally organized during 1835 and the first true ranger expedition was carried out during that summer.

Many books have been written on the rangers and the Texas Indian wars, but none have taken a comprehensive look at the pivotal period of 1835-1839. Indian depredations and frontier conflicts reached a climax during this period. Ranging battalions were organized and battle tactics were refined. By late 1839 some Indian tribes had been driven from the republic. Some of the brightest Texas Ranger leaders, fabled for their exploits in the 1840s, cut their teeth in battles during the 1830s.

Savage Frontier is the first in-depth study of the Texan leaders, the expeditions, and the battles that shaped the frontier systems of future decades. Select fights and a few leaders of the late 1830s have previously received great attention. Other Indian fights, ranger leaders, and entire campaigns have received little to no attention in histories of this period.

Walter Prescott Webb's *The Texas Rangers*, published in 1935, paints a broad picture of this force from its creation through the early 1900s. Webb's pioneer account gives a compact history of the 1830s rangers. Subsequent works have only delved a little deeper, focusing primarily on the battles for which there is ample documentation available.

For this manuscript, numerous military, county, and social histories of early Texas were consulted on the early Texas Indian wars in order to bring new details to each battle covered. As often as possible, the events of the 1830s are allowed to be told firsthand through the participants whose stories were captured in newspaper articles, diaries, letters, or by early historians. We are fortunate in that some early rangers, such as George Bernard Erath and Noah Smithwick, left vivid memoirs that detail the 1830s ranging service. Such recollections are even more powerful when accurate dates are added via the use of available republic-era documents.

Original letters and documents quoted are done so in the language of the original authors. However, I have chosen to correct spelling and add punctuation in many cases for readership. No words are added to such quotes, with any exceptions denoted by [ ] brackets. Some historians may argue against this methodology, but these quotes are more significant when the reader can clearly understand what was being expressed in the writer's limited grammar and spelling abilities.

Setting the record straight on dates and service periods for the various ranger and riflemen companies was accomplished with the cooperation of Donaly Brice and the staff of the Texas State Archives. Over the course of several years, Mr. Brice has furnished copies of numerous muster rolls, company pay rolls, and other primary source material.

Considerable information was obtained from the Republic of Texas Audited Claims, Public Debt Claims, Pension Papers, and Unpaid Debt microfilm series. These files contain the original service papers filled out by the men and their companies during their service period. These documents give insight into the locations of companies, their tenure of service, payroll information, personnel losses, recruitment efforts, and eyewitness accounts of various battles or skirmishes. They were also vital in my efforts to reconstruct some of the missing muster rolls of the 1830s.

These records helped to clarify dates of key events, which have in some cases been recorded inaccurately. For example, the 1839 mounted rifleman expedition led by Colonel John Neill is often shown as having occurred in 1838. Just as often, the leader of this expedition is erroneously listed as James Clinton Neill. Oftentimes these mistakes were made from someone's use of a second-hand-source, such as a participant's recollections passed along to them by another person.

Numerous ranger records, army papers, muster rolls, and other military documents were forever lost when the Adjutant General's office was burned in 1855 and during a fire in the Texas Capitol in 1881. Other records have disappeared from the Texas Archives over time. Setting the record straight between fact and folklore is thus much more difficult.

My interest in the Texas frontier wars originally stemmed from family research. Great-great-great grandfather Thomas Alonzo Menefee and his father Laban Menefee both served as Texas Rangers during the Indian campaigns of 1839. Great-great-great-great-great grandfather John M. Morton served in an 1839 Houston County ranger battalion and fought in the Cherokee War that summer. Great-great-great grandfather William Turner Sadler was active in the 1830s Indian wars as a ranger, militia, and army captain. Great-great-great-great grandfather Armstead Bennett, a veteran rifleman of the 1811 battle of Tippecanoe in Indiana, supplied early ranger and militia companies with goods from his fortified home, known as Bennett's Fort, in present Houston County.

The earliest men fought with what little they had for everything they did not have: independence, freedom from Indian depredations, and security for their families.

Distinguishing who was truly a "Texas Ranger" during the 1830s has often been a subject of interpretation. The rangers of the Republic of Texas were at times formally commissioned in battalions by the republic's congress. Some served in militia districts during times when regular militia units were not on active campaign. Others served in conjunction with regular army units.

A few units consisted primarily of *Tejanos*, or Texas settlers of Spanish descent. There were even Indian units that served as scouts and rangers, including braves from Cherokee, Shawnee, Choctaw, Lipan Apache, and Delaware tribes.

Some men served with the early ranger companies as guides, teamsters, and volunteers, although their names were not officially entered on muster rolls. In this sense, these men were truly serving as rangers but were not hindered by the legal requirement of fulfilling a service enlistment should they chose to move on to other endeavors. Many early Texans thus served the Texas Rangers without ever having their names scribed to a roll for history's sake.

Historians of the rangers and Indian wars will find new material in this study. Campaign rosters and casualty lists have been compiled from archival data for such events as Colonel John H. Moore's 1835 Indian campaign, his 1839 Comanche offensive, and other expeditions made by the militia. Personal accounts help accent the drama of the time. An 1839 Texas hill country expedition led by Henry Karnes, for example, is enlivened by the details of the diary of one of the participants.

Volume 1 traces the evolution of the Texas Rangers from the earliest days to the legendary unit's legal creation during the Texas Revolution. One of the earliest movers for an organized Texas Rangers corps was Robert Morris Coleman. He commanded a company in 1835 and in July of that year called for a formal organization of the ranging forces. This was followed up on by Congress, and during the Texas Revolution three different ranger battalions were approved. This study does not exclusively focus on ranger history but does, however, reveal which companies truly served as such. For example, prior ranger histories have only identified a few of the companies operating during the Texas Revolution. A closer study reveals that as many as fourteen different companies of Texas Rangers served between October 1835 and April 1836.

More than forty men who had served as rangers under seven different captains either fought at San Jacinto or guarded the baggage at Harrisburg. An eighth company organized by the officer commanding the Texas Rangers should be considered, which would push this number to more than eighty rangers present for San Jacinto.

The revolutionary rangers played an important role in maintaining peace on the Texas frontiers during the absence of regular army companies. They were instrumental in building or manning at least four frontier outposts. Two ranger companies had skirmishes with Indians during the Texas Revolution. Another little-known fact is that a thirty-two-man ranger company from Gonzales, officially raised by a government-appointed ranger recruiter, paid the ultimate price for Texas independence in being sacrificed at the Alamo.

The ranger superintendent based at Fort Parker was killed soon after the revolution in one of the most well known Indian depredations of Texas history. A new battalion of rangers was soon formed under

Colonel Robert Coleman to cover the Colorado River frontier. His command would be short-lived. While he was away tending to new military installations, one of his junior officers allowed a man to die on the post. Coleman, the organizer of the Texas Rangers, was court-martialed and he died before he ever reached trial.

By mid-September 1836, thirteen ranger companies were in service on the frontiers. Collectively, these comprised approximately 450 men in four battalions, a new strength for this service. By the spring of 1837, however, only one battalion of five companies remained in service under Major William H. Smith. A full ten-company rifleman battalion was authorized by congress in June 1837, but the battalion never fully developed.

The rangers of 1837 were not able to carry out major campaigns against the hostile Indians but did engage in a number of fights. An expedition carried out during the approach of winter ended with a detachment of the rangers suffering terrible losses at the battle of the Stone Houses.

In Volume 2, *Savage Frontier* examines the key years of 1838 and 1839. The ranger battalion dwindled during late 1837 as men's enlistments expired. President Sam Houston was not interested in maintaining the army or regular ranging companies. Major Smith retired from the service, as did the ranger captains, until the senior lieutenant remaining discharged the balance of his rangers in April 1838.

Within months of the disbanding of the Texas Rangers, Major General Thomas Rusk began authorizing the use of his revamped Texas militia. During 1838 the Texas militia was out in force on a number of expeditions. In between periods of alert, Rusk allowed his militia brigades to maintain small battalions of mounted rangers.

These ranger battalions and the militia conducted offensive expeditions to the Kickapoo village in East Texas, up the Trinity River to the Cross Timbers area of present Dallas and Fort Worth, and even chased Caddo Indians across the United States border into Louisiana.

Continued depredations throughout Texas compelled newly elected President Mirabeau Lamar to adopt an extermination policy toward hostile Indians upon his taking office in December 1838. He immediately appropriated funds to build up a new Frontier Regiment of the Texas army, comprising both infantry and cavalry. During early 1839, Lamar's Congress also authorized numerous companies of Texas Rangers to serve the more troubled counties. One such unit in Houston County was that of Captain John Wortham. According to orders, Wortham's ranger company was "organized to protect and defend lives and property and whose duty was to die in such defense thereof."

The year 1839 was very active in the Indian wars of Texas. Depredations were particularly deadly for settlers, but the white settlers aggressively retaliated. Campaigns and offensive strikes were carried out by the army, cavalry, rangers, and even hastily-assembled civilian volunteer groups.

The new Frontier Regiment made two major offensive thrusts during the year—the Cherokee War during the summer and another campaign in December. Ranger companies also had a number of encounters during the year. Lamar authorized several other expeditions against Comanches and other hostile tribes. By year's end, the Cherokees had been largely driven from Texas and the Shawnees had been removed. The Comanches, however, would remain a formidable presence for some time.

The fabled Texas Rangers continue to serve the state on into the twenty-first century. Along the way they have evolved from the mounted frontiersmen to special lawmen. Today this small force falls under the supervision of the Texas Department of Public Safety. As recently as July 1999, the Texas Rangers received national recognition for ranger Drew Carter's peaceful apprehension of one of the FBI's most wanted murderers.

This modern perspective on the Texas Indian wars does not seek to justify the persecution or prejudices that prevailed in the 1830s. It uncovers new detail on the men that served during this time and should aid genealogists tracing their early ancestors' adventures on the old frontiers.

The spelling of names on muster rolls contained within this text has been corrected where possible. When in doubt, the original spelling from the roll is used. Although the majority of the 1830s rangers were of Anglo-European descent, there were many *Tejano* and Indian rangers as well. The enlistment officer often recorded their names by transliteration and translation. When an Indian name was difficult, the recruiter often scribed the brave's Anglo nickname, his adopted Spanish name, or a crude translation of his name via interpreter.

The modern conveniences and spreading cities of Texas make it more difficult with each passing decade to appreciate the duress of living on such remote frontiers where neighbors once banded together to fight "savages" with whatever weapons they could quickly muster.

Few of the Indian battlefields of early Texas history have received any more attention than a commemorative marker. One notable exception is the Cherokee War's Neches battlefield near Tyler, which the Dallas-based American Indian Heritage Center purchased in 1997 and is working to preserve. The battleground will remain intact, with a cultural center planned near the entrance to the property.

AIHC board member Kenneth Cade gave my wife, father, and I a tour of the battlefield in 1996. He took us to the site of the old Delaware village on the hill above the river, the ravine that the Indians used to hold off two Texan charges, and the open field where Chief Bowles was slain.

I remember reflecting on the irony of my own lineage. Present on one side of a musket had been great-great-great grandfathers Sadler and Morton. Firing back with bows and rifles from across the Neches battlefield were the people of my great-great-great grandmother Moore, who had descended from the Cherokees.

Standing near the monument to Chief Bowles on this hot, windless July afternoon, Cade read aloud a little poem called "Gathering" which he had written in tribute to the Indians. Visitors to this battleground have reported extreme temperature differences on even the hottest summer days. Some feel that this is the spirit of Bowles and his Cherokee warriors who died in this sacred graveyard while fighting to keep their land.

...The Great Spirit is calling to you and me. Do we hear the voice?
It is like the beat of a distant drum moving closer every day.
It echoes like the love song of the flute on the still air of
the East Texas night. The Great Spirit speaks, saying:

> *"Children, you must gather and unite.*
> *You are of the Real People family,*
> *You must secure the sacred site!"*

As Cade read his poem's last stanza, a healthy breeze began to blow over the little field, strong enough to bring a little relief from the relentless sun. The others of my little group made no comment, but it seemed to be more than chance. Perhaps, somewhere in the wind's whisper, the spirits of our Native American ancestors were trying to send a message. We should honor those who fought and died for their beliefs in the past, but we should not repeat the mistakes of such prejudices and persecutions in the future.

Acknowledgments

I must first acknowledge the tireless efforts of Donaly Brice of the Texas State Library and Archives Commission in Austin. He continually fulfilled search requests for muster rolls and various archival documents over the years that helped fill in the blanks in this manuscript. Dr. Frank Edens supplied many interesting documents, including an unpublished biography of Daniel Parker Sr. I am grateful to Elliott Kagen for loaning numerous copies of periodicals that contained articles on the rangers and Texas Indian wars.

For the illustrations, I had plenty of assistance. John Anderson of the Texas Archives helped in digging up old photos and provided advice on reproduction of artwork. Thanks also to Tom Shelton of the University of Texas Institute of Texan Cultures in San Antonio and Linda Peterson of the Center for American History, the University of Texas at Austin. My parents, Marshall L. and Kathy Moore Jr., were always willing to take a trip in search of photos or information. I also appreciate the continued support of Eliza Bishop of the Houston County Historical Commission and the photo she provided of her great-grandfather, Major John Wortham. Wilfred Clapp of Houston was kind enough to allow me to reproduce her painting of her great-grandfather, Captain Elisha Clapp. Mike Hiatt of the Old Fort Parker State Historical Park provided assistance in finding early illustrations relating to the Parker's Fort massacre. Special thanks to Mike Johnson for his help in scanning and retouching old illustrations.

For offering advice and reviewing the manuscript prior to publication, special thanks are due to historians Chuck Parsons, Bill O'Neal, Donaly Brice, and Allen Hatley. Ed Timms of *The Dallas Morning News* offered helpful information on the revolutionary rangers.

Aside from primary archival data, research for this book was greatly aided by published works of the leading authorities of Texas Indian Wars history. These authors had the foresight to record much of the eyewitness accounts, folklore, and memoirs of the early frontiersmen. Such crucial guides included John Henry Brown's *Indian Wars and Pioneers of Texas* (1880); J. W. Wilbarger's *Indian Depredations in Texas* (1889); James T. DeShields' *Border Wars of Texas* (1912); and A. J. Sowell's *Texas Indian Fighters* (1900) and *Rangers and Pioneers of Texas* (1884).

More recently, Dr. Walter Prescott Webb's *The Texas Rangers* (1965) was the forerunner of the modern histories of this state's fabled lawmen.

The following is a list of the key published sources from which eyewitness accounts and recollections have been extracted to add flavor to the campaigns and battles.

American Indian Heritage Center (courtesy of Eagle Douglas)
"Gathering." A poem written August 1995 by Kenneth R. Cade.

Naylor Company
DeShields, James T. *Tall Men with Long Rifles.* San Antonio: Naylor Company, 1935.

Pemberton Press
Gulick, Charles A. Jr., Winnie Allen, Katherine Elliott, and Harriet Smither. *The Papers of Mirabeau Buonaparte Lamar*, six volumes, 1922. Reprint. Austin: Pemberton Press, 1968.

Lane, Walter Paye. *The Adventures and Recollections of General Walter P. Lane.* Austin: Pemberton Press, 1970.

Reagan, John H. *The Memoirs of John H. Reagan.* Edited by John F. Jenkins. Austin: The Pemberton Press, 1968.

Presidial Press
Jenkins, John Holland. *Papers of the Texas Revolution 1835-1836.* Ten Volumes. Austin: Presidial Press, 1973.

State House Press (courtesy of Tom Munnerlyn)
Brown, John Henry. *Indian Wars and Pioneers of Texas.* 1880. Reprint. Austin: State House Press, 1988.

DeShields, James T. *Border Wars of Texas.* 1912. Reprint. Austin: State House Press, 1993.

Sowell, A. J. *Texas Indian Fighters. Early Settlers and Indian Fighters of Southwest Texas.* 1900. Reprint. Austin: State House Press, 1986.

_____. *Rangers and Pioneers of Texas.* 1884. Reprint. Austin: State House Press, 1991.

Wilbarger, John Wesley. *Indian Depredations in Texas.* 1889. Reprint. Austin: State House Press, 1985.

Texas State Historical Association
Benedict, J. W. "Diary of a Campaign against the Comanches." *Southwestern Historical Quarterly.* Vol. 32 (April 1929) 300-10.

Erath, George Bernard as dictated to Lucy A. Erath. *The Memoirs of Major George B. Erath, 1813-1891.* Austin: Texas State Historical Society, 1923. Reprinted by The Heritage Society of Waco in 1956.

Looscan, Adele B. "Capt. Joseph Daniels." *Texas Historical Association Quarterly*, Vol. V, No. 1 (1901-1902), 19-21.

Reagan, John Hunter. "Expulsion of the Cherokees from East Texas." *Quarterly of the Texas State Historical Association,* Vol. I (1897), 38-46.

University of Texas Press
Ford, John Salmon, edited by Stephen B. Oates. *Rip Ford's Texas.* Austin: University of Texas Press, 1994.
Jenkins, John Holland. Recollections of Early Texas. *The Memoirs of John Holland Jenkins.* Edited by John Holmes Jenkins III. Austin: University of Texas Press, 1958. Reprint. 1995.
McDowell, Catherine W. (ed.). *Now You Hear My Horn. The Journal of James Wilson Nichols, 1820-1887.* Austin: University of Texas Press, 1961.
Procter, Ben H. *The Life of John H. Reagan.* Austin: University of Texas Press, 1962.
Smithwick, Noah. *The Evolution of a State/Recollections of Old Texas Days.* Austin: University of Texas Press, 1983.
Williams, Amelia W. and Eugene C. Barker. *Writings of Sam Houston.* Austin: University of Texas Press, 1938-43.

University of Texas at Arlington (UTA Press)
McLean, Malcolm D. *Papers Concerning Robertson's Colony in Texas.* Published by the University of Texas at Arlington. Arlington, Tex: The UTA Press.

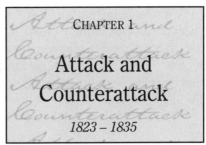

CHAPTER 1

Attack and Counterattack

1823 – 1835

The campground was ominously quiet as the first rays of sunlight filtered through the trees along Sandies Creek. The dawn air was cool on the mid-April morning in South Texas. The tranquility was violently interrupted by the sudden report of rifles and resounding war whoops as more than sixty Comanche Indians descended on the scene.

The men of the camp scrambled to make a stand. Improvising breastworks of carts, packsaddles, and trading goods, the besieged fired back at the howling Indians who outnumbered them by upwards of six to one. The contest was fierce, but it was over before it had begun.

From a small porthole type window in his pioneer cabin several hundred yards away, John Castleman could only watch the massacre in anguish. He was frustrated that he could not assist the besieged and that they had not heeded his advice.

His gut instinct was to open fire with his rifle, however futile the effort may prove to be. Only the pleading of Castleman's wife restrained him. The first shot he fired would only ensure that he, his wife, and his children would also be slaughtered. Even still, it was difficult to watch as others died before him.

Castleman and his pioneer family had become bystanders to a bloody Indian depredation in south central Texas. It was April 1835 when the Indians descended near his place and slaughtered a party of traders.

John Castleman, a backwoodsman from Missouri, had settled with his wife, four children, and his wife's mother in the autumn of 1833 fifteen miles west of Gonzales. His cabin often served as a place of refuge for travelers moving down the San Antonio Road from Gonzales. Castleman's place was located in present Gonzales County on Sandies Creek, a good watering hole. Indians were known to be about the area, and they had even killed his four dogs in one attempt to steal Castleman's horses.

On about April 15, 1835, a thirteen-man trading party with loaded pack mules from Natchitoches, Louisiana, made camp a few hundred yards from Castleman's cabin. The group included a French trader named Mr. Greesier, his two partners, and ten Mexican cart drivers and muleteers. Having noted Indian tracks about, he warned these traders that their lives were at stake if they did not use his place as a fortification for the night.[1]

The traders declined the offer to use Castleman's cabin, choosing to retire for the night near the waterhole. The Indians attacked these traders right at daylight, the yelling from which had awakened Castleman. The traders fired back and continued to hold their ground for some four hours while the Indians circled them. The attackers slowly tightened their circle as the morning sun rose, falling back temporarily whenever the traders managed to inflict damage on their own numbers.

The traders suffered losses and drew to a desperate point. The furious Comanches finally took advantage of their enemies' desperation and made an all-out onslaught from three sides. They succeeded in drawing the fire of the party simultaneously and left them momentarily unloaded. During this brief instant, the Indians rushed in with victorious war whoops and fell upon the traders in hand-to-hand combat.[2]

Raiding to acquire fine stock and other goods became a ruthless sport to the Comanche (translatable as "the real people" in Indian tongue) as settlement of Texas began to encroach upon the hunting lands the Indians had long claimed. By 1830 the Indian population in the territory of Texas was perhaps fifteen thousand compared to about seventeen thousand settlers of Anglo-European, Mexican national, and black origin. In combat with early settlers, the Comanche warriors had learned to exploit any advantage a battle might offer them, such as lengthy time required to reload weapons in the case of the French and Mexican traders. The determined Indians could accurately fire a half dozen arrows in the time it took an opponent to reload his rifle a single time. The battlewise Comanches forced the traders to discharge all their weapons at once before moving in to slaughter the men before they could reload.[3]

This last terrific charge was witnessed by Castleman from his window, and he immediately realized that it was all over for the poor traders. The victims were brutally mutilated and scalped. The Comanches stayed long enough to dispose of their own dead, round up the traders' mules, and collect all of the booty that was desired. As they slowly rode past his house single file, Castleman counted eighty surviving warriors, each shaking his shield or lance at the house as they passed.

Castleman waited until he thought it safe before visiting the battle-ground. He found no men still alive and found each to be horribly mutilated. The area was drenched in blood, littered with the strewn goods, and peppered with arrows stuck through boxes, saddles, and carts and lying broken on the ground. The Indians had only thrown the bodies of their own dead into a pool of water for the fiends of nature to dispose of.

John Castleman hurried back to his house, gathered his family, and set out immediately for Gonzales to carry the news.

In the early days of Texas, those who ventured into the prairies did so at their own risk. White settlements were only beginning to flourish. Those starting homes or farms farther north and west were venturing into territories long considered that of the local Indian tribes.

★ ★ ★ ★ ★

Battle on the Rio Blanco: April 1835

Castleman's story spread rapidly, and by the following morning a party of between twenty-seven and thirty men was saddled up in Gonzales and ready to go. The two principal early accounts of this episode differ slightly on the details of what followed and even as to who was in command.

Early Indian wars chronicler Andrew J. Sowell, whose uncle was among those in this party, wrote that Bartlett D. McClure, who had arrived in Texas in 1830, was elected captain of a twenty-seven-man pursuit party. John Henry Brown, another early Indian wars historian who likely obtained his account from less direct sources, says that Dr. James H. C. Miller was in charge. In the absence of good documentary evidence to support either man, McClure will be used here as the posse commander since Sowell knew many of the men who participated in this event.

Known participants of this party from Gonzales were Captain McClure, Dr. Miller, Mathew Caldwell, John Castleman, George Washington Cottle, James C. Darst, John Davis, Almeron Dickinson, William S. Fisher, David Hanna, Tom Malone, Daniel McCoy, Jesse McCoy, Jonathan Scott, Andrew Jackson Sowell, Landon Webster, Robert White, and Ezekiel Williams.[4]

Arriving at the scene of the battle near Castleman's, McClure's posse followed the trail of the Indians into the Guadalupe valley. They crossed the Guadalupe at a spot later called Erskine's Ford located some twelve miles from Seguin in present Guadalupe County. They proceeded toward Gonzales and crossed Darst Creek, where they soon found evidence of the Indians before them. For amusement, the Indians had apparently tied spools of thread to their horses' tails and let the string unwind itself as they passed over the prairies. This made for an easy trail, which the Texans pursued rapidly toward the northwest to the headwaters of Mill Creek.

The Indians continued onward slowly day and night, while Captain McClure's pursuers were forced to camp at night near the York's Creek divide when the trail was lost to darkness. While scouting out ahead on the second night, Andrew Sowell detected Indians singing and rode back to inform Captain McClure. The next morning the Texans found that they had only been about two miles from the Indians' camp. This camp was found on a high ridge overlooking the present town of San Marcos in Hays County.[5]

From this point, the Indians were entering the hill country where pursuit was becoming much more difficult. The Texans camped on the third night on the Blanco River in the cedar brakes. The scouts found plenty of sign that the Indians were just ahead of them. They moved forward cautiously the next morning and entered a valley just as a dense morning fog began to lift. As they did so, the yell of an advance Indian scout on the mountain across the river signaled to all that they had been discovered.[6]

Captain McClure ordered an immediate advance into the cedar brake near the river. The thick woods soon compelled his men to dismount their horses and proceed on foot. Two or three scouts were sent ahead. Sowell claims that these men were Almeron Dickinson and James Darst, while Brown's version has these men being Mathew Caldwell, Dan McCoy, and Ezekiel Williams. The remainder of the party moved slowly forward in single file, stooping and crawling as they went.

The scouts soon happened upon the Indians, who had stopped to eat. The scouts turned to sneak away but were discovered, and gunfire quickly erupted behind them as they fled. McClure and the others following prepared themselves at the sight of the spies, who were literally running for their lives from pursuing Indians. McClure, Miller, and others are said to have laid in ambush until their own men came running past. At that moment McClure then raised his rifle and fired at the first Indian to come in range.

Brown states that Caldwell, having been hotly pursued, passed through the small clearing and then immediately wheeled and fired a deadly shot into one of the Indians.[7] John Castleman, the witness to the horrible massacre of the traders just a week previous, is said to have also shot and killed an Indian. After losing two of their number to the Texans, the Indians shouted warnings to their fellows and fled.[8]

Andrew Sowell Sr. was among the settlers waiting as the Indians ran toward their ambush. His nephew, A. J. Sowell, later wrote:

> Several shots were fired, and a third Indian had his bow stick shot in two while in the act of discharging an arrow. Andrew Sowell attempted to fire with a flintlock rifle, but it flashed in the pan. He had stopped up the touch-hole to keep the powder dry in the fog, and had forgotten to take it out. The other Indians now ran back towards the river, yelling loudly. By this time most of the men had gotten clear of the brush and charged with McClure across the open ground.[9]

The early weapons used by the Texan volunteers in 1835 did not lend themselves to rapid firing. Most of the men who made up such hastily organized pursuit parties were settlers who survived by farming and hunting. Therefore their weapon of choice in the 1830s was most often a flintlock rifle such as the one described by Sowell. The early versions, commonly known by modern collectors as "Kentucky rifles," were generally made of polished maple or cherry wood with ornamental brass fittings. The caliber ranged from .36 to .45, and the gun's octagonal barrel was forty-four to forty-six inches in length.[10]

Monikers such as Kentucky rifle or Tennessee mountain rifle evolved due to the fact that the guns often arrived in Texas with immigrants from those American states. All were actually versions of the Pennsylvania long rifle, designed by German craftsmen who settled in Pennsylvania.[11]

These early rifles were considered extremely accurate. A good marksman could kill his prey from three hundred yards and could be especially deadly from one hundred yards. This was in comparison to those who carried the basic musket, which was considered inaccurate beyond fifty yards.

The smoothbore musket was better suited for infantrymen, who could quickly load the powder and ball. The Texans who became rangers and Indian fighters largely carried rifles, but some carried muskets. Muskets were much cheaper. By the time a new mounted ranger battalion was called for in December 1836, they were required to use rifles. The rifles were time-consuming to load; the rifle ball had to be carefully rammed down the muzzle with a greased patch.

Almost all of the early weapons in Texas were of the flintlock variety,

TEXAS FRONTIER WEAPONS

(*Above*) Cross-section of the 1830s rangers' tools of the trade. At top is an 1820s era .48-caliber Pennsylvania/Kentucky flintlock rifle. Directly below is a .60-caliber Ketland flintlock pistol. The slightly shorter barreled pistol is a .52-caliber derringer pocket pistol. Noted for his quality craftsmanship, Henry Deringer Jr. began manufacturing large caliber pistols in Philadelphia in 1806. Also shown are a nineteenth-century powder horn and a bowie knife. A staple of the early ranger's equipment, such a knife was an important secondary weapon, as well as an early camp tool.

(*Below*) Nineteenth-century Indian peace pipe tomahawk and Lipan Apache arrows. The arrows are distinguishable as Lipan by the colors around their shafts.

Author's photos, courtesy of the Texas Ranger Hall of Fame and Museum, Waco, Texas.

both muskets and rifles. During the 1820s, percussion caps were introduced to fire the powder charge in a weapon. The caps were more expensive and much harder to find supplies of, so flintlock continued to be the largest source of means to ignite the powder during the 1830s in Texas.

A flintlock rifle could be converted to percussion cap rifle by unscrewing the old lock and removing the hammer, powder pan, and frizzen. A new hammer was placed in the old fittings and a special plug was threaded into the old touch hole to hold the cap. The required parts were mass produced by several United States gunsmith plants. Texas gunsmiths and blacksmiths were capable of converting older rifles into percussion arms.

Aside from muskets and rifles, a smaller number of men also carried pistols. Most early 1830s pistols were also flintlocks, but these began converting to percussion caps by late in the decade. Henry Deringer's single shot pistol was a "belt pistol" for use in very close fighting. Samuel Colt patented the first practical repeating firearm in 1836, but there is little evidence of Colt revolvers being used by Texas military until late 1839 and early 1840.

Captain McClure's volunteer forces pursued the Indians to the Blanco River, where the fighting became more general. More of the fifty-odd Comanches were killed as they tried to cross the water with their stolen goods. Andrew Sowell shot and killed one Indian as he tried in vain to climb a steep bank on the far side. In the end, they left much of their spoils behind and moved swiftly from the area. The whites chose not to cross the river and continue their pursuit. They were fortunate to have not had any man killed or any serious injuries sustained.[12]

The colonists returned to their horses and found that only one had escaped, and it was soon recovered. They gathered up the more valuable of the goods that they could carry. Many Indian bows, shields, blankets, and buffalo robes were stashed along a bank on the river for another party to return for later.

The date of this 1835 Indian battle was a few days before April 20, as on this date William H. Steele wrote to empresario Sterling Robertson with details of the fight. Steele, who was just passing through en route to Béxar, wrote that the Gonzales citizens were said to have killed five Indians.[13]

The volunteer party had not relieved the area of its Indians problems, but it had made a statement to the raiders: The developing settlements of Texas were not about to give up without a fight.

★   ★   ★   ★   ★

Early Texas Rangers and Indian Battles: 1821-1834
Clashes between settlers and Indians were building to a new level of
intensity by the spring of 1835. Hostile encounters between the native
Americans and the newly arriving Texas settlers, however, had been
occurring for many years. One of the earliest clashes was reported in
1821 between a party of white settlers who attacked some coastal
Karankawa (translatable as "they live in the water" in native tongue)
Indians inhabiting Galveston Island.[14]

As the settlement of Texas progressed, encounters between colonists and the more hostile Indian tribes increased. White colonization of
Texas was arranged by empresario Moses Austin in 1821, but his son
Stephen Fuller Austin became known as the "Father of Texas" for fulfilling his father's land grant. Austin's original three hundred families,
known as the "Old Three Hundred," started colonies on land situated
along the Brazos River near present Washington County and along the
Colorado River near Columbus.

During the early days of colonization in Texas, settlers formed civilian posses to strike back against Indian raiding parties. The Mexican
governor organized the early settlers into two militia districts in late
1822. Male immigrants to Texas between the ages of eighteen and
fifty-five were soon included into the militia system, which boasted six
districts by November 1824.[15]

The roots of the legendary Texas Rangers can be traced back to two
early Texas settlers, John Jackson Tumlinson and Robert Kuykendall.
Tumlinson was serving as the *alcalde*, or civilian leader, of the Colorado
River settlement, and Kuykendall was an early militiaman who had led a
posse against Karankawa Indians in 1822. These two men wrote to Governor José Trespalacios on January 7, 1823, to ask permission to raise
fifteen men to serve with ten regular soldiers from San Antonio. The plan
was for these men to build blockhouses and small boats to make a combined land and sea attack on coastal Indians.

Thirty-year-old Lieutenant Moses Morrison, one of Austin's Old
Three Hundred settlers and the second-in-command of the Colorado settlement's militia district, became commander of the volunteers
requested by Tumlinson and Kuykendall. Morrison, a veteran of the U.S.
Army, was able to muster in ten men, who are credited by some with
being the first true rangers of Texas.

By definition, rangers were a group of armed men who operated
independently from a regular military organization. They were generally

self-armed, non-uniformed squads of civilians who patrolled the outer frontiers of a settled area to protect against Indian hostilities. Stephen F. Austin first used the term "rangers" to describe an employment offer for ten men under Lieutenant Morrison to provide protection. This note was written on the back of a proclamation by the Baron de Bastrop, another empresario born in the Netherlands, that was dated August 1823.

Moses Morrison's force was employed for the three-month period spanning May 5 - July 5, 1823. His muster roll shows the company to also include Corporal John McCrosky and Privates Caleb R. Bostwick, Pumpry Burnitt, John Frazer, William Kingston, Aaron Linville, Jesse Robinson, Samuel Sims, and John Smith.

An engraving of Stephen Fuller Austin (1793-1836). Dubbed the "Father of Texas," Austin was also instrumental in organizing the early militia of Texas and the first Texas Rangers. (From James T. DeShields' *Border Wars of Texas*.)

Of these men, Bostwick and Robinson had arrived in Texas the previous year. Linville had just arrived in 1823 and received a one-third league of land in present Matagorda County. John McCrosky was another of Stephen F. Austin's Old Three Hundred colonists in the present Brazoria and Austin Counties area. After serving in Morrison's company, he later was elected third lieutenant of a militia company at San Felipe de Austin on July 10, 1824.[16]

Lieutenant Morrison's men spent much of their three months hunting for food to survive on. They struggled with finding powder suitable for their guns and were not able to build any blockhouses. The men camped and explored near the mouth of the Colorado River but were brought back to the Colorado settlement in August.[17]

Austin's note was a plan to employ ten mounted rangers to be

The muster roll of Moses Morrison's ten-man company is on display at the Texas Ranger Hall of Fame in Waco. This unit is credited by some as being the first true Texas Ranger company. Bexar Archives (1717-1836). *The Center for American History, University of Texas at Austin*, CN Number 10095.

attached to the men under command of Lieutenant Morrison. They would act both as mounted scouts and as a rapid deployment force to pursue raiders while the militia guarded the settlements. The early colonists did not favor such a standing unit, and there is no evidence that this unit was ever properly formed. Austin's vision for companies of mobile rangers who remained on constant duty on the outer frontiers did not die, but his idea would take several more years to fully develop.[18]

John Jackson Tumlinson, who had requested the need for a ranger-type system in January 1823, was killed on July 6, 1823, by a band of Indians near the present town of Seguin in the Colorado settlement. Tumlinson and a companion, aide Joseph Newman, had been en route to San Antonio to secure ammunition requested by Moses Morrison's men when he was killed by Karankawa and Huaco Indians. His son John Jackson Tumlinson Jr., later a respected ranger captain, collected a posse and led them against a band of thirteen Huaco (Waco) Indians who had camped above the present town of Columbus. The posse leader's teenage brother, Joseph Tumlinson, acted as a scout for this unit and managed to kill the first Indian when the Texans surprised the Waco camp. Captain Tumlinson's posse killed all but one of the Indians.[19]

In June 1824 Austin reorganized his militia into five companies. Soon thereafter, Captains Jesse Burnam and Amos Rawls fought nine Karankawa Indians on the Colorado River, killing eight. Austin also sent Captain Aylett C. Buckner with a party of volunteers to the Waco Indian village to make a treaty with the Waco, Tawakoni, and Towash Indians.[20]

Captain Randall Jones' twenty-three-man militia company was authorized by Austin to make an expedition against a force of Indians who had killed several immigrants en route to Austin's Colony. Jones' men fought two skirmishes with the Indians in September 1824. In the first, the whites killed or drove away all of their attackers. On the following day, Captain Jones and his men made a surprise dawn attack on the Indians. They managed to kill an estimated fifteen Indians before losing three of their own killed and several wounded, forcing Jones to order a retreat.[21]

One of the little settlements that would remain a centerpiece for Indian troubles and revolution was Gonzales, the capital of Green DeWitt's young Texas colony. The area of DeWitt's Colony as contracted with the Mexican government included all of present Gonzales, Caldwell, Guadalupe, and DeWitt Counties and portions of Lavaca, Wilson, and Karnes Counties.

The peace in this area was shattered on July 2, 1826, when a party of Indians attacked a group of pioneers, stealing their horses and personal effects. Bazil Durbin was wounded by a rifle ball that drove so deeply into his shoulder that it remained there for the next thirty-two years of his life. The Indians next plundered the double log home of James Kerr, where John Wightman had been left alone in charge of the premises. Wightman was killed, mutilated, and had his scalp removed by the Indians. The fear spread by this depredation was enough to prevent the Gonzales area from being permanently settled again until the spring of 1828.[22]

The most serious encounter of 1826 occurred when Tawakoni Indians came into the settlements stealing horses and hunting the Tonkawa Indians they so hated. The Tonkawa name was derived from "they all stay together" but has been translated as "men who eat men." They were also reported to have killed and scalped a Mexican resident while on their depredation. The Indians made their camp in the bed of Ross Creek in present Fayette County near the town that later became La Grange. Captain James J. Ross led thirty-one militiamen out to fight these Indians on April 4, 1826. His party was composed of many future Fayette County settlers, including John J. Tumlinson Jr., John Cryer, and

S. A. Anderson. When Ross's men raided the Indian camp, they caught them by surprise. Some of the Indians were dancing around with fresh scalps, while others were parching corn or lying down. Of an estimated sixteen Indians, the Texans killed eight and wounded most of the others.[23]

Following Ross's raid, Stephen F. Austin proposed to wage an aggressive campaign against the hostile Waco and Tawakoni Indians, enlisting the help of the more friendly Cherokees, Shawnees, and Delawares. By June 1826 his militia had grown to five companies with 565 total troops. Captains Rawson Alley, William Hall, Horatio Chriesman, and Bartlett Sims did carry out one campaign but found the Indian villages empty.[24]

When a Mexican commandant ordered a suspension of the campaign until help could arrive from Mexico, Austin called a meeting of representatives in August from his militia districts. From this meeting the representatives decided to keep a force of "twenty to thirty mounted men" in service continually, with each landowner either serving or furnishing a substitute for one month for each league of land he owned. There is no record that these recommendations were ever approved by the Mexican government or that such ranging commands served in the late 1820s.

Perhaps the earliest confirmed existence of a true Texas Ranger company was in January 1827. Austin had taken his militia out to maintain order during the Fredonian Rebellion in Nacogdoches. To protect his colony from surprise Indian raids in his absence, Austin ordered Captain Abner Kuykendall and eight other men (John Walker, Early Robbins, Thomas Stevens, Barzillai Kuykendall, John Jones, William Kuykendall, James Kiggans, and John Furnash) "to range the country" between the Brazos and the Colorado along the San Antonio Road.[25]

The balance of 1827 and 1828 found Austin Colony settlers and the native Indians on somewhat better relations. In July 1829, however, a battle was fought against Indians who had taken control of Thomas Thompson's small farm near present Bastrop on the Colorado River. Thompson led ten men in a fight against the Indians, killing four and chasing away the others. Colonel Austin ordered two volunteer companies of fifty men raised. The companies were under Captains Oliver Jones and Bartlett Sims and under the supervision of Colonel Abner Kuykendall. Captain Harvey S. Brown raised another volunteer company during this time due to murders and depredations committed by Indians around the Gonzales area. Although Captain Sims and his company scouted extensively in pursuit of the Indians, these combined forces only managed to kill one Indian while on their offensive.[26]

The homes of Charles Cavina, who had immigrated to Texas in 1828 and received a league in Matagorda County, and neighbor Elisha Flowers were attacked by an estimated seventy Karankawa Indians in 1830 near Live Oak Bayou on Old Caney Creek in Austin's Colony. Four women in the Cavina house were killed, as was Mrs. Flowers. Two badly wounded girls survived the assault. Cavina raised sixty of Austin's settlers, and command was given to Captain Buckner. At the site of present Matagorda on the Colorado River, Buckner's men fought a heated battle with the raiding Indians. Among his volunteers who narrowly escaped death in this battle was Moses Morrison, who had been the organizer of what was arguably the earliest Texas Rangers. In the ensuing massacre, the vengeful Texans killed Indian men and women. As many as forty or fifty Indians were killed and the riverbanks literally ran red with blood.

By the early 1830s the volume of immigrants flowing into Texas strained the relationships between Mexican officials and the white settlers. Texas colonists seized the heavily fortified Mexican post on the Gulf Coast at Velasco on June 26, 1832, marking the first armed conflict between colonists and the Mexican government. A convention of delegates from most of the Texan settlements was soon held. The representatives reorganized Stephen Austin's militia and even suggested forming a forty-man ranger company to cover the territory between Austin and DeWitt Colonies.[27]

The colonists held another convention in 1833. When Austin went to Mexico City to present the convention's resolutions, he was arrested and held there for twenty-eight months. By the time he returned to Texas, colonists were growing more resentful of Mexican authorities. William Barret Travis led a small group of men with a cannon, who forced the surrender of a coastal Mexican garrison at Anahuac on June 29, 1835. Most settlers, however, continued to cooperate with Mexican authorities. Several more months would pass before Texans were provoked enough to start a revolution.

CHAPTER 2

The Original Ranger Battalion

May - September 1835

Indian encounters began to accelerate throughout 1835 in the wake of the Rio Blanco battle. Noted Texas Ranger George Bernard Erath wrote in 1844 that, "The war with the Indians began in 1835."[1]

While battles with Indians had occurred since the first white settlers had arrived many years before, Erath was correct in noting that 1835 was a true turning point in "the war." The continued heavy flow of immigrants, the continued Indian depredations, and the revolution with Mexico during this year forced the provisional government of Texas to take new steps to protect its frontier settlements.

Among the more important steps was the legal creation of the Texas Rangers during 1835. This fabled body was organized in several stages, as will be seen.

★　★　★　★　★

The Killing of Chief Canoma: May-June 1835

Within two weeks of the San Marcos battle, another party of traders bound for Brazoria was attacked by a party of Tawakonis, who were armed with bows and arrows. The traders fired on the Indians, killing one and causing the others to flee. A description of this battle was published in the May 2, 1835 edition of *The Texas Republican* in Brazoria.[2]

The Indians considered to be "wild tribes" by the early Colorado River settlers were the Wacos, Tehuacanas (Tawakonis), Ionis, Anadarkos, Towash, and other related tribes of the Caddoan confederation. These tribes along the upper Brazos and Trinity Rivers had become openly hostile toward white settlers by the spring of 1835. They even felt that the white settlers along the Colorado were a separate "tribe" of whites who were more hated than those along the Brazos River.[3]

The settlers along the Falls of the Brazos River, in present Falls County near the town of Tenoxtitlan, experienced relative peace with the local Indians in the early 1830s. One noteworthy exception occurred when a stranger named H. Reed from the United States was slain by Tonkawa Indians in 1832 near Tenoxtitlan following a horse trade between Reed and the Indians in which they felt cheated. Revenge against this small band of Indians was exacted by a small band of Caddos led by the friendly Chief Canoma.

Canoma pursued these Indians, recovered Reed's horse and saddle, and brought them back to his father. Canoma's faithful Caddos, numbering about thirty, were living near Tenoxtitlan in 1835 when tensions again increased in Robertson Colony.

The Bastrop area citizens were concerned enough with the presence of hostile Indians to form a committee of safety and correspondence, with an initial meeting held on May 8, 1835. In a second meeting on May 17, a formal committee of five was created, of which Edward Burleson was a member. These members were charged with handling communications concerning Indian hostilities.[4]

The colonists in late May 1835 employed Chief Canoma of the Caddos to go among the hostile Indians to make peace talks and to try and return two small children who had been taken captive. After visiting several tribes, Canoma returned and reported that the Indians he had seen were willing to make peace with the settlers along the Brazos River. At least half of the Indians, however, very much opposed making peace with the white settlers along the upper areas of the Colorado River. Canoma further reported that a band of these most unsettled Indians were on the move toward the white settlement at Bastrop.[5]

From the Falls of the Brazos, the townspeople selected Samuel McFall to run ahead and warn the Bastrop citizens. Bastrop was the uppermost white settlement of any size on the Colorado River in 1835. The local residents had been forced to band together to protect themselves from neighboring Waco, Tawakoni, Kichai, and Comanche raids. Consequently, a strong log stockade or fort was erected in the center of the little town. In the event of a serious Indian attack, the townspeople could take shelter inside.[6]

McFall, a lean and quick man of six feet, three inches, ran the distance on foot and is fabled to have been a faster runner than most saddle horses of the time. Before he could arrive, a party of eight Indians made a vicious attack on June 1. On the road from San Felipe to Bastrop, they attacked the wagon of Amos R. Alexander near Cummins Creek.[7]

Alexander, a Pennsylvania native, had brought his wife and two sons to Texas in the spring of 1833. They settled in Bastrop and eventually opened a store and hotel. In April 1835 Amos and son Amos Jr. went to the coast to get a supply of goods they had ordered. They hired two other men to serve as teamsters to haul their goods. The Alexanders were attacked by Indians on June 1 at Pin Oak Creek about thirty-five miles from Bastrop.[8]

Amos Alexander was killed outright. His son was on horseback and was shot through the body. The younger Alexander rode full speed from the scene of the attack toward Moore's Fort at La Grange, the last town they had passed. He met the second wagon being hauled by the two brothers his father had hired as teamsters. The three started for Moore's Fort, but the young Alexander died from his wounds. His body was laid under a tree and covered with leaves and moss.

The teamsters reached La Grange, and John Henry Moore helped them raise a party of men. Moore, thirty-five, was a native of Tennessee who had settled on the Colorado River in 1821 as one of Austin's Old Three Hundred. By 1828 he owned the twin blockhouse known as Moore's Fort, which was located in La Grange, the town he had laid out and named in 1831.[9]

As this attack was going on, two immigrants had stopped at the home of frontiersman John Marlin near the Falls of the Brazos. While these men lay sick, their horses managed to wander off beyond the Little River toward Brushy Creek. Marlin then employed Canoma and Dorcha to attempt to bring the horses back. In good faith for their services, Marlin presented one of the Indian chiefs with a new shirt.[10]

As Chief Canoma, his wife, son, and his other Indian companion set out to assist the white settlers, other frontiersmen were unwittingly on a collision course with these do-gooders. A party of volunteers from Bastrop was formed under forty-six-year-old Captain Edward Burleson, a North Carolinian who had migrated to Texas in 1831. A soldier under General Andrew Jackson in the Creek Indian War of 1813-1814, Burleson would become one of the most respected frontier leaders in early Texas history. This Bastrop party included Stephen Townsend, Spencer Burton Townsend, Moses Townsend, John York, William Isbell, Jesse L. McCrocklin, and George A. Kerr, among others. Captain Burleson's men set out to follow the trail of the Indians who had killed the wagoner and his son. Finding the bodies of the Alexanders, they buried them and rode in pursuit of the killers, tracking them as far as the three forks of the Little River, where the trail was lost.[11]

Burleson's force met up with the small group of La Grange area volunteers under Captain John Moore. The united force of sixty-one men proceeded up the Little River to a spot about fifty miles above the Falls of the Brazos. One of Moore's volunteers, John Rabb, described Burleson's men as a "don't care a-looking company of men as could be found on the top of the ground."

While the party rested at camp for two days, volunteer John Bate Berry and several others went out hunting. In the process, they encountered a lone Caddo Indian whom they captured and brought back to Captain Burleson. The Indian professed to being honest and friendly, even offering the fact that he was traveling with several other Indians. Burleson and Moore's men went to the Indian camp, taking the Caddo, two Cherokees, and two Indian women as prisoners. These prisoners, of course, included Chief Canoma and Dorcha. Several volunteers trailed one of the Indians into the bush near Brushy Creek and found that the Indians had two well-shod and cared for American horses. Most Indians did not possess horses that had been properly shoed unless the horses were acquired from more civilized persons.[12]

Assuming their possession of shod horses made them guilty, Robert Morris Coleman of Captain Burleson's Bastrop company decided Canoma's party was guilty of the Alexander murders and tried to shoot one of them on the spot. John Rabb intervened, and Canoma's party protested that the horses they had were runaways. The Texan party thereafter held them captive.

The Indians were taken into custody, and the volunteer party proceeded on its hunt. Burleson reportedly promised Canoma and his son a fair trial once the party returned to Bastrop. Moses Cummins wrote to empresario Sterling Robertson on June 10 in hopes that Robertson could dispatch a letter to Burleson immediately to "prevent some mischief" from befalling those he considered "innocent Indians."

It was too late. Despite Burleson's good intentions, he was unable to control the wild want for vengeance some of his men displayed. Ignoring control of their captains, the volunteers voted forty to twenty-one to execute these prisoners for the murder of the Alexanders. Coleman and eight others carried out the actual executions, lashing Canoma and his son to trees and shooting them to death. Canoma's wife was left to wander back to the settlements alone. At least two of the white volunteers, Stephen Townsend and John Rabb, were opposed to the killings and left their party rather than watch. Rabb later noted that one of the executioners took a piece of skin from a dead Indian's back and formed it into a razor strop. As for the psychology of these eye-for-an-eye killings, settler Cummins wrote, "Such men, in such a state of mind, are not apt to discriminate between guilt and innocence."[13]

This eye-for-an-eye vengeance mentality was typical of the early Texas Indian wars. The killing of Chief Canoma set the stage for a marked increase in Indian hostilities and expeditions during the summer of 1835.

Oldham/York Company Takes the Offensive

Chief Canoma's wife, upon returning to the Falls of the Brazos, quickly informed the other Caddos of the murder of her husband and son. Choctaw Tom, the most senior Indian leader left among them, stated that he could not blame the Coloradian settlers for the mishap, but that all the Indians would now make war on the settlers.[14]

Choctaw Tom's Caddos then left the settlement and joined other Indians out in the country. The younger Indians promised settler John Marlin that they did not intend any harm upon him or other "friendly" settlers near the Falls.[15]

Shortly thereafter, Major William Oldham raised a company of twenty-five men from the town of Washington-on-the-Brazos. It is interesting to note that both Major Oldham and Captain John York claimed to have been in command of this party of Washington volunteers. Neither, however, left a muster roll that has survived time. This company marched to the Kichai (Keechi) village located on Boggy Creek, a tributary to the Trinity River in present Leon County. As they approached, they had a friendly exchange with Indian representatives. When accused of stealing white settlers' horses, the Indians produced a contract signed by empresario Sterling Robertson to prove their good terms.

According to volunteer Joel Walter Robison, Oldham's party was preparing to leave peacefully when some of the men recognized several stolen horses about their village. Upon being questioned, the Indians replied, "Oh, those. Those were stolen from the people on the Colorado. We don't have any treaty with them."

The Indians immediately seized their arms, and the whites opened fire. In the ensuing battle, two Indians were killed while the rest escaped into nearby thickets. The whites withdrew, taking about thirty horses with them and all of the camp equipage before burning the Kichai village down. Joel Robison:

> None of our men were injured. Papers were found in the village which were known to have been on the person of a young man named Edwards who was killed by the Indians twenty miles

below Bastrop, a few months previously.[16]

When the Oldham/York party made camp that night on the return to Washington, a frightened sentry fired his gun and ran into camp screaming, "Indians!" In the dark and confusion, the half-asleep Texans frantically grabbed guns and fired. One man, Benjamin Castleman, was killed and another volunteer wounded in the confusion of friendly fire.

Coleman's Rangers Attack Tawakonis: July 11, 1835

In the wake of the Canoma episode, another volunteer group was organized to protect the frightened settlers. Texas records show that Robert Morris Coleman was elected captain of a small frontier ranger company in Robertson's Colony. Although no muster roll of Coleman's company has survived, he reportedly employed between eighteen and twenty-five men. From June 12, 1835, Coleman served two months and fifteen days "on the frontier as Capt. of Mounted Riflemen." He had been ordered to assume this command by the Committee of Safety upon his return from the Burleson/Moore expedition in which Chief Canoma had been killed.[17]

Captain Coleman, thirty-six, was from Christian (later Trigg) County, Kentucky, and had come to Texas in 1830. He had been granted twenty-four labors of land in Robertson's Colony on February 1, 1835, located in present Lee County on the West Yegua River, not far from Bastrop. Three of his rangers were Bastrop citizens well known to the Indians.

Coleman later wrote to Safety Committee Chairman Henry Rueg of his company's activities.18

> The wanton outrages of the Indians not only upon our frontier, but in the midst of our settlements call for redress. I on the 2nd July left the town of Bastrop with a company of men for the purpose of chastising those menaces to civilized men.

Coleman's men crossed the Brazos River at Washington on July 4, 1835, and made a campaign against the Tawakoni Indians living near Tehuacana Springs in present Limestone County. His men were not discovered until they were east of the Brazos and near the village on July 11. There, they fell in with an estimated one hundred Indians, mainly Tawakonis, with some Caddos and Ionis also.

According to early pioneer John Holland Jenkins, Coleman's men used the cover of darkness to crawl up into the very midst of the Indians and wait for daylight before starting the battle. The point man was Jesse Halderman, a store owner in Bastrop who had come to Texas from Kentucky in 1831. Halderman was appointed to give the signal for attack, but actions hastened his signal. Jenkins later wrote:[19]

> Some dogs commenced barking, and one of the Indians arose and walked out to see what was the matter. He soon showed that he discovered the concealed whites, so Halderman, realizing their danger, fired, thereby giving signal for the fight to begin. It was a fierce and heavy fight, although Coleman's eighteen men were struggling against an entire tribe. He was at last forced to retreat; three men—Halderman, Bliss and Wallace being badly wounded, and one Mr. Wallace being killed.

Other sources state the name of the ranger killed to have been John Williams and that as many as four others were wounded. In return, Captain Coleman's men managed to kill a number of the Indians in the village. The Indians were too numerous for the remainder to fight and were reportedly spurred on by the fact that they recognized three Brazos men among their assailants.[20]

"We had a severe battle," Coleman wrote. "One fourth of my men was killed and wounded. We took their encampment by a charge and the battle ended." Coleman's party fell back to Parker's Fort, where they arrived on July 11. The wounded men of his company were left under charge of a doctor, and Coleman headed back to Robertson's Colony to report the events of his campaign.[21]

Coleman returned to Viesca, the capital of Robertson's Colony, where he wrote a letter to Henry Rueg, the political chief for the Department of Nacogdoches, on July 20, 1835. Coleman outlined a plan for a ranger battalion to attack the Indian threat he and his men had just encountered.

> Those Indians must be chastised or this flourishing country abandoned, and again become a wilderness. I now, Sir, propose to levy a general tax on the citizens of Texas, sufficient to pay and provision 200 men. Let them be stationed in four garrisons [with] 50 men in each. Let those garrisons be established high up on the different rivers and placed under the command of a man calculated to command and the country will be safe.

Coleman's call to action is significant because it laid the groundwork for the formal ranger battalion that became known as the Texas Rangers. His plan for organizing the troops under a central command was an idea that was legally put into effect several months later on October 17, 1835. Coleman, in fact, was immortalized on the historical marker for Coleman County, Texas (named after him) as the "organizer of the first company of Texas Rangers."[22] Since loosely organized ranger companies had operated since the 1820s, this statement on the marker is best clarified as Coleman being the organizer of the first Texas Ranger company *legally recognized by the provisional government of Texas*.

Ironically, Coleman would be commissioned one year later as the colonel commanding a three-company ranger battalion serving in remote frontier outposts, just as he had recommended.

★　★　★　★　★

Colonel Moore's Ranger Expedition

Word of Captain Coleman's fight at the Tawakoni village spread quickly through the Texas colonies. Within days of his appeal for the creation of a ranger battalion, volunteers began assembling at Tenoxtitlan in Robertson's Colony.

Four volunteer companies are known to have been organized at Tenoxtitlan during the latter days of July 1835. The first of these companies organized was that of Captain Philip Haddox Coe on July 9, 1835. His twelve-man unit was later considered to be "Rangers under the command of Col. John H. Moore." Coe was born on January 10, 1800, in Georgia, from where he had recently come to Texas and settled in present Washington County. One of his rangers, forty-three-year-old William Tom, was a veteran of the Horseshoe Bend and New Orleans battles of the War of 1812 and had only moved his family to Washington-on-the-Brazos as of February 1835.[23]

The second company, under Captain George Washington Barnett, was raised on July 20. Barnett's muster roll shows that he took command of a "Co. Volunteers raised for the purpose of defending the frontier against Indian depredations, under the command of Col. J. H. Moore."[24]

Two other volunteer companies were mustered into service on July 25 under captains John Henry Moore and Robert McAlpin Williamson. Frontiersman Edward Burleson was also reported to have raised some volunteers from the upper Colorado settlements who joined these forces.[25]

Captain Moore, who had led volunteers during the recent June expedition, again raised a company of men from La Grange. Captain Williamson, for whom Williamson County was later named, commanded a "mounted rifle company." Born in Georgia in 1806, Williamson had been stricken at age fifteen by an attack of white swelling, which confined him to home and left him a cripple for life. His right leg was drawn back at the knee, which forced him to be fitted with a wooden leg from his knee to the ground. While confined, he studied law, mathematics, and foreign languages. By age twenty he was practicing law in Georgia. He emigrated to San Felipe de Austin in 1826, mastered the Spanish language, and edited *The Cotton Plant* from 1829-1831, one of the first newspapers in Texas. His wooden leg earned him the nickname "Three-Legged Willie," although most of his closer friends just called him Willie.[26]

On July 31 these four companies marched from Tenoxtitlan for Parker's Fort on the Navasota River to join up with Captain Coleman's company. Captain Williamson was later reimbursed for spending forty-five dollars cash for beef for the troops. According to Edward Burleson, Williamson bought the cattle from Samuel Frost, who was then living near Parker's Fort about the last day of July.[27]

Upon arriving at Fort Parker, the volunteer companies were formally organized in a battalion. This became the first true ranger battalion ever organized in Texas, although independent ranging companies had been employed during the past decade to supplement militia forces operating from the various colonies.

The men elected John Moore as the colonel commanding the five small companies. Moore's spot as commander of the La Grange rangers was filled by twenty-seven-year-old Michigan native Michael R. Goheen. Captain Goheen's company of "volunteer rangers" was confirmed by James Neill to have participated in the campaign against the Indians from July 25 to September 13, 1835.[28]

Goheen was assisted in his command by First Lieutenant William Mosby Eastland. John Moore was later paid $294.66 for one month and twenty-two days of service as colonel at the rate of $170 per month. Forty-five-year-old James Clinton Neill, who had fought in the 1814 Seminole Indian battle at Horseshoe, was elected adjutant of this command.[29]

Although some men had fought Indians in Texas previously, thirty-four-year-old William Isbell, a Colorado River area settler new to Texas, was typical of the men of this ranger campaign.

> In the spring of 1835, I went on my first campaign with Capt.
> R. M. Williamson, who was called Three-Legged-Willie. John H.
> Moore, Lester, Rabb, Eastland, Goheen, Ned Burleson, R. M.

Fort Parker, also known as Fort Sterling, was the rendezvous site for Colonel Moore's ranger companies and that of Captain Coleman. The pioneer cabins within the fort were protected by a split cedar stockade and two-story blockhouses at either corner of the grounds. The reconstructed fort stands at Old Fort Parker State Historical Park in Limestone County. *Author's photo.*

Coleman, Col. Neill, and others were in the company. We were absent about sixty days on the upper Brazos, and lived mainly on beef.[30]

Although some accounts of Colonel Moore's 1835 Indian campaign only mention four ranger companies participating, a study of the audited military claims of men participating in this campaign clearly shows that there were five total companies. This includes the company originally under Moore that passed to Captain Goheen. Moore later gave testimony of the service of the other companies under his command. In a deposition written by him before the Fayette County court, it states that

in the year 1835, he commanded an expedition against the Indians, which said expedition was composed of the companies of captains Williamson, Barnett, Coe, Goheen and Coleman.[31]

Military papers of Captain Robert Coleman show that he was still at Parker's Fort on August 5, 1835. He wrote a note this date that said, "I bought of Silas Parker, for the use of the company under my command" more than one thousand pounds of beef at three cents per pound, thirty-seven bushels of corn at two dollars per bushel, and twenty-five pounds of bacon. He also acknowledged that two men at Parker's Fort had

Colonel Moore's Ranger Campaign: July - September 13, 1835

| John Henry Moore | Colonel | James Clinton Neill | Adjutant |

Captain Barnett's Company: July 20 - August 28, 1835

Captain:
George W. Barnett
Lieutenant:
William Warner Hill
Privates:
Isham G. Belcher
Abram B. Clark

Christopher Haner Clark
Abraham Dillard
George Bernard Erath
Samuel Evetts
William W. Hawkins
Richard Hope
William Isaacs

Samuel McFall
James Moore
Lucien B. Outlaw
Robert A. Toler
David Thompson
Felix Wright

Captain Coe's Rangers: July 9 - August 31, 1835

Captain:
Philip Haddox Coe
Privates:
Lewis Chapman Clemmons
Bryant Daughtery

George Givenn
Ennes Hardin
John Henderson
Obediah Hudson
James Hughes

Jacob Long
Joseph Lynch
William Tom
James Walker

Captain Goheen's Rangers: July 25 - September 13, 1835

Captain:
Michael R. Goheen +
First Lieutenant:
William M. Eastland
Privates:
Lyman W. Alexander*
Leander Beason
David Berry
Jesse Billingsley
Edward J. Blakey
Edward Burleson
John W. Burton
Robert M. Coleman*
William Connell
Wiley Cummins

James P. Davis
Absolom C. Deloplain*
Patrick Durst
Vincent L. Evans
Joseph Highland
Malcolm M. Hornsby
Moses Smith Hornsby
William W. Hornsby
Michael Kinnard*
David Smith Kornegay
James Seaton Lester
William Lewis
George W. Lyons
James H. Manning*
Charles Mason*

James McLaughlin*
James Robert Pace
William Pace
Elisha Marshall Pease*
John Rabb
James C. Ragsdale
Henry P. Redfield
Joel Walter Robison*
Thomas Thompson
John Jackson Tumlinson
Wayman F. Wells *

*+Captain Moore elected
colonel by August 1.*

Capt. Williamson's Mounted Riflemen: July 25 - September 13, 1835

Captain:
Robert M. Williamson
First Lieutenant:
Hugh M. Childress
First Corporal:
Nicholas Wren
Privates:
John Bate Berry
William Bridge

Henry Bridgers
Oliver Buckman
Aaron Burleson
Robert M. Cravins
Leroy V. Criswell
William Criswell
Thomas Davey
William Duty
Elijah Ingram

William Isbell
William Harrison Magill*
George Neill
Samuel C. Neill
David F. Owen
William J. C. Pearce
John G. Robison
John H. Scaggs
Robert Townsley

* Known member of Captain Robert Coleman's rangers from June 12 - August 28, 1835. His rangers and volunteers under Edward Burleson merged into other companies when the Texans were organized at Fort Parker. *Sources:* Daughters of the Republic of Texas, *Muster Rolls of the Texas Revolution*, 134-35. Rosters for Goheen and Williamson's companies constructed from author's research of audited military claims of the Republic of Texas.

cared for the wounded men of his company "from the 11th day of July up to this time" for which was claimed fifty-five dollars.[32]

A search of available Republic of Texas records fails to reveal a complete list of those men who served under Captain Coleman on Moore's campaign. A large percentage of his men appear to have joined with the companies of Captains Goheen and Williamson before the campaign's end. The pension papers of Michael Kinnard, for example, state that he participated in an 1835 Indian expedition led by Captain Robert Coleman. Kinnard's audited military claims, however, show that he was later honorably discharged from active service by Lieutenant William Eastland of Captain Goheen's company on September 13.

One of the men under Captain Barnett's command was George Bernard Erath, who had arrived in Texas in 1833 at age twenty. He had been born in Vienna, Austria,

Colonel John Henry Moore (1800-1880) of La Grange led the first true Texas Ranger campaign in 1835 against the Indians. He would later become a hero of the Texas Revolution and lead two future expeditions against Comanche forces.

Prints and Photographs Collection, The Center for American History, University of Texas at Austin, CN Number 03821.

and sailed to New Orleans in 1832. He left Austria partially because of the country's mandatory military service yet now volunteered his service. Once in Texas, he became a partner of Alexander Thomson in surveying the new territory.[33]

Colonel Moore's ranger expedition departed Parker's Fort in early August. The mounted volunteers moved northeast toward the Tawakoni village as George Erath later recorded.

> After waiting for the swollen Navasota to run down, we marched on to the village. Texas Indians never allowed themselves to be attacked by a hundred men together; they had evacuated the village, and we had nothing to do but occupy it. We found sixty acres in corn, which was just hard enough to be

gritted, and by making holes in the bottom of the tin cups we carried we fashioned graters, and supplied ourselves with bread. There were also numbers of pumpkins, watermelons, muskmelons, peas and other vegetables, such as were then raised by Indians in their primitive agriculture.[34]

Colonel Moore's troops left the Indian village two days later and moved about twenty miles over the prairie. Late in the afternoon, the troops came within a mile of a belt of timber that extended along Post Oak Creek, a tributary to the Trinity River. Advance scouts suddenly reported Indians up ahead in the timber. All of the men were formed into battle lines.

Moore and his adjutant, James Neill, "took as much precaution as if we were about to fight such formidable foes as Creeks, Cherokees, and Seminoles—foes the two had faced in their younger days under Jackson," wrote volunteer Erath. After approximately fifteen minutes of parading and maneuvering, the order was passed to charge across the two to three hundred yards through post oak timber over boggy soil.

The officers were strict about keeping the men in line. From Captain George Barnett's ranger company, Privates Samuel McFall and George Erath darted far ahead of the rest of the volunteers on their horses. It was not, however, by their own choice, as Erath recalled.

> I was riding a young horse which had been caught a colt from the mustangs, that was fiery. When the order came to charge, it darted forward ahead of all the rest, and I found myself alone in the advance. Next came McFall, who was also on a wild horse, too eager for the fray. The officers shouted to us to come back into line, but our efforts to obey were in vain. Our steeds had determined to give us a reputation for bravery which we did not deserve.[35]

Erath's daughter recalled that this incident even helped earn her father the nickname "The Flying Dutchman." Around the Texan campfires that night, the episode drew great laughter. The charge against the Indians itself proved futile. As the companies advanced across the field, they were met by their own scouts, who brought news that the half dozen or so Indians they had found had since fled while Moore's troops had prepared for their charge. Nearly one hundred strong, the Texas volunteers succeeded only in capturing one Indian pony this day.

Colonel Moore's troops continued marching for several more days in pursuit of the Indians. Time spent waiting for swollen streams to run down and for mud bogs to become passable brought grumbling from the troops that Texas Indians could easily keep out of sight of such a large party.

The expedition did encounter a small camp of Wacos. They attacked immediately, killing at least one Indian and capturing five or six others. Moore's force learned from their prisoners that a larger body of Indians was camped shortly ahead of them. With darkness falling, the troops waited until daylight to pursue. They found the remains of a large Indian encampment a short distance away. It had been abandoned so precipitously that some Indians had even cut the stake ropes to their horses.[36]

The Texans and their horses were well worn from weeks of pursuing the Indians. Among the volunteer companies, there arose a division among those wishing to end the campaign and those desiring to return home. Colonel Moore was harshly opposed to turning back on this expedition. A split among the troops resulted, and many of the men from the Brazos area turned back for home in late August.

Captain Barnett's company disbanded on August 28, and Captain Coe's company mustered out of service on August 31. Captain Robert Coleman was paid as a captain of rangers through August 28, 1835. George Erath of Captain Barnett's company later summarized the balance of the Moore expedition.

> The main body of the Indians were never overtaken; but several small scattering parties were met, with which there was some skirmishing. The Texan forces kept daily diminishing, and in two months the expedition closed.[37]

Although Captain Coleman turned for home at the same time as Captains Coe and Barnett, a portion of his men continued on. Some of them are shown to have been later discharged by Lieutenant William Eastland of Captain Goheen's company. As first lieutenant of the "First Company of Volunteers," Eastland was paid at the rate of two dollars per day for this expedition. When the expedition was closed out, he signed the discharge papers. He also signed a promissory note for Private George W. Lyons, who had "by an unavoidable accident lost his rifle gun" during the campaign. Another of his men, Private William Connell, lost "his rifle, gun pistol and other property" during the expedition.[38]

Colonel Moore continued his expedition against the Indians for another two weeks before turning home. He commanded the companies of Captains Goheen and Williamson during this time. They covered the countryside up the Trinity River as far as to its forks, where the present city of Dallas stands. Passing over to and down the Brazos River, Moore's expedition crossed to where Fort Graham was later constructed, without encountering more than five or six Indians on several occasions.[39]

The volunteers experienced several incidents with the Indians during their return home. The Indians captured at the Waco village created their own problems for their Texan captors. Notable among the prisoners was a Waco woman and her bright young girl of about three years of age. The Indian woman, apparently distraught over her captivity, somehow managed to steal a knife one night in camp on the Brazos River, and she brutally killed her own daughter before attempting to kill herself.[40]

This attempt did not succeed, but the Texans found her near death by morning when they checked. Edward Burleson, deciding that the suffering Indian woman would bleed to death shortly, asked for a volunteer to kill her to spare her further suffering. Oliver Buckman of Captain Williamson's company came forward for the mercy mission. Taking her to the edge of the river, he drew his large, homemade hack knife. Gazing straight into her face, Buckman "severed with one stroke her head from her body, both of which rolled into the water beneath."

En route home, Moore's rangers discovered two Indians on foot about a half mile from them. The Indians were moving toward a timber grove another half mile beyond. Those of the company with the best horses immediately took off in pursuit. The young Indians were fast and swiftly raced into the woods to take cover ahead of their pursuers. The whites attempted to surround the thicket and then selected several of their men to enter the thicket and drive the Indians out.

The Texans found and shot one Indian and continued hunting the second one in the woods. Moses Smith Hornsby of Captain Goheen's company finally spotted him and fired but missed the Indian. The Indian quickly returned fire and struck Hornsby in the shoulder. Suffering from his wound, Hornsby hollered, "Here's the Indian!" and stumbled from the brush.

One of Williamson's rangers, William Magill, heard the cry of "Indian" and raised his rifle. In his haste to kill, he fired at the first person to rush from the brush, hitting his fellow ranger. Magill's shot shredded poor Hornsby's arm. A physician attached to the company examined him and decided that an amputation would be required to save his life. Hornsby solidly refused to lose his arm, stating that he preferred death. "After lingering along in great pain for a day or two," he got his wish and was buried with the honors of a volunteer soldier.

Lieutenant Eastland wrote that Smith Hornsby

> faithfully discharged the duties of a soldier until about the first of
> September, at which time in an encounter with a parcel of
> Indians, said Hornsby was badly wounded and in a few days
> thereafter died in consequence of said wound.[41]

The Texans practiced an interesting burial custom in the field in
order to protect a body from being further mutilated by Indians. After
covering up the corpse, the ground was packed smooth and flat above it.
A campfire was then kindled on this spot and left burning to conceal the
fact that a body lay underneath.[42]

Adjutant James Neill took up his own little experiment for returning
destruction to the enemy tribes. He had procured some type of smallpox
virus and had this bacteria injected into one of the Indians his men had
captured. This Indian was then released and allowed to carry the infec-
tion back to his tribe. Neill was never able to ascertain the success or
failure of his little experiment.

Without any further incident, Moore's men made their way back to
their settlements and disbanded. The volunteers were drummed out of
service on September 13, 1835, in the town of Mina in present Bastrop
County. Captain "Willie" Williamson was later paid for service through
September 13, and Republic of Texas auditors determined he was due
$1,005 for his expenses as company commander.[43]

Early historian Henderson Yoakum wrote that this early ranger
expedition was a great service in its display of force to the Indians. This
campaign "also tended to discipline the volunteers, and prepare them for
the toils and triumphs that awaited them at home."[44]

★　★　★　★　★

Depredation on the San Gabriel

During late September, surveyor Thomas A. Graves set out from
Bastrop in Robertson's Colony with a party of seventeen land surveyors
and speculators. After surveying ten leagues near the San Gabriel River,
one of the small groups of surveyors was attacked by a party of Indians.
An Irishman named Lang was killed and scalped while working his com-
pass. One of the men of the party of four escaped and ran to the men
under Graves to spread the news. The other two men being unaccounted
for, the men under Graves decided to go in search of them.

One of Graves' surveyors was George Erath, who had joined his surveying party after serving in the Moore expedition through August 28. Erath felt that "there was little danger in our whole party remaining a few days longer," as the Indians were believed to have fled after lifting their scalps. Graves' men went to the scene of the attack but didn't find any bodies. The Indian attack was enough to cut short this surveying trip, as Erath recalled.

> We paused there and, after another deliberation, Graves cut the matter short by declaring he had fitted out the expedition, would have to pay the hands, and did not propose to be at unnecessary expense in public service. So we turned back. Had we gone but a few hundred yards farther we would have found Lang's body.[45]

Before returning to Bastrop, Graves' surveying party did find two other badly frightened survivors of this Indian depredation.

Graves, Erath, and the other surveyors returned from their expedition early in October and made town at Hornsby's settlement. There, they found events that would forever change the future of Texas had occurred in their absence.

CHAPTER 3

Frontiersmen of the Texas Revolution

September 29 - December 10, 1835

Freshly returned from their Indian campaign, Colonel John Moore's volunteers immediately became engaged in a confrontation that ignited the opening shots of what became known as the Texas Revolution. This action would serve as a uniting force to enlist thousands into the effort to gain Texas independence. It also forced the provisional government of the frontier territory to establish a formal military system.

Mexican troops under General Martín Perfecto Cos had originally landed at Copano Bay near Gonzales about September 20 and had marched into San Antonio. In San Antonio de Béxar, Colonel Domingo Ugartechea, the Mexican military commander in Texas, sent a force of one hundred soldiers under Lieutenant Francisco de Castañeda about seventy miles east to the town of Gonzales. Their mission was to retrieve a bronze cannon that had been given to the citizens of Gonzales four years earlier to protect themselves against hostile Indians. In light of declining relations between Texas settlers and the Mexican authorities, Ugartechea considered it wise to remove this weapon from the possession of the settlers.[1]

When Castañeda's men arrived in Gonzales on September 29, 1835, they were surprised to be prevented from crossing the Guadalupe River by eighteen local citizens, later immortalized as the "Old Eighteen." They were Captain Albert Martin, William W. Arrington, Simeon Bateman, Valentine Bennett, Joseph D. Clements, Almond Cottle, Jacob C. Darst, George Washington Davis, Almeron Dickinson, Gravis Fulcher, Benjamin Fuqua, James B. Hinds, Thomas Jackson, Charles Mason, Thomas R. Miller, John Sowell, Winslow Turner, and Ezekiel Williams.

These eighteen men informed Castañeda that his men would have to wait on the west side of the river for the return of *alcalde* Andrew Ponton. The Texans buried the cannon in a peach orchard while more volunteers arrived. Captain Robert Coleman arrived with thirty men from Bastrop on the night of September 29, as did Captain John H. Moore with another forty or more men. The following day, September 30, Captains Martin, Coleman, and Moore sent word from Gonzales to the citizens of San Felipe and Lavaca.

> A detachment of the Mexican forces from Béxar amounting to about 150 men are encamped opposite us. We expect an attack momently. Yesterday, we were but 18 strong; today, 150 and forces constantly arriving. We wish all the aid and despatch that is possible to give us that we may take up soon our line of march for Béxar and drive from our country all the Mexican forces.[2]

Once Castañeda received word that the Texan forces were growing, he moved his men seven miles upstream in search of a better spot to cross. The Texans dug up their cannon and crossed the Guadalupe with it, carrying with them a newly made flag with the slogan "Come and Take It." Old John Sowell, one of the eighteen who had originally repulsed the Mexican forces, picked up scrap iron from his blacksmith shop to use in the Texan cannon. According to fellow Gonzales volunteer David Darst, Sowell made wrought-iron balls for the Texas cannon.[3]

On the morning of October 2, the Texans attacked the camp of Castañeda near the farm of Zeke Williams. The Mexican commander eventually removed his men back toward Béxar. The opening shots of the Texas Revolution had thus been fired in what became known as the Battle of Gonzales. The little town of Gonzales earned the sobriquet "Lexington of Texas," and the bold "Come and Take It" flag became legendary. Although the whole affair was little more than a skirmish, the movement to drive the Mexican forces from Texas was well under way. Volunteers continued to stream into Gonzales over the next weeks, and Stephen F. Austin was elected commander of the volunteer army.

The surveying party under Thomas Graves returned soon after this Gonzales action to find that the retreating Mexicans were being followed back toward San Antonio by newly formed Texan companies. A party of twenty Colorado River area volunteers was formed under Captain Edward Blakey, who had come to Texas in 1832 from Kentucky, to go against the Indians in the vicinity where the surveyor party had been attacked. Among Blakey's volunteers was surveyor George Erath, who recalled

> We found Lang's body and buried it, and scouted around for some time. On our return we found that little had been going on at San Antonio.[4]

Southeast of San Antonio toward the Gulf Coast, plenty was going on at Goliad, where the next round of the Texas Revolution occurred on October 9. Previously known as La Bahía, Goliad lay on the important route from the Gulf of Mexico to San Antonio de Béxar. La Bahía was crucial in that it guarded the principal supply line from the port of Copano on Aransas Bay to San Antonio.[5]

Captain George M. Collinsworth organized a company of men from the Matagorda area and marched to Victoria, picking up recruits along the way. General Cos had departed Goliad for San Antonio, leaving only a small garrison at the old Presidio La Bahía. Collinsworth ultimately commanded about 120 men, including well-known former Mexican prisoner Benjamin Rush Milam, when his men assaulted the garrison at La Bahía about 11:00 p.m. on October 9.

In a half-hour assault, the Texans captured the fortress and suffered only several wounded. The Mexicans lost three killed, seven wounded, and twenty-one made prisoners, including the two senior officers. Texan reinforcements soon arrived at Goliad, including companies under Captains Ben Fort Smith and John Alley. A regiment of about one hundred men was organized and they elected Smith colonel, Collinsworth major, and Philip Dimmitt captain.

General Austin ordered that the Goliad garrison be maintained under Captain Dimmitt, while the rest of the Texas volunteers were ordered to join the preparation for Austin's planned siege against General Cos's forces in San Antonio.

★ ★ ★ ★ ★

General Council Establishes "Corps of Texas Rangers"

Just days after the Gonzales and Goliad battles, the provisional government of Texas assembled in San Felipe de Austin. Elections were held on October 5 to elect fifty-five representatives from thirteen jurisdictions, or "municipalities," of Texas. These men began arriving in San Felipe for the opening session on October 15. On this date a temporary body called the "Permanent Council" was formed, and on October 11 Richardson Royster Royall was elected president of this convention.

These representatives would pass the laws that would direct the efforts of the Texas Revolution. One of the more important acts that the Permanent Council took under consideration was a move to create a frontier ranging force to contend with Indian hostilities during the revolution.

On October 17 Nacogdoches representative Daniel Parker Sr.

Daniel Parker Sr. (1781-1844) organized the first non-Catholic church of Texas in 1833. As a representative of the new provisional government, he introduced legislation to create a corps of Texas Rangers in October 1835. Two of his brothers, Silas Mercer and James Wilson Parker, would command rangers from Parker's Fort during the Texas Revolution.

Courtesy of Old Fort Parker State Historical Park.

offered a resolution to create a corps of Texas Rangers. Parker's resolution appears to be the result of the proposal from Captain Robert Coleman of July 20, 1835. Parker's resolution called for "creating a corps of Texas Rangers to consist of small detachments stationed on the Indian frontier."[6]

Three men were selected as superintendents of the regional ranging units. Silas Mercer Parker, brother of Daniel Parker, was selected as superintendent over twenty-five rangers between the Brazos and Trinity Rivers. Daniel Boone Friar was named superintendent of another thirty-five rangers to serve between the Brazos and the Colorado Rivers. Garrison Greenwood would oversee a ten-man unit to serve in the east between the Trinity and Neches Rivers. These three superintendents were authorized to draw on the Council for money to defray personal expenses.

After the resolution was presented to the Council, a special five-man committee was formed to consider it. They were Daniel Parker, Alexander Thomson, John Goodloe Warren Pierson, William Pettus, and Albert G. Perry. Perry reported back to the Council on the afternoon of October 17 that the committee had decided on the specifics of these ranger districts. The companies under Friar and Parker would both rendezvous at the Waco Indian village on the Brazos River, while Greenwood's men would be based out of the developing little East Texas settlement of Houston, in present Anderson County. Those volunteering for ranging duty would be paid $1.25 per day of service. Each company was to elect its own officers and report to the regional superintendent every fifteen days. The superintendents were to report to the Council every thirty days via an express courier.[7]

The companies under Friar and Parker were to rendezvous at the Waco village every fifteen days, unless detained by some engagement with or pursuit of the Indians. The Waco village, on the upper frontier of Robertson's Colony, was likely given strong consideration as a central point due to the fact that four of the five committee members resided in that colony. The rangers were not to bother the friendly tribes of Indians living along the Texas borders. The superintendents were to "watch over the conduct of the officers and report accordingly and see that full justice is done in the bounds assigned them." The General Council, upon hearing the recommendation from the special committee, proceeded on October 17 to adopt the ranger resolution. The Council then made a motion that the secretary furnish a copy of this resolution to the editor of the *Telegraph and Texas Register*.[8]

Additional agents from the upper settlements of Texas had joined the General Council in San Felipe by Sunday, October 18. Some of these men were dispatched to inform those in the field of the newly appointed ranger leaders. Among those dispatched to spread the news of the rangers' creation was delegate James Wilson Parker, whose brother Silas had been elected one of the three regional superintendents. Parker was given a leave of absence from the Council. The Council felt that providing the line of rangers was for the "safety and welfare of the country" on its frontiers "to protect the inhabitants from the savage scalping knife."[9]

Council President Royall wrote to General Stephen Austin on October 18 that the Council had appointed Jacob Garrett, Joseph L. Hood, and Peter J. Menard as commissioners to council with the Indians of Texas. They would seek to avoid "unwarrantable encroachments made upon the lands" by the Indians, while assuring them that the Council would respect their rights and privileges. Upon their departure from San Felipe, these commissioners carried with them printed "pledges of public faith" for the Indian leaders. These three commissioners would also transact any other business that promoted the cause of the people of Texas in their travels through the different municipalities.[10]

Royall also informed Austin that John Durst had been among the Cherokees and their associate tribes and found that "they intended to be neutral." Durst did find, however, that the Indians' opinion was that if the white men of Texas were defeated in their revolution, "they would turn against us." Thankfully, for the moment, Durst found that some of the Cherokees were out hunting and "appearing entirely indifferent" to the whole revolution.

The General Council continued in session through October 26. It adjourned until November 1, lacking a proper quorum to conduct business. The establishment of the ranger corps was announced in the third issue of the newspaper *Telegraph and Texas Register*, published in San Felipe de Austin on October 26, 1835.

> To secure the inhabitants on the frontiers from the invasions of the Hostile Indians, the General Council has made arrangements for raising three companies of Rangers.

The three new ranger superintendents were appointed to select company commanders and then supervise and provide for their companies. One of these three, Daniel Friar, actually served as both superintending contractor *and* captain of his first company. Friar, thirty-five, was a native of Georgia who had settled in 1828 at Washington-on-the-Brazos as a member of Austin's second colony. He was also an early settler of Robertson's Colony, who had entered into an agreement on April 21, 1835, with empresario Sterling Robertson, Joseph L. Hood, and George Campbell Childress to recruit three hundred new families to settle in Robertson's Colony.[11]

The other two ranger leaders, Silas Parker and Garrison Greenwood, were content to appoint others to take direct command of their companies. Both of these men had come to Texas together with the first Protestant church, the Pilgrim Predestinarian Regular Baptist Church. Since Mexican law forbade non-Catholic churches in Texas territory, Baptist preacher Daniel Parker Sr. had found that the laws could not prevent the immigration of an *already organized* Protestant church. Therefore, Elder Parker and family formed the Pilgrim Church in Jefferson County, Illinois, on July 26, 1833, and made immediate preparations to move it to Texas.[12]

Greenwood, born in Franklin County, Georgia, on December 19, 1799, was already an ordained minister in the Parker church. The Parker wagon train left Illinois and made its way to Texas with a large number of families joining along the way. Reuben Brown and some of the Parker immigrants settled on San Pedro Creek in present Houston County and began construction of Brown's Fort in 1834.[13]

Elder John Parker and sons James Wilson, Silas Mercer, and Benjamin Parker settled near the Navasota River in present Limestone County, where they began building what became known as Parker's Fort near present Groesbeck, Texas. By 1835 another group of the Pilgrim Church immigrants, consisting of the families of Garrison Greenwood, Joseph Jordan, John Crist, and William M. Frost, had moved into present Anderson County, near the present county seat of Palestine, Texas. Jordan and Frost were granted headrights there during June 1835, and this small colony of pioneers began to form a community.

Garrison Greenwood (1799-1859), early East Texas settler and Baptist preacher, was one of four government-appointed regional ranger superintendents during the Texas Revolution. Greenwood's ten-man unit was based out of Fort Houston. From *Garrison Greenwood: Ancestors and Descendants*.

The little community in East Texas took shape, and the settlers built primitive cabins of the native pine. John Crist made the boards for the first homes in present Anderson County from logs chopped by William T. Sadler, who had arrived from Georgia in July 1835. The next few months were spent developing the settlement, which became known as the Fort Houston settlement. To attract settlers, Joseph Jordan and William McDonald laid out a new town they named Houston, for the prominent leader in Nacogdoches, where the settlers had recently embarked.[14]

Both the Parker's Fort and Houston settlements are significant in that they served as the rendezvous sites for the ranger companies directed by superintendents Parker and Greenwood. One of these sites would serve as a major staging area for Texas troops during future Indian expeditions. The other would long be remembered as the site of one of the more tragic Indian depredations in Texas history.

Parker's Rangers Take to the Field

About the time that the new regional ranging service was set up, an Indian depredation occurred against the McLellan family during October, which stressed the need for such a system.[15]

The McLellan family had immigrated to Texas in 1835 and settled in a remote section of present Williamson County. When the family ran short of meat, Mr. McLellan went out hunting one afternoon with one of his young sons. He became lost and did not return to the family's camp until after dark. In his absence, Indians had seized his family, stripped them, and tied them up. Mrs. McLellan, her other small son, and her infant were left alone while the Indians plundered the family's wagon. While the Indians were entertaining themselves with the settlers' belongings, Mrs. McLellan took the opportunity to untie herself and flee with her children.[16]

They hid throughout the night in the San Gabriel River bottoms, shivering in the cold air from their lack of clothing, while the Indians searched in vain for them. Mr. McLellan, assuming that his family had been killed or taken hostage, hurried back to the settlements with his young son to raise a volunteer party. Mrs. McLellan and her other two children returned to her abandoned camp the following morning and found a few rags of clothing for herself and the children to wear. She fed the children remnants of corn found in the dust about camp over the next few days.

Mr. McLellan returned within a few days with a volunteer party. He found his wife and children in pitiful condition from the lack of food and proper clothing in the October weather. The family had a joyous reunion. J. W. Wilbarger describes the McLellan attack in his early history of Texas Indian depredations but gives no details on who comprised this volunteer party.

The first new ranger company went into service within days of the act passed on October 17 by the General Council. From Fort Sterling, which by mid-1836 became popularly known as Parker's Fort, superintendent Silas Parker received word of his appointment from his brother James. His family's fort was but a series of wood cabins surrounded by a bulletproof stockade fence. The fort was home to Silas and Lucy Duty

Parker, their four children, and his elderly parents. The colony also included a number of women and children and a handful of adult men, including Silas's brothers Benjamin, James, and Joseph Parker.

Parker's Fort had recently served as a gathering place for troops during Colonel John Moore's Indian campaign in August 1835. The departure of these companies, however, left the families at the fort very exposed to the wilderness and the neighboring Indians, who were becoming less peaceful by this time.

The ordained place of rendezvous for Silas Parker's rangers was the Waco village, and it was at this location that his men were scheduled to be properly organized. Due to the recent Indian hostilities, Parker appointed Eli Hillhouse as captain of his unit and ordered volunteers raised immediately to protect against the hostilities. The Texas government would later approve the fact that this first company was organized outside of its scheduled rendezvous area.

One of the privates of Captain Hillhouse's new company was forty-one-year-old Joseph A. Parker, an older brother of Silas Parker. In a written statement in February 1836, Parker offers some insight of the formation of this early company:

> On the 23rd day of October 1835, I marched under the command of Captain Eli Hillhouse in pursuit of the Indians and on the 25th was sent back for me to get ammunition, guns and more men.[17]

At the time Hillhouse's unit marched on October 23, he had only six other rangers: William B. Billows, Joe Parker, John Richardson, Jesse G. Thompson, Samuel Bowman, and William Peterson. These seven men were the first to be employed as Texas Rangers under the new laws of the provisional government of Texas.

It is likely that Parker sent his first company in pursuit of the Indians who had attacked the McLennan family in October. This event was known to have compelled some of the settlers to go against the Indians. The *Telegraph and Texas Register*, in fact, printed an editorial in its October 17 issue advising men to ignore this action and instead report themselves to San Felipe to join Stephen F. Austin's army.[18]

When Captain Hillhouse's small ranger unit marched out against the Indians, the residents of Fort Sterling were protected by a handful of armed men. Evan W. Faulkenberry later stated in his pension papers that the fort was protected by his father, Captain David Faulkenberry. These papers show that Evan Faulkenberry served under his father during

Capt. Hillhouse/Seale's Rangers: Oct. 23, 1835 - Jan. 25, 1836

Date Enrolled:	Name:	Remarks:
Oct 23, 1835	William Peterson	Discharged January 25.
Oct 23, 1835	Jesse G. Thompson	Discharged January 25.
Oct 23, 1835	Joseph Allen Parker	Discharged January 25.
Oct 23, 1835	William B. Billows	
Oct 23, 1835	Samuel Bowman	Discharged December 31.
Oct 23, 1835	Eli Hillhouse, Capt.	Died December 24.
Oct 23, 1835	John Richardson	Discharged January 25.
Oct 26, 1835	Eli Seale	Succeeded Hillhouse as captain.
Oct 26, 1835	James A. Head	Discharged on January 25. Became captain of small unit on January 27, 1836.
Oct 26, 1835	John Loyd	Discharged January 25.
Oct 26, 1835	Caleb M. Tinnon	Died December 26.
Oct 27, 1835	George Cox	Discharged January 18.
Oct 27, 1835	Andrew M. McMillan	Discharged January 25.
Oct 27, 1835	Edward D. McMillan	Discharged January 25.
Nov 2, 1835	Abram Anglin	Discharged on January 25. Continued in ranger service under Captain Parker.
Nov 2, 1835	Silas H. Bates	Discharged on January 25. Continued in ranger service under Captain Parker.
Nov 16, 1835	Luther T. M. Plummer	Served under Captain Parker.
Nov 16, 1835	Letson Purdy	Served under Captain Parker.
Nov 16, 1835	Richard Duty	Served under Captain Parker.
Nov 16, 1835	Robert B. Frost	Under Capt. Parker to 4/22.
Nov 17, 1835	Francis Holland	Discharged January 25.
Nov 17, 1835	Hugh Chandler	Discharged December 31.
Nov 17, 1835	George Allen	Discharged January 25.
Nov 17, 1835	James Wilson Parker	Promoted to captain of ten-man unit January 1.
Nov 24, 1835	William Fullerton	Discharged January 25.
Nov 24, 1835	Henry Fullerton	Discharged January 25.
Nov 24, 1835	James M. McMillan	Discharged January 25.
Dec 4, 1835	James Emory	Died December 31.
Dec 4, 1835	Lorenzo D. Nixon Jr.	Discharged January 25. Later served under Captain Head.
Dec 20, 1835	Benjamin Parker	Under Captain Parker to May 19, 1836.
Dec 27, 1835	Catfish (Cherokee)	Discharged January 25.

October 1835 and that his service was affirmed by Abram Anglin and Silas H. Bates, both of whom would long serve the Republic of Texas as frontier rangers.[19]

Captain Faulkenberry's tenure is believed to have actually been an informal command of only the week that Hillhouse's men were in the field. Company muster rolls show that Anglin and Bates were enrolled into Hillhouse's company on November 2.

From Fort Sterling, Silas Parker sent his first report to the General Council of Texas on November 2.

> I return to you my hearty thanks for the honors bestowed on me in appointing me Superintendent of the rangers. I have used my utmost exertion to raise the company and a large majority of the company is now in the woods pursuant to my order. I took the responsibility on myself to instruct the officer to pursue a fresh Indian trail that had been made by late depredators.[20]

There is no record of Hillhouse's men getting into any serious Indian engagement. Joe Parker recorded that he spent three dollars of his own money between October 25 and October 30 in gathering ammunition and guns. Parker was apparently successful in rounding up some men, for company muster roll records show that six men—John Loyd, James A. Head, George Cox, Andrew M. McMillan, Edward McMillan, and Caleb M. Tinnon—joined on October 26 and October 27. Tinnon had come to Texas in November 1829 and was granted a one-third league in present Robertson County.

Captain Hillhouse's company apparently returned to Fort Sterling by November 2, on which date Anglin and Bates joined the company. Bates later testified that he enlisted and "performed service in Captain Hillhouse's company of rangers raised for the purpose of frontier defense in 1835."[21]

Captain Hillhouse continued to recruit new men for his ranger company after returning from his brief venture out against the Indians. In his ranger records, Silas Parker later affirmed the service of seven rangers who were briefly stationed at Fort Sterling while Hillhouse was in the field. He stated that these men were "left with me when their captain was recruiting" and these men, plus a Cherokee scout named Catfish, were temporarily "subject to my command."[22]

★   ★   ★   ★   ★

Friar's Rangers and the Taylor Fight: November 1835

The second ranger company to be organized was that of superintendent Daniel Friar, who had been authorized by the Council to organize twenty-five men between the Brazos and Colorado Rivers. He was the only superintendent who doubled as captain of his ranger unit. The site of his company's rendezvous spot was shared with that of Silas Parker's men, the Waco Indian village on the Brazos River.

Daniel Friar's rangers were organized on November 1, 1835, in the settlement of Viesca in Robertson's Colony. Sarahville de Viesca was founded in 1834 by Sterling Robertson and named for his mother, Sarah, and for the recent Mexican governor of Coahuila and Texas, Agustín Viesca. The site of this settlement was at the Falls of the Brazos on the west bank near present Marlin. By year-end 1835 the municipality of Viesca was renamed Milam.[23]

Ennes Hardin was appointed as first lieutenant of Friar's rangers. Pay records for Captain Friar's rangers during 1835 indicate that Curtis A. Wilkinson served two months apparently in the role of sergeant. Friar personally covered the company's first two months of expenses and provided some of the horses used. Lieutenant Hardin later wrote that he

> joined the company of rangers under the command of D. B. Friar between the Brazos and Colorado on the first day of November 1835 and that said Friar furnished all the provisions and ammunition for his company out of his own private money.[24]

Within two weeks of the company's formation, the Kickapoo Indians were on the warpath in Robertson's Colony. They attacked the home of Joseph Taylor, whose family had settled near the Three Forks of the Little River, formed by the juncture of the Leon, Lampasas, and Salado Rivers. The home was located some three miles southeast of the present city of Belton and about the same distance from the Falls of the Brazos. The Taylor home was a double log cabin of the dogtrot style with a door to each cabin opening to the floored passage in between. The window shutters were made of riven slats, which did not quite reach the top but left an opening of several inches.[25]

Joseph and his wife, Nancy Frazier Taylor, had not been married very long. She, in fact, brought two grown daughters and two sons, including fourteen-year-old Stephen Frazier, to live with her from her previous marriage, her husband having passed away.

The Taylor attack occurred on the night of November 12, 1835, in the moonlight just after the family had retired for the night. The parents and girls slept in one room, while the two boys slept in the other. A party of about eleven Kickapoo Indians, whose approach was warned by the faithful family dog's fierce barking, attacked them. An arrow quickly silenced the dog, and the Indians crept up to the house.

Upon their demand to know how many men were in the house, Taylor replied, "We have plenty of men, well armed and ready to fight."

The Kickapoos were ready for a fight and had been led to believe that Taylor had stolen some of their horses. Tonkawa Indians, who had placed the blame on Taylor, had actually stolen their horses.

The Indian, peeking through a crack, called Taylor a liar, whereupon Taylor jabbed at his face with a board. During this interchange, Nancy Taylor threw open the bedroom door and called the boys into her room amid a shower of arrows and rifle balls. The family then prepared to battle to the end against the Indians, with Mrs. Taylor bravely directing the efforts of the children. She pushed a table against the door, armed her younger twelve-year-old son with a gun, and instructed him to shoot the first Indian that came through the door. The two little girls were put to work molding more bullets to keep up the supply.

Older brother Stephen stood on a table and directed his fire from one of the window vents. One Kickapoo snatched an ax from the woodpile and headed for the front door, where he was shot dead. Another Indian rushed forward to drag away his comrade's body but was shot dead in the process by Joseph Taylor. With two of their party killed, the Kickapoos resorted to driving the whites from their home rather than making a direct assault.

They set fire to the vacant room and danced about with exultant yells as the flames quickly spread. Sensing their doom, Taylor announced that they should rush out and surrender, assuming that he would be killed and the women and children would at least survive as prisoners. His wife refused this option and instead jumped on a table and climbed the log wall to the roof. She removed key poles and riven shingles that led from one side of the dogtrot to the other, trying to prevent the fire from making it across the breezeway. The children passed up the family's milk supply and a small barrel of homemade vinegar, which she used to quench out the flames and prevent them from reaching their room.

As his wife was valiantly fighting flames while exposed to enemy gunfire and arrows that nicked her clothing, Joseph Taylor and stepson Stephen Frazier continued to fire back on the Indians. Taylor wounded a Kickapoo who attempted to steal a horse, while young Frazier also wounded an Indian. Another Kickapoo was discovered peering through a

A party of Kickapoo Indians attacked the Joseph Taylor home near present Belton on November 12, 1835. The family fought off their attackers and managed to kill two Indians. This early illustration, "Heroic Defense of the Taylor Family," was originally published in James De-Shields' 1912 book *Border Wars of Texas*.

hole in the cabin while trying to light their cabin on fire. The dauntless Nancy Taylor sent him howling with a wooden shovel full of live coals and embers, which seared his eyes and face.

The Indians, having suffered two dead and as many as three wounded from their small tribe, decided that this frontier family was not worth the fight and moved out. About an hour later the family cautiously emerged from the charred remnants of their home. They stashed their bedding and other valuables in the Leon River bottom and quickly made their way toward their nearest neighbor's house, that of Goldsby Childers. Childers had built a cabin on Little River, about seven miles below, near present Rogers.

The Taylor family arrived at the Childers home just after daylight on November 13, 1835. Having survived their assault, they stayed for a time at the home of Goldsby Childers, where they were well treated. One of the daughters later related, "After we had been there sixteen days our dog came to us, but he never recovered from his wound." The depredation apparently had a pronounced effect on fourteen-year-old Stephen Frazier, who joined a ranger company under Sterling Robertson two months later to fight Indians in his colony.

In the forenoon of November 13, George W. Chapman and a company of rangers arrived at the Taylor cabin. This ranger company is said to have been "stationed at the Falls of the Brazos" and also under command of Chapman. It is true that there was a newly formed Texas Ranger company stationed at Viesca at the Falls of the Brazos; it was actually commanded by Captain Daniel Friar, rather than George Chapman. Famous ranger John Salmon "Rip" Ford later wrote an account of the Taylor family fight based on statements of one of the daughters present at the battle. Ford's account seems to make sense of the situation. He explains that "Chapman made his home with the Taylor's, but was absent when the fight occurred."[26]

Suspecting trouble between the Kickapoos and Tonkawas, Chapman had left the Taylor home for Nashville to secure extra guns for protection. Upon his return after daylight, he found the home partially burned, stripped, and vacant. Assuming the family to have been murdered or carried away as hostages, he rode to Nashville to seek help. By Ford's account, a "company of rangers and citizens was quickly en route to the scene."

Some accounts of the Taylor fight incorrectly report these rangers to have been under Captain George Chapman. While he did serve as a Texas Ranger officer several years later, Chapman was not at this time employed as a ranger.

Chapman did accompany Captain Friar's rangers back to the Taylor house. One of the surviving Taylor daughters, who later married George Chapman, recalled:

> My late husband came to us at the home of Mr. Childers. He had been to our house. The bodies of the two Indians were being eaten by the hogs.[27]

The rangers reportedly cut the heads off the two charred Indian corpses, stuck them on long poles, and raised them as a gruesome warning to any other hostiles that should pass that way.

Friar's company did not find any hostile Indians to engage. By November 19 his men were back in Viesca, the central town of Robertson's Colony. Friar on this date submitted his first ranger superintendent's report to the Permanent Council, read on November 23, which described the growth of his company.

> I on the 1st day of Novr. procured 16 men who assembled at this place and proceeded to elect their officers, whereupon I was duly elected the Captain of said Company and we proceeded immediately to the Waco village and from thence have performed one trip across to the Colorado and back again

without meeting any Indians. On this morning, 6 more persons from the United States of the North have added their names to the list of Rangers under my charge. From the activity and courage of the Company I anticipate great benefit will result from the expedition.[28]

The six new men joining Captain Friar's company on November 19 from the United States were Benjamin Franklin Fitch, William Cox, Louis B. Franks, Gilbert Wright, Calvin Brallery Emmons, and Stephen Jett. Jett was enrolled "for two months service in Capt. D. B. Friar's company of rangers in the northwestern frontier" and was discharged on January 15, 1836.

Captain Friar also submitted a report of his first month's expenses, totaling $1,350, to the Council on November 24. This included payment for the first sixteen rangers, shoeing of twenty-five horses, two hundred bushels of corn, $250 for necessary packhorses, and $200 for sundry articles. Friar also submitted a voucher of $154.77 for his first month's expenses in procuring corn, beef, and pork for his troops.

These notes he sent via Indian commissioner Joseph Hood from Viesca to San Felipe with instructions for the Treasurer of Texas to "at sight pay the above to J. L. Hood."

As of the end of November, Captain Friar and First Lieutenant Hardin had twenty enlisted rangers, all Robertson colonists, under their charge. One of the company's early pay vouchers lists the names of these rangers but does not include Friar or Sergeant Wilkinson, whose service is affirmed by audited military papers.

Shortly after his first report was issued to the Council, a party of Captain Friar's men had an encounter with hostile Indians while out on a scouting patrol. Lieutenant Hardin wrote, "the Indians made the attack on us near the San Gabriel." The rangers apparently made a hurried escape from the area, as Hardin noted that his horse "was wounded so that he could not travel and was left and died without any doubt."

The horse lost by Hardin was one of the ones that had been supplied for company use by Captain Friar. The company apparently escaped without injury but did lose at least one other horse in the brief encounter. Private Calvin Emmons was later given a promissory note from "The Provisional Government of Texas" for forty dollars for "1 horse killed by Indians."[29]

★   ★   ★   ★   ★

Original Payment Voucher of Captain Daniel Friar's Rangers:

Employed:	*Name:*	*Pay:*	*Drew in their favor:*
Nov. 1, 1835	Montgomery Shackleford	$75.00	$43.75
Nov. 1, 1835	David Wilson Campbell	75.00	
Nov. 1, 1835	Napoleon Darneill	75.00	40.75
Nov. 1, 1835	Ennes Hardin	75.00	
Nov. 1, 1835	William Brooks	75.00	
Nov. 1, 1835	John H. Pierson	75.00	
Nov. 1, 1835	William C. Neill	75.00	
Nov. 1, 1835	William H. McGee	75.00	
Nov. 1, 1835	William Moffitt	75.00	
Nov. 1, 1835	Peterson Lloyd	75.00	
Nov. 1, 1835	Warren Lyman	75.00	37.50
Nov. 1, 1835	Richard S. Teal	75.00	
Nov. 1, 1835	Thomas H. Barron	75.00	
Nov. 1, 1835	James Matthew Jett	75.00	
Nov. 19, 1835	Benjamin Franklin Fitch	52.00	
Nov. 19, 1835	William Cox	52.00	23.75
Nov. 19, 1835	Louis Franks	52.00	24.75
Nov. 19, 1835	Gilbert Wright	52.00	170.50 total
Nov. 19, 1835	Calvin Brallery Emmons	52.00	
Nov. 19, 1835	Stephen Jett	52.00	
Source: Daniel B. Friar AC, R 33, F 463		1,362.00	

Concepción and an Indian Ambush

The Texas Revolution continued to grow in scope during the time that these first two ranger companies were taking to the field. Soon after the October 2 Gonzales battle, General Austin's volunteer army had grown to more than three hundred men. On October 12 Austin moved his troops toward San Antonio de Béxar, where General Martín Perfecto de Cos had recently concentrated some 650 Mexican soldiers. The Texans made camp along Salado Creek east of San Antonio, where more volunteers continued to join them. Among the newer arrivals were companies under Captains James Bowie and Juan N. Seguín, the latter commanding a company of Mexican Texans.[30]

On October 27 Bowie and James Walker Fannin Jr. were sent by Austin from the mission San Francisco de la Espada south of Béxar to secure a position for his army closer to the Mexican forces in Béxar. Another four volunteer companies under Captains Andrew Briscoe, Robert Coleman, Valentine Bennett, and Michael Goheen explored the other missions and briefly engaged Mexican scouts before reaching Nuestra

Señora de la Purísima Concepción.[31] Coleman and Goheen, of course, had been ranger captains during Colonel Moore's recent Indian campaign.

Near the Mission Concepción, Fannin's ninety men became engaged in a skirmish on October 28 with a 275-man Mexican force under Colonel Domingo de Ugartechea. The Texans initially occupied a wooded bend in the San Antonio River. After several hours of fighting infantrymen and two cannons, the Texans succeeded in forcing the Mexicans to retreat. During the Battle of Concepción, Bowie's men even managed to capture one of the two Mexican cannons. General Austin, arriving with more troops a half hour after the fighting ceased, was persuaded by his junior officers not to pursue the retreating Mexican forces back into Béxar. The Mexicans suffered fourteen killed and thirty-nine wounded, some of whom later died. The Texans lost Richard Andrews of Captain Coleman's company killed, the first Texan death in the revolution, and another man wounded.

In the wake of this victory, a small Texas army detachment suffered an attack by hostile Indians. Major George Sutherland departed the main fort at Goliad on October 28 with twenty-five men and twelve teams of supplies for the main camp of the army. One of the companies, which continued to operate from this post since the Texans had seized it on October 9, was a spy company under Captain Ira Ingram. The afternoon after Sutherland's departure, Ingram sent a six-man detachment to report to the army headquarters near Béxar.[32]

Early in the evening of October 29, this detachment was attacked by Indians at a point about twelve miles from the Goliad fort. First Lieutenant David M. Collinsworth yelled out, "Oh, Lord!" as he was hit and fell from his horse. Second Lieutenant Augustus H. Jones and the other four surviving company members rushed back to the fort. The following day, October 30, they returned with eight others from their company and retrieved the body of Lieutenant Collinsworth. "He was shot in the neck, and probably killed instantly," related Captain Ingram. "The head and face, however, bore several marks of savage violence."

Ingram reported to General Council President Royall that Collinsworth was buried "with the honors of war." He also related that of the three men recently appointed as Indian commissioners—James Kerr, John Joseph Linn, and Thomas G. Western—the former two had departed for the Nueces with Colonel James Power, a General Council committee member of land and Indian affairs. They were to talk the Karankawa Indians out of committing attacks on the livestock around the

Guadalupe River area. The resulting treaty with the Karankawas was later deemed to be mostly successful during the revolution.[33]

The Mexican army did not immediately react to their loss at the Battle of Concepción. Texans continued to collect near Béxar during late October and early November. Captain Thomas J. Rusk arrived with a force of East Texas volunteers, bringing Austin's total numbers to more than six hundred. Some of the volunteers returned home during November to secure winter clothing, but other newly arriving companies continued to offset the losses. Texas and Mexican cavalry skirmished on occasion during this buildup period. The most significant skirmish occurred on November 8 when William Barret Travis and other Texans managed to capture some three hundred Mexican mules and horses grazing beyond the Medina River.[34]

★ ★ ★ ★ ★

Council Adds Fourth Ranger District

After a short hiatus, the General Council of Texas reconvened on November 1 at San Felipe and continued in session through November 14. The role of the Texas Rangers would be further defined, and this legislative body of the provisional government of Texas would add another ranging district. The Council received a report from the temporary council meetings, which had ended the week prior, including the report authorizing the formation of volunteer frontier rangers.

Representing the Nacogdoches municipality was James Parker, who was a brother to ranger superintendent Silas Parker. He carried with him recommendations for the Council on certain improvements that the Fort Sterling rangers desired. For starters, Silas felt that the superintendents should have some say in the designated rendezvous site of the companies. Parker felt that the Council-designated rendezvous spot of the Waco village was not in the best interest of the public they were to protect.

Silas Parker also asked for an increase in the allotted number of rangers in his Brazos-to-Trinity district.

> I should say that the company ranging from Brazos to Trinity should be at least 40 strong. We are nearly out of ammunitions and provisions. For further particulars, I refer you to Mr. J. W. Parker, who has been here in person and discovered the most of the difficulty under which we are at this time laboring, and have personally instructed him what I think to be the most advisable course.[35]

After approving what acts had already been passed, the Council then set to work establishing a proper military structure for Texas to handle its current revolution with Mexico. On November 6, 1835, it was resolved to create a five-man committee to "provide for the necessities of our army and troops on the road." This important committee was authorized to borrow money and originate debts to cover the costs of providing for a proper army. These special committee members were Henry Millard of Liberty, Richardson Royall of Matagorda, Joseph D. Clements of Gonzales, William Plunket Harris of Harrisburg, and Robert Williamson of Mina municipality.[36]

The Council also held an election to replace Colonel John Moore in the field. Edward Burleson was the overwhelming choice to succeed Moore as colonel, or General Austin's second-in-command of the Texas army.

Representative Clements of the special military committee presented a new resolution on November 6 pertaining to the ranger system that had been created on October 17. This act proposed that the territory covered by the regional rangers be extended "from the Colorado river, their present limits, to the settlements on the Guadalupe river." Clements also requested that a "proportionate number of men" be assigned to cover this new district.[37]

This resolution was then referred to a committee under Daniel Parker that was charged with studying the amendments to the "acts of the council on the subject of rangers on the frontiers." This latest proposal would stretch the boundary covered by the Texas Rangers from the Neches River westward to Cibolo Creek, a tributary of the San Antonio River.[38]

Parker read the ranger resolution early in the morning on November 9, at which time it was adopted by the Consultation. The councilmen recognized the prior acts of the General Council on this subject and considered the present resolution "sufficient for the present emergency." George Washington Davis, the representative serving the Gonzales municipality, was selected as this fourth ranger superintendent to join Greenwood, Parker, and Friar in the field. The November 9 resolution effectively extended the line of frontier rangers

> from the Colorado river to the Cibolo, with a company of twenty rangers under the superintendence of G. W. Davis, who shall be governed by the same resolutions and instructions of the other superintendent heretofore given; and that the said George W. Davis, make his place of rendezvous at the place known by the

big spring or head of St. Mark's [San Marcos] river.

The Consultation next was asked to approve the organization of the company of rangers under Silas Parker. Parker's first company under Captain Hillhouse had been organized to scout against the Indians before actually reaching the "proper place of rendezvous" as required. It was also recommended that Silas Parker be allowed to add another ten men to his company "by and under the former authority and rules."[39]

Parker's extra rangers were approved, and his shortage of ammunition was addressed. Committee Chairman Henry Millard sent written instructions to William Smith on November 8.

> Please forward to the Rangers, under the command of Capt. Silas M. Parker—seventy-five lead and twenty-five powder and present your account to the Govt of Texas.[40]

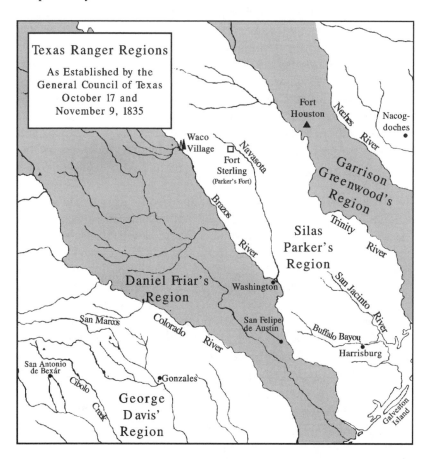

Texas Ranger Regions

As Established by the General Council of Texas October 17 and November 9, 1835

In other acts concerning the present revolution, the Consultation resolved that all volunteers under command of General Stephen F. Austin who continue "in service until the reduction of San Antonio or until they receive an honorable discharge" should be entitled to twenty dollars per month. These volunteers were to be paid from the day they left their home until the day they returned and would also be reimbursed for personal expenses while in service and for the loss of any private property.[41]

On November 12, 1835, the Consultation elected Henry Smith as the provisional governor of Texas, James W. Robinson as his lieutenant governor, and Sam Houston as the major general of the Texas army. The Council appointed Branch Archer, William Harris Wharton, and Stephen Austin as commissioners to solicit help from the United States for the current crisis. This new appointment would necessitate Austin passing his immediate command of the Texas army to Colonel Edward Burleson.

This General Council broke up on November 14 for a two-week hiatus. Some members would be replaced before the next legislative body was seated. Among them was James Parker, who departed San Felipe for the 170-mile return trip to his residence at Fort Sterling. He was there by November 17, on which day he enlisted as a ranger in Captain Hillhouse's company. Parker, as related, had been selected to take over as captain of the newly approved ten-man unit under his brother Silas's superintendence. Parker would not formally be considered a captain until the time that his new company was mustered into service weeks later.

★   ★   ★   ★   ★

"Ready, Armed, Equipped": Williamson's Ranger Battalion

The regional frontier ranging system established in October and expanded to four districts in November did not have the time to reach full strength before the provisional government of Texas passed further acts restructuring this system.

The buildup of army forces in the vicinity of San Antonio left the frontier settlements very loosely protected. When the General Council reconvened on November 21, a new proposal to protect the citizens with an organized ranging corps was presented. John A. Wharton of the Committee on Military Affairs presented this ordinance, which called for a three-company ranger battalion of 168 men, to be headed by a commanding major.[42]

On November 24, 1835, the General Council passed "An Ordinance and Decree to establish and organize a Corps of Rangers." It stated in short

That there shall be, and there is hereby created and established a Corps of Rangers, which shall consist of three companies of fifty-six men each, with one Captain, one Lieutenant, and one second Lieutenant for each company; and there shall be one Major to command the said companies, who shall be subject to the orders and direction of the Commander-in-Chief of the Regular Army.[43]

Section Two decreed that the privates of the ranging corps "shall be enlisted for one year" and would be paid $1.25 per day in compensation for "pay, ration, clothing and horse service." Each ranger was required to be "always ready armed and equipped, and supplied with one hundred rounds of powder and ball." The private was required to have a dependable horse that was properly accoutered and equipped with a saddle, bridle, and blanket. Should he be unable to provide his own horse, the captain of the company "shall cause a horse to be purchased for said private and charge him with the same, in the settlement of his quarterly accounts."

Section Three of the new ranging corps act specified that the officers, in addition to the same per diem compensation of the privates, would receive the same pay as officers of equal rank in the cavalry of the U.S. Army.

This act was passed at San Felipe, signed by James W. Robinson, lieutenant governor and ex-officio president of the General Council, and approved by Peter B. Dexter, secretary of the General Council, on November 26, 1835. This new ranger battalion differed from the one passed during the October Council session in two main ways. First, it eliminated regional ranger superintendents and placed command of the individual companies under one commanding major. Second, the major commanding the ranger battalion reported directly to the commander in chief of the Texas army versus the provisional government. This revised reporting structure would continue to serve as the basic ranger structure for years.

The passage of the November 24 ranger ordinance did not immediately eliminate the ranging system previously established in October. The districts presided over by superintendents Parker, Friar, and Greenwood would field rangers into 1836. The newly appointed superintendent, George Davis, does not appear to have had time to establish his regional company. This new ranger act and the buildup of Texas troops near San Antonio during late November and early

December likely negated the need for his company.

The Council also passed an ordinance and decree on November 24 to raise a regular army. This Texas army would consist of 1,120 men who were to be enlisted for two years or the duration of the war. The army would contain one regiment of artillery and one of infantry, each presided over by a colonel. Each regiment was to be broken into two five-company battalions, each led by a lieutenant colonel. Upon honorable discharge from the army, every noncommissioned officer and private was entitled to 640 acres of land in Texas. Interestingly, each company was also to include one drummer and one fifer, who were entitled to bounty land, rations, and pay equal to that of a sergeant.[44]

On November 28 the Council's Select Committee under Daniel Parker appointed John Dunn in charge of purchasing provisions for the volunteer army. Provisions were to be carried over water to the Copano Bay landing and then delivered to Dunn.[45] Ammunition for the regional ranger companies was to be drawn by the four superintendents from John Lott in Washington-on-the-Brazos, where a vast quantity of ammunition was deposited.

The Council met again at 7:00 p.m. in San Felipe on November 28 to handle special elections for municipal judges and for the election of company officers of the regiment of infantry of the army of Texas. The Council then proceeded to the elections of officers for the newly approved corps of rangers.

Three captains were elected to lead the new ranging corps. The first was Isaac Watts Burton, a thirty-year-old Georgia native, who had settled between the Sabine and Nacogdoches in 1832. Having led a volunteer company against the commander of the Mexican garrison in Nacogdoches soon after his arrival, Burton was now charged with forming a ranger company in the more eastern areas of Texas. The second new captain was John Jackson Tumlinson Jr., oldest son of the Colorado Colony's slain *alcalde* and already a veteran Indian fighter in Texas. He had also served on Colonel John Henry Moore's Tawakoni campaign the previous summer before being commissioned to organize rangers from key Colorado River settlements such as Bastrop. The third man elected captain was William W. Arrington, who had arrived in Texas as a bachelor in 1831 and settled in Green DeWitt's colony. Arrington, the General Council representative for the Gonzales municipality, was also known for being one of the eighteen defiant Gonzales citizens who had helped initiate the Texas Revolution.

Officer Appointments: November 28, 1835
Texas Army - Regiment of Infantry

Captain:	*First Lieutenant:*	*Second Lieutenant:*
James Carter	Henry Teal	Madison G. Whitaker
John Bird	John York	McHenry Winborne
Ezekiel Williams	William H. Smith	Benjamin F. Sanders
Andrew Briscoe	Franklin Hardin	Milton Hardin
James Collinsworth	Leander H. McNeil	Pleasant Bull
Robert Boyd Irvine	George English	Leonard H. Mabbitt
Robert M. Coleman	Amasa Turner	Benjamin C. Wallace
George M. Collinsworth	John Bowman	William E. Hooth
John W. Martin	J. W. Shepard	Jefferson Allcorn
George F. Richardson	Robert Wilson	David L. Kokernot

Corps of Texas Rangers

Captain:	*First Lieutenant:*	*Second Lieutenant:*
Isaac Watts Burton	Horatio M. Hanks	Thomas Robbins
William W. Arrington	Jesse McCoy	Littleton Tumlinson
John Jackson Tumlinson Jr.	Launcelot Smither*	Joseph W. Rogers

* Declined position. Replaced by George M. Petty by Council.

Source: Proceedings of the General Council, 51-53.

For major of the corps of rangers, three men were nominated: Robert Williamson, James Kerr, and John G. W. Pierson. Pierson was another member of the council, present as representative for the municipality of Viesca. Williamson, captain of one of the ranger companies of Colonel Moore's Tawakoni campaign, was representing the municipality of Mina (later Bastrop). Wyatt Hanks submitted a letter recommending Williamson for major that had been signed by a large number of citizens. In a close vote, "Willie" Williamson received six votes to Kerr's five and was thus duly declared major of the ranger corps by the Council.[46]

Despite his zeal for recruiting, it will be seen that Williamson was never able to completely raise the designated ranger corps to full strength. This was due partially to the scarcity of available recruits and the dissatisfaction of the men in not being able to elect officers.[47]

During the morning session of December 1, the Council received a request from Dr. Benjamin Briggs Goodrich requesting that a surgeon be appointed to the corps of rangers. The Committee on Military Affairs, however, decided that the rangers should use an army surgeon if one was needed.[48]

Major Robert McAlpin Williamson (1806-1859) was named the senior commander of a new regiment of Texas Rangers that would serve during the Texas Revolution. Known as "Three-Legged Willie" due to a wooden leg he wore, Williamson had previously commanded a ranger company on Colonel Moore's summer 1835 campaign. *The UT Institute of Texan Cultures at San Antonio, No. 70-497.*

Daniel Parker also called on the Council this day to fill a void in the new ranger corps' officers. Ranger nominee Launcelot Smither, engaged with the army as a messenger and spy near Béxar, declined his position as first lieutenant of Captain John Tumlinson's company. On a motion of Wyatt Hanks, the Council went into a closed-door election, and Stephen Townsend was selected to fill this void in a vote of six to five over George M. Petty.

It was quickly pointed out, however, that a quorum of Council had not been present during this voting. A quorum was then formed, and the House proceeded to ballot again, with different results. George Petty was elected first lieutenant of rangers over Townsend by a vote of eight to five. Townsend, however, would later serve as a ranger officer during the revolution.[49]

From his army headquarters in San Felipe, General Sam Houston issued orders on December 1 to his freshly appointed ranger commander. Major Williamson was to lead his rangers to the sources of Mill Creek, where Indians were lurking "with intentions no doubt to murder and steal horses." Williamson was to solicit from thirty to seventy men for this campaign.

> Should you obtain a sufficient number to pursue the Indians, you will do so, as far as policy will justify but you will not expose your command, where there can be no benefit result to the Country.
>
> Should you overtake the Indians, you will chastise them, in such sort, as will prevent them, from future incursions into our

frontier settlements and give security, to our inhabitants.[50]

These orders were sent via Colonel Almanzon Huston to Williamson in Mina. Upon reviewing these orders, Williamson penned an immediate response to General Houston on December 1. He promised to "immediately repair to the point designated for the purpose indicated" and that he would exert every effort to engage these Indians. He signed his letter as "Major Commanding the Ranging Corps of Texas."

Little is recorded of Williamson's efforts to engage these Indians about Mill Creek during December. He later related one story of he and five of his rangers attacking some Indians on an unspecified date. His small party, having been stalked by a band of Indians for several days, decided to lay an ambush for their enemy. Knowing that these warriors preferred surprise attacks just before dawn, the rangers built a large campfire one night that could be seen for some distance. Then each man wrapped his blanket around a log of the approximate size of a man's body.

The rangers concealed themselves, and just before dawn the Indians approached their camp. Without making a sound, they crawled forward and attacked what appeared to be six sleeping frontiersmen. By the time the Indians realized their knives were hitting solid wood, the rangers had opened fire with their rifles and killed them. Williamson considered this to be his most satisfactory Indian fight of all.[51]

★ ★ ★ ★ ★

Béxar Siege: December 5-9, 1835

When Williamson returned from his Indian scout to begin recruiting men for his new ranger corps, he would have more than a little difficulty finding volunteers during December. The bulk of the Texas army and the volunteer companies arriving from the United States had become engaged in the battle to wrestle San Antonio from Mexican forces.

Mexican and Texan forces had been sparring with each other around San Antonio throughout November without any major battles. General Cos used his time to fortify the town plazas west of the San Antonio River at Béxar and to fortify the former mission known as the Alamo east of the stream. Stephen F. Austin had pushed for an assault on San Antonio, but his wishes were not fulfilled before he was called away from his command in November to assume diplomatic duties in the United States. In his absence, Colonel Edward Burleson assumed command of the Texas army.[52]

When Texan spy Erastus "Deaf" Smith reported Mexican cavalry approaching on November 26, Burleson ordered troops out to cut them off. The ensuing skirmish near Alazán Creek west of town became known as the Grass Fight because the captured Mexican supply animals were found to carry only fodder for horses rather than the rumored pay for Mexican soldiers.

During the next few days, Colonel Burleson debated on moving his troops back to Goliad due to limited supplies and winter conditions. Intelligence of declining Mexican morale in San Antonio, however, prompted Benjamin Rush Milam, who had been put in charge of a company of scouts by Austin, and Captain William Gordon Cooke to call for volunteers to proceed with the storming of Béxar. During a meeting at an old mill on the night of December 4, Milam uttered his inspirational call of "Who will go with old Ben Milam to Béxar?" The attacking party was organized into two divisions.

Milam and Cooke assaulted San Antonio on December 5 with approximately three hundred volunteers while the reluctant Burleson and another four hundred men scouted, protected the camp and supplies, and forced Cos to keep his 570 men divided between the town and the Alamo.

Colonel Milam took charge of the first division, assisted by Lieutenant Colonel Louis B. Franks of the artillery and Major Robert C. Morris of the New Orleans Grays. Sam Maverick and Hendrick Arnold guided the first division. The first division company commanders were Captains John York, Thomas Alley, William H. Patton, Almeron Dickerson [Dickinson], John English, and Thomas W. Ward. The second division was placed under Colonel Francis W. "Frank" Johnson, assisted by Colonels James Grant and William T. Austin. Deaf Smith and John W. Smith served as their guides. The companies of this division were under Captains William Gordon Cooke, Plácido Benavides, Thomas H. Breece, John W. Peacock, James G. Swisher, and Haden Harrison Edwards.[53]

The siege at Béxar attracted men from all over Texas to join the fight, including some who had recently been named to take other military commands by the government on November 28. John York, for example, had been named as first lieutenant of an infantry company but actually was commanding a volunteer company from the Brazos area during early December. Captain York's company included John Jackson Tumlinson Jr., one of the three appointed to take command of a frontier ranging company under Major Williamson. Tumlinson would later draw pay as a ranger captain beginning November 28, although he would not formally organize his rangers until January, weeks after the fighting in San

Antonio had ceased. Several of the other new ranger officers, including Jesse McCoy and Littleton Tumlinson, also were participants in the Béxar siege.

The morning of December 5 opened with Colonel James Clinton Neill leading a division of artillerymen in a feint against the Alamo, opening fire on it to divert the enemy's attention. The other two divisions swept in to seize two key houses north of the plaza in San Antonio. The firing soon became tremendous as the Mexican army was engaged. During the first day, the Texans suffered one killed, plus twelve privates and three officers wounded. The enemy kept up a constant firing during the night, while the Texan divisions reinforced their positions.

The other companies under Burleson, including a division under Colonel John Moore, were soon called in to reinforce the efforts. Commanders of other Texan companies called in to fight the Mexican army in San Antonio following the initial sweep were those of Captains Henry W. Augustine, John M. Bradley, James Chessher, John Crane, Peter Duncan, Michael Goheen, Manuel Leal, Mark B. Lewis, Thomas Lewellen, Albert Martin, Thomas J. Rusk, Juan Seguín, Thomas Splane, and William B. Travis.

After daylight on December 6, the Mexicans were discovered to be occupying the rooftops in key positions around the plaza. From these positions, they maintained a steady small arms fire upon the Texans. A detachment under Lieutenant William McDonald from Captain John Crane's company took a key house after a hard fight and managed to extend the Texan line. Five more Texans were wounded throughout the course of the day. Captain John Peacock was seriously wounded during the Béxar siege and later died.

The fighting was intense again on December 7. About noon Henry Karnes led a charge against a house near the plaza with a crowbar while under heavy fire. Followed by Captain York's company, these men took this house and held the position. The Mexicans' firing was heavy again late in the evening, and Ben Milam was fatally hit in the head while passing from his division's position to that of Johnson's. Johnson thereafter took overall control of the fighting forces. This loss seemed to set the Texans off with a new fury for vengeance. A large party consisting of men from the companies of Captains Lewellen, English, Crane, and York charged on foot to take possession of a key Mexican house on the north side of Main Street.

During December 8 Ugartechea returned to San Antonio with more than six hundred replacements, although the majority were untrained conscripts. The Texans pierced the thick partitioning walls between houses and steadily advanced on Mexican positions about the central part of town. After dark on December 8, Burleson sent reinforcements from the companies of Captains Swisher, Alley, Edwards, and Duncan who moved in to help hold the command of the enemy's northwest portion of defenses.

Fighting continued until the remaining Mexicans retreated into the Alamo before daylight on December 9. Four companies of Cos's cavalry decided not to fight and rode away. At 6:30 a.m. General Cos sent up a flag of truce, whereupon General Burleson proceeded into town later that day to hold peace talks. The talks were concluded by the early morning hours of December 10. Cos and his soldiers were allowed to retire southward under the provision that they did not oppose any further.

Of an aggregate force of perhaps fourteen hundred soldiers, the Mexicans had lost as many as one hundred fifty soldiers in the Béxar siege. Texan casualties numbered thirty to thirty-five men. The capture of San Antonio was a moral victory for the Texas settlers and the United States soldiers who had come to fight. Those who believed that Santa Anna had been demoralized and would give up were, however, mistaken.

CHAPTER 4

"Loathsome Trophy"

December 11, 1835 -
February 23, 1836

Parker's Rangers Form Second Company

During early December the new ranging corps under Major Willie Williamson was still in the early stages of organizing. There were only two companies of the previously approved regional rangers in the field, those of Captains Daniel Friar and Eli Hillhouse.

The company of Hillhouse continued to operate from Fort Sterling and add new recruits during the month under the superintendence of Silas Parker. Parker had been authorized by the Council to bring an additional ten-man company under his charge, but this group would not assemble before year's end.

Silas Parker wrote from Fort Sterling on December 17, 1835, to the General Council in San Felipe, informing them of the latest efforts of his rangers.

> Through much difficulty, I have engaged about thirty of the rangers under my superintendence. Several of them have lost their horses and the horses continue dying, so that it is extremely difficult to keep horses for them. I find it very difficult to procure provisions. Indeed, I cannot engage any beef or pork for them though store is plenty in the country. Such is the indifference of the people as to the cause of Texas. I have no other chance but to go to those that has cattle to spare and have them valued myself; and the people of my vicinity has turned out all the beef that we had—the amount of which I shall make out in my next. I have drawn about 100 Lbs. Lead & 1 ½ Keg. of powder from Mr. Lott. The Indians has committed no depredations since my last. The boys are zealously engaged and I hope their labors will be of the most vital importance to those fe[ar]less adventurers that has reclaimed this fertile country from savage haunts.[1]

Parker also pointed out that establishing a mail route from Viesca to Washington would be beneficial, as the cost for him to send expresses had become considerable. "It would afford us a great satisfaction to have the public news at any rate conveyed to our seat of justice," he wrote. Parker also noted that he had furnished all supplies to his company thus far and would send a full account of all his expenditures with his next communication.

Parker's note was read before the Council on December 19. The Council's Committee on Military Affairs also decided that the rangers did not need a separate surgeon to be furnished, as had been proposed. Should these frontier companies be called to act with the regular army, "they will be entitled to the services of the surgeon of the regiment to which they are attached."[2]

Securing provisions for these companies out on the extreme Texas frontiers was no simple task. Parker furnished much of the early provisions for his rangers. He furnished a hog, valued at five dollars by rangers Elisha Anglin and Samuel Frost, to Hillhouse's company on October 30. Between October 30 and December 15, he also furnished fourteen bushels of corn totaling fifty-six dollars and twenty-five dollars' worth of fresh beef, salt, and salted pork to his rangers.[3]

For more complete provisioning, Silas Parker was forced to send his brother Joe Parker 170 miles to San Felipe with his wagon and horse team. Joe Parker wrote:

> On the 18th of December I was dispatched for services at Mr. Tinnons on the San Antonio Road by Silas M. Parker and Captain Hillhouse for the purpose of coming to San Felipe with the charge of wagon and team to lay in necessaries for the company.[4]

Parker's audited claims show an order signed by Silas Parker dated December 18, 1835, at Fort Sterling that appointed "Joseph A. Parker my agent to contract for all necessary provisions for the rangers under my superintendence." Silas would accept all contracts and orders, and Joe was to convey the provisions to Fort Sterling. Another audited paper shows that Joe Parker was given temporary leave from Captain Hillhouse's company to fulfill these orders.[5]

Joe Parker set out from Tinnons' place down the San Antonio Road for San Felipe, covering expenses for food and forage for his horse and for the wagon team out of his own pocket. On December 21 he secured five bushels of corn at two dollars per bushel and twenty-five pounds of pork at four dollars per hundredweight. On December 23 in Washington he picked up more forage and horse feed before pushing on for San Felipe, where he arrived on December 24 and spent three days. While in town, he brought the latest news from home to his brother Daniel Parker Sr., who was still serving on the General Council.

Loaded with supplies, Parker departed San Felipe. He paid for the wagon crossing twice and for his horse on December 27, a total of $2.25. On December 28 he purchased meal and bacon and on December 30 he provided five more bushels of corn, twenty-five pounds of pork, and fifteen pounds of beef. On January 5, 1836, he paid $1.25 for forage and crossing fees at the Navasota River and arrived at Tinnon's place on January 6. Parker arrived with his wagonload of provisions on January 9 at Fort Sterling. The seemingly routine task of securing provisions for a frontier ranger company had thus taken a full three weeks.

By the time Parker arrived back at Fort Sterling, he found that his company had undergone changes. Captain Eli Hillhouse had died. The company's muster rolls simply states that he was "discharged" as of December 24, 1835. Hillhouse was succeeded by Eli Seale, who had been with the company since its inception in October. A muster roll signed by Captain Seale before Judge Joseph Baker on February 5, 1836, in San Felipe de Austin, shows that he was in command through January 25, 1836.

It appears that the Hillhouse/Seale company was at the ranger headquarters at the Falls of the Brazos at the time command was passed to Seale. Service records for ranger Lorenzo D. Nixon show that he had supplied his own provisions since joining the company on December 4. His monthly allowance was later deducted, however, for provisions he received at the Falls on December 29, 1836. Nixon became the lieutenant, or second-in-command, of Captain Seale's company and served as such for the next month.[6] Seale's ranger company, under charge of Silas Parker's superintendence, operated from Fort Sterling during January 1836.

One of the more interesting men serving under Captain Seale after Hillhouse's death was a Cherokee Indian named Catfish, who was used for scouting. Seale signed his discharge from "my company as a ranger" on January 25, 1836, at Fort Sterling.[7]

Also on January 1, Captain James Parker took command of the secondary company of rangers under Silas Parker that had been approved by the General Council on November 9. His audited claims show that he was elected Captain of a part of a company of rangers on about January 1 1836 under the superintendence of Silas M. Parker in pursuance of an ordnance and decree of the General Council.[8]

Parker's rangers would remain in service through the Texas Revolution, although he would later have trouble securing payment as a captain due to the fact that he did not at all times have the prescribed complement of ten men under his charge.

New Companies Form Under Burton and Sadler

In the wake of the Béxar siege, the General Council in San Felipe was asked on December 17 to add another ranging company to the service. This resolution, introduced by Asa Mitchell, called for ten men to range on the headwaters of Cummins and Rabb's Creeks, northeast of Mina. The company was to be commanded by a first and second lieutenant, who would be instructed "to range no longer than they conceive it necessary for the protection of the citizens in the immediate vicinity."[9]

This proposal, however, was struck down the following day by Joseph Clements and the Committee on Military Affairs, who felt that "the additional corps of rangers is altogether unnecessary." It was their opinion that the corps already created under Major Williamson "is sufficient for the protection of the country, which the said resolution contemplates."

Although the Council deemed Williamson's corps to be sufficient coverage for the frontiers on December 17, it was not until two days later that official orders went out from Washington-on-the-Brazos to the appointed ranger officers.

Major Williamson was sent orders on December 19 to "proceed to Mina and there establish your Headquarters for recruiting" his corps of rangers. Similarly, the other ranger officers were given their respective orders. Captain Isaac Burton, for instance, was issued orders from acting Adjutant General George W. Poe on December 19 to "proceed to Sabine and there establish your Headquarters for a recruiting station." Burton was to send weekly reports of his progress to Major Williamson at Mina and receive his future orders directly from him.[10]

There is little record of the men or activities of Captain Burton's company during the Texas Revolution. The officers originally appointed under his command, however, were First Lieutenant Horatio M. Hanks and Second Lieutenant Thomas Robbins. In the December 28, 1835 session for the General Council, Horatio M. Hanks declined his nomination. The Council in his place elected Wade Horton as first lieutenant of the ranger corps.[11] Burton had established his recruitment station by early January and began the slow process of building a company.

Another man organizing a ranger company at the turn of the new year was Captain William Turner Sadler at Fort Houston in East Texas. A veteran of the Seminole and Creek Indian wars, he had been selected in December 1835 by superintendent Garrison Greenwood to organize the ten-man company designated to patrol between the Neches and Trinity Rivers. Republic records show that Captain Sadler's rangers were officially mustered into service on January 1, 1836, in present Anderson County.

Sadler, one of the early pioneers who had helped establish the little settlement of Houston, had arrived in Nacogdoches in July 1835. Born in Lincoln County, North Carolina, on July 27, 1797, he and his family had moved on to Putnam County, Georgia, in 1817. He made an early scouting trip to Texas and surveyed the land around present Anderson and Houston Counties. Sadler sold his own Georgia farm in 1834 and left his family behind to start a new life in Texas. En route, he met a fellow Putnam County traveler named Mirabeau B. Lamar, future president of Texas, aboard the steamboat *Little Rock* on the Alabama River on June 19, 1835. Together, Sadler and Lamar traveled until parting ways in Natchitoches, Louisiana, about July 5.[12]

The members of Captain Sadler's small ranging company were enrolled on January 1, 1836, for a three-month period. Although no muster roll has survived for this unit, Sadler and seven of his other men later joined a company known as the Nacogdoches Volunteers near the

Captain William Turner Sadler (1797-1884) commanded a ten-man ranger company that worked on Fort Houston during the Texas Revolution. He would later command companies during the Kickapoo War and the Cherokee War in East Texas. *Author's collection.*

Captain Sadler's Mounted Rangers: January 1 - March 16, 1836

Captain:	William Calvert Hallmark
William Turner Sadler	James Madden
Privates:	Philip C. Martin
Daniel LaMora Crist	Daniel Parker Jr.
Daniel Doubt	Dickerson Parker
John Crawford Grigsby	Samuel G. Wells

Source: Based on author's research of available Republic of Texas military records. See Moore, *Taming Texas*, 39-41.

Colorado River prior to San Jacinto but *after* that company had originally formed.

The names of several men of his company are shown in Republic of Texas pension papers. Twenty-one-year-old Daniel LaMora Crist stated that he "was a private in Captain William T. Sadler's Company No. 10 of Mounted Rangers of independent volunteers under order of the Government." Samuel G. Wells also joined the Fort Houston rangers on New Year's Day. His service was later affirmed by company mate Daniel Parker Jr., a brother of ranger superintendent Silas Parker.[13]

These rangers, all residents of present Houston and Anderson Counties, are listed on several documents as "Company No. 10," a name that would have been indicative of size and not number of total ranger units in existence. Captain Sadler referred to his men as the "Houston Company" in a document he signed in March 1836. His company was assigned to construct a blockhouse, the main fortification for what would become known in East Texas as Fort Houston.[14] The early cabins of Fort Houston had already been started by the settlers during the fall of 1835.

The pioneers of the new town of Houston needed the support of these rangers and the fortification that they were building. The citizens were exposed to Indians, as superintendent Greenwood noted of Houston weeks later on March 7.

> This place and the adjoining frontier is exposed from the Indians who inhabit in great numbers this part of the country—the Ionis, the Caddos, Anadarkos, the Kickapoos, the Ayish, and the Kichais and Tawakonis are supposed to be not far north and frequently through the country. These all range the woods and now and then steal horses, and with them there has that I know of been as yet no settled principal of action nor of friendship established—which leaves us without any grounds of confidence to expect anything more of them than has ever been

the practice of the savage when the times and circumstances afforded a favorable opportunity of venting their malignant spleen.[15]

★ ★ ★ ★ ★

Captain Daniel Friar's ranger company was still in service at the first of the year and appears to have been stationed at Sarahville de Viesca, a little settlement at the Falls of the Brazos, northeast of present Temple, Texas. Fort Viesca, the settlement's only fortified blockhouse, was renamed Fort Milam in December 1835 to honor the only Texan killed in the Béxar siege.

As superintendent as well as captain, Friar used his own money to furnish ammunition, pay, food, and supplies for his men. First Lieutenant Ennes Hardin noted that at the end of his company's first two months of service, Captain Friar was

> requested to take the Account of all his men and present them to the delegates of all Texas then in session at San Felipe and make the best disposition of them he could.[16]

Some of Friar's men, including privates Peterson Lloyd and William Brooks, were discharged from his company at this time. Friar signed a discharge paper for Private Peterson Lloyd stating that Lloyd had joined the "company of rangers under my command on the 1st day of November 1835 and faithfully performed the duties of soldier" through January 1. This discharge was signed by Friar as "Captain Mounted Rangers" on January 2, 1836.[17]

Friar traveled to San Felipe de Austin to present his expenses to the General Council of Texas, leaving Lieutenant Hardin in command. Audited military papers of Friar show that he was in San Felipe for about a week trying to settle his expenses with the Council.

One of these documents (see following page) recaps Captain Friar's expenses through year end 1835. This document shows the costs for provisioning early rangers with necessities such as food, ammunition, and even the shoeing of horses. Of special note is the fact that some of Friar's rangers used a combination of the traditional flintlock and percussion caps rifles. A ranger could purchase one box of the rare percussion caps for seventy-five cents or three-dozen traditional gunflints for the same price.

His claims were initially rejected by the auditor and controller of public accounts for Texas on January 5. The auditor rejected Friar's

Summary of Expenses for Captain Daniel Friar's Rangers
November 1 - December 31, 1835
Source: Daniel B. Friar AC, R 33, F 463

The State of Texas
To D. B. Friar Dr.
for the use of the Rangers:

133 lbs. coffee at	33¢ pound	43.89
30 lbs. powder	$1	30.00
100 lbs. seal(?)	25¢	25.00
4 doz gun flints	25¢	1.00
1 box percussion caps		.75
6 Bushels of corn & peas	$2	12.00
400 lbs. beef	.35	14.00
4 ½ bushels corn at Taylors	$2	9.00
227 Beef (?)	3¢	6.00
3 ½ bushels corn at Hornsby		3.50
200 pork	5¢	10.00
10 bushel corn of F. Smith		20.00
100 pork		5.00
100 dried beef		10.00
27 bushels corn of J. L. Hood		54.00
10 lbs. powder of Daniels		10.00
100 lbs. salt		8.00
4 bushels potatoes Hornsby		4.00
2 pack horses 40 & 35		75.00
Shoeing 5 horses		10.00
10 bushels corn & peas		20.00
20 bushels of corns/peas Hornsby		20.00
Paid J. L. Hood 35 for his services to bear the ____		
from Viesca to San Felipe		35.00
		$426.14

(Signed) D. B. Friar

payment records due to his expenditures not being admitted to record in "conformity with the existing laws." On January 6 the General Council went through the accounts of Captain Friar. A select committee under Alexander Thomson, having reviewed his claims, made their report on this date. They decided to deduct from his request

> ten dollars to be deducted from said account for sending an express, and also ten dollars for shoeing horses; the balance of the account your committee would recommend to the Honorable the General Council to receive, as your committee find nothing incorrect in it.[18]

Friar was in due time paid for his expenses, but by the time he left the Council he had only drawn a draft from the government for $170.50 out of $1,788.14 that he claimed for provisions, ammunition, and payments made for his rangers.

It is important to note that the General Council considered Captain Friar's company and his superintendence to be a temporary condition that would only exist until the new ranging corps under Major Williamson was raised. Friar still had on hand as of January 6 two packhorses, thirty-one bushels of corn, ammunition, and other provisions. The Council felt that these goods should

> be used by the rangers who are now in the service, until the regular corps of rangers can be raised and organized for the protection of the frontier, and if any should remain, at that time, it can be disposed of, and the proceeds thereof paid over to the Government.

Upon returning to his company in the second week of January, Captain Friar stated "that he had got each man's account audited except the amount that he had previously drawn on the Treasury of Texas." The accounts of his rangers and the expenses he had incurred previously for the use of the company "was all in a consolidated draft and in his own name, all of which appeared to be satisfactory."[19]

Captain Friar's rangers remained on duty for three months, through February 1, 1836. By this time new companies under the supervision of Major Williamson had been organized to begin replacing the regional ranger units.

★   ★   ★   ★   ★

Riley Massacre and Robertson's Rangers: January 1836

During the early days of 1836, Governor Henry Smith and the General Council of Texas were in such a rift that the Council suspended him from acting as governor. Among the main areas of conflict were a proposed expedition to invade Matamoros under Frank Johnson, money donated to Texas that Smith refused to release, and the fact that Smith refused to release the state archives. He elected to be tried by the next Convention, which was slated to meet on March 1. In the interim, Lieutenant Governor James W. Robinson took over as acting governor.

On January 14, 1836, Robinson wrote to the General Council of Texas, accepting his new duties and addressing ranger needs.

> The defenseless situation of our oppressed country calls for

your prompt attention and speedy relief. Surrounded on one side by hordes of merciless savages, brandishing the tomahawk and scalping knife, recently red with human gore; and on the other, the less merciful glittering spears and ruthless sword of the descendants of Cortes, and his modern Goths and Vandals, make it in my opinion your paramount duty as Council, to remain permanently in session until the Convention meets, as there is no other authority to provide for the speed[y] organization of the ranging corps, and particularly for the security and protection of the inhabitants of the frontier of Red River, where no force is yet stationed or raised.

And I would respectfully recommend to your consideration the propriety of raising and officering the detachments of rangers from the inhabitants of the frontier where they are designed to range; that it would operate to increase the activity and vigilance of the corps and promote their harmony, I entertain little doubt.[20]

Governor Robinson's appeal indicates that Major Williamson's ranging corps was finally beginning to take shape. There is evidence that two of three designated captains, John Tumlinson and Isaac Burton, were organizing their companies by the middle of the month. As for the third captain officially appointed by the Council on November 24, there is no evidence that William Arrington ever fully organized his ranger command.

Arrington had served as a Council representative for the Gonzales municipality during November 1835. He was still in Gonzales as of March 1836, at which time he provided a pack mule for the use of Byrd Lockhart. Arrington's home area was short of the volunteers needed to staff such a company. By the first week of January 1836, the townspeople of Gonzales had supplied all the food and goods to the various army companies that the townspeople could possibly give. Stationed in Gonzales at this time was army recruiter Mathew Caldwell, who was recovering from his "wounds and afflictions," received during the early Béxar campaign. Caldwell found on January 7 that "there is now no more than is immediately needed for the families in this [com]munity" and there were no funds available which had not already "been applied to public use."[21]

Caldwell also found that Gonzales could not support a ranger company, further indication that Captain Arrington's company never formed. He sent notice to the General Council that the locals were not in favor of the government having already appointed the officers of these ranger companies.

> If your Honorable body will see fit to permit us to elect our own officers to command the company, up to a Captain, in that event I think a company may be made, which we need much.

While Arrington's third company of government-appointed rangers was not formed, another company was put together in mid-January in Robertson's Colony by empresario Robertson. The creation of this extra body of rangers was the result of a deadly Indian depredation carried out in Robertson's Colony during early January 1836.

This event happened along the upper tributaries of the Little River, a hunting grounds the Indians called "Teha Lanna" or "the Land of the Beauty." The pioneers they attacked were brothers James and Thomas Riley, who were traveling with two loaded wagons and their wives, children, and another young man.[22]

Near the mouth of Brushy Creek on the San Gabriel River, the Rileys met surveyor William Crain Sparks and his servant Jack. These three were returning from Sparks' camp near the Little River, where they had encountered Indians. Sparks and Jack had set out from Tenoxtitlan with a man named Michael Reed and an ox wagon loaded with corn. As dusk fell on their camp on the Little River, Reed crossed the river to visit the camp of newly arrived emigrant John Welsh. During his absence, Indians attacked the camp of Sparks and Jack, who both hid in a thicket.[23]

Sparks and Jack survived then set out after morning for Tenoxtitlan. En route, near where Brushy Creek met the San Gabriel, these two happened upon the Rileys. They advised the Rileys to turn back, but their warning was not heeded. Within another mile the Rileys encountered a band of about forty Caddos and Comanches. The Indians claimed to be friendly and stated that they were only following Sparks and his black man.

The Riley party decided to turn back at this point, but the Indians attacked them just as they reached the Brushy Creek bottom. One of the Indians leaped onto the lead wagon horse and cut loose the harness. Before he could strike, one of the Riley men shot him dead and thus started the general fight. Thomas Riley managed to kill two Indians before being mortally wounded himself. James Riley also killed two of his attackers but was severely wounded in four places before the remaining Indians fled.[24]

The younger man accompanying the Rileys fled with the women and children during the engagement. They reached the settlements on the Brazos safely within two days. The seriously wounded James Riley laid his brother Thomas's body on a mattress and wrapped it before mounting a horse and heading for Yellow Prairie in present Burleson County. After reaching safety the next day, he returned with a party to bury his brother.

Riley survived with severe wounds that kept him confined for a long period of time. A petition was presented to the Congress of Texas in 1840 for the republic to provide aid to the crippled James Riley in supporting his wife and six children.

Empresario Sterling Clack Robertson organized a ranger company to defend the citizens of his colony. The unit's muster roll shows that they were mustered into service on January 17, 1836. The Riley death was reported in the January 23 issue of the *Telegraph and Texas Register*, noting that the Indians had taken eight of the Rileys' horses. The paper reported that a company of twenty-five men had gone immediately in pursuit of the Indians. This number obviously increased as more men joined Robertson's company, for his muster roll, signed by Robertson as "Captain Rangers," shows a total of sixty-five men.[25]

Among the members of the company was Elijah Sterling Clack Robertson, the fifteen-year-old son of the captain. The company also included rangers who had recently served under Captains Daniel Friar and Eli Seale. Friar's reduced company remained in service throughout January, although at least eight of his men had enlisted in Robertson's new company.

Robertson's company had returned back to town by January 26, on which date empresario Robertson was conducting colony business. It is unknown exactly how long Robertson's ranger company remained in service, but it was disbanded by late February. Sterling Robertson was elected to the Convention of March 1 on February 1. Correspondence of Captain Robertson further places him at Milam as of February 7 and at the Falls of the Brazos as of February 18.[26]

The Riley attack was reported to the Council Advisory Committee on January 27 via a letter from John G. Robison. This five-man committee consisted of Don Carlos Barrett, Joseph D. Clements, Alexander Thomson, Elijah Simmons Collard, and George A. Pattillo. They recommended that another ranging company, not to exceed fifty-six men, should be immediately raised to offensively remove the Indians from the area, serving along Mill Creek, the Colorado River, and the Yegua. It was to be raised "under the agency of" Captain John York, Colonel John

Captain Sterling Clack Robertson (1785-1842) served as a soldier, colonizer, and legislator for Texas. He also twice commanded ranger companies in 1836 and was a key ranger recruiter following the Texas Revolution.

From DeShields' 1912 *Border Wars of Texas*.

Captain Robertson's Rangers: Muster Roll of January 17, 1836

Captain:	Nathan Campbell	Daniel Monroe
Sterling Clack Robertson	Michael Castleman	Andrew J. Morgan
First Lieutenant:	Eli Chandler	John C. Morgan
John A. F. Gravis [1]	Francis Childers	William J. Morgan
Second Lieutenant:	James Robertson Childress	Jesse Munford
Montgomery Shackleford [1]	Robert Childers	John Needham
First Sergeant:	Willis Collins	Elijah B. Reed
Thomas Hudson Barron [1]	Augustus A. Cook	Joseph Reed
Second Sergeant:	James Conall	Thomas J. Reed
Philip Walker	Britton Dorson	Elijah S. C. Robertson
Third Sergeant:	David Dorson	Thomas Ross
Warren Lyman [1]	James Dunn	John David Smith
Fourth Sergeant:	Stephen Eaton	William Crain Sparks
Calvin Boales	Benjamin Franklin Fitch [1]	Levi Taylor
First Corporal:	Stephen Frazier	Richard S. Teal [1]
James Hudson	John Fulcher	Jasper N. M. Thomson
Second Corporal:	Henry Fullerton [2]	John Walker
Enoch M. Jones	Robert Furgeson	Skeaugh Walker
Third Corporal:	Thomas A. Graves	Ezra Webb
Moses Griffin	John Marlin	John B. Webb
Fourth Corporal:	Jeremiah McDonald	James A. Wilkinson
George W. Morgan	Hardin McGrew	John Wilkinson
Privates:	John McLennan	[1] Previously under Captain Daniel Friar.
Samuel Tabor Allen	Edward D. McMillan [2]	
Paton Byrne	James M. McMillan [2]	[2] Previously under Captain Eli Seale.
Patrick T. Camell	Robert Moffitt	Source: *Muster Rolls of the Texas Revolution*, 128-29.
David Wilson Campbell [1]	William Moffitt [1]	

Henry Moore, and Stephen Townsend, who were all residents of this area. The company was to make Gotier's Camp and Robison's home their points of rendezvous.[27]

In further response to the increased Indian tensions, acting Governor Robinson had appointed Byrd Lockhart, Edward Burleson, James C. Neill, John W. Smith, and Francisco Ruiz as co-commissioners to treat with the Comanche Indians, who were rumored to be preparing for attack. They were required to repair to San Antonio de Béxar and treat with these Indians.

These commissioners were given little if any bargaining value with the Indians. There is no evidence the commissioners ever met with the Comanches, who continued to attack settlers sporadically throughout the balance of 1836.[28]

On January 24 Robinson also commissioned Hugh Love to proceed to Nacogdoches. There, he was to seek the assistance of John Forbes and James Cameron in treating with the northern Indians to assist Texas in protecting its northern and western borders from hostile Indian tribes and marauding bands of Mexicans.

★   ★   ★   ★   ★

Tumlinson's Rangers to the Rescue: January 20, 1836

The first company of Major Williamson's ranger corps to see action was formed in present Bastrop County in the town originally known as Mina. This unit was under command of Captain John Jackson Tumlinson Jr., who had been appointed on November 24 by the General Council. Tumlinson, a Tennessee native who immigrated to Texas in November 1821 with his wife and three sons, had served as a private under Captain John York in the Béxar siege during December 1835.

James Edmundson, a youth of fifteen years, later stated that he enlisted in January 1836 for a one-year term in "Captain John Tumlinson's company of Texan Volunteers in the war of independence between the Republic of Texas and Mexico" at Hornsby's Station. Tumlinson recruited from the Colorado River settlements and ordered his men to assemble at Hornsby's, located along the Colorado below present Austin in Travis County.[29]

The other senior officers of Tumlinson's company were First Lieutenant George M. Petty and Second Lieutenant Joseph W. Rogers. No complete muster roll has survived for his company, although the ranks of Tumlinson's unit included many Mina area citizens. Among them was Hugh M. Childress, who had previously served as first lieutenant of

Captain Willie Williamson's company during the summer Indian campaign under Colonel Moore. According to the military papers of Childress and others, Captain Tumlinson's "first division of the ranging corps" was mustered into service upon rendezvous at Hornsby's Station on January 17, 1836.[30]

The privates of the company were paid the designated rate of $1.25 per day. Captain Tumlinson's records show that he was paid $50 dollars per month as captain, an additional $1.25 per day for himself, $8 per month for one private servant, $2.50 per month for the servant's clothes, and $24 per month for forage for three horses. His records show that he also carried a sword. Although he had served in Captain York's company during the December siege of Béxar, Tumlinson later drew pay as a ranger captain beginning the day of his appointment, November 28, 1835.[31]

One of Tumlinson's rangers, Noah Smithwick, later wrote a detailed autobiography of his early days in Texas, including his experiences during the Texas Revolution. Born in North Carolina in 1808, he had immigrated to Texas in 1827, where he became a blacksmith in San Felipe de Austin. He left Texas for four years but returned in the fall of 1835 as the Texas Revolution was in its infancy and fought in the Battle of Concepción. As the army prepared to storm San Antonio during the winter, Smithwick received a furlough from Captain Thomas Alley's company in order to return to Bastrop to secure proper winter gear.

While in Bastrop, he took a fever that prevented him from engaging in the Béxar siege of December. With the army committed to engaging the Mexican army, the Indians took advantage of the weakened state of the frontier settlements to commit a number of depredations against the

Noah Smithwick (1808-1899) was part of Captain John Tumlinson's ranger company during the rescue of the Hibbins boy in January 1836. In his memoirs, Smithwick offers considerable insight into the early Texas Rangers of the 1830s.

Prints and Photographs Collection, Center for American History, University of Texas at Austin, CN Number 01542.

Captain Tumlinson's Rangers: January 17 - March 1836

Captain:	James Curtis Sr.	William Leech
John J. Tumlinson Jr.	Hugh M. Childress	Robert B. Owen [2]
First Lieutenant:	Andrew Dunn	Henry P. Redfield [2]
George M. Petty	James Edmundson	James O. Rice
Second Lieutenant:	Felix W. Goff	Conrad Rohrer
Joseph W. Rogers	James P. Gorman [3]	Noah Smithwick
Orderly Sergeant:	Daniel Gray [2]	Joseph Tumlinson
Oliver Buckman	Joshua Gray [2]	Joseph Weeks [2]
Privates:	Thomas Gray [2]	John Williams
John T. Ballard [1]	Howell Haggard [2]	
Calvin Barker	James Haggard [2]	[1] Joined in March. Transferred to
Joseph Berry	James Hamilton	Capt. Hayden Arnold's company
___ Cain	Reuben Hornsby	before San Jacinto.
Joseph Cottle [2]	Elijah W. Ingram [4]	[2] Enlisted between Feb. 1 - 10.
Ganey Crosby	William Johnson	[3] Enlisted Feb. 11, 1836.
James Curtis Jr.	James Leech	[4] Discharged Feb. 14 at Hornsby's
		due to injuries.

Source: Incomplete roster based on Noah Smithwick's memoirs, *Muster Rolls of the Texas Revolution*, and author's research of audited military claims of the Republic of Texas.

---

pioneers. The provisional government protected them as best it could "with the means at its disposal," Smithwick wrote, "graciously permitting the citizens to protect themselves by organizing and equipping ranging companies." He, in fact, became one of Captain John Tumlinson's earliest recruits.

> We were assigned to duty on the head waters of Brushy Creek, some thirty miles northwest of the site of the present capital, that city not having been even projected then. The appointed rendezvous was Hornsby's station, ten miles below Austin on the Colorado, from which place we were to proceed at once to our post, taking with us such materials as were necessary to aid us in the construction of a block house.[32]

When Captain Tumlinson's ranging company rendezvoused at the cabin of Reuben Hornsby, only eighteen were originally mustered into service.[33] Tumlinson informed his men that they had orders to proceed to the headwaters of Brushy Creek to begin erecting the new fort. This location was in Robertson's Colony, within present Williamson County, about thirty miles north of the future site of Austin.

His company would not be long in finding their first Indian battle as Texas Rangers. On January 19, two days after Tumlinson's men had made camp at Hornsby's, a tattered, blond-haired woman stumbled into camp and made her way to the cabin of Jacob Harrell. She reported that members of her family had just been killed by a band of Comanches while en route to their home on the Guadalupe River.

This woman had bad luck when it came to Indians. Born Sarah Creath, she married John McSherry in Illinois and moved to Texas in 1828. Her husband was killed by Indians the following year and left her with young son John Jr. to survive the attack. She was remarried to John Hibbins, who adopted her little boy. Returning from a trip up north to see her family in 1835, Sarah Hibbins, her son, an infant, and brother George Creath were picked up at Columbia-on-the-Brazos by her husband. Together, they proceeded via Hibbins' oxcart along the La Bahía road toward their home in present DeWitt County.[34]

Within about fifteen miles of their home, they made camp on Rocky Creek in present Lavaca County. They were then attacked by some thirteen Comanche Indians, who immediately killed Creath and John Hibbins. Sarah Hibbins, her new infant, and her older son, John McSherry, were taken prisoners after the Indians finished looting their belongings. As the Indians moved them between the Guadalupe and Colorado Rivers, the crying of the Hibbins infant compelled one of the Comanches to dash the baby's brains out against a tree.

Resolving to find help, Mrs. Hibbins escaped from camp that night while the Indians slept, making the painful choice to leave her boy behind as a hostage. During the next twenty-four hours, she stumbled through the wilderness until finding a herd of cattle which she hoped would lead her to white civilization. Her clothes ripped and her flesh lacerated, Sarah Hibbins happened upon Tumlinson's rangers. Describing the band of Indians, she begged the men to save her child. The frontiersmen set out immediately into the night with guide Reuben Hornsby at the lead. They moved swiftly to gain ground on their foes, pausing only a short while before daybreak to rest their horses.

With dawn's first light on January 20, Tumlinson sent out scouts to search for the Indians. They found a fresh trail that indicated the Indians were not exercising any caution in retreating from the area. They were believed to have spent a good deal of the previous day in searching for the escaped Sarah Hibbins. At about 9:00 a.m., the small ranger company happened upon the party of thirteen Indians as they were preparing to depart their camp on Walnut Creek, located about ten miles northwest of the future town of Austin.

Both parties were equally surprised. The Indians quickly fled their camp, as related by Captain Tumlinson.

> The Indians discovered us just as we discovered them, but had not time to get their horses, so they commenced running on foot towards the mountain thickets. I threw Lieut. Joseph Rogers, with eight men, below them—and with the others I dashed past and took possession of their route above them.
>
> The Indians saw that the route above and below them was in our possession, and struck off for the mountain thicket nearest the side of the trail. I ordered Lieut. Rogers to charge, and fell upon them simultaneously.[35]

Racing through his enemy's camp, Tumlinson noted a Comanche aiming his rifle at him. He leaped from his horse to take aim at the Indian just as the brave fired. "The ball passed through the bosom of my shirt and struck my horse in the neck, killing him immediately," the ranger captain wrote. Tumlinson took deliberate aim and shot his opponent. "The Indian sprang a few feet into the air, gave one whoop and fell dead within twenty-five feet of me. The fight now became general."

Private Noah Smithwick, who had just reached his twenty-eighth birthday, had an equally close call in the Indian camp.

> I was riding a fleet horse, which, becoming excited, carried me right in among the fleeing savages, one of whom jumped behind a tree and fired on me with a musket, fortunately missing his aim. Unable to control my horse, I jumped off him and gave chase to my assailant on foot, knowing his gun was empty. I fired on him and had the satisfaction of seeing him fall. My blood was up and, leaving him for dead, I ran on, loading my rifle as I ran, hoping to bring down another. A limb knocked my hat off and one of my comrades, catching a glimpse of me flying bareheaded through the brake on foot, mistook me for a Comanche and raised his gun to check my flight; but, another ranger dashed the gun aside in time to save me.[36]

The Indian whom Smithwick had shot loaded his gun again while lying wounded on the ground. Conrad Rohrer, a burly Dutchman from Pennsylvania, then snatched the gun from the Indian and used the firearm to crush his enemy's skull with one powerful blow.

"Of the Indians, four were killed," wrote Captain Tumlinson. He also noted "two of my men were wounded." Private Elijah Ingram, an early pioneer of Texas who had served as a ranger as early as 1829 under

Captain Abner Kuykendall, had his arm shattered by one of the bullets, "the ball ranging upwards to the shoulder." Ranger Hugh Childress, a Tennessee native and Methodist minister, was shot through the leg.[37]

The remaining Indians escaped into the cedar thicket, which Tumlinson felt "was so dense that it would have been madness to have attempted to penetrate it." Abandoning pursuit, he sent Lieutenant Joe Rogers after the captive Hibbins boy. Tumlinson and several sentries "remained watching the thicket to guard against surprise."

The rangers managed to capture all of the Indians' horses, their camp goods, and the Hibbins boy. The youth, wrapped by the Indians in buffalo robes and tied to a mule, was very nearly killed by one of the rangers when the mule ran from camp following the brief battle. Fortunately, the rifle of the man attempting to kill this fleeing "brave" misfired and he killed the mule.[38]

The rangers had a grisly drawing in the Comanche camp for the scalp of the Indian wounded by Smithwick, as he recalled.

> The boys held an inquest on the dead Indian and, deciding that the gunshot wound would have proved fatal, awarded me the scalp. I modestly waived my claim in favor of Rohrer, but he, generous soul, declared that, according to all the rules of the chase, the man who brought down the game was entitled to the pelt, and himself scalped the savage, tying the loathsome trophy to my saddle, where I permitted it to remain, thinking it might afford the poor woman, whose family its owner had helped to murder, some satisfaction to see that gory evidence that one of the wretches had paid the penalty of his crime. That was the only Indian I ever knew that I shot down, and, after a long experience with them and their success at getting away wounded, I am not at all sure that that fellow would not have survived my shot, so I can't say positively that I ever did kill a man, not even an Indian.

From the spoils of the Indian camp, Rogers and his men "selected the best horse in the lot" to replace the one killed out from under their captain. Captain Tumlinson's victorious men made their way back to Hornsby's Station.

> We watched the Indians a while longer; and in the meantime sent a runner for the doctor to see the wounded. I sent a portion of the men under the command of Rogers with the child, and the wounded men and I brought up the rear.[39]

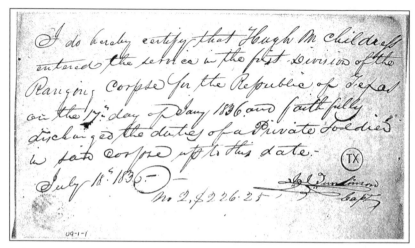

Evidence of John Tumlinson's duration as captain is shown by this service voucher he signed on July 18, 1836. Hugh M. Childress AC, R 17, F 551.

Tumlinson's rangers arrived back at Jacob Harrell's cabin that night, and the "dazed and bewildered" boy was returned to his mother. Captain Tumlinson found it a reunion to remember.

> Lieutenant Rogers presented the child to its mother, and the scene which here ensued beggars description. A mother meeting with her child released from Indian captivity, rescued, as it were, from the very jaws of death! Not an eye was dry. She called us brothers, and every other endearing name, and would have fallen on her knees to worship us. She hugged the child—her only remaining treasure—to her bosom as if fearful that she would again lose him.

Captain Tumlinson's rangers proceeded with building the block-house, which was named after their captain. The location was on the headwaters of Brushy Creek on the league of land originally owned by John Tumlinson, which had originally been surveyed in May 1835. He had transferred the eastern half of this league to Sheaswood J. Dover on August 27, 1835, and it was on this plot that the blockhouse was built.[40]

The fort consisted of a cedar blockhouse and stockade built near what became known as Block House Creek. A few steps away from Tumlinson's blockhouse was a huge live oak tree, which the rangers used for a lookout perch. They cut steps into its trunk and climbed it to view the countryside. The view was open for miles, as the only nearby timber was that which grew along the banks of the creeks. Scars from these "steps" were still visible in this tree for more than 130 years!

There is little other information on this early blockhouse, but Noah Smithwick indicates it remained until 1837, when Indians burned it down. The state of Texas erected a centennial marker in 1936 that describes Tumlinson's blockhouse. The spot is south of Block House Creek and about one-fourth mile east of present Highway 183. The marker is located between two driveways on Block House Creek Drive West in Leander. The huge live oak lookout tree, once estimated to be at least five hundred years old, disappeared sometime after 1973.

Tumlinson's rangers completed the blockhouse and patrolled from west of the Colorado River to east of the Brazos River. This post served as their headquarters for the next two months, during which time they saw no further encounters with the Indians.

Tumlinson's fight on January 20, 1836, had been the first ranger versus Comanche skirmish.[41] These two parties would continue to battle each other for nearly forty more years.

★ ★ ★ ★ ★

Other Ranger Companies Created

The original ranger company of superintendent Silas Parker's district fulfilled its three months of service on January 25, 1836. Captain Eli Seale, who had taken command of the company in late 1835, discharged the men of his company on this date at Fort Sterling. Captain James Parker's smaller unit, including some men originally under captains Eli Hillhouse and Seale, would remain in service for several more months.

One early record shows that Captains Hillhouse, James Parker, and Daniel Friar commanded the earliest ranger units of the Republic of Texas. These three men "were the commandants of the first rangers, afterwards Seal and Head."[42]

Some of Captain Seale's men formed another small ranger unit at Fort Sterling on January 27, two days after their discharge from the original company. James A. Head was made captain of the company by superintendent Silas Parker. Captain Head's company was enlisted for the three-month period of January 27 - April 27, as reflected by the service record of Lorenzo D. Nixon Jr.[43]

After the breakup of Captain Seale's company, ranger Joe Parker was active during the end of January, securing provisions for Silas Parker's men. He arrived back at Fort Sterling on January 30 and made preparations to head out again. On February 1 he left home for San Felipe, traveling with Seale and superintendent Silas Parker. En route, Joe Parker paid for forage and other expenses in Washington, signing a payment voucher at San Felipe with, "I have served as a ranger between the Brazos and Trinity for 90 days and found my own provision."[44]

Before the General Council, Seale presented muster rolls prepared by himself and Captain Hillhouse as testament to their company's service since October 1835. The Council was also presented papers entitled, "Report of Silas M. Parker, Superintendent of the Company of Rangers Between the Brazos and the Trinity." He was allowed by the Finance Committee $343.41 on February 3, 1836, for the expenses he had incurred.[45]

His first receipt, labeled Voucher # 1, detailed his own personal expenses of providing corn, beef, pork, salt, and other food to his rangers during their first six weeks in the field. Voucher No. 2 covered Silas's expenses of sending his brother Joe Parker to San Felipe with his wagon team to haul back a complete surplus of goods. The second voucher was noted with:

> I will leave to the Council to allow me what they may think proper. The provisions purchased were not all used as appears by the Voucher No. 2 referred to but remains at this time for the use of the Rangers; in fact they are now using it.

Superintendent Daniel Friar, who also served as captain of his ranger company, discharged the remainder of his men on February 1 after they had completed a three-month enlistment. Elections were held on this date for delegates to the Convention at Washington-on-the-Brazos, scheduled for March 1. Election returns for the town of Milam on February 1 show a large number of rangers present from Friar's company: Daniel Friar, Ennes Hardin, James Jett, Stephen Jett, Benjamin Fitch, Thomas Barron, Warren Lyman, William Moffitt, William Neill, John Pierson, William Brooks, Ansel Darniell, and David Campbell.[46]

Two other men who had served under Captain Friar, Calvin Emmons and Richard Teal, cast their ballots on February 1 in the town of Tenoxtitlan. During these elections, the precinct of Tenoxtitlan also cast ballots for officers for a company of rangers to patrol their district. Louis B. Franks was elected captain, with Thomas Morrow being elected his first lieutenant. James Bowen received the most votes for second lieutenant, followed by Alford Benton, Absolom Henson, and J. Trudo.[47]

Captain Franks was a resident of Robertson's Colony who owned a league of land on the Brazos River. He had also served at times as assistant surveyor to John G. W. Pierson. Colonel Edward Burleson had appointed Franks on November 27, 1835. During the Béxar siege of December 5-9, Colonel James C. Neill fell ill, and Franks stepped in to command the two cannons and fifteen gunners. Franks was a fighter, and he was openly critical of Burleson's aide-de-camp Peter W. Grayson for not forwarding more troops to Béxar to join the fight.

The ranger company under Franks was apparently stationed as "high up the country as the Waco village" during February. Due to a scarcity of provisions "and the difficulty of conveying the small quantity of necessaries of life, they were forced to fall back to the Falls."[48]

During early February the General Council was reviewing the progress of the ranger service. Three of the four regional ranger superintendents had by this time successfully organized companies in their districts. The three-company ranger battalion under Major Williamson, authorized by the act of the General Convention in November, however, had been less successful.

A special advisory committee headed by Don Carlos Barrett made a report of their findings to acting Governor Robinson on February 4. Captain Tumlinson's company had been formed and was operating in the field. Captain Burton was actively recruiting new men during January, but his company was not completely raised. The third company of Captain Arrington had not been organized. Barrett's committee found that Williamson's service had "failed of the designed effect" for several reasons.

> Men cannot be found who are willing to serve in the corps at such pay as is provided for by the laws. Second, objection is that they—the rangers—are not privileged to elect their own officers. Those are the reasons for them not being in the field. This committee viewing it as a matter of the first importance that our frontiers should by all means [be] protected from the incursions of hostile Indians, and seeing no probability that a corps of rangers will be raised, are clearly of opinion that some prompt and decisive measures should be adopted.[49]

Barrett's committee therefore proposed that two new ranger companies be formed. Commissioners were appointed for the municipalities of Gonzales and Milam to raise these companies. The commissioners were Mathew Caldwell, Byrd Lockhart Sr., and William A. Mathews for the municipality of Gonzales and Daniel Friar, David Faulkenberry, and Joseph Parker for Milam.[50]

The Council's Advisory Committee decided that these ranger commissioners would recruit men and then let the men elect their own company officers. As soon as twenty-eight men were raised in each municipality, the rangers were to elect a lieutenant, "who shall be entitled to pay from the time they are mustered into service." The company would then immediately proceed into service under the command of its lieutenant.

The commissioners would then recruit another twenty-eight men, at which time the combined fifty-six men would elect their captain and two lieutenants. The commission of the lieutenant first elected would thereby end, unless he was re-elected to his same post or that of unit commander. Thereafter, sergeants and corporals would be elected for the company. The commissioners were responsible for forwarding the results of such companies to the government. These men were to be employed for three months at a time. Privates were to be paid $1.25 per day, plus an extra $5 per month for provisions, covering their arms, horse, and ammunition. The company captain would be paid $60 per month, the first lieutenant $55 dollars, and the second lieutenant $50 dollars per month.

Prior to the ranger commissioners being appointed, another small volunteer ranging company had formed on February 1 at the previous request of John G. Robison. These men elected thirty-six-year-old Stephen Townsend as captain. His recruits included younger brothers William T., Moses, and Spencer Burton Townsend, and nephew Stephen Townsend, son of the captain's older brother. The new ranger commissioners decided that this company was needed and should be stationed at the head of Mill Creek. Major Williamson, commander of the corps of rangers, seconded their recommendation. Both of these recommendations were forwarded to acting Governor Robinson at Council Hall in San Felipe on February 11.

Robinson was informed on February 11 that by recently approved rules of raising ranger companies, "Captain" Townsend should be considered a first lieutenant. The committee felt that Townsend's rangers were subject to the same rules for raising a company and same payment fashion that had been instated for the Milam and Gonzales municipalities. Robinson felt commissioners

> should continue to engage men and send them on to the said Lieutenant until the number of 56 be engaged, then proceed to hold an election for Captain first and Second Lieutenant —according to the instruction given to the other companies.

Despite being legally considered a first lieutenant, Stephen Townsend was allowed payment in October 1837 for having served as captain of rangers from February 1 to March 16, 1836.

The committee further found that Captain Daniel Friar, who had been appointed superintendent of rangers by the previous council, now had a surplus of provisions, pack animals, and "various other articles of public property" obtained for his ranger company on the west side of the Brazos River. Niles F. Smith was authorized to take this government property into his possession, advertise it for ten days, and sell it at an auction for the best possible price. Friar, one of the new ranger recruiters, had disbanded his company on February 1.

The committee noted that there were still on "the east side of the Brazos five men ranging now in service and some provisions which they are now using." These were likely the rangers under either Captain James Head or James Parker. These men were advised to remain in service until a proper company of twenty-eight men was raised. If there were any remaining provisions, superintendent Silas Parker was recommended to then dispose of them in a fashion similar to that of Friar's unused supplies.[51]

The Advisory Committee on February 14 took steps to define the roles of Major Williamson's rangers. They sent a note to Governor Robinson that they had "learned with much regret of the late Indian depredations and murders committed on our frontiers, and deeming it of the greatest importance that prompt and efficient measures should be taken to organize and put into service the Ranging corps." For that purpose, the committee sent forth a set of five orders to Major Williamson that Robinson approved.[52]

Williamson's clarifying orders set the standard with which the ranger service would run throughout the revolution. First, he should continue to maintain his headquarters at Mina, leaving one of his subaltern officers in Mina to act as his secretary. After so doing, Williamson was to proceed "to the frontier and make such arrangements for building block houses and fortifications" at points as he deemed best calculated for the "protections of the frontiers."

Williamson was to also get involved in the recruiting and organizing of the companies that had been approved for his corps. Williamson was also ordered to appoint a corps paymaster and a contractor, who would act in the role of ranger commissary, supplying the corps of rangers with provisions.

Fourth on Williamson's new set of orders was that in cases of emergency or in the prospect of a general enemy engagement, he would have the

> power to call on the mounted volunteers, to call out the militia of the country—and to concentrate his command at such points as may be necessary for the protection of the frontier.

Finally, Williamson was to regularly report his proceedings to the governor and to the Council. This report of the Advisory Committee was approved by Governor Robinson on February 15. Two days later, on February 17, Major Williamson met up with Colonel William F. Gray of Virginia, who was journeying down to San Felipe. He noted in his diary, "Williamson, of the Rangers, seems to be an intrepid Indian fighter. Has a wooden leg." Williamson offered to trade half a league of his land to Gray for his horse, but Gray declined the offer.[53]

★　　★　　★　　★　　★

Cherokee Nation Created: February 23, 1836

Mexican authorities took the new provisional government of Texas as a serious threat from its inception. Early on, Mexico called upon the Cherokee Indians and their associated bands to work with them against the Texans.

More than six thousand Cherokees, led by Chief Bowles, and their related tribes had settled into eastern Texas between Nacogdoches and the Neches River. The leader's name "Bowl" was a rough translation of his native name "Duwali." His people had migrated to Texas from Virginia, Georgia, and the Carolinas around the time that Stephen F. Austin was settling the area. The Cherokees were intelligent people who used an alphabet system and educational standards far above that of most Texas-based tribes.

The land on which they farmed and hunted in East Texas had been promised to the Cherokees by the Mexican government, but clear title was never given. Mexican agents continued to visit Chief Bowles. During the Texas Revolution, the Cherokees were even encouraged to wage war against the Comanches to stir up the frontier and distract the Texan revolutionaries with defending their own frontier simultaneously.[54]

Governor Henry Smith in November 1835 had decided it would be wise for Texas to win the favor and allegiance of the Cherokees. He therefore appointed General Sam Houston, Colonel John Forbes, and John Cameron as commissioners to meet with and form a treaty with the Cherokees and their associates.[55]

Houston and fellow commissioners were successful in their talks with Chief Bowles during early 1836. The Indians and the Texans agreed to a firm and lasting peace. The Cherokees were given a territory of land in East Texas, which they owned exclusively and within which they were governed by their own regulations and laws. This land comprised the entire area of present Smith and Cherokee Counties, the western portion of Rusk and Gregg Counties, and the northeastern portion of Van Zandt County.

This area, known as Cherokee Nation, was approximately fifty miles long and thirty miles wide. Within this perimeter, the Indians were free to live, hunt, and carry on life as they so chose. Forbes and Houston signed the agreement at Bowles' village near present Henderson on February 23, 1836.

Cherokee leaders signed the document for several other nations claimed as their "associate bands." Those signing for the Indians were Colonel Bowles, Big Mush, Samuel Benge, Osoota (Utsidihi in Cherokee or "Mankiller"), Corn Tassel (Utsitsata), The Egg, John Bowles, and Tunnetee (or Kanati). These chiefs represented the Cherokees, Shawnees, Delawares, Kickapoos, Quapaws, Biloxies, Iowanes, Alabamas, Coushattas, Caddos of Neches, Anadarkos, and possibly the Chickasaws who lived on Attoyac Bayou outside the Cherokees' claim.[56]

At the time of the treaty with Houston, Bowles' Cherokee village was located in present Rusk County on Caney Creek about nine miles north of Henderson and nine miles southeast of Kilgore. The main village was located about three-quarters of a mile west of the confluence of Towisky Creek and Caney Creek.

During the course of concluding his treaty with the Cherokees, Sam Houston presented a testament of his good will to Chief Bowles. The Indian leader was given a black military hat, a silk vest, a handsome sash, and a fine sword. Bowles would continue to proudly wear these new symbols of friendship and peace until his death several years later, when he died near the spot of this treaty while fighting Texans for the very land that had been given to him by Texas.

CHAPTER 5

The Alamo's "Immortal Thirty-Two"

February 23 - March 6, 1836

"Victory or Death"

By February 23 the Texan forces in San Antonio were aware that something big was up. The citizens of San Antonio began slipping out of town, having been warned by a Mexican courier that General Santa Anna's advance cavalry was only eight miles away. Lieutenant Colonel Travis, Dr. John Sutherland, and scout John W. Smith slipped out of town to spy on the advance Mexican forces.[1]

Travis and his co-commander, Jim Bowie, decided to use the security of the Alamo for a defensive stronghold. Travis scribbled a note appealing for help to Colonel James Fannin in Goliad and sent it off with a young courier named Johnson. That afternoon around 3:00 p.m., Dr. Sutherland left the Alamo, joining company with John W. Smith. They carried a note to Gonzales, some seventy miles away, stating that the enemy force was in sight. Travis also noted that his 150 men were "determined to defend the Alamo to the last."

The first Mexican troops were starting to pour into San Antonio's Military Plaza as Sutherland and Smith headed out for reinforcements. Later in the afternoon of February 23, Launcelot Smither, one of the men who had turned down a commission as a ranger officer, left with another appeal to Gonzales. Smither rode through the night to arrive in Gonzales on February 24. He wrote on one note that made its way to Nacogdoches, "If every man cannot turn out to a man, every man in the Alamo will be murdered." He also added, "If you do not turn out, Texas is gone."[2]

During the day, several representatives from both sides held brief talks, but the Texans had no intentions of surrendering the Alamo. After the last interchange between Captain Albert Martin and Colonel Juan Almonte, Martin returned to the fortress, and Travis had his men fire a cannon shot into town to signify their desire to fight versus surrender.[3]

The Mexican army began its assault on the Alamo on the afternoon of

February 24 with long-range artillery firing at the fortress. The Texans fired only occasionally, choosing to reserve their ammunition. They suffered no casualties, and the firing died off after nightfall. Travis had by now assumed command from his ill co-commander Bowie.

Travis's little Texan garrison at the Alamo held little more than 150 gallant defenders, who pledged to "never surrender or retreat." The one-thousand-plus Mexican troops who first arrived in San Antonio were continually augmented over the next few days until Travis estimated that his forces could not last more than two more weeks. He thus decided on February 24 to send out an urgent appeal for help to Gonzales via Captain Martin. Addressed to "the people of Texas and all Americans in the world," the letter clearly stated Travis's desire to fight to the bitter end.

> I call upon you in the name of liberty, of patriotism and everything dear to the American character, to come to our aid with all dispatch... If this call is neglected, I am determined to sustain myself as long as possible and die like a soldier who never forgets what is due his own honor and that of his country.
> Victory or death.[4]

Martin rode from the Alamo with this message on the night of February 24. On the back of this dispatch, he noted that since he slipped out he had "heard a very heavy cannonade during the whole day. I think there must have been an attack made on the Alamo." Martin also scribbled, "We were short of ammunition when I left. Hurry on all the men you can get in haste."

Upon his arrival in Gonzales, Martin's message from Lieutenant Colonel Travis was handed off to Launcelot Smither. Smither was rested up, having arrived in Gonzales during the early morning hours of February 24 with Travis's previous message. Smither then carried this latest message on to San Felipe. At some point he passed it on to another courier, adding his own message to the back:

> I hope that everyone will rendezvous at Gonzales as soon as possible, as these brave soldiers are suffering. Don't neglect them. Powder is very scarce and some should not be delayed one moment.

★ ★ ★ ★ ★

Lockhart Forms Gonzales Mounted Rangers

The desperate appeals originating from the Alamo did not go unnoticed. In Gonzales, a new ranger company was organized the very day that Santa Anna's troops were entering San Antonio.

Fifty-four-year-old Byrd Lockhart Sr. had been busy forming a company since being appointed on February 4 as a recruiter for the ranger service. Lockhart had previously served in the army from October 14 to December 19, 1835, "for most of the time as one of our most efficient spies," according to Colonel Edward Burleson. He had also entered Béxar during the siege on December 5 as part of Captain John York's company.[5]

In the wake of the Béxar siege, a number of men ill-prepared for a winter campaign had gone back to Gonzales in order to secure heavier winter clothing. Thus, there were men available for service during February that were not attached to the regular army. By February 23 Lockhart had recruited twenty-two men. A surviving muster roll of this company shows that these men called themselves the "Gonzales Mounted Ranger Company."

As per recent direction from the General Council on how to form new ranger companies, the original enlistment of men would select their initial officer, who would be commissioned as a lieutenant. In the case of the Gonzales company, the men selected George C. Kimbell as their second lieutenant. He is incorrectly referred to as "Captain Kimbell" in a number of historical accounts. He was, however, a captain of sorts as he was senior officer commanding this ranger force.

Kimbell, born in 1803, had traveled to Texas from New York in 1825 and settled in Gonzales. He owned and operated a hat factory on Water Street in partnership with Almeron Dickinson, who was currently commanding an artillery company in the Alamo. Kimbell married Prudence Nash in 1832, and they had two young children as of 1836.[6] Some of the other men joining his company were farmers and others were merchants. Marcus Sewell was an English shoemaker. Another member, Jesse McCoy, had recently served as the town sheriff. He had also been commissioned as an officer in Major Williamson's ranger battalion, but the company had never been properly formed.

The day after the Gonzales rangers were formed, Captain Albert Martin arrived in town during the early morning hours of February 25 with Travis's desperate appeal for help. He then spent some time scouring the countryside for more volunteers. The latest news from Martin was not good. George Kimbell rushed to tell his wife the bitter news. The Alamo was besieged and Travis needed help. His new company, slated to protect the frontiers from Indians, must answer the call and ride to Travis's relief. Prudence Kimbell understood that her husband might not return.[7]

The Gonzales rangers formed the nucleus of the relief force Travis needed. Lieutenant Kimbell and Captain Martin spent several days rounding up new recruits and persuading men to join them for the desperate mission to Béxar. From the original twenty-two members mustered into the Gonzales rangers on February 23, nine members, including Sergeant William Irvin, decided to stay behind and protect their families. Kimbell and a dozen of his other rangers ultimately made the trip, but new volunteers who were eager to fight joined them.

Among the new volunteers was young surveyor Jonathan Lindley. Thomas R. Miller, the richest man in Gonzales, also felt the urge to join up. The youngest member of the company was sixteen-year-old Galba Fuqua. Two other teenagers joined, seventeen-year-old Johnnie Gaston and his brother-in-law Johnnie Kellogg, nineteen. Another from Gonzales who joined the rangers was George W. Tumlinson, cousin of Captain John Tumlinson.

Lieutenant Kimbell's rangers departed the Gonzales town square at 2:00 p.m. on Saturday, February 27. Kimbell rode at the head of the mounted group with Captain Albert Martin alongside him. Historical accounts alternately refer to "Captain" Kimbell or Captain Martin being in command of the volunteer rangers organized in Gonzales. Martin merely accompanied these rangers to the Alamo, and scout John W. Smith led them there. Martin had procured some of the men who joined the Gonzales volunteers, but Lieutenant Kimbell was properly in command of the Gonzales rangers raised by Byrd Lockhart.

Loaded with rifles, blankets, and food, twenty-five men rode out of town. Kimbell carried with him fifty-two pounds of coffee provided for the Alamo defenders by Stephen Smith. As fate would have it, the coffee would not survive the ride into the Alamo.

Lieut. Kimbell's Gonzales Rangers: February 23 - March 6, 1836

Second Lieutenant:	William Fishbaugh *	William Morrison
George C. Kimbell *	Galba Fuqua *	James Nash
First Sergeant:	John Harris *	Marcus L. Sewell *
William A. Irvin	Andrew Kent *	William E. Summers *
Privates:	David Kent	Robert White *
John T. Ballard	John G. King	
Jacob C. Darst *	Daniel McCoy Jr.	* Entered the Alamo on
John Davis *	Jesse McCoy *	March 1 with company.
Andrew Duvalt *	Prospect McCoy	*Source: Muster Rolls of the*
Frederick C. Elm	Isaac Millsaps *	*Texas Revolution, 25.*

As the company reached the home of John G. King, his fifteen-year-old eldest son begged his father to let him take his place. With nine children at home, the elder King was needed to look after the family. Lieutenant Kimbell approved the switch and William Philip King took his place among the Gonzales volunteers.[8]

By the following day, February 28, the rangers had crossed the prairies to Cibolo River, where Kimbell and Martin stopped long enough to look for extra recruits. They found some, including David Cummings, who had previously been in the Alamo garrison. The men rested during much of February 29 and prepared to make an evening dash into Béxar.

The Gonzales rangers crossed the river at sunset and moved west toward the Alamo. They could only guess how desperately their services would be needed.

★　★　★　★　★

Williamson Calls in Tumlinson's Company

Major Willie Williamson, commander of the Texas Rangers, was also in Gonzales at the time Travis's message arrived on February 25 via Albert Martin.

As required by his recent orders, Williamson was quick to report to Governor Robinson and the Council his actions. The latest note he received from Travis was enough to make him act. Under the fourth rule of his instructions from the governor dated February 15, Williamson considered this enough of an emergency to put his ranger troops in motion.

He sent word on February 25 to Captain Tumlinson, commanding the "first detachment of the ranger corps."

> Information directed from San Antonio under date of yesterday is calculated to call forth the united efforts of all Texas. Two thousand troops under the command of Sesma have arrived in that place and are in possession of the public square, compelling our troops (150 in number) to retire to the Alamo, where they are at present and determined to remain until death or victory. Provisions and men is the cry.[9]

Williamson questioned Tumlinson whether the Colorado frontiers were safe from Indian threat at the moment. If so, Tumlinson was to "forthwith fall down to Bastrop and wait further orders from me." It was also suggested to him that spies be kept out in advance of Bastrop to be on the watch for Mexican troops. Williamson suggested that the remaining settlers should concentrate in various settlements and build blockhouses or forts for better protection. As a final note, the ranger commander penned, "Rest assured that no exertions on my part will be wanting to give the earliest aid practicable to our fellow soldiers in the Alamo. Citizens of Texas, arouse, save your country and your liberties." His orders to Tumlinson were endorsed with, "R. M. Williamson, Comdg. the Rangers."

Private Noah Smithwick of Captain Tumlinson's company recalled these orders from Williamson reaching their company at their remote outpost. Smithwick's recollections reveal that "the invasion of Santa Anna necessitated our recall" and that all advance positions "were ordered abandoned, and the forces to concentrate at Gonzales, whither every available man was urged to repair forthwith."[10]

Williamson himself then departed Gonzales on the morning of February 26 and set forth for Mina (Bastrop) to direct the actions of his ranger forces. He sent a copy of his orders to Captain Tumlinson to the governor and General Council in San Felipe. This letter was referred to the Advisory Committee, which recommended on February 27 to order "Captain Tumlinson to proceed immediately to Béxar to aid the army there." Tumlinson does not appear to have ever received these orders, perhaps because Williamson had departed Gonzales before the papers arrived from San Felipe.[11]

★ ★ ★ ★ ★

Barron's Company and the Graves Fight

Captain Sterling Robertson's self-formed ranger company appears to have disbanded by mid-February. He did not receive any orders related to aiding the Alamo. In this area, however, the settlers were still forced to deal with Indian problems.

Robertson was en route by late February to Washington-on-the-Brazos for the Convention. Another Indian attack in Robertson's Colony soon motivated the colonists to organize another volunteer company to deal with the depredators. Command of the this company was apparently passed on to Thomas Hudson Barron, who had been on the original muster of January 17 as a sergeant. Born in 1797, Barron had enlisted in the Kentucky militia in 1814 and participated in the Battle of New Orleans on January 9, 1815. He and his wife were early members of Austin's Colony in 1821 but returned to Arkansas soon thereafter. Barron returned to Texas in January 1831 and settled permanently in present Brazos County in Robertson's Colony near the Old San Antonio Road. He joined Captain Friar's rangers in 1835 and later Captain

Robertson's company, serving on the frontier from Viesca, Nashville, and Washington-on-the-Brazos.[12]

Barron is known to have commanded a detachment of rangers at Tenoxtitlan during March 1836. He organized his men near Washington-on-the-Brazos as other companies were formed in the different localities of the colonies for protection. Some of the men requested Albert G. Gholson for their first lieutenant. Captain Barron stated that if enough votes were received for him, he would try to have him transferred from the army.

Gholson had been born in Kentucky on May 25, 1818. He and his family had made their way to San Felipe in late July 1832 with an emigrant wagon train from Tennessee and then settled in Robertson's Colony. Gholson had enlisted in the company of Captain Carey White in Gonzales and had participated in the Battle of Concepción and the Béxar siege. He received the necessary votes and was allowed to transfer to being second-in-command of Barron's company. Gholson was just shy of his eighteenth birthday at the time.[13]

Barron apparently took command of his volunteers in the wake of another Indian depredation committed in Robertson's Colony on February 26. Surveyor Thomas A. Graves had organized a ten-man party in late February to survey claims near Brushy Creek, a tributary to the Brazos River. Most of these men had been sworn in as Robertson's colonists during December and January and were eager to properly stake their land claims.

Graves' men had pitched their tents in the open post oak timber about eight and a half miles from the mouth of the creek on the evening of February 25. Shortly before daylight on the following morning, a large party of Indians attacked the survey party. Graves wrote a letter to Sterling Robertson from the Little River two days after the attack.

> I suppose from appearances there could not have been less than one hundred. I had pitched my tent cloth in the open post oak timber within eight miles and a half of the mouth of Brushy Creek and having made [no] particular discovery of Indian sign previously, we laid down carelessly as we had done before; and on Friday morning a little before daylight they charged up within twenty paces and discharged 15 or 18 guns and killed two of the company and wounded two others.[14]

James Drake from North Carolina was killed, and a black servant of Bernard Warner Holtzclaw was also killed. Holtzclaw, age thirty-five, was from Jackson, Tennessee, and had been sworn in as a Robertson colonist on December 10, 1835. The wounded were Montgomery Shackleford, who was shot through the thigh, and a young man named James Shaw, the latter hit in the knee. The other surveyors in this fight were William Moore, William Griffin, Willis Bruce, and a Mr. Webb.

Graves and his party had only a short period of time to take shelter before the Indians attacked again.

> On the first attack we retreated back to some timber perhaps one hundred yards or upwards and had taken a position with a view of fighting and after an intermission of about 15 minutes there was a second attack by not less than one hundred. I had on the first attack left my shot pouch and Shaw had left his and Moore had also left his. They had Drake's and Shackleford's guns and among the whole we only had four guns that we could have shot more than once.

Feeling he and his other seven surviving men had no chance to hold out against such superior numbers, Graves told his men to flee for their lives. They escaped in two groups and made their way to a raft on Little River and returned to the nearest settlements, some thirty miles away. The two wounded men survived. Bernard Holtzclaw narrowly escaped injury when a bullet passed through his pantaloons.

Graves warned Sterling Robertson, "I think you had best make some speedy arrangement to have a company of rangers fitted out as soon as possible or I haven't a doubt but what they will destroy the families on Little River within the course of this spring." Graves was furious, as the Indians had stripped him of everything he had from his camp, including almost one thousand dollars' worth of field work in the form of surveying notes.

The mention of a need to fit out a company of rangers thus indicates that Captain Robertson's company had disbanded prior to February 26. This request would also lend credence to Captain Barron forming a new volunteer company during early March to serve in Robertson's Colony.

Colonel Benton's Ranger Regiment

Three days after Congressman Robertson received news of the attack on Thomas Graves' surveyors, the Convention at Washington-on-the-Brazos passed an act to create an additional ranger corps for the Texas frontiers. These rangers would be a supplement to the ranging corps previously authorized under Major Williamson.

The act approved on Thursday, March 3, stated:

> Col. Jesse Benton and Lieut. [Col.] Griffin Bayne be and
> they are hereby, authorized to raise a Regiment of rangers, the
> officers of which shall be commissioned by the authority of this
> convention; the said Regiment of rangers to receive the same
> pay and rations that are provided for the regular army; the said
> regiment to enroll themselves during the war, and to be subject
> at all times, to the orders of the Commander-in-Chief of the
> public forces.[15]

Jesse Benton and Griffin Bayne, an older doctor originally from Tennessee, were both old acquaintances of empresario Robertson, who had recruited them for settlement in his colony. Benton, his wife, and their children departed from Memphis in October 1835 for Texas with a number of other families, including those of Colonel Francis M. Weatherred, John Chalmers, Thomas Ross, and his brother Samuel Benton. Jesse Benton had brought these families with him from the United States with his wagon teams and planned to help clear their land titles in exchange for half their land.[16]

These Tennesseans traveled by water to Natchitoches, Louisiana, and then took horses and oxen to the mouth of the Red River. Benton fell ill during the journey and was recovering in Nacogdoches as of February 22. He continued his journey through Robertson's Colony down to Washington-on-the-Brazos to see Robertson in time to be named colonel of rangers.

Griffin Bayne was in Milam in Robertson's Colony on February 20 with a large group of new settlers who were awaiting the colony's land office to reopen. Bayne and many men who later served under him as rangers—including Weatherred, William C. Wilson, and Joseph Clayton—signed a petition to Robertson on this date. Ranger recruiter Daniel Friar was also in Milam on this date, presumably organizing the ranger company he, David Faulkenberry, and Joe Parker had been ordered to organize on February 4.[17]

A number of these men organized a new ranger company at Milam on March 1 that would fall under Benton and Bayne's command. William C. Wilson was elected captain of this unit, and his enlistees enrolled for a three-month period. Among those known to have served under Lieutenant Colonel Bayne in Captain Wilson's company are George W. Anderson, Joseph A. Clayton, William Sherrod, William D. Thomson,

Francis Weatherred, and William C. Weatherred. The latter served during the month of March as a private in Wilson's company and thereafter as orderly sergeant. Other men continued to join Bayne's ranger corps during the month, such as Daniel T. Dunham, who enlisted on March 27.[18]

★ ★ ★ ★ ★

The Fall of the Alamo

The Mexican troops resumed firing on the Alamo on February 25 and began moving troops ever closer, forcing brave Texans to run forth and burn nearby huts that offered cover to Sesma's troops. Travis had only a few men nicked by flying rocks. During the cover of night, Mexicans dug trenches and planted batteries within firing range of the Alamo. That night Captain Juan Seguín and his orderly, Antonio Cruz, were sent by Travis with a message to Sam Houston, begging for help.[19]

Fighting at the Alamo resumed on February 26, and sharpshooters like Davy Crockett carefully picked off Mexican soldiers who too carelessly exposed themselves. There was little firing against the Alamo on February 27, but Santa Anna himself arrived in town this day. Travis penned yet another call for help that night and sent it off with courier James Butler Bonham, who had made one previous trip with a message prior to the Mexican army arriving in town.

From the Alamo, the top-ranking Mexican-Texan, Captain Juan Seguín, and an aide slipped out again and rode to Gonzales on February 29 for reinforcements. Juan Seguín was chosen after lots had been cast for who should serve as the messenger.[20] Unbeknownst to Lieutenant Colonel Travis, the town of Gonzales had already dispatched all that it could spare in the form of Second Lieutenant George Kimbell's Gonzales Mounted Rangers. Captain Albert Martin and other volunteers joined Kimbell's company en route to San Antonio.

Scout John W. Smith joined the Kimbell party outside of Gonzales and guided them into San Antonio. The company moved through the brush and cautiously skirted Mexican soldiers during the bitterly cold night until arriving within sight of the Alamo. They rushed into the old fortress at 3:00 a.m. on March 1. In a letter written two days later, Travis noted:

> A company of thirty-two men from Gonzales, made their way to us on the morning of the 1st instant, at 3 o'clock, and Colonel J. B. Bonham, a courier from the same place, got in this morning at 11 o'clock.[21]

Modern view of the Alamo in San Antonio. From Gonzales, a government-recruited company of Texas Rangers joined the garrison on March 1.

Author's collection.

Bonham arrived with a note from Major Williamson, who told Travis and his men "to hold on firmly" by their "wills until I go there."[22]

Travis apparently did not count Captain Martin and scout John Smith, since both were returning couriers versus new defenders for the Alamo. Ranger recruiter Byrd Lockhart may have been in the Alamo after recruiting the Gonzales rangers on February 23. One source states that Lockhart left the Alamo at a late date with Andrew Sowell for Gonzales to secure some cattle to drive into San Antonio for the garrison's use. The *American Sketch Book*, published in Austin in 1881 by Bella French Swisher, states that

> Sowell, and one other, was detailed and sent out after beef to supply the fort, but before they had time to procure the beef, the fort had been surrounded.[23]

At the time Captain Martin and Lieutenant Kimbell entered the Alamo, there were eight other organized companies stationed in the mission. Captains Almeron Dickerson (Dickinson) and William R. Carey commanded artillery companies, Captains William Blazeby and Robert White commanded infantry companies, Captains William Charles M. Baker and William B. Harrison each headed a volunteer rifleman company, and Captains John Hubbard Forsyth and Juan Seguín commanded cavalry companies.[24]

The other officers of Bowie and Travis's Alamo staff were Majors Robert Evans and Green B. Jameson, Sergeant Major Hiram James Williamson, Captains John J. Baugh (adjutant) and Samuel Blair, and Lieutenants Charles Zanco and Eliel Melton.

The newly arrived Gonzales rangers were amazed at the strong showing of the Mexican army. "The Mexicans are here in large numbers," wrote forty-one-year-old Isaac Millsaps on March 3. "They have kept up a constant fire since we got here."[25]

Millsaps had been among the first to join the Gonzales Mounted Ranger Company on February 23, hoping to protect his blind wife and seven children. Once in the Alamo, he and companion "Wash" Cottle were reacquainted with Jim Bowie, who was trying to keep morale up despite his own illness.

> Col. Bowie is down sick and had to be to bed. I saw him yesterday & he is ready to fight. He didn't know me from last spring but did remember Wash. He tells us all that help will be here soon & it makes us feel good.
>
> We have beef & corn to eat but no coffee; bag I had fell off on the way here so it was all spilt. I have not see[n] Travis but 2 times since here. He told us all this morning that Fannin was going to be here early with many men and there would be a good fight . . .
>
> There is no discontent in our boys. Some are tired from lack of sleep and rest. The Mexicans are shooting every few minutes but most of the shots fall inside and do no harm. I don't know what else to say. They is calling for all letters.

Scout John Smith was sent out through the south wall on the night of March 3 with a final message for help to the delegates of the General Convention of Texas being held at the small town of Washington-on-the-Brazos.

Travis and roughly 188 brave Alamo defenders were overrun by the superior Mexican forces on March 6. The fighting became hand-to-hand, with the Texans killing as many as 1,544 enemy soldiers before being overwhelmed. Cannon fire kept Santa Anna from personally joining the fray until organized resistance had been crushed. Santa Anna ordered no prisoners, and at least six Texans in the hospital barracks were executed with bayonets. The bodies of the slain Alamo defenders were ordered to be burned that night.

Santa Anna released three survivors: Susanna Dickinson, wife of

The Alamo's "Immortal Thirty-Two" Gonzales Rangers			
Name:	*Age:*	James George	34
Isaac G. Baker	32	Thomas Jackson	
John Cain	34	John Benjamin Kellogg	19
George Washington Cottle	31	Andrew Kent	38
David P. Cummings	27	George C. Kimbell, Lt.	33
Squire Daymon	28	William Philip King	15
Jacob C. Darst	42	Jonathan L. Lindley	22
John Davis	25	Albert Martin, Capt.	28
William Dearduff		Jesse McCoy	32
Charles Despallier	24	Thomas R. Miller	41
Andrew Duvalt	32	Isaac Millsaps	41
William Fishbaugh		George Neggan	28
John Flanders	36	Marcus L. Sewell	31
Dolphin Ward Floyd	32	William E. Summers	24
Galba Fuqua	16	George W. Tumlinson	22
John E. Garvin	27	Robert White	30
John E. Gaston	17	Claiborne Wright	26

Note: The centennial marker in Gonzales County lists John G. King and John McGee in place of Andrew Duvalt and Marcus L. Sewell.

slain Captain Almeron Dickinson, her fifteen-month-old daughter, and Travis's slave Joe. He sent them to Gonzales to serve as a grim warning about what would happen to other rebels who dared to resist the Mexican army. In a boastful report to his government in Mexico City, Santa Anna claimed that more than six hundred Texans had been killed at Béxar.[26]

Among the fallen heroes of the Alamo fortress were all thirty-two volunteers from Gonzales under Lieutenant George Kimbell. Texas later named Kimble County in his honor, although his name was incorrectly spelled by Congress.[27]

The names and ages, where available, of Kimbell and his men were carved into a marker in Gonzales during the centennial year of 1936 by the state of Texas. Further research shows two of these names to be in error. The marker does not include Marcus Sewell and Andrew Duvalt, who are on Lieutenant Kimbell's ranger muster roll. These should replace the names of John G. King and John McGee. King had stayed at home in Gonzales and allowed his young son to replace him. McGee, an Irish native, had been in Béxar since the siege and died on March 6.

At least forty men from Gonzales died at the Alamo, making it difficult to accurately name each who entered with Kimbell. Lieutenant Kimbell and his rangers were commemorated on the marker as the "Immortal Thirty-Two."[28]

CHAPTER 6

The Road to San Jacinto

March 7 - April 22, 1836

The message of Alamo courier John Smith was read before the Convention at Washington-on-the-Brazos on March 6, 1836. The delegates had declared the independence of Texas on March 1 and had worked non-stop writing and signing their formal Declaration of Independence for Texas. The convention would then spend the next seventeen days and nights forming the draft for the Republic of Texas's constitution. These men, however, had no way of knowing at the time that the desperate appeal of Travis was now too late to respond to.

General Sam Houston, who had been appointed by the Convention as commander in chief of the Texas army, departed for Burnham Crossing on the Colorado River on March 6. He planned to take command of his Texas forces to repel the threat of Santa Anna's advancing troops.

At the time of the Alamo's fall, the ranger company under Captain Louis Franks was operating near the Little River settlements in Robertson's Colony. He wrote a letter from the home of Goldsby Childers on March 8, informing Convention members that he had taken the liberty to form his own ranger company on February 1. This was due to the fact that Captain Franks had seen "the many depredations daily committ[ed] on the frontier."

His thirty-man company was armed with a small cannon, which had been left when the Mexicans abandoned their Tenoxtitlan garrison in 1832. Franks and Alford Benton had mounted the cannon at their own expense. By March, Thomas Pliney Plaster had become second-in-command of Captain Franks' company. Plaster was enrolled as a lieutenant on March 1 and served as such until joining the Texas army on April 1.[1]

Unaware of how severe the crisis was in San Antonio, these rangers were preparing to go against the Indians from the Childers settlement. Captain Franks wrote that he and his rangers had been equally responsible for the team, baggage, and wagon.

I shall proceed today from this place towards the Colorado Mountains, and the headwaters of the Little River in search of the Indians and having no scarcity of ammunition I shall endeavor to keep my men concealed in the wagon and let them approach us as a moving family.

Franks hoped to fool the Indians into attacking their moving train. He planned to keep "eight on horseback, two in advance, two in the rear and two on each flank." With this number of mounted men surrounding the wagon, it would only be a large band of Indians brave enough to attack them.

Nonetheless, Captain Franks was intent on routing the Indians "from this part of the country." He also proposed that a campaign should immediately be fitted out against their villages. By these two methods, Franks felt that "we shall be able to get rid of savage cruelty on our frontier."

Franks' letter of March 8 was sent to the Convention via Orville Tyler, son-in-law of Goldsby Childers. It was addressed to Representative George C. Childress, who read it before the Convention president on March 10. On the motion of Childress, this letter was referred to the Committee on Military Affairs. Records of the Convention make no further references to the deployment of Captain Franks' company. There is also no indication that his men ever succeeded in drawing an Indian attack against their wagon train. Franks would later serve as an Indian agent for President Houston among the Lipan and Tonkawa Indians.

While the Texas Declaration of Independence was being drafted at Washington-on-the-Brazos, the Convention representatives addressed other relevant issues concerning their new nation. Foremost among these was the state of Texan military forces. On March 10 a special committee, which had been appointed to give an exact condition of the army including numbers of officers and privates, gave a report.

The committee members reported that they could not "obtain the requisite information" to make an accurate report "under the present circumstances" of the revolution. They therefore only reported on the "number of officers now in commission."[2]

The officers in commission for General Houston's army were reported in five categories: infantry, artillery, cavalry, rangers, and volunteers. As for the ranging service, only the corps under Major Williamson was presented in this accounting of the Texas military. The Convention's report showed that Wade Horton had replaced Horatio M.

Corps of Texas Rangers
Officers in Commission as of March 10, 1836 *

Robert McAlpin Williamson   Major Commanding

Captain:	*First Lieutenant:*	*Second Lieutenant:*
John Jackson Tumlinson Jr.	George M. Petty	Joseph W. Rogers
William W. Arrington	Jesse McCoy *	Littleton Tumlinson
Isaac Watts Burton	Wade Horton	Thomas Robbins

* Per Convention's reporting. McCoy was killed in the Alamo March 6, 1836.
Source: McLean, *Papers Concerning Robertson's Colony*, XIII: 600-604.

Hanks as first lieutenant of Captain Burton's company. Captain Arrington and the officers commissioned to form his ranger company were listed, although this unit had never formed. In fact, Arrington's appointed first lieutenant, Jesse McCoy, had already perished at the Alamo four days prior.

This convention report made no mention of the second ranger battalion authorized on March 3 under Colonel Jesse Benton. In a letter written several weeks later, Benton related his first actions in this new billet.[3]

> After my appointment by the Convention of Col. of rangers, I remained several days at Washington for the purpose of knowing the features of the land law. Unless liberal provision was made for all persons then in the country, or who would come and assist in the defense of it, I knew that it would be in vain to attempt the enlisting of a regiment of men.

Benton, in fact, appears to have had little involvement in the recruiting of men for his ranger battalion. He left this task to Lieutenant Colonel Griffin Bayne, who would eventually take acting command of Benton's battalion. After leaving Washington-on-the-Brazos, Colonel Benton set out with some of his recruits to complete a military road to the United States border. This road led from the Falls of the Brazos in Robertson's Colony, passed through Washington, continued on past the new Fort Houston settlement near the Trinity River, and continued to Pecan Point on the Red River. Benton sent a letter to his wife on March 9 from a point on the road near Nacogdoches. He explained to her his intent on working so hastily on this new road.

> I intended with a few volunteers to pass directly over to Red River, marking as I went a new trail, to lead from the Falls of the

Brazos to Red River for the purpose of connecting it with what we call the military road from Memphis, Tennessee to Fulton on Red River. This route would pass over grounds of a firmer character, and also shorten the distance several hundred miles. My object was further to try and bring men this route from Red River in order to show the Indians that they would be placed between two fires, and that the people of Texas and those of the U[nited] States were still one and the same people.

Benton later stated that the panic following the fall of the Alamo helped stall his efforts. By March 31 he had reached Leonard Williams' Neches River crossing on the Old San Antonio Road. There, Williams was "enrolled in Benton's Reg't of Regular Rangers on March 31, 1836 to serve the Republic three months upon extra duty at his crossing."[4]

Despite delays, Benton's new road was already open by this time, as indicated by an article in the March 29 *Arkansas Gazette*. Colonel Benton later wrote to Secretary of War Thomas Rusk on April 3 from John Durst's. He had completed working on his road from the Falls of the Brazos, but his commission from the Convention of Texas had not caught up with him.

I have no commission as Col. of Rangers and no instructions. But I have established myself here to receive volunteers and to watch for Indians and Mexicans.[5]

★   ★   ★   ★   ★

The Great Runaway Scrape

By the second week of March, the frontier forces of Texas were largely joining the move to reach Sam Houston's army. Captain John Tumlinson's ranger company had received orders from Major Williamson about February 26 to abandon their new frontier post and proceed to Bastrop for further orders.

They had joined Williamson in Bastrop by early March and there awaited further orders. Tumlinson detailed three men of his company—John Williams, Howell Haggard, and Cain—to stay and help families in the present Bastrop County area move to safety. These three men would stay actively involved with assisting settlers during the crisis of the next month and would not rejoin the company.[6]

The Texas army was on the move in the meantime. General Sam

Houston arrived in Gonzales on March 11 from the convention, and he took command of 374 men. While he awaited definite word on the fate of the Alamo defenders, Houston began organizing his troops. He placed Colonel Edward Burleson in command of the First Regiment of Texas Volunteers.[7]

Houston sent out three of his best scouts on the morning of March 13. They were Erastus "Deaf" Smith, Henry Karnes, and Robert Eden Handy. On the road to San Antonio, the scouts found Susannah Dickerson and her small party of Alamo survivors. When Mrs. Dickerson (Dickinson) reached Gonzales, wives of Lieutenant Kimbell's rangers quizzed her on their husbands' fates. By the time she finished describing the thoroughness of the executions, the women understood the painful truth that none of their men had survived.

Word that Travis's forces had been completely annihilated sent a surge of panic through men, women, and children alike. The citizens of Gonzales began packing up what they could carry away, fearful that Santa Anna's army might sweep into their town next at any moment. General Houston also decided to have his small army depart Gonzales during the night of March 13. He needed to organize and concentrate his scattered forces, but it appeared for the moment that the Texas army was on the retreat. The ensuing rush of citizens fleeing eastward ahead of the slowly progressing Mexican army was a mass chaos that became known in Texas history as the "Runaway Scrape."

The day after Houston's army departed Gonzales, Texan forces fought another battle with Mexican troops on March 14 at the old mission in Refugio called La Bahiá. Fifteen Texans were killed, and more than eighty enemy soldiers were killed or wounded. After dark, the Texas soldiers slipped out of the old mission and tried to escape. Captain Amon King's company was spotted by Indians who reported them to General Jose Urrea's troops. King's men fought desperately for twelve hours but were ultimately forced to surrender after suffering five casualties.

Urrea promised to treat Captain King's men as prisoners of war after their surrender. Urrea, however, had previous orders from Santa Anna on how to handle such rebels. Soon after their surrender, the Texans were marched two by two in front of the La Bahiá mission and executed.[8]

During March, Tumlinson's rangers operated from Bastrop with Major Williamson. Private Noah Smithwick was put in charge of eight rangers from Tumlinson's company about March 13. They were detailed as a "picket guard out on the San Antonio Road, beyond Plum Creek, to give notice of hostile approach" of Mexican troops. Taking supplies for two days, they started out on their mission. En route to this station, a courier overtook Smithwick's men with news that the Alamo had fallen and an order to send all men back to Bastrop except for two.[9]

Reading the orders to his men, Smithwick asked for a volunteer to stay with him. Young Jim Edmundson, a youth of about sixteen years, spoke up, "By gumie, Cap, I ain't afraid to stay with you anywhere." Smithwick then reluctantly sent the remainder of the men back to Major Williamson in Bastrop. Being in possession of two good horses, Smithwick and Edmundson rode out ahead, keeping a sharp lookout for Indians. Smithwick relates:

> On reaching our station, we carefully reconnoitered the country in every direction, selecting a position on a rise overlooking the road for several miles. We loosened our saddles without removing them, only slipping the bridle bits to allow our horses to eat corn we had brought with us. By that time it was growing dark, and, not daring to light a fire, we ate a cold bite. I then told Jim to lie down, and I kept watch with eye and ear all night long, unwilling, under such circumstances, to trust a growing boy to keep awake.

After morning, the rangers made a fire and had their morning coffee. After tending to the horses, Smithwick slept while Edmundson stood post. Another night and day of their lonely vigil passed without event. Having seen neither Indians nor the Mexican army, the duo saddled up late the second afternoon and returned back as far as Cedar Creek, where they stopped for the night. With the citizens having fled this area of the country, the rangers found bountiful chickens and eggs with which to make their supper.

Returning to Bastrop about March 17, Smithwick found that his ranger company had dwindled down to only twenty-two men. Captain Tumlinson and Second Lieutenant Joe Rogers had received permission to help move their families to safer ground once the Runaway Scrape had commenced. Smithwick claimed that Tumlinson did not return to ranger service, but military records show that Captain Tumlinson remained in command of a portion of his company for another five months. He was later paid by Texas for service as a ranger captain from the date of his commission on November 28, 1835, through August 16, 1836.[10]

The roads about this area were filling with settlers who were moving out as Houston's army retreated. Major Williamson and First Lieutenant George Petty took command of the remaining Tumlinson rangers in

Bastrop. The rangers sunk all the boats on the nearby Colorado River to prevent Mexican soldiers from having an easy crossing. They then proceeded down the east side of the river. After covering perhaps ten miles, they were met by a courier who had orders for them to remain in Bastrop and get as many cattle across to the east bank of the Colorado as possible.

Noah Smithwick and four others moved up to Webber's place, where a large dugout was known to be. They tied lariats to the dugout and dragged the clumsy raft down to the river, which was swollen from recent showers. Smithwick and Ganey Crosby, who was known as "Choctaw Tom," manned the raft while the others took control of the horses. The boat dumped its occupants into the river, but they managed to save their guns and right the craft, eventually piloting it down to old Marty Wells' place.

Here, the rangers took up shelter for the night and found additional supplies. The next morning they sailed the raft down to John Caldwell's place, where they found a better canoe. Using this, they finally reached Bastrop without further incident. There, they found the river in such a state that they were unable to get any cattle across. Instead, the men took up station near the river and kept a lookout for Mexicans.[11]

They did not have long to wait. One morning they awoke and found about six hundred Mexican troops on the opposite side of the river who had captured their little boat. The rangers fled so fast that sentry Jimmy Curtis Sr., an older settler of the colony, was left behind at the river. Major Williamson ordered Noah Smithwick to return and bring the guard with him. Smithwick galloped back to the river and found Curtis propped against a tree with a bottle of whiskey and looking "as happy and unconscious as a turtle on a log."

Smithwick shouted at the man to mount his horse and flee, as the Mexicans were on the other side of the river. "The hell they are!" shouted Curtis. "Light and take a drink." Smithwick eventually managed to get the old man on his horse, and they rode back to join the balance of the company.

Williamson and his rangers assumed a rapid pace for the Texas army. Two of the older men, Andy Dunn and Jim Leech, had lost their horses. Some of the younger men took turns walking in order to let these men ride. The pace was slow, as the horses continually bogged down on the muddy roads.

Taking company with old Jimmy Curtis and "Choctaw Tom" Crosby, Major Williamson decided to leave the slow pace behind. Together, the trio pressed on to join General Houston's troops, leaving Lieutenant

Petty and his men to move at their own pace.

Rangers Called to Join the Army

The Convention at Washington-on-the Brazos met through March 17, after which time the members frantically scurried off to either help their families or join General Houston's army. The delegates had declared their independence from Mexico and drafted a constitution for the new Republic of Texas. Their new nation, however, was in a serious state of panic by this date.

The Alamo had fallen and settlers on the extreme frontiers were preparing to flee at the first sight of enemy forces. Volunteers were arriving from the United States in groups and companies, but the Texas army was still struggling to organize itself for a real stand against President Santa Anna's army.

Representative Sterling Robertson, who had commanded rangers prior to serving the convention, hurried back to his colony in company with two others. He rounded up all his papers, land titles, and maps and entrusted his fifteen-year-old son Elijah Robertson to take them safely beyond Texas borders until the revolution was ended. These important details complete, the elder Robertson would next help organize and equip colonists over the next few weeks to join the army of Sam Houston.[12]

When word of the Alamo's fall reached the Convention on March 15, it was apparent that every available man would be needed to make a stand against Santa Anna's army. Word was sent to all ends of Texas for those who could fight to join General Houston. Captain Stephen Townsend's twelve-man ranger company in Robertson's Colony was issued orders on March 16 to join the army. The word reached Townsend at his camp on the east bank of the Colorado River on March 19, and his rangers soon joined with Sam Houston's main army forces.[13]

News of the Alamo's fall also reached Captain William Sadler's Fort Houston rangers in remote East Texas about the same time. Sadler's men were busy working on the main blockhouse of what had become known as Fort Houston. His grandson, Robert Roach Sadler, related in 1921 to Anderson County's historian, "I've heard my grandfather say they were working on the house when they got news that San Antonio had fallen." The message was that help was needed for the Texan forces in this area. Upon this word, Captain Sadler "and a party of men started to their relief."[14]

He disbanded his company at Fort Houston just two weeks short of fulfilling their three-month commitment. In pension papers filed more than thirty-five years later, several of these men stated the date to be either March 1 or "about the first day of March" 1836. Private Daniel Crist's papers state that Sadler's men were "discharged at Fort Houston on the first day of March A.D. 1836 by reason of the fall of the Alamo, when they were called to the Army of San Jacinto."[15]

These dates were obviously approximations made decades after the actual event. It is certain that the Houston company was still in the present Houston County area until March 19.[16]

The breakup of Sadler's company left Fort Houston virtually open to any invaders. Garrison Greenwood had already written to the Convention on March 7 that the people in his little community were in a "defenseless condition." Of the approximately seventy people using the fort, there were only a small number of armed men, "most of them late emigrants to the country." In the event of a major Indian raid, Greenwood had stated that serious losses were likely. Their post was "twenty five miles from the nearest white settlement" from which they could expect reinforcements. Greenwood wrote:

> Being thus surrounded with danger and difficulty, unless something is done speedily by the Convention for the protection of our frontier families, I think that an abandonment of the place and perhaps of the country will probably be the result.[17]

In a postscript to this note, Greenwood had added a note in which he felt that twenty-five or thirty rangers employed between the Neches and Trinity Rivers "would secure a large and much exposed and scattered settlement below."[18] Although he had been commissioned as one of the four ranger superintendents by the General Council in October of 1835, Greenwood had not taken an active part in his jurisdiction after the November act creating the corps of rangers had been passed.

A search of Republic of Texas documents shows that Garrison Greenwood did not submit any claims for having incurred expenses for outfitting rangers. There are also no records of the General Council showing reports he submitted. Greenwood did acknowledge his having been named a superintendent, "but under another arrangement have been superceded and there remains now no probability of any Rangers to these bounds until there is still a third arrangement made for that purpose."

The other "arrangement" Greenwood refers to is the corps of

rangers that was called for in late November of 1835. Since this corps never reached full strength and was only beginning to organize itself during the first days of January 1836, Captain Sadler and his ten-man unit apparently operated without the direct supervision of Greenwood.

Their work on Fort Houston remained incomplete and would not be resumed until other rangers took up station there in the summer of 1836. Sometime around March 16 or thereafter, Captain William Sadler's small "Houston Company" ranger outfit at Fort Houston struck out on the old San Antonio Road to join the Texas army. Two of his privates, Sam Wells and Daniel Crist, stayed behind to help protect the women and children of the Fort Houston settlement.

Sadler and seven of his rangers crossed the Trinity River with their horses at the community of Randolph on March 19. Sadler wrote a promissory note to ferry keeper Nathaniel Robbins that his men had crossed the river "for the purpose of joining the army of Texas, for which we did not pay." Interestingly, he did not sign this note as "Captain," since his company had officially disbanded, but as "Paymaster for the Houston Company."[19]

During the Runaway Scrape, the white settlers in this area abandoned Fort Houston. According to Creed Taylor, a Béxar siege veteran who was witness to the great Runaway Scrape, "Greenwood held a quasi command at Fort Houston to watch the movements of the Indians during the war."

After Sadler's small party departed to join the Texas army, Greenwood was left to handle the settlers during the Runaway Scrape. Taylor stated that Greenwood

> conducted quite a party of settlers from that vicinity towards the Sabine. While the party was halting on the Angelina, a body of armed men rode up and camped. They were volunteers from Tennessee led by Captain Crockett, a nephew of Davy Crockett, en route to the Alamo. News traveled slowly and they had not heard of the fall of the fortress.[20]

Greenwood and the Fort Houston settlers left their homes vacant for about two months during the Runaway Scrape crisis. When they finally did return later, they found that the Indians had ransacked their log cabins.

While the small groups under Captains Sadler and Townsend were moving to join the army, Lieutenant Colonel Griffin Bayne was still recruiting men for his new ranger battalion. Most of his efforts were in the old Robertson's Colony, which had been newly named the municipality of Milam. His first company under Captain William Wilson had been organized at the beginning of March. On March 16 Bayne appointed Eleazor Louis Ripley Wheelock as "second lieutenant of rangers."

Wheelock, an early member of Robertson's Colony, would serve as such through May 7, 1836, at which time he would receive command of his own company. Joining Bayne's ranger battalion on this date with him were his son George Ripley Wheelock and his son-in-law Samuel A. Kimble. It is possible that Wheelock may have become second lieutenant of Captain Isaac Burton's rangers.[21]

During March a large group of men assembled at the town of Tenoxtitlan in present Burleson County to form a company that would march to join General Houston's army. Among those men in this group were Herman Chapman, George W. Chapman, Robert Childers, William Frazier, Stephen Frazier, John Needham, Jefferson Reed, William Reed, Josiah Taylor, and Orville T. Tyler. Several of these men had previously served in Captain Robertson's rangers during January and February.[22]

The company organized at Tenoxtitlan was likely that of Captain Tommy Barron, who had organized a volunteer ranger company following the Graves fight. Barron had previously served as first sergeant of Captain Robertson's rangers. It is also possible that Ripley Wheelock was the second lieutenant of this company. At the height of the Runaway Scrape, Captain Barron and a number of the others were allowed to return to their homes. Barron helped his family, slaves, and others in moving their property and families. He turned command of his company over to Lieutenant Albert Gholson, who was unmarried. Within a few weeks his small band of volunteers would join Lieutenant Colonel Bayne for the march to join the main Texas army.[23]

The commanders of the small volunteer companies formed during March in Robertson's Colony remain sketchy at best. Enough military papers have survived to verify Captain Wilson's rangers serving under Lieutenant Colonel Bayne. The mounted spy company of Captain William H. Smith was formed on March 16 as a cavalry company of the Texas army. Some of his men, however, would describe the company as a ranger type unit.

The mass exodus of settlers from the western settlements of Texas during the Runaway Scrape went largely without incident from the Indians. One exception was an attack made in present Lavaca County, about twelve miles from the present site of Hallettsville, where all the settlers departed except for two families. These were the Irish families of a Mr.

Daugherty, a widower with three children, and John Douglas with his wife and children. Both families had come to Texas in 1832, and both were forced to flee their homes in March 1836.[24]

John Douglas sent his teenage sons Augustine and Thaddeus out on the range to fetch the oxen. When they returned hours later, they found their home in flames and a band of painted Indians in the process of massacring their family. The boys approached after dark to find their parents, two siblings, and the entire Daughtery family butchered and scalped. The two surviving boys wandered about vacant settlements until they were eventually taken under charge of a Mexican army detachment. The surviving Douglas boys were not liberated until after San Jacinto, when scouts under Henry Karnes found them.

Major Williamson and a few of his rangers had reached Washington-on-the-Brazos by the time the Convention was broken up. Secretary of War Thomas Rusk on March 17 had authorized an army officer in Washington "to organize a company of Rangers or Spies and observe the approach of the enemy."[25] The ranger unit that Williamson hastily assembled became known as the "Washington Guards." Among the volunteers was Ennes Hardin, who was recently first lieutenant of Captain Friar's rangers. Three others—Peterson Lloyd, John Gravis, and Calvin Emmons—had served in Captain Robertson's ranger company.

The Washington Guards were placed under command of Captain Joseph Bell Chance on March 20 and ultimately joined Sam Houston's army as part of the Second Regiment of Texas Volunteers. The fact that the company was organized by ranger commander Williamson and that it included veteran rangers gives support to considering Chance's Washington Guards to be a ranger unit prior to joining the Texas army at San Jacinto.

Private Amos Gates was among several who were not present when Captain Chance's company was mustered in, but were instead acting in "obedience to" the commands of Major Williamson. Gates and others "were detailed to go with the families" to the Trinity River. These rangers did not return from shepherding families until after April. In a note written May 29, Gates was surprised at what he then discovered.

> Shortly after my return, I learned that the volunteers under Williamson had been ordered to headquarters and that myself and several others had been reported by Capt. Chance as deserters.[26]

Williamson and Captain Chance's men remained stationed at

Washington for the time being. Since the start of the Runaway Scrape, Sam Houston's army had been steadily moving easterly ahead of the advancing Mexican army. By March 19 the bulk of the army had reached the Colorado River near present La Grange.

Colonel James Fannin's three hundred Texas troops would never make their intended rendezvous with General Houston. They engaged Mexican troops east of San Antonio near Coleto Creek, about ten miles from Goliad, on March 19. The fighting lasted into the night, and Fannin's men killed or wounded an estimated 250 Mexican infantrymen and cavalrymen. He lost approximately sixty men killed or wounded, and Fannin's remaining men were overwhelmed and taken prisoners of war. They were marched to the fortress of La Bahía. Another group of Texans, the company of Captain William Ward, which had participated in the La Bahía fight of March 14, were captured by General Urrea's men on March 23.[27]

General Santa Anna considered these rebellious bands of Texan troops to be "pirates." From Goliad, some 350 Texans were thus marched outside of the La Bahía fortress and fired upon. The Mexican soldiers turned their swords and bayonets on the wounded men, although a small number of Texans did manage to escape from the massacre. Another fifty-odd Texans inside La Bahía were executed a short time later, including Colonel Fannin.

Captain Chance's Washington Guards: March 20 - June 1, 1836

Captain:
Joseph Bell Chance
First Lieutenant:
John Campbell Hunt [1]
Second Lieutenant:
Moses Evans
Orderly Sergeant:
John H. Scaggs
Second Sergeant:
Ennes Hardin [2]
Privates:
George Bond
David Wilson Campbell [3]
Thomas Cannon
James K. Chelaup
James R. Childress [3]
John R. Cockrill
Sylvanus Cottle [4]
Josiah G. Dunn
Calvin Brallery Emmons [2]

Edwin B. Emory
Massillon Farley
Benjamin C. Finley
Lankford Fitzgerald
Samuel S. Gillett
John A. F. Gravis [3]
Dr. James D. Jennings [1]
David J. Jones [1]
Garrett Law
Theodore Staunton Lee
Peterson Lloyd [2]
James H. Manning [5]
James Maury
Robert Merritt
Spencer Morris
Richard Rodgers Peebles
J. M. Pennington
Stephen R. Roberts
Thomas M. Splane
Thomas Thompson

Richard Vaughn
John Walker [3]
Josiah Walker
Robert Winnett
Joseph H. Woods
William Riley Woods
Gilbert Wright [2]

[1] Fought at San Jacinto.
[2] Previously in Captain Friar's ranger unit.
[3] Previously in Captain Robertson's rangers.
[4] Enlisted Feb. 4 in Capt. Burton's rangers.
[5] Enlisted Feb. 11 by Capt. Burton for twelve months' service.

Source: *Muster Rolls of the Texas Revolution*, 208-209.

The month of March 1836 had been catastrophic for the Texans. Close to six hundred Texans had been slaughtered, most after having been taken prisoners of war, by Santa Anna's troops at the Alamo, Refugio, and Goliad. As news of the latest massacres slowly filtered down to the volunteers, they became increasingly anxious to rendezvous with Houston.

Noah Smithwick had plenty of reason to be distressed with his situation. Two senior officers of his company and other company members had long since departed to assist families during the Runaway Scrape. The battalion commander, Major Willie Williamson, had ridden ahead with two other rangers in search of the main army.

Smithwick and about eighteen others originally of Captain Tumlinson's company had been left under command of First Lieutenant George Petty, a man they felt was "destitute of experience." Their detachment could move only as fast as those without horses could walk.

Protecting the frontier settlements from Indian depredations was the farthest thing from these rangers' minds. Behind them the whole Mexican army was slowly pursuing the retreating Texas army. Ahead of them lay nothing but empty homes, wandering cattle, and scattered belongings of settlers who had fled in sheer terror. The scene before Smithwick and his comrades told only too vividly how hastily the citizens had fled.

> Houses were standing open, the beds unmade, the breakfast things still on the tables, pans of milk moulding in the dairies. There were cribs full of corn, smoke houses full of bacon, yards full of chickens that ran after us for food, nests of eggs in every fence corner, young corn and garden truck rejoicing in the rain, cattle cropping the luxuriant grass, hogs, fat and lazy, wallowing in the mud, all abandoned. Forlorn dogs roamed around the deserted homes, their doleful howls adding to the general sense of desolation. Hungry cats ran mewing to meet us, rubbing their sides against our legs in token of welcome. Wagons were so scarce that it was impossible to remove household goods; many of the women and children, even, had to walk. Some had no conveyance but trucks, the screeching of which added to the horror of the situation. One young lady said she walked with a bucket in hand to keep the trucks on which her mother and their little camping outfit rode from taking fire.[28]

When Lieutenant Petty's rangers reached Cole's Settlement (present Independence), they found a note that Major Williamson had stuck to a tree near the road. It told them of the surrender and subsequent massacre of Fannin's men. One of his older men, John Williams, who had fought in "several revolutions," became overly paranoid of capture by the Mexican army. Smithwick reported that Williams' fears

> so worked upon the natural timidity of our commanding officer, that he saw a Mexican soldier in every bush. He actually tore up his commission, lest it be found on him, and condemn him to certain death.

Smithwick and others sneered at the cowardice of Lieutenant Petty but did not let it deter them from their course of ensuring that all settlers made it safely away from the oncoming enemy.

The remaining rangers moved slowly on during early April. The two with the best horses, Felix W. Goff and Noah Smithwick, offered to ride out ahead and see what forces they could find in Washington-on-the-Brazos. This offer was turned down, so the company made camp in the Brazos River bottom above Washington that night. With two men still on foot due to Dunn and Leech not having horses, the men could not move fast enough to stay ahead of the Mexican army. After sighting a large body of enemy forces moving down the road toward Washington, these rangers were forced to dodge the soldiers. "There was nothing for us but to try and keep out of the way," wrote Smithwick.

The rangers found that their only course to avoid the enemy was to move upriver. They proceeded on up to the settlement of Tenoxtitlan, where they could at last cross the Brazos and make a turn for the south.

William T. Sadler and the remnants of his Fort Houston ranger company finally caught up with Colonel Sidney Sherman's regiment of the Texas army on the Colorado River on March 20. Sadler recalled that this was "at or near the DeWees Crossing on the Colorado River" and that he soon became "a private soldier in the company commanded by Captain Leander Smith." Private Daniel Parker Jr. affirmed that they joined "Sherman's regiment at Colorado."[29]

Captain Smith was promoted to major of artillery on April 1, and command of the Nacogdoches Volunteers passed to Captain Hayden S. Arnold. Private William Hallmark, another former Sadler ranger, said they were formally "enlisted about the first day of April 1836 for the term of three months" in Captain Arnold's Nacogdoches Volunteers.[30]

During the early days of April, Major Willie Williamson was still in Washington-on-the-Brazos. He busied himself enlisting recruits for General Houston and sending out spy patrols for the purpose of gathering information on the approaching Mexican army. The information was relayed down to General Houston, where he and the army had made camp at Groce's Plantation.

On April 7 Williamson sent two letters to General Houston on the activities he had been engaged in at Washington. He sent with Major Robert Barr a list of the new recruits he had put together in this town, including those of Captain Chance's Washington Guards.

When Barr departed, he traveled in company with four men whom Williamson had enlisted as volunteer rangers. Three were considered dutiful soldiers who were acting as guards over the fourth man named Murphy. This man had apparently pleaded guilty to petty larceny and disobedience of orders from Williamson. When this man was sent to Houston, Williamson sent the note in which was stated that Houston should "release him and make a soldier of him. I believe he will do his duty as such, for he is much alarmed."[31]

Williamson sent his first letter on the morning of April 7 with Major Barr. In the afternoon he wrote a second letter. In this, he gave details that one of his ranger spies, Daniel Gray, had returned that morning from an overnight scout. Gray, who had originally enlisted under Captain Tumlinson, had been chased by eight mounted men whom he believed were Mexicans. Williamson actually felt that his scout was mistaken; he noted, "five men are still out in the same direction and well mounted and have had time to report." Williamson noted to Houston of this chase, "I take them to be a party of your spies that have given chase—in a few hours we will know the truth."

From the headquarters camp west of the Brazos River, General Houston and Secretary of War Rusk sent their own communication back to Major Williamson on April 7 via Major James Collinsworth, an aide-de-camp of General Houston. Houston was displeased that drunken men under Williamson's command had killed two Mexican soldiers who were captured during a scouting mission.

Houston and Rusk ordered Major Williamson to report himself to their headquarters "forthwith." Williamson's command at Washington was relinquished to Major Collinsworth, who had been given specific new orders.

He has orders to keep out spies and to adopt such measures as he may see proper for the safety of the place. I disapprove the killing of those two Mexicans. They should have been sent to me for examination. I have no idea, but that they were deserters from the enemy and important information might have been obtained from them. I order without exception the destruction of all ardent spirits at Washington and wherever it may be found. I have not delegated any power to any person or persons to arrest and try persons for offenses. The discretionary powers given to Maj. Collinsworth are the first issued by me. I wish Col. [William] Pettus to repair to camp and report to me. Major Collinsworth has power to call all persons into service, and to act to his discretion, saving life.

Thus, Williamson relinquished his command of the rangers and headed to join the Texas army and face Sam Houston. He remained with the army as it marched eastward until Houston turned at the fork in the road and headed for Harrisburg on April 16. One of Houston's staff, Dr. Nicholas D. Labadie, wrote that about six miles down the road to Harrisburg, Houston ordered Williamson to "go with all possible speed to the Red Land Company, with directions that they should join the army, as it had now changed its course to Harrisburg."[32]

By April 17 Captain John Tumlinson and a few of his men had caught up with Major Williamson and the two rangers who had kept company with him, Crosby and Curtis. Tumlinson had taken leave from the main body of his company during the Runaway Scrape to help escort his and other families to safety ahead of the Mexican army. Private Joseph Cottle's military papers show that he served under Captain Tumlinson through April 25, 1836. Cottle, however, does not show up on muster rolls as having fought at San Jacinto. The military papers of Private Ganey Crosby show that Captain Tumlinson discharged him from service on April 17 to join the regular army. Crosby was immediately enlisted by Lieutenant Colonel Joseph Bennett into Captain William Heard's Company F of the Second Regiment.[33]

Members of the other ranger regiment headed by Lieutenant Colonel Griffin Bayne were preparing to join the Texas army by this time. Bayne and his Robertson Colony rangers had joined with Captain Isaac Burton's rangers by April 13 as evidenced by military claims later filed by Bayne for Captain William Wilson's ranger company. On this date Bayne, Burton, and John Hart signed papers attesting to horses that had been secured for members of Wilson's ranger company.

Private William Sherrod received "one horse and equipage" worth $100. Griffin Bayne received two horses valued at $200, George W. Anderson received a horse valued at $160, Joseph A. Clayton and Captain Wilson each received a horse and rigging valued at $125 each, and William D. Thomson received a horse valued at $130. These horses became "property belonging to a part of Capt. Wilson's Company and to be used for the benefit of the Texian Army." Colonel Bayne also received "one negro man slave and gun" valued at $1,220, as witnessed on April 13 by J. Hart and I. W. Burton.[34]

At least a few of Captain Wilson's rangers joined the Texas army instead of staying to escort the settlers. Private Daniel T. Dunham, who had entered Lieutenant Colonel Bayne's ranging corps on March 27, had left the rangers by April 18 to join the artillery company of Captain George W. Poe. Papers of Francis Weatherred indicate that he also served for a time under Benton's ranger corps before joining Captain Poe's company.[35]

One of the small bands of rangers that likely joined with Bayne's party was that of Lieutenant Albert Gholson, who had taken command of the Tenoxtitlan company after Captain Barron's departure to assist the fleeing families. Gholson's son later wrote of his father's recollections, stating that Gholson's rangers arrived in time to join in some of the April 21 fighting at Vince's Bridge. Gholson's men are not listed on any roster of the participants of the San Jacinto battle but may have reached the battlefield just ahead of Griffin Bayne's other rangers. Following San Jacinto, Gholson would serve in the cavalry company of Captain John Pierson from June 30 to July 30 and then under Captain Thomas Robbins.[36]

Griffin Bayne and his rangers were "near the Brazos" on April 19, on which date Bayne received of Captain John Dix a gray mare for public service. The two men with Bayne who were called upon to place a value on the horse, decided upon as twenty-five dollars, were Alpheus Rice and Daniel Arnold.[37]

After crossing the Brazos south of Tenoxtitlan, Noah Smithwick and his remaining rangers ran into Bayne's rangers. This would have been about April 19, based on the movements of Bayne's men. Smithwick wrote that the rangers of "Captain Bob Childers" and Lieutenant Colonel Bayne "had been conveying the families from their district."[38]

Smithwick's reference to Captain Bob Childers is puzzling. Goldsby Childers was referred to as "Captain" Childers during the Republic of

Texas era and even signed his name as such on one 1836 document. Bob Childers, who served with Smithwick later in 1836 and 1837 in another ranger company, was a young son of Goldsby Childers. It is very doubtful that he would have been old enough to be considered for captain of a ranger company by the older men around him. During a mounted gunmen campaign in 1839, Bob Childers had only reached the rank of first lieutenant. His pension papers make no mention of his holding any command during the Texas Revolution. Childers was among the men who had gathered in Tenoxtitlan in March under Tommy Barron and Albert Gholson, the latter likely being truly in charge of these volunteer rangers when Smithwick encountered the party.

Lieutenant Colonel Bayne had two men without horses. These two, plus Andy Dunn and Jim Leech from Tumlinson's old company, were forced to construct a raft on which to ride down the river. The rest of the men started down the Brazos River in pursuit of General Houston's army.

Their first indication that they were close came on April 21, when they could hear the booming of guns. A messenger arrived the next day and informed these men of the recent events. They discovered, to their dismay, that they had just missed one of the most historic battles in Texas history.

★ ★ ★ ★ ★

Santa Anna Defeated: April 21, 1836

General Sam Houston's army of more than nine hundred men was ready for action near the San Jacinto River by the afternoon of April 20. The army's cavalry and some of the infantrymen did fight a skirmish with Santa Anna's troops late in the day.

The following day, April 21, found the Texas army preparing for a major battle with the Mexican army. A large group of men was left at the burned-out town of Harrisburg to guard the army's baggage and to tend to the numerous sick men who were unfit for battle. The baggage guard was placed under command of Major Robert McNutt. Aside from sick men and guards from various units, the principal companies under his command were Captain Gibson Kuykendall's Company E of the First Regiment of Texas Volunteers, Captain Peyton R. Splane's volunteer company, and Captain Joseph Chance's Washington Guards, which had been organized by Major Williamson on March 20.

Some of the men forming Major McNutt's baggage guard were Texas Rangers. Among them was Sylvanus Cottle, who had enlisted as a private in Captain Isaac Burton's rangers on February 4. Due to the small size of most revolutionary ranging companies, it is interesting to note that the rangers moved fluidly into various companies for the San Jacinto battle and then returned to their ranger duties. Cottle, for example, is listed as a member of Captain Chance's baggage guard. Military papers signed by Captain Burton, however, show that Cottle served continually under Burton's supervision in the ranger service through October 28, 1836.[39]

The officers of the ranger service were equally fluid in their roles with the main army. Both Captains Burton and Tumlinson would serve as privates during the battle of April 21, but both would resume command of ranger companies in the immediate wake of the battle. Burton and his first lieutenant, Thomas Robbins, both joined the cavalry company of Captain William H. Smith for the battle. It appears that most of Burton's company, however, remained with Lieutenant Colonel Bayne in escorting the fleeing civilians. It is possible that Burton's men were under command of Second Lieutenant Wheelock, whose detachment did not make the battle. A pay certificate on display at the Texas Ranger Hall of Fame in Waco shows that Private Richard Young served under Captain Burton from January 1 through July 10, 1836, although he was not present at San Jacinto.

Another of the cavalry recruits at San Jacinto was George Washington Davis, one of the four men who had been slated in 1835 to become a ranger superintendent. Major Williamson and two of Captain Tumlinson's former rangers, Ganey Crosby and James Curtis Sr., also joined the army as buck privates. Curtis, who had lost his son-in-law Wash Cottle (a member of the Gonzales Mounted Rangers) at the Alamo in March, would use San Jacinto to his utmost for revenge. Once the rout was complete, he used his rifle as a club to bash skulls.[40]

Of the other revolutionary rangers, five men previously serving under Captain Daniel Friar and some of Captain Stephen Townsend's men served as baggage guards at Harrisburg. Three others formerly under Friar fought at San Jacinto, and three men who served under Captain Eli Seale also fought. Sterling Robertson and four men who had served under his command were guarding baggage at the time of the battle. At least eight of Captain Robertson's former rangers fought at San Jacinto in various companies. Captain William Sadler and seven of his former rangers had joined with Captain Hayden Arnold's Nacogdoches Volunteers and would fight as privates on April 21.

More than forty men who had served as rangers under seven

different captains thus either fought at San Jacinto or guarded the baggage at Harrisburg. This number can be increased to more than eighty if Captain Chance's company, organized by Major Williamson, is viewed as a ranger unit. The fact that the Texas Rangers played a role at both the Alamo's fall and the victory at San Jacinto has received little attention in past frontier histories.

Private Moses Townsend was later paid for serving three months and twelve days in Captain Townsend's rangers, which had been ordered to the army on March 16. His public debt file shows that he was paid for duties in

> Capt. Stephen Townsend's company in the year A.D. 1836 [and] service in guarding the baggage wagons in the Battle of San Jacinto.

Moses Townsend's papers further show that Captain Townsend's rangers served through May 12, 1836. Captain Townsend and his brother Spencer Townsend actually fought in the battle as part of Captain William H. Smith's cavalry company.[41]

General Houston moved his army across the battlefield at 3:30 p.m. on April 21. They swept in from all sides on Santa Anna's unsuspecting army, catching them completely off guard.

Ranger Companies of the Texas Revolution
October 1835 - April 1836

Commander:	*Length of Service:*
Eli Hillhouse	Oct. 23 - Dec. 24, 1835
Daniel Boone Friar	Nov. 1, 1835 - Feb. 1, 1836
Eli Seale	Dec. 24, 1835 - Jan. 25, 1836
Isaac Watts Burton	Dec. 19, 1835 - June 24, 1836
James Wilson Parker Sr.	Jan. 1, 1836 - May 19, 1836
William Turner Sadler	Jan. 1, 1836 - March 16, 1836
John Jackson Tumlinson Jr.	Jan. 17, 1836 - August 16, 1836
Sterling Clack Robertson	Jan. 17 - Feb. 1836
James A. Head	Jan. 27 - April 27, 1836
Stephen Townsend	Feb. 1 - May 12, 1836
Louis B. Franks	Feb. 1 - April 1, 1836
George C. Kimbell, Lieutenant	Feb. 22 - March 6, 1836
Thomas Hudson Barron	Late Feb. - March 16, 1836 *
William C. Wilson	March 1 - June 1, 1836
Albert G. Gholson, Lieutenant	March 16 - May 7, 1836 *
Joseph Bell Chance	March 20 - June 1, 1836

* Estimated dates of service. Specific dates unavailable. Each company commander held rank of captain unless otherwise noted.

Most of the various groups of Texas Rangers employed during the revolution joined the Texas army in time to defeat the Mexican army at San Jacinto on April 21, 1836. "Charge at San Jacinto" by E. M. "Buck" Schiwetz. *Courtesy of the San Jacinto Museum of History Association.*

Houston, who suffered a painful leg wound while leading the charge, stated in his battle report that the main battle lasted only eighteen minutes. The killing went on for more than an hour, however. Mexican soldiers were pursued through the trees back to Peggy's Lake, where they were slaughtered like animals until control could be brought to the Texans who rallied under the cries of "Remember Goliad!" and "Remember the Alamo!"

Official battle reports would show only eleven Texans killed and thirty-two wounded in two days of fighting at San Jacinto. The Mexican army lost an estimated 630 soldiers killed, 208 wounded, and another 730 men captured. The prisoners of war were held in a crude barricade overnight while Texan spies fanned out to search for President Santa Anna, who had momentarily escaped the battlefield.

The Mexican leader, disguised as a private soldier, was captured the next day and brought into the Texan camp, where his true identity was immediately revealed by his own men. Santa Anna was brought before the wounded General Houston on April 22 for surrender conditions. Santa Anna agreed to order the withdrawal of all Mexican troops from Texas, although he would remain a prisoner of war until a formal treaty could be worked out that ensured the true independence of Texas.

★ ★ ★ ★ ★

Throughout the Texas Revolution, the frontier ranging corps played an important role, which has been largely played down in previous histories of the rangers. Most accounts only mention the companies of Captains John Tumlinson and Isaac Burton as having served any length of time.

The General Council of Texas legally created three separate ranging systems during the course of the revolution and at least a few other special companies. The three ranging systems created included the four-district superintendent system, Major Williamson's three-company ranging corps, and the ranging battalion under Colonel Benton. One of the constants of each of these systems was the fact that the ranger leaders ultimately reported to the commander of the Texas army.

None of these three systems ever reached its full capacity during the war, but each played an important role on the frontiers in maintaining peace during the absence of regular army companies. These rangers were instrumental in building or manning at least four frontier outposts: Fort Sterling, Fort Houston, Tumlinson's Blockhouse, and Fort Milam in Viesca.

Two companies had skirmishes with hostile Indians during the course of the revolution, and one thirty-two-man ranger company paid the ultimate price for Texas independence in being sacrificed at the Alamo.

CHAPTER 7

Parker's Fort and Little River Depredations

April 23 - June 5, 1836

Lieutenant Colonel Griffin Bayne's rangers arrived on the San Jacinto battlefield one day after the historic conflict. The group included Captain Wilson's company and a ranger detachment that had been commanded by Captain Tumlinson prior to the Runaway Scrape.

Noah Smithwick, who had recently joined Bayne's party, later described the carnage they witnessed.

> The dead Mexicans lay in piles, the survivors not even asking permission to bury them, thinking, perhaps, that, in return for the butchery they had practiced, they would soon be lying dead themselves. The buzzards and coyotes were gathering to the feast, but it is a singular fact that they singled out the dead horses, refusing to touch the Mexicans, presumably because of the peppery condition of the flesh. There they lay unmolested and dried up, the cattle got to chewing the bones, which so affected the milk that residents in the vicinity had to dig trenches and bury them.[1]

In the immediate wake of the battle, the Texas soldiers were variously occupied in guarding Mexican prisoners and in splitting the spoils of war from their great victory. Scouts and patrols were busy rounding up additional prisoners and monitoring the retreat of other Mexican forces. President Santa Anna, now a Texas prisoner of war, signed a surrender dispatch that ordered Generals Vicente Filisola, José Urrea, and Antonio Gaona to fall back to Victoria and San Antonio to await his further orders. During the process of delivering this message to the enemy, Texas scouts under Deaf Smith managed to capture General Cos, a brother-in-law to Santa Anna, and haul him back to the army's camp.[2]

As word of the Texan victory spread, the massive Runaway Scrape was slowly contained. From Robbins' Ferry on the Old San Antonio

Road, George P. Digges wrote to General Houston on April 23 of the movement of some of these families. Digges wrote that he had "formed two companies of spies from among the men moving on their families." One he placed under the direction of Louis B. Franks, who had recently commanded his own ranger company during the revolution, to watch the road near Gonzales. The other was under William Robinson, to spy on the road between Bidai Creek and the La Bahía Road on to the Brazos River. Neither company found any signs of advancing Mexican troops, and the companies were not maintained for any length of time.[3]

Lieutenant Colonel Bayne assumed command of the various ranging companies that had joined the Texas army for the battle of San Jacinto. Payment papers of William Weatherred of Captain William Wilson's rangers show that the company was stationed at "Headquarters Battle-ground" on April 28, where Bayne signed off as "Lt. Col. of the Army."[4]

During this time there was a steady shuffling of personnel between the army and the ranger service. Captain Isaac Burton, who had fought as a private in the cavalry at San Jacinto, resumed command of his company. Payment records for Privates James Gorman and Felix W. Goff, who fell in briefly with other companies at San Jacinto, show that both did continue their service in Burton's company.[5] Some of the newer arrivals formerly under Captain Tumlinson were added to Captain Burton's command.

Lieutenant Thomas Robbins, originally the second lieutenant of Burton's rangers, was promoted from Captain William H. Smith's cavalry company into his own command on April 25. Although Captain Robbins would sign military papers as a captain of cavalry, his company operated on the frontiers in the fashion of a ranger unit during its existence. Several of his new men, in fact, were taken directly from Lieutenant Colonel Bayne's ranging service. Joseph Clayton, George W. Anderson, James Shaw, and William Sherrod all transferred from Captain Wilson's ranger company into Robbins' on April 25. Another who enlisted under Robbins was former ranger superintendent Daniel Friar.

Many of the senior officers of the Texas army were eager to pursue and mop up the remnants of the Mexican forces. General Sam Houston, however, sent only cavalry scouts under Henry Karnes and Juan Seguín to monitor the retreat of enemy forces. David Burnet, the interim president of Texas, reached the army headquarters near San Jacinto on May 1. He found that Secretary of War Tom Rusk, eager to give chase to the enemy, was being held back until a peace treaty could be signed by Santa Anna in Velasco, located at present Surfside.[6]

This agreement would not be signed until May 14. During that time, Tom Rusk was appointed brigadier general in charge of all Texas armed forces to replace General Houston, who resigned from the army on May 5 to seek treatment in the United States for his leg wound. Mirabeau Lamar, who had commanded the cavalry at San Jacinto, took over Rusk's billet as secretary of war. Lamar then instructed General Rusk to organize his troops and to follow the retreating Mexican forces at a safe distance without provoking them.

★   ★   ★   ★   ★

Ranger Regiment Revamped: May 8, 1836

As the main body of the army departed to chase the Mexican army, the Texas Rangers were reorganized on May 8. Major Willie Williamson had ceased to be involved with the ranging service prior to San Jacinto. The previous regional ranger system with area superintendents largely lapsed also. Three of the four Council-appointed superintendents—Daniel Friar, Garrison Greenwood, and George Davis—had ceased to function in such a role. Only the fourth, Silas Parker, was actually still in charge of a small ranger company under Captain James Parker as of May 1836. Captain James Head's small ranger unit, also under Silas Parker's direction, had disbanded on April 27.

Colonel Jesse Benton, commissioned by the Constitutional Convention to raise a battalion of rangers, was still absent in the vicinity of the United States border on the Red River. His second-in-command, Lieutenant Colonel Griffin Bayne, therefore became the active organizer and commander of the various units of rangers in the vicinity of the San Jacinto battlefield.

Bayne promoted several officers including Second Lieutenant Ripley Wheelock to captain on May 8. A native of New England, Wheelock had completed college at West Point. He later served in the War of 1812 and in the Black Hawk War. Afterwards he had been involved in trading in Illinois, even spending three years trading in Mexico. In 1833 he came to Texas and settled in Robertson's Colony on a prairie that was soon named Wheelock Prairie, where a town named for him was later laid out. He, his son George Ripley Wheelock, and son-in-law Samuel Kimble had joined up with Bayne's rangers on March 16.[7]

Captain Wheelock formed his three-month company on May 8 from available volunteers and from many of the men who had served with him in his prior ranger company. He promoted his son-in-law Samuel Kimble to second sergeant. Wheelock also promoted Francis M. Doyle to second lieutenant. Prior to May 8, Doyle had been

> a private in my company of Texas Regiment of Rangers ordered to be raised by a resolution of the Convention, to be commanded by Col. Benton and Lt. Col. Bayne.

Captain Wheelock further stated that his company was under orders of General Rusk, commanding the Texian army but "attached to the command of General [Thomas] Green." He would sign military papers while in command as "E. L. Ripley Wheelock, Captain Regular Ranging."[8]

Griffin Bayne directed three other ranger companies as of this date, those of Captains William Wilson, John Tumlinson, and Isaac Burton. Among the men serving under Burton were rangers Dickinson Putnam and Samuel Smith, both enlisted since March. Both of these men would

---

Captain Wheelock's Rangers: May 8 - August 8, 1836

Captain:	Charles Baker [1]	Stephen Rogers [3]
E. L. Ripley Wheelock	Levi Barrow	Joseph Routch
First Lieutenant:	Reuben Barrow	Nicholas James Ryan
Thomas Cantwell	Solomon Barrow	William D. Smith
Second Lieutenant:	Joseph T. Bell [1]	Frederick Springer
Francis M. Doyle	William Bloodgood	Joseph Taylor
First Sergeant:	Washington Brask	John Teer [2]
Seth Carey	Therence Carlin [1]	Napoleon B. Thompson [1]
Second Sergeant:	Lorenzo H. Clark	Willis Vaughn
Samuel A. Kimble	William B. Crabtree	Joseph Walker [1]
Third Sergeant:	John Davis	Nathaniel Whitcher [1]
John Archer	George W. Davis	George Ripley Wheelock
Fourth Sergeant:	J. M. Finch	Jackson Williams [1]
George W. Lyons	Chester S. Gorbet [1]	John Williams [1]
First Corporal:	John Hynes [4]	Samuel Williams [5]
John Williams	Peter Hynes [4]	
Second Corporal:	Edward B. Jackson [1]	[1] Served six months.
Jacob Townsend	Joseph (Indian)	[2] Deserted by Aug. 23.
Third Corporal:	W. A. Lagrone	[3] Left sick; not officially
Elijah Allen	John Lawrence	discharged.
Fourth Corporal:	Henry Linney	[4] Joined June 1 for six-
Isaac Garner	Dewitt C. Lyons	month enlistment.
Musician:	William L. Moss [1]	[5] Furloughed as of August
Alfred Pride	Milo Mower [1]	23 to take charge of
Privates:	James Murray	Capt. Wheelock's family.
John Adams	William T. Neal [1]	Pay charged to Capt.
William H. Arthur	John R. Rhea	Wheelock.
William H. Attree	John W. Rial [1]	
Burton Baker	Robert Rogers [3]	Source: *Muster Rolls of the Texas Revolution*, 141-44.

soon command their own ranger companies. Contrary to previous published ranger histories, Captain Tumlinson did remain in command of rangers immediately prior to the battle of San Jacinto and in the months following. The audited military papers of Private Hugh Childress, for example, show that he was discharged from Tumlinson's company on July 18, 1836. Tumlinson noted that Childress had "entered the services in the First Division of the Ranging Corps for the Republic of Texas on the 17th day of Jany 1836."[9]

Empresario Sterling Robertson was again involved with the rangers in the weeks following San Jacinto. A signer of the Texas Declaration of Independence, he had been among those detailed to guard the baggage at the time of the battle. Robertson joined a reconnoitering party that slowly pursued a large contingent of enemy soldiers who were making their way back to Mexico. The Texans collected a sizable stock of discarded goods and even pack mules still fully loaded that had been abandoned. Robertson felt that Santa Anna's soldiers fled in great haste, leaving behind wagons and at least one thousand stands of arms thrown into the San Bernard River.[10]

Ranger Noah Smithwick, now part of Captain Burton's company, later wrote of the pursuit of the Mexican army.

> The country being deserted, we helped ourselves to anything in the way of provisions we found lying around loose; but, the Mexican army having marched and countermarched through that section, there was little, except livestock, left to forage on . . .
>
> All danger from the Mexicans being over, our men were strung out across the prairie, sometimes a mile ahead of the wagons. The sedge grass, which in many places was waist high, was getting dry, furnishing material for a terrible conflagration if by chance a spark should light among it.[11]

In his memoirs, Smithwick did not list his post-San Jacinto ranger commanders. They are, however, identified in military papers he later filed for payment from the Republic of Texas. One pay certificate was issued him for $190 "for services in I. W. Burton's Company of Rangers." These records further show that Smithwick was with the ranger corps long enough to have the command of his company pass from Burton to Dickinson Putnam in June. He was later paid $112 on November 2 for services rendered "in the Company of Rangers commanded by Capt. Dick[in]son Putnam in 1836."[12]

Bayne's ranger companies trailed the main Texas army body as it moved slowly westward toward Victoria while following the Mexican army. As new troops continually arrived from the United States, some of the frontiersman became eager to return to their homes. Settlers were beginning to return from the Runaway Scrape, and there was still time to plant crops for the growing season.

From Victoria, General Rusk reported the requests of three companies "now applying to me to go home" on May 12 to Secretary of War Lamar. They were the companies of Captain William Fisher of Velasco, Captain Jesse Billingsley's Mina Volunteers of Robertson's Colony, and Captain William Ware of San Jacinto. On May 14 Rusk furloughed these companies and Colonel Edward Burleson, commander of the army's first regiment. The men of Captain Billingsley's unit still had two weeks left of their original enlistment, but he willingly gave most of his men these last two weeks as furlough. Two weeks later Burleson signed the discharges of these men on June 1, 1836, in Bastrop.[13]

As the growing Texas army continued to drive the remaining Mexican troops toward the Rio Grande, the Bastrop area citizens tried to return to a normal life on the frontiers. At least a small portion of the Mina Volunteers remained under Captain Billingsley's direction even after the company officially disbanded. These men were likely motivated to stay armed by a rash of Indian depredations, which began to escalate. A new menace had returned to the prairies to replace the revolution. In a matter of weeks, Billingsley would be forced to organize yet another company of Mina area men to range the local frontiers against Indians.

★ ★ ★ ★ ★

Indians Attack Near Bastrop: May 14, 1836

Almost as soon as the Runaway Scrape ended and settlers began returning to their fields, the Indian attacks resumed. During late April and early May, settlers had made their way back to the San Antonio Road at the settlement of Tenoxtitlan. From there, many of the families moved back to Bastrop and prepared to work their fields again.[14]

It was in the Hornsby neighborhood in the Bastrop area that Indian violence renewed on May 14. The attack occurred in a field about a half mile from the home of Reuben Hornsby. The men working this field were John Williams, Howell Haggard, nineteen-year-old Malcolm Hornsby, seventeen-year-old Billy Hornsby, twelve-year-old Reuben Hornsby Jr., and a man about eighteen years of age named Cain. Cain, Williams, and Haggard had previously been rangers of Captain

Tumlinson's company until they were ordered in March to assist the Bastrop area settlers during the Runaway Scrape.[15]

A party of ten to fifteen Comanche warriors was seen to ride up into the field of these white men. The Indians carried a white flag, giving the appearance that they came in peace. Williams and Haggard were closest to the approaching Indians and some distance away from the other men. They were suddenly speared and shot down by the Comanches. The Hornsby brothers and the other men immediately ran for cover and swam the river with the Indians in pursuit.

The Hornsby brothers hid in the river bottom until after dark. They cautiously crept back to their father's house, expecting to find the occupants murdered. It was a joyous reunion when Reuben Hornsby Sr. saw three of his sons return unharmed that night. Hornsby, his wife, Cynthia Castner Hornsby, and their younger children had defiantly stood outside their home displaying their rifles. The Indians had decided not to approach this armed force. They instead stole all the cattle from the neighborhood, numbering as many as one hundred head, and then moved on.[16]

★ ★ ★ ★ ★

Rangers Massacred at Parker's Fort: May 19, 1836

As the Mexican troops withdrew and the Texas army reorganized, the frontier settlements had been left largely to fend for themselves in the days following the Texas Revolution. Most of the ranger companies formed during the revolution were now attached to the army in some capacity. The only small group of rangers on the eastern frontier still on duty was the ten-man company of thirty-nine-year-old Captain James Parker, under the superintendence of Silas Parker.

The Parker rangers were stationed at Parker's Fort, which had been known as Fort Sterling during the early months of the Texas Revolution. The name Fort Sterling was dropped over time in favor of the more popularly known sobriquet of "Parker's Fort." The compound itself, located near the headwaters of the Navasota River in present Limestone County, consisted of a number of small native wood cabins surrounded by a bulletproof stockade designed to keep the Indians out.

The settlement's patriarch was seventy-nine-year-old Elder John Parker, who had organized the Pilgrim Predestinarian Baptist Church, the first non-Catholic church in Texas. Parker's church records noted on April 2 during the Runaway Scrape that "members of this church are like to scatter by reason of the apparent danger and unsettled state of the country."[17]

The end of the Runaway Scrape and the victory at San Jacinto had scarcely been celebrated before chaos shook this little community. One of the most famous Indians assaults in Texas history occurred at Parker's Fort on May 19, 1836.

There were thirty-eight settlers residing at Parker's Fort at the time of this attack. Most of the adult men were or had previously been attached to Captain James Parker's command. For example, settler Robert B. Frost's Republic of Texas audited claims show that he had initially joined Captain Hillhouse's company on November 16, 1835, and later served under Captain James Parker until being discharged on April 22, 1836.

James Parker later wrote that he had disbanded his small ranger company a few days before the Indian attack, "as there appeared to be but little danger of an attack, and as the Government was not in a condition to bear the expense of supporting troops."[18] This statement conflicts with

---

Parker's Fort Massacre: May 19, 1836

Residents:	Sarah Parker Nixon
Elisha Anglin	*Benjamin Parker* [1]
Abram Anglin	*Capt. James Wilson Parker Sr.*
Seth Bates	Martha Duty Parker
Silas H. Bates	James Wilson Parker Jr.
George E. Dwight	Francis Marion Parker
Mrs. G. E. Dwight	Martha Patsy Parker
Dwight children	Elder John Parker [1]
Mrs. Duty [2]	Sallie White Parker [2]
David Faulkenberry	Silas Mercer Parker Sr. [1]
Evan Faulkenberry	Lucy Duty Parker
Samuel Frost [1]	Cynthia Ann Parker [3]
Mrs. Samuel Frost	John Parker [3]
Robert B. Frost [1]	Silas Parker Jr.
S. Frost children	Orlena Parker
Elizabeth Kellogg [3]	*Luther Thomas Martin Plummer*
Oliver Lund	Rachel Parker Plummer [3]
Mrs. Lorenzo D. Nixon Sr.	James Pratt Plummer [3]
Lorenzo D. Nixon Jr.	

[1] Killed by the Indians May 19, 1836.
[2] Wounded May 19, 1836.
[3] Taken hostage May 19, 1836.
Note: Italics indicates name of a man who served as a ranger under superintendent Silas Parker during 1836. Some of these men were still serving under Captain James Parker at the time of the attack. Names that are indented indicate young children of their parents listed immediately above them. The names and exact number of children of Samuel Frost and George Dwight are unknown.

the fact that audited military claims show Captain Parker to have been paid as a ranger through May 19, 1836. His brother Benjamin Parker is also shown as a ranger who served from December 28, 1835, to May 19, 1836. Serving as the only guardians for this remote Navasota River settlement, these men were caught too widely scattered to provide an effective defense when the depredation occurred.

With morning's first light on May 19, a number of men left the fort to work their fields. Rachel Parker Plummer's husband, Luther, went with her father, James Parker, Lorenzo Nixon, and her little brother Wilson Parker to work on a farm about a mile from the fort near the Navasota River. The Faulkenberrys, Bates, Anglins, and Oliver Lund also went to work the crops about a mile farther and a little below.[19]

It was about 9:00 a.m. when a combined force of hundreds of Comanches and Kiowas appeared in the prairie near Parker's Fort. As the Indians approached, Sarah Parker Nixon quickly ran for her father James Parker's farm to give the alarm. Most of the other women departed, also, with the exception of Captain Parker's younger daughter Rachel because of her inability to run with her infant son. She chose to stay in the shelter of the fort.

Rachel Parker Plummer in 1838 wrote an account of her family's ordeal, which was printed in 1839. She recalled that her grandparents Elder John Parker and wife and several others quickly departed across the farm of Silas Parker, which immediately adjoined the fort. George E. Dwight also departed with his wife, children, and mother-in-law, despite a protest from Silas Parker of, "Good Lord, Dwight, you are not going to run!"

Dwight insisted that he was only escorting the women and children to the woods. Silas Parker insisted that the other man stay and "fight like a man," to which Dwight promised that he would return. At this point, ranger Benjamin Parker volunteered to go forward and greet the approaching Indians. They had stopped some two hundred yards from Parker's Fort, displayed a white flag, and sent two Indians forward with the ruse of making a peace treaty with the whites.

There were only four men left in the fort, Silas and Ben Parker plus Samuel Frost and his son Robert B. Frost. Rachel Plummer later wrote:

> The Indians halted; and two Indians came up to the fort to inform the inmates that they were friendly, and had come for the purpose of making a treaty with the Americans. They instantly threw the people off guard, and Uncle Benjamin went to the Indians, who had now got within a few hundred yards of the fort.

In a few minutes he returned, and told Frost and his son and Uncle Silas that he believed the Indians intended to fight, and told them to put everything in the best order of defense.[20]

These men prepared themselves as best they could. Ben Parker then said he would try to go work out a compromise with the Indians, although his brother Silas warned him not to go. Fearing the worst, Silas hurried back into his house to fetch one of his shot pouches for his rifle. He told Rachel to keep watch of the proceedings while he prepared for the fight. Passing through the small back gate, the sight she next witnessed was painful, as the Comanches and Kiowas attacked her uncle.

I ran out of the fort, and passing the corner I saw the Indians drive their spears into Benjamin. The work of death had already commenced. I shall not attempt to describe their terrific yells, their united voices that seemed to reach the very skies, whilst they were dealing death to the inmates of the fort. It can scarcely be comprehended in the wide field of imagination.

Before Rachel could make a run back into the fort, Indians got ahead of her and blocked her escape. One of them knocked her unconscious with a hoe and tore her fifteen-month-old son, James Pratt Plummer, from her arms. When she came to momentarily, the Indians were dragging her by the hair toward the fort. She was escorted past the body of Ben Parker in the process. "His face was much mutilated, and many arrows were sticking in his body," she later wrote. "As the savages passed by, they thrust their spears through him."

The Indians eventually drug her back into the fort, where for a desperate half hour or so, the one-sided fight had taken place. Ranger superintendent Silas Parker was killed while bravely fighting outside the fort. To his last effort, he tried to protect Rachel Plummer, but he was soon killed and scalped. Young Comanches were taught to prove themselves as being brave in combat, with physically striking an opponent in battle being far more courageous than merely shooting the same person from a distance. Scalping an enemy while still alive was considered a great feat. This grisly act involved using a sharp knife to remove the entire scalp with ears if possible, although the raiding process often left insufficient time to take the entire scalp.

During the assault on the interior of the fort, Samuel Frost and his son Robert were also killed while trying to defend some of the women and children who had stayed.

One of the two restored blockhouses at Old Fort Parker State Historical Park. In the famous Comanche raid on this ranger fortress on May 19, 1836, three men were killed outside the fort's perimeter and two others were killed within the stockade. Two women were seriously wounded, while another woman and four children were taken as hostages by the Indians. *Author's photo, courtesy Old Fort Parker State Historical Park.*

The last bunch of settlers to leave the fort did not make it far. Elder John Parker and his wife, Sallie White "Granny" Parker, and Elizabeth Kellogg, made it less than a mile before they were overtaken. They were stripped and then John Parker was shot through with an arrow and scalped. Mrs. Duty, Silas Parker's mother-in-law, was stabbed with a knife and left for dead. "Granny" Parker, stripped to her underwear, was speared and otherwise violated by the Indians, who then left the poor eighty-year-old woman for dead. The youngest of the party, Elizabeth Kellogg, was taken captive and dragged back toward the fort.

Inside Parker's Fort, captive Rachel Plummer had the horrible anxiety of seeing braves sporting bloody scalps as souvenirs. "Among them I could distinguish that of my old grandfather by the grey hairs, but could not discriminate the balance." Other Indians then returned with captive Elizabeth Kellogg.

When the Indians first appeared, Sarah Nixon had hurried away to the fields to alert some of the men who were working away from the fort, including James Parker, Luther Plummer, and her husband, Lorenzo Nixon. Plummer then hurried to inform the others in the field: Silas Bates, Abram Anglin, David Faulkenberry, and the latter's son Evan

An early artist's rendering of the massacre within Parker's Fort. Originally published in 1912 in DeShields' *Border Wars of Texas*.

Faulkenberry. He first met David Faulkenberry, who turned and headed immediately back for the fort alone.

Once Plummer reached the others, these men also rushed back toward Fort Parker. En route, James Parker met his fleeing family, and he took them to shelter in the Navasota River bottom. Luther Plummer was sent to spread the warning to the others, who were about a half mile away, while Nixon hurried for the fort. Nixon arrived back at the fort unarmed in time to see Lucy Parker, wife of the murdered Silas Parker, and her four children just as the Indians were overtaking them.

Two of Lucy Parker's children, Cynthia Ann and John Parker, were lifted onto horseback behind two Indians and were carried inside the fort. Nixon, desperately following on foot in some vain attempt to help them, had his life spared by David Faulkenberry, who appeared with his rifle.

Faulkenberry, left alone to defend Lucy Parker and her two remaining children, bravely made charges at the Indians with his rifle to keep them back. Mrs. Parker's dog lunged into the face of a horse ridden by one of these braves. The dog succeeded in causing the horse and rider to stumble, the Indian being thrown into a gully. At this fortunate time, Silas Bates, Abram Anglin, and Evan Faulkenberry arrived from the field with their rifles, followed by Luther Plummer, who was unarmed. The pursuing Indians made more hostile advances but in time chose to retire from the armed party.

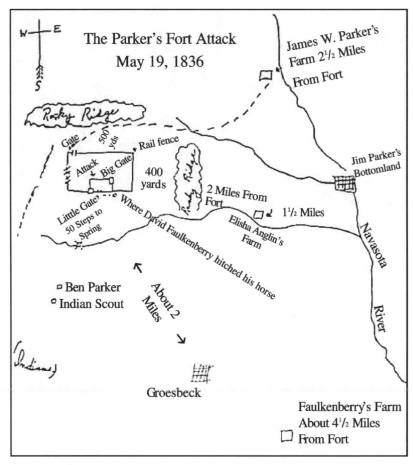

Among the family stories about the Fort Parker engagement in the Texas State Archives is an old, unsigned map of the attack on the fort. The original handwritten text has been replaced here for readability.

This little bunch made their way back towards the river bottom with Lucy Parker and her two small children. Soon after David Faulkenberry had helped save Lucy Parker, Lorenzo Nixon became excited and set out in search of his own wife. He did manage to find the badly wounded Mrs. Duty, who had been stripped and stabbed. Nixon took her to Plummer, who helped dress Mrs. Duty's wounds. She was gathered along with the other women and children and would manage to recover from her wounds in time.

Plummer, whose wife and son had been carried away by the Indians, wandered off on his own to search for them, armed only with young Abram Anglin's butcher knife. He finally ended up at Tinnon's, a little settlement located on the land grant of Jeremiah Tinnon on the west bank of the Navasota River at the crossing of the San Antonio-Nacogdoches Road. This was some ninety miles from Parker's Fort.[21]

During this time, the last of the massive band of Indians moved away from Parker's Fort. They carried away with them five captives: Elizabeth Kellogg, Cynthia Ann and John Parker, Rachel Plummer, and her infant son, James Pratt Plummer. Five men of the Parker and Frost families had been killed. Two other women, "Granny" Parker and Mrs. Duty, had been badly wounded and left for dead. The raiders had also stripped the fort of all worthwhile plunder, destroyed many of the settlers' cattle, and caught some of their horses. With the Indians estimated

Luther Thomas Martin Plummer (1811-1875) served as a ranger under Captains Hillhouse, Seale, and James Parker during the Texas Revolution. His pregnant wife and son were both taken hostage by the Comanches on May 19 from Parker's Fort. Plummer served in Ranger Company E during 1837 on the Navasota River. *Courtesy Old Fort Parker State Historical Park.*

at seven to eight hundred strong, these few whites did not think to follow them.

At twilight Abram Anglin and Evan Faulkenberry decided to make their way back to the fort to look for survivors. About three-quarters of a mile from the main fortress, they found poor Granny Parker, who had fooled the Indians into thinking that she was dead. With her long white hair and bloody appearance, poor young Anglin at first took her for a ghost in the fading light. Recovering from his initial fright, Anglin later related:

> I took some bed clothing and carrying her some distance from the house, made her a bed, covered her up, and left her until we should return from the fort. On arriving at the fort, we could not see a single individual alive, or hear a human sound. But the dogs were barking, the cattle lowing, the horses neighing, and the hogs squealing.

Mrs. Parker had told me where she had left some silver, $106.50. This I found under a hickory bush, by moonlight.

Finding no one at the fort, we returned to where I had hidden "Granny" Parker. On taking her up behind me, we made our way back to our hiding place in the bottom, where we found Nixon.[22]

Silas Bates, Abram Anglin, and Evan Faulkenberry returned to the fort again the following morning, May 20, securing five horses and supplies. They, along with Nixon, Lund, Seth Bates, Granny Parker, Mrs. Duty, Lucy Parker, and her two children rode to the safety of Fort Houston. Poor Granny Parker did not live long after reaching Fort Houston. A party of twelve from Fort Houston then returned to look for survivors.[23]

The second group of survivors, headed by Captain James Parker, had a more desperate time reaching safety. His party consisted of himself, George Dwight, and nineteen surviving women and children. Captain Parker later wrote of the family's hardships in reaching safety.

> We started from the fort, the party consisting of eighteen in all, for Fort Houston, a distance of ninety miles by the route we had to travel. The feelings of the party can be better imagined than described. We were truly a forlorn set, many of us barefooted and bareheaded, a relentless foe on the one hand and on the other a trackless and uninhabited wilderness infested with reptiles and wild beasts, entirely destitute of food and no means of procuring it.[24]

Parker stated that his wife "was in bad health" and that "Mrs. Frost was in deep distress for the loss of her husband and son." Briars ripped at the skin of the women and children as they wandered through the wilderness. During the next five days, these survivors had no food to eat except for two skunks and two small terrapins, which were killed during this time and roasted.

By the evening of the fifth day, the women and children were so exhausted from fatigue and hunger that they could not go on. "After holding a consultation it was agreed that I should hurry on to Fort Houston for aid, leaving Mr. Dwight in charge of the women and children," wrote Parker. He set out the following morning and estimated that he covered some thirty-five miles before reaching Fort Houston.

James Parker returned to Parker's Fort on June 19, exactly one month after the massacre. The crops had been destroyed, the horses were gone, and most of the cattle had been killed. The houses were still standing within the fort, although every piece of furniture was gone. He gathered the bones of his father John and brothers Benjamin and Silas,

Cynthia Ann Parker (1827-1864), daughter of ranger superintendent Silas Parker. Among the captives taken from Parker's Fort, she would later marry a chief and live more than two decades with the Comanches. From DeShields' *Border Wars of Texas*.

Early East Texas settler Elisha Anglin was a resident of Parker's Fort in 1836. He was working the fields at the time of the massacre. From DeShields' *Border Wars of Texas*.

plus those of Robert and Samuel Frost. After constructing a crude box, he buried the remains of all except his younger brother Silas. James wrote that he and his brother had made a pact that whichever of the two survived longest would see that his brother's body was not buried, however strange the request may have seemed.[25]

Perhaps the first documented account of the Parker massacre was dated June 18, 1836, less than a month after the event. Three citizens of the Fort Houston area heard the account from Lucy Parker and other survivors who had made their way to Fort Houston. These men were Daniel Parker, Armstead Bennett, and Thomas Lagow. Lucy Parker informed them that at least some of the attacking Indians were Caddos.

As for the Indian captives, Elizabeth Kellogg was eventually ransomed and delivered to Nacogdoches six months later, where Sam Houston paid $150 to a band of Delawares for her return.

James Parker went to the First Congress of Texas in December 1836 with a petition asking for the means with which he could recover his daughter Rachel and other prisoners of the Indians. The grieving father would make three perilous trips into Indian Territory before finally recovering her. About six months after being captured at Parker's Fort, Rachel Plummer gave birth to a child, but the baby was brutally murdered in her presence. She was finally ransomed by Mexican traders in Santa Fe on June 19, 1837, and then taken to St. Louis. Rachel returned with her brother-in-law on February 19, 1838, twenty-two months after her capture.[26]

In September 1838 Rachel Plummer dictated a narrative of her ordeal with the Indians; she died one year after being returned to her husband. Her son, James Pratt Plummer, was also ransomed, taken to Fort Gibson in 1842, and delivered to his family in February 1843. James lived out a full life as a respected citizen of present Anderson County.

Two of the other Parker's Fort hostages, Cynthia Ann and John Parker, became the most well known Indian captives of Texas. Captain James Parker spent years trying to ransom them. He even published a little book in 1844 describing his efforts to recover his daughter Rachel Parker Plummer, hoping to make enough money to ransom his niece Cynthia Ann.

John Parker became a famous Indian warrior. He married a Mexican girl, led his own tribe for a time, and later quit his tribe before finally fighting for the Confederacy with a Mexican company. His nine-year-old sister, Cynthia Ann Parker, lived for twenty-five years with the Indians, giving birth to two sons and a daughter. One son became the famous Comanche chief Quanah Parker. Upon her return to civilization, her family tried to help her adjust. She was brought back to Anderson County, but she continued to grieve for her former life and family.[27]

The Parker's Fort massacre brought about the end of the ranger companies that had operated under superintendent Silas Parker. His brother Captain James Parker would later have trouble securing proper payment for his service. While in Houston in 1838 settling his unpaid claims, he opted to take pay as a common ranger for the period of November 17, 1835, until May 19, 1836. Papers show that since his former company commander Eli Hillhouse had passed away in December 1835 and "owing to the massacre of Silas M. Parker he has been unable to procure the necessary vouchers." Comptroller Francis R. Lubbock decided that James Parker should not be paid as a private but as a captain on June 14, 1838.[28]

Texas eventually paid Captain Parker on a $294.50 claim for his service as a ranger, six months of boarding others, and for providing corn and beef. Silas Parker's widow, Lucy Parker, was later paid $164.38 by Texas for military goods and supplies he had furnished his rangers.[29]

Post San Jacinto Military Movements

The plight of the Parker's Fort settlers was unknown to the Texas army. The infantry companies under General Rusk straggled into the main army camp at Victoria by late May on foot. Ahead of them, work had already been completed by rangers in setting up camp, building barracks and even a stock pen.

Those with special trades, such as blacksmiths, were ordered into special duty out of their ranger companies. One of these was blacksmith Noah Smithwick, who was detached from Captain Burton's company to make use of his special skills.

The cavalry units, headed by Colonel Sidney Sherman, had already moved on out from Victoria to trail General Filisola's retreating troops. Sherman's mounted forces included a spy company under Captain Henry Karnes, cavalrymen under Juan Seguín, a newly arrived cavalry company under Captain William Strickland from Mississippi, and at least a portion of Lieutenant Colonel Bayne's ranger battalion.

General Rusk promoted Juan Seguín to lieutenant colonel in charge of raising and maintaining two cavalry companies to be stationed at Béxar. His troops were to monitor Mexican activity from San Antonio toward the Rio Grande. Seguín had taken up station in San Antonio as of June 4, 1836.[30]

After a brief rest in Victoria, Rusk's troops marched twenty-five miles farther to Goliad. There, on June 3, a proper military funeral, including a general parade of the troops, was held at 9:00 a.m. The bones of the Goliad defenders had been collected and placed into a single grave, and several of Fannin's command who had miraculously escaped the massacre were in attendance as mourners.

Lieutenant Colonel Bayne and Captain Wilson's company of rangers are known to have accompanied Rusk into Goliad.[31] It is likely that the companies of Captains Tumlinson and Wheelock also accompanied Bayne's command. Captain Burton's ranger company, reduced in size by men assigned to special detail at Victoria, had been ordered to scout coastal activity near Copano Bay. The frontier company of Captain Joseph Chance, which had been organized in March by ranger commander Willie Williamson, was reorganized on June 1. Several of Chance's men continued in service in the new volunteer army company of Captain John Campbell Hunt, Chance's former first lieutenant.

General Rusk was interested in further developing a proper frontier ranging system to support settlers who were beginning to return to their homes following the Runaway Scrape. During May he commissioned former ranger captain Sterling Robertson to raise new volunteers for the service. Robertson found during his travels to Nacogdoches and San Augustine that the men were "lukewarm and have but little notion of turning out." From Robertson's correspondence, it is noted that Colonel Jesse Benton was with him at least part of the time while he was in Nacogdoches.[32]

Robertson wrote to Rusk on May 27 from San Augustine,

> I am afraid that I shall not get many, if any, to march to the field, though it is admitted on all hands that men are necessary at this time to enable you to follow up the blow at San Jacinto.

Robertson did learn of a large contingent of men from New Orleans who were en route to join the Texas army. He sent his note via Judge Joseph Hood, who had accompanied him in recruiting as far as San Augustine.

Robertson wrote that Major James Smith, who had joined him for the recruiting trip, felt it unnecessary to continue on to Natchitoches. Smith and Robertson instead sent Thomas Dillard on ahead to Natchitoches with a printed proclamation from Rusk calling for volunteers. Major Smith headed for Nacogdoches on May 27, while Robertson headed back for the main army. "On the way out at least 50 will accompany me from my colony and the upper part of Austin's," Robertson promised.

These men traveling back to empresario Robertson's colony were enlisted into the ranging service. Military papers for some of these men show them serving under Captain Robertson during late May and early June, although Robertson was not properly in command of a ranger company until July 15. The papers of Leroy Bogguss, for example, show that he "joined in the ranging corps on the 28th May A.D. 1836 and that he [served] as a private from that time [until] the 30th day of June 1836." After being discharged by Robertson, Bogguss was enrolled in the cavalry company of Captain John Pierson.[33]

The fact that General Rusk had Robertson recruiting new frontier fighters during late May and early June was important. The services of the Texas Rangers would become more crucial during the rise of a renewed Indian threat beginning to return to the white settlements.

★   ★   ★   ★   ★

Little River Settlers Attacked: June 4, 1836

Within weeks of the deadly Parker massacre, another Indian attack occurred in June 1836 near the settlement of Nashville. During the winter of 1835-1836, several settlers had cleared patches of about four acres each along the Little River and planted corn. These people had fled during the Runaway Scrape or served in the army. Afterwards they returned as a group and collectively worked these crops for mutual protection while restoring their little community.

Nashville was the most major settlement in this area during the summer of 1836. The town consisted of a number of small stores, log homes, sheds, stock pens, and tilled fields arranged about a centrally located cedar blockhouse known as Fort Nashville. Early resident George W. Tyler described this fort as being

> constructed in the usual way of frontier forts, with port or gunholes through which the besieged could defend themselves against the enemy's approach.[34]

This frontier settlement also had a small cannon, which had been sent out by the ladies of Nashville, Tennessee, to defend their city's Texas namesake. The settlers occasionally loaded and fired their cannon at sunset, but it had never been used in battle.

Nashville-on-the-Brazos remained relatively safe from Indian attack in the months after San Jacinto, but such was not the case for the more remote settlements surrounding this town.

Two messengers, John Beal and John H. "Jack" Hobson (or Hopson), departed from Nashville about June 1 to warn others that a large party of hostile Indians was moving through the area. It is possible that they were spreading the word about the attack near Hornsby's. The word was also out on the Parker's Fort massacre. Jack Hobson had come to Texas in December 1835 and had just completed service with Jesse Billingsley's Mina Volunteers. After the revolution, he later served in several ranger companies, including that of Tommy Barron.[35]

The settlers that Beal and Hobson warned, a family centered around Goldsby Childers, lived about eight miles east of the present town of Cameron, in present Milam County. Childers is referred to as Captain Childers in various early accounts. There are no records to indicate that he ever formally commanded an army or ranger company. His title was more likely for being in charge of volunteers in the area of his fortified home whenever they were called together. The title stuck with him, as evidenced by a petition signed in the Nashville colony on September 26, 1836. His name is entered as "Capt. G. Childers."

The Childers household took heed of the warning and made preparations on June 3 to move down to Nashville for protection. They had with them one wagon drawn by a pair of oxen, plus a few horses, although not enough to mount the entire party. Captain Goldsby Childers took command of the seventeen-person volunteer settler party.

This party included Childers, his wife, their seven children, an older man named Henry Rhoads who had come to Texas with the Childers, a minister named "Parson" Isaac Crouch, and Ezekiel Robinson, a single man staying with the Childers. Messengers Hobson and Beal plus three single men (Orville Thomas Tyler, Robert Davidson, and Montgomery Bell Shackleford) who were temporarily living at the Childers home also constituted this party. Twenty-seven-year-old Shackleford, a native of Virginia, had been sworn in as a Robertson Colonist on August 25, 1835. He had previously served as a ranger under Captains Friar and Robertson during the Texas Revolution.[36]

This party departed and camped the first night at the house of local settler William Henry Walker, where the families of James "Camel Back" Smith and Daniel Monroe had already taken refuge. Walker's home was located on the east bank of the Little River at the present site of the town of Cameron, Texas. The cabins of Smith and Monroe were located perhaps one hundred yards apart from that of Walker's. The Childers party stayed the night and then moved out early the next morning, June 4. The Walker, Smith, and Monroe families were not yet ready to depart when Childers set out.

The Childers party encountered Indians at a point about two or three miles southeast of Walker's house on the road to Nashville near Smith's Crossing of the Little River. Robert Davidson and Parson Crouch were riding on horseback about three hundred yards ahead of the party. Two hundred yards behind them was Captain Childers, who was riding in advance of the wagon and those on foot. Two or three men trailed the whole procession, driving the cattle. These men suddenly discovered about two hundred mounted Indians bearing down on them from the rear.

These men shouted an alarm and rushed forward to join the wagon. Captain Childers yelled ahead to Crouch and Davidson before turning back to help guard the wagon. The Indians split into two groups and began encircling the wagon. The little party crouched around their wagon and attempted to defend themselves against the Indian party that surrounded them. Only eleven of the Childers party were able to bear arms, although Henry Rhoads was very old and in poor health.

Crouch and Davidson were separated and were unable to rejoin the others in time. They tried to escape but did not make it. In a statement made two weeks later, Montgomery Shackleford described the attack.

> When they approached within two hundred yards, they divided, one half to the right, the other half to the left—passed us shooting at us—and pursued and killed Crouch and Davidson, who were some three hundred yards ahead of us. Before they could gain, those of us who were near the wagon made our way to some timber that was near. The Indians drove off our cattle and took one horse; the balance of the company escaped without further injury.[37]

Orville Thomas Tyler (1810-1886) came to Texas in 1834 and settled along the Little River. He was among the Childers party that was attacked by Indians on June 4, 1836. From DeShields' *Border Wars of Texas*.

The Indians scalped Crouch and Davidson after killing them. They reportedly became excited and quarreled among each other over who would keep the scalps and plunder of these two men. During this distraction, Captain Childers hastened his party and their wagon into a small grove of oak trees located about a quarter of a mile away.

Under cover of the trees, the Childers group released their oxen to prevent their escape from being slowed down. Beal and Hobson chose to escape into the woods and abandoned the party. The Indians galloped about the stranded party, firing shots and attempting to entice the settlers to fire back at them. Shackleford, who knew some of the Indian language, shouted challenges for the warriors to approach closer. The Indians evidently believed that the settlers had good pistols or extra arms stashed in the wagon, as they chose not to approach closer than one hundred yards. Shackleford later stated that he was well acquainted with the Caddo tribe, knowing them "by their dress and manner." He felt that some of those attacking his party were Caddos, and that others were

Childers Party Depredation: June 4, 1836	
Capt. Goldsby Childers	John Beal
Elizabeth Thomas Childers	Isaac Crouch *
Robert Childers	Robert Davidson *
Frank Childers	John H. Hobson
William Childers	Henry Rhoads
Prior Childers	Ezekiel Robinson
Catherine Childers	Montgomery Bell Shackleford
Amanda Childers	Orville Thomas Tyler
Caroline Childers	* Killed by the Indians.

Kichais, Tawakonis, and Wacos.

John Beal made it to town and excitedly reported that the whole party had been massacred, he being the only survivor to fight his way out. He became the hero of the town, until Captain Childers arrived later with other survivors and the truth was realized. During his escape, Jack Hobson had been thrown from his horse and had to alternately run and walk all the way to Nashville barefooted, a slow, painful process.[38]

Soon the Indians withdrew from the area and Childers led his party on toward Nashville, choosing a different route to the spot where they swam the river. They camped that night and reached Nashville the next day, June 5, without further attacks.

When the Indians turned back, they headed for the Little River houses that the Childers party had just abandoned. There, they found the Monroe, Smith, and Walker families still packing up to leave. The families took shelter in the Walker house and fired back at their attackers through the portholes when the opportunity presented itself.

In a deposition given on June 15 in Robertson's Colony, Daniel Monroe related:

> They used guns, bows and arrows, and spears. Whilst defending themselves in their house against the Indians, William Smith was shot on the outside of the door through the leg by a rifle ball. They shot and killed deponent's horse whilst tied to the house—killed many cattle—drove the balance off—and plundered a wagon.[39]

The Indians perpetrating these attacks were believed by Monroe to be Caddos, due to the fact that the braves wore shirts "which is rarely done by any of the tribes of Indians who live in Texas." His testimony also stated:

The Caddos have a peculiar manner of wearing their hair, by cutting it closely on both sides of the head, and leaving a top-knot, which is most generally worn in a silver tube, and they have silver in their nose. [Monroe] is strengthened in the belief that a portion of them were Caddos, as he recognized in the crowd an old Indian named Douchey of the Caddo tribe, whom he knew well. He believes that it was Douchey [Dorcha], as he shot cross-fire—a manner of shooting peculiar to Douchey.

The Indians continued to fire on the Walker house until night came on. After their attackers retired, the three families set out for Nashville and arrived without further attacks on June 5. Daniel Monroe stated that three or four days after the attacks, he and others assisted in burying the dead. Wilson T. Davidson, the son of Robert Davidson, later wrote of his father's death to historian James DeShields.[40]

He recalled that Jasper Crouch was a Missionary Baptist preacher and close friend of his father's. Davidson and Crouch

were buried in the same grave on the prairie where they were slain about 7 or 8 miles north of the present town of Cameron. Judge O. T. Tyler and a few others performed the last sad rites.

CHAPTER 8

Burleson's Battalion

June 6 - August 9, 1836

Coastal Defense: Captain Burton's "Horse Marines"

Sprawled in the dunes hugging the coast of Copano Bay, the sentinels studied the outline of the silent *Watchman* as day broke. The two-masted schooner had slipped into the key deep-water Texas seaport and was awaiting a signal to begin offloading its valuable cargo, provisions to supplement the retreating Mexican army.

At 8:00 a.m. on June 3, two Texans sent a distress signal to the Mexican vessel, which was anchored in the bay. The schooner's skipper had his crew run the American Stars and Stripes flag up the mast. When this received no response from the men ashore, he then hoisted the red, green, and white Mexican flag. Upon sighting the Mexican flag, the two men on the beach excitedly beckoned for the sailors to come ashore.

The *Watchman*'s skipper and four other sailors quickly lowered a small boat and boarded it. The Mexican sailors rowed strongly for shore, likely eager for word of how the Texans were holding out against Santa Anna's superior army.

The greeting ashore was a far cry from what the *Watchman* sailors anticipated, however. To their surprise, they were taken prisoner by their "comrades" onshore, men who proved not to be Mexican soldiers but instead Texas Rangers!

The arresting party was a twenty-man ranger detachment under the command of Captain Isaac Burton, who had become an old hand with the rangers by this time. His "3rd Co. of Rangers," originally raised in early 1836, had been ordered by General Rusk on May 29 to patrol the flat coastal plains from the Guadalupe to Mission Bay near Refugio, watching for Mexican incursions.[1]

Mexican army forces were resupplied by merchant ships sailing into Texas ports during the revolution. The Mexican forces at Goliad were supplied from nearby Copano Bay. The General Council in November

1835 had authorized a Texas navy of four ships to deal with this threat, and they had thus far been effective in thwarting Mexican reprovisioning efforts, although some supplies still made it through.[2]

The Texas navy was outperformed by Isaac Burton's small detachment of Texas Rangers in one of the more unusual cargo seizures of Texas history. His men had arrived at the coast three days prior. Private Samuel Rayner "near Copano ran down and caught a wild mule." Captain Burton claimed that it was "the finest and among the largest animals ever saw by me." Rayner managed to break the mule and put it to the company's use, although it was later pressed for army service by General Rusk's commissary in Victoria.[3]

Burton's men received word of a suspicious vessel in the Bay of Copano on June 2 and had spent the night hours preparing their clever ambush. Keeping a cold camp, they had watched the schooner from a bluff overlooking the bay while their horses were kept tied off in the brush nearby until the sailors were captured.

Leaving four rangers to guard the five Mexican sailors ashore, Captain Burton led a sixteen-man party back into the bay. His men rowed the small boat out to the *Watchman*, climbed aboard, and seized the remaining sailors and the ship's cargo. As expected, the sailing ship was found to be loaded with supplies intended for the Mexican army. Burton's men took control of the ship, guarding their prisoners and proudly sending word via a courier of their seizure to General Rusk.[4]

At La Bahía, Rusk was less than pleased to hear that the rangers had actually seized the Mexican sailors and their cargo. He feared negative repercussions with any Americans held prisoner by the Mexican army and also worried that this seizure was in violation of the armistice recently signed following San Jacinto. He sent orders back to Burton the same day, dated June 3.

Captain Isaac Burton's Coastal Rangers: May 8 - June 24, 1836

Captain:	Calvin B. Emmons	Samuel M. Rayner
Isaac Watts Burton	C. D. Faris	George M. Roberts
Privates:	William Fitzmania	Christian Rockwell
John Walker Baylor Jr.	Andrew Jackson Grey	Samuel Smith
Jacob Buckman	Alexander G. Hale	P. B. Stephenson
Samuel L. Burns	Ennes Hardin	John Swarty
Williamson Daniels	Willis Hockenday	Source: *Muster Rolls of the*
James Duncan	Dickinson Putnam	*Texas Revolution*, 183.

Return the provisions on board the vessel and permit her to proceed as she may choose under directions of those who had the charge of her. You will return as early as possible to Headquarters, keeping a good look out, as the rear division of the Mexican Army are within nine miles of this place proceeding on towards Matamoros. On your march up to this point, you will lose no time and keep a vigilant lookout.[5]

Captain Burton either did not receive these orders in a timely fashion or chose to ignore them for the time being. His adventures along the Texas Gulf Coast were only beginning.

By June 13 Rusk was back in Victoria. He wrote to President Burnet on his frustrations with Captain Burton.

I had sent him out simply on a scouting expedition when he ran foul of the ship. You have enclosed copies of the letters and order which I transmitted to him upon the subject. He has not yet returned from Copano.[6]

The captured *Watchman* was ordered around to Velasco, but the ship was detained by contrary winds until June 17. Twelve men remained behind with the horses, while Captain Burton and seven other rangers stayed aboard the *Watchman*. Republic records show these other seven men to be Samuel Burns, Andrew J. Grey, Christian Rockwell, Samuel Smith, William Fitzmania, Willis Hockenday, and John W. Baylor. That afternoon, sails were sighted as two other Mexican vessels, the *Comanche* and *Fanny Butler*, approached Copano Bay.

Both schooners, also loaded with supplies for the Mexican army, soon anchored off the sandbar. Burton ordered the captain of the *Watchman* to invite the other captains, via signals, to come aboard his ship for a glass of grog. The unsuspecting skippers soon obliged and made their way to the *Watchman* in their small boats. Once aboard, of course, they were made prisoners of the Texas Rangers.[7]

The *Comanche* and *Fanny Butler* made it over the sandbar soon thereafter and were also captured by Burton's rangers, who rowed over and boarded both vessels. Thus were three Mexican supply ships captured by only a handful of frontiersmen without ever a shot being fired!

Captain Burton and seven other men of his company were split between the three schooners. They set sail from Copano on June 19 to the northeast for the port of Velasco at the mouth of the Brazos River. Once in Velasco, the vessels were seized and ordered to Galveston for condemnation proceedings, where their cargoes were forfeited to the Republic of Texas. The American-owned vessels, which had been chartered by the Mexican government, were ordered released to their American owners.

The freight, valued by Texan auditors at $25,000, was of great service in supporting the Texas army. The schooners carried barrels of pickled pork, beef jerky, thirty containers of rice, ninety barrels of beans, and four hundred barrels of bread. This was in addition to a large quantity of muskets, gunpowder, ammunition, and bayonets.

Captain Burton's men soon earned the nickname "Horse Marines" after word of their dramatic seizures spread. This name may be attributed to Colonel Edward J. Wilson, who had recently arrived in Texas in command of Kentucky soldiers. In a letter published in the *Kentucky Gazette* on July 28, 1836, Wilson describes the rangers' capture of the *Comanche* and *Fanny Butler*.

> They saw two other vessels coming; they hoisted the Mexican flag on board the vessel they had taken. The coming vessels seeing this, came up carelessly, and cabled, when they in turn were visited by this company of Horse Marines—a new kind of troops, you will say—and the last two shared the same fate as the first.[8]

During the seizures at Copano Bay, Private Calvin Emmons managed to lose his horse, an eight-year-old black mare of Spanish breed, while out on expedition with Captain Burton. Weeks later in camp, Captain Dickinson Putnam and company mate George Roberts assessed the value of this horse at one hundred dollars. He signed Emmons' note as "Comd of 2 Comp of Rangers." From the Office of the Quartermaster General in Columbia on July 31, 1836, Isaac Burton was also allowed $150 for the loss of his horse, no doubt during his two weeks aboard the Mexican vessels, while in service to Texas.[9]

If General Rusk was upset with the ocean captures, Lieutenant Colonel Bayne seems to have been more pleased with his rangers. After returning with his troops to camp, Captain Burton was promoted to major, commanding Bayne's ranger battalion on June 24, 1836.

Pay receipts show that Major Burton served in this role for three months through September 24 and that command of his ranger company was passed on June 24 to another of his newly promoted "horse marines," Captain Dickinson Putnam. Joining Burton's company on May 19, Putnam was quickly promoted to second lieutenant. On July 12 he furnished three horses for the use of his new company. Among the men Captain Putnam would command were some of John Tumlinson's earliest rangers, including Noah Smithwick and Sylvanus Cottle.[10]

President David Burnet later allowed Burton and his men a share of the booty they had seized from the Mexican schooners. An original quartermaster note from Post Velasco shows that Major Burton was to be paid $9,496.35. This was split

> in the proportion of 3/10 to himself as commanding officer and one seventh to each of his men for the capture of the cargos of the schooners *Comanche* and *Fanny Butler*.

The other seven rangers receiving a cut of this booty were Burns, Grey, Rockwell, Smith, Fitzmania, Hockenday, and Baylor. Burton's share amounted to $2,848.90, approved by a note signed July 10 by President Burnet in Velasco. Major Burton was initially paid in three drafts totaling two thousand dollars, and he settled his claim with an auditor in Velasco on July 11.

★　★　★　★　★

Texas Army Restructuring

While Isaac Burton's rangers were conducting their unique coastal defenses, General Rusk's regular army spent about a week in Goliad. By mid-June most of these forces moved back to the Guadalupe River near Victoria, an area Rusk felt to be a more secure staging area for the newly arriving troops than Goliad had been. Camp Victoria was established during the second week of June at a point about three miles above town on Spring Creek.[11]

The only flurry of excitement for the troops during June came in the form of the so-called "whip-handle dispatch." In accordance with the Velasco treaty between Santa Anna and Texan forces, captains Henry Karnes and Henry Teal had been sent to Matamoros as commissioners to negotiate with General José Urrea about a prisoner exchange. Because General Rusk following San Jacinto had detained General Adrian Woll, Urrea held Karnes and his men prisoner. While imprisoned, Karnes learned of Urrea's preparations to begin another Texas invasion, and Karnes enlisted William P. Miller and other scouts to send out a letter concealed in a whip handle. This warning letter was conveyed by messenger to Rusk, and the dispatch became known as the "whip-handle dispatch."[12]

The letter made it to Secretary of War Alexander Somervell in

Velasco, and it detailed Mexican plans for four thousand troops to depart Matamoros for La Bahía. An equal number of troops were to depart by ship for Vera Cruz and proceed to Copano or some other Texas port. This threat compelled acting President David Burnet to ask for volunteers to hurry from New Orleans and on June 20 for every able-bodied man between the ages of sixteen and fifty to enroll for military duty. The threat of troops arriving by water even forced Burnet to proclaim a blockade of the port of Matamoros as of July 21.

As for Karnes and Teal, they were eventually released from Mexico. Karnes was issued a promissory note on September 26, 1836, by General Rusk's Lavaca headquarters for $1,439.16 in expenses for his part in the Matamoros expedition. This included four months salary, one hundred dollars for a saddle that was lost, thirty dollars for a gun and shot bag lost, and payment for the guide who had initially taken his party to Matamoros.[13]

The whip-handle dispatch initiated by Karnes did serve to help drum up new recruits. At a time when the Texas government was struggling with how to deal with prisoner of war President Santa Anna of Mexico, the Texas army was struggling with changes of leadership.

General Rusk found that by June 17, his forces in Victoria numbered just over three hundred men. He asked to be relieved of his command on June 25, and Burnet appointed Mirabeau B. Lamar, who had previously served a brief term as secretary of war, to take command of the army. Lamar was viewed as restrained in his desire to engage the Mexican army, and the troops in the field refused to accept him as their commander.

The men instead chose Felix Huston, a Kentucky native who later immigrated to Mississippi, as their general. General Huston had recently arrived in Camp Victoria with a large group of mounted men from Natchez, Mississippi, under his charge and another two hundred volunteers under General Thomas Jefferson Green of North Carolina.[14]

As new troops moved in from the United States, Rusk changed his decision and remained in command of the army. During July and August 1836, muster rolls show that the army's new strength comprised fifty-three companies with 2,503 officers and men, in addition to regimental and staff officers. Of these, only fourteen companies were comprised of men who were largely Texans and had fought in the Texas Revolution.[15]

★ ★ ★ ★ ★

Robertson Recruits for the Ranger Service

On June 15 a hearing was held to take the depositions of some of those involved in the two June 4 Indian attacks on the Little River residents of Robertson's Colony. Empresario Sterling Robertson was back in his namesake colony by this date, having most recently been out recruiting for the ranger forces in Nacogdoches and San Augustine. He was present for these hearings and signed an affidavit that he was familiar with these families and vouched for the credit of their testimony.

On June 16 Robertson wrote to General Edmund Pendleton Gaines, enclosing the depositions of these atrocities carried out by the Caddos in his colony. Gaines was in command of the U.S. Army forces at Fort Jesup, Louisiana. Robertson hoped that Gaines would take his army forces against the Indians. He sent this letter to General Gaines via Philip Walker, who had been an officer of his ranger company formed in January 1836.

From Nashville, Robertson wrote to General Rusk on June 18 that he had succeeded in raising a few men during his recruiting trip over the weeks previous, but that the most luck had come from a draft that Major James Smith had ordered. Smith let the men sign on as volunteers after they were drafted.[16]

Robertson had conferred with Major Smith about using the approximately fifty men who had been recruited in San Augustine, as well as those men from Nacogdoches, as Robertson's Colony rangers until the danger passed. Smith had granted Robertson permission, but upon his overtaking these men, he was less than impressed.

> I found part without guns and part without horses and but few of them of but little use as rangers and some thought it would be right to assist the suffering inhabitants if they would furnish them with horses, guns and ammunition. I saw but little to them, particularly when I found they had a notion that they were authorized to press horses, guns or anything that they wanted for their private purposes—although it was the only horse that a man had to plow and make a support for his family or the only gun that he had to defend himself and family against the Indians that would at any hour make an attack on his house.

Robertson found that pioneer families were angered and afraid rather than being cheered by the sight of volunteers marching through the countryside. Some families went as far as to hide their horses in the woods as soldiers marched past. Many a family traveling west into Texas had their horses and only firearms "pressed" into government service by newly arriving United States volunteers. Thus the pioneers were often left on foot and even more vulnerable to Indian attack than they had been before.

Robertson also informed Rusk of the recent Parker's Fort massacre and the fresh assaults on Little River settlers in his own colony.

> Every settlement in my colony is broken up and are forted in this place and on the San Antonio Road. The Indians have taken nearly all the horses and drove off and killed the greatest part of the cattle in the colony.

Robertson noted that Major Smith was still in Nacogdoches, where he felt that he could employ some of the Mexican citizens there into service against the Indians if Rusk would approve. Robertson felt that the Caddos had been involved in the recent attacks in his colony, and he requested that General Rusk allow him to raise another ranger company under his own immediate command.

> Be so good as to order a draft in this Colony, for there are many that will not assist in any way whatever—as they and their families are safe. And if there is any law to press, let some man be commissioned that will not abuse the power given him. If you think your humble servant competent to take the command of the rangers, you will confer a favor on me by giving the command to me. I think I can find the Indians and bring them to battle, which has rarely been the case in all the campaigns that has been made against them. Please, if you should think proper to order a draft, let it be for three months' service and if the public has to furnish them with either guns or horses, it comes out of their wages.

Robertson sent this message on to General Rusk from Nashville via courier on June 18. He asked permission to use some or all of the volunteers raised in San Augustine that he had accompanied to Nashville prior to writing his letter.

One of the men who joined Robertson during June was San Jacinto veteran George Erath, who had been with Captain Jesse Billingsley's Mina Volunteer company until it disbanded in mid-May. Erath had only begun helping another farmer with his crops when word came of the Parker massacre. "It created general consternation," recalled Erath, and "for the protection of the frontier companies were at once formed."[17]

Erath later wrote that when he joined Captain Robertson, the ranging service was largely filled with volunteers from the frontier settlements of Texas. Within two weeks of Robertson's appeal to Rusk, a new ranging battalion would be properly assembled for service in the field.

★ ★ ★ ★ ★

The Rise in Frontier Violence: June - July 1836

The need for ranger companies dedicated solely to protecting the outermost settlements was made abundantly clear during the summer of 1836. The attack on the Childers party in early June and the terrible massacre at Parker's Fort in May were significant attacks which terrified many pioneer families. Aside from these widely reported attacks, there was a growing number of smaller scale attacks and killings committed in post-revolutionary Texas between late May and the first days of July 1836.

June was particularly bloody in terms of Indian and settler clashes near Bastrop and among the Colorado River area settlements. The persistence of Indian attacks and cattle stealing caused many families, who had only just returned from the Runaway Scrape, to move from their homes yet again back to the relative safety of Bastrop. Only parties of armed men dared to venture from town to work the fields. Those who ventured out alone did so at their own risk.

On June 7 Indians plundered the house of Nathaniel Moore, and on the next day, June 8, attacked the house of Thomas Moore. Veteran ranger Conrad Rohrer was outside Moore's house at this moment attempting to saddle his horse. Rohrer had served Sam Houston's army as a special wagon master and had been among Captain John Tumlinson's early rangers during the revolution. He was shot down dead in the yard.[18]

In another depredation, Bastrop area citizen Matthew Duty was killed while riding out alone one night to look over his crops. He had barely gotten out of sight of town when shots were heard. His horse returned on the run, its saddle splattered with blood. When an armed party rode out to look for Duty, he was found murdered and scalped.

Also during the summer of 1836, Indians killed Texas pioneer John Edwards, who had been traveling in company with Bartholomew Manlove from Bastrop to Washington. Manlove rode for his life, but the Indians killed Edwards. He was repeatedly speared and then scalped. The Indians took his horse and rifle.[19]

Also during this period, Laban and Jarrett Menefee and John Marlin had an encounter with Indians near the Colorado River in which they killed four. The trio was out to cut bee trees for food when they were surprised by an Indian who suddenly rose and fired at them. The shot missed. Marlin and Laban Menefee immediately returned fire at the same instant. Each man claimed to have dropped the Indian with his shot. Upon examining the body, they found that two bullets had penetrated the Indian's chest no more than two inches apart![20]

The men reloaded their guns and proceeded along their trail, only to be ambushed by more Indians within minutes. Marlin and the Menefees managed to kill two more Indians and drive the others from their hiding places in the ensuing battle. The remaining two Indians were chased back into a timber thicket. As the trio of whites prepared to go after them, another man who happened to ride up on the action joined them. One of the remaining Indians was eventually killed and the other managed to escape the Texans pursuing him. Marlin, the Menefees, and their other companion returned to the settlements unhurt that night. They had killed four out of five Indians encountered.

Indians attacked three other men in this same area shortly after Marlin and Menefee's battle, but these men did not share the same good fortunes. Harris, Blakely, and another man had spent the night at Hornsby's on the Colorado before proceeding down to the river to kill a cow. A party of Indians attacked them in a ravine. At the first firing, Blakely dug spurs into his horse and escaped back to the settlements.

Harris and the other man were shot and then brutally dismembered. The Indians cut out their entrails and strewed them about the bushes. They also cut off the men's arms and removed their hearts from their chests. From bones and remains at a campfire found shortly thereafter, it appeared that the two luckless Texans were roasted and eaten by the cannibalistic Indians.

One of the more serious battles near Bastrop during the summer of 1836 claimed the lives of other Texans. Brothers Joseph and Braman Reed had both lived in Bastrop before settling near Davidson's Creek in present Burleson County. While riding out on the range one day to drive some of his cattle, Joseph Reed was attacked by an estimated forty or more Indians.

He raced for his home with them hot in pursuit, managing to reach the gate in his own yard before arrow wounds killed him. His wife bravely rushed out and dragged his body into the house to prevent scalping or other mutilation. Braman Reed was very upset by the murder of his brother, and he immediately organized a volunteer pursuit party. The

Indians were attacked in their camp. Reed was killed and others were wounded. The Texans managed to kill the leader of the Indian party and several others before the Indians fled the battleground. On this occasion, some of the Texans took the liberty of removing an Indian scalp in their exasperation.

★ ★ ★ ★ ★

Colonel Burleson's Ranger Battalion Forms

The sharp increase in Indian violence following the Texas Revolution required attention. Some settlements were better protected than others. For example, General Thomas Rusk authorized Captain John Goodloe Warren Pierson to raise a company of mounted men to protect the town of Washington-on-the-Brazos.

Captain Pierson raised a sixty-seven-man mounted cavalry company, which was composed largely of old settlers from the Washington area. They were mustered in on June 30, 1836, and manned a fort dubbed Post Washington. These men patrolled both sides of the Brazos for three months but had no documented Indian battles. Post Washington was deactivated on September 30, when Pierson's volunteer company was discharged.[21]

Stephen F. Austin would write on July 4, 1836, that the Indians had "commenced active hostilities" on the whole line of the frontier along the San Antonio Road.[22] In order to check the activities of the Indians, Edward Burleson was commissioned in late June as a colonel in charge of a new ranger battalion to serve between the upper Colorado and Brazos Rivers. He had only just quit the military life to return to his farm on June 1, at which time he had discharged a large number of men from army service.

The six companies soon under Colonel Burleson's command would be stationed at Fort Milam on the west banks of the Brazos River in central Falls County. The first of his rangers began organizing into frontier companies on July 1, although some would not be properly mustered into service until as late as July 20. His battalion would soon consist of companies under Captains Jesse Billingsley, John McGehee, John York, William Hill, Sterling Robertson, and Byrd Lockhart Sr.

Since his own home was but a few miles from the ransacked town of Bastrop, Burleson kept his ranger headquarters at his home. He even periodically had some of his ranger troops camped out at his farm, as evidenced by payment vouchers of some of Captain John McGehee's men.[23]

The major settlement of Bastrop, formerly known as Mina, was a

Colonel Burleson's Ranging Corps of Mounted Riflemen
July 1 - December 1, 1836

Captain Hill's Texas Rangers: July 3 - October 3, 1836

Captain:	Francis Clampet	David Lawrence
William W. Hill	David Clark	Shubael Marsh
First Lieutenant:	John P. Coles	Parrott W. McNeese
Richard Hope	Aaron Colvin	John Miller
Second Lieutenant:	Charles Covington	Diadem Millican
George W. Barnett	James Dallas	Nathan Mitchell
First Sergeant:	Lee R. Davis	James Moore
Horatio Chriesman	Absolom C. Deloplain	Cicero Rufus Perry
Privates:	George Bernard Erath	Levi Pitts
John Quincy Adams	Gary D. Gary	Samuel Seward
Elliott Allcorn	David Frost	J. W. Simpson
John H. Allcorn	Charles Furnash	Jacob J. Stevens
Samuel Anders	Joshua Graham	Thomas Stevens
Abedingo Bedy	George Green	James Gibson Swisher
Alfred Berry	William Anderson Hall	William C. Walker
John Bate Berry	Isaac Hawkins	William Woodford
Thomas Blakely	William W. Hornsby *	
Robert Bowen	Andrew Houston	Per Texas audited claims.
William Bridge	David Houston	
Samuel P. Brown	John H. Jones	

Captain McGehee's Rangers: July 1 - November 20, 1836

Captain:	James Crawford	Peter F. Wade
John G. McGehee	William M. Eastland	James P. Wallace
First Sergeant:	William A. Faires	Martin Jones Wells
Russell B. Craft *	Burleson Gage	Gonzalvo Woods
Privates:	Jesse Halderman *	Montraville Woods
Micah Andrews *	Wiley Harris	Nicholas Wren
Thomas Barnett	Abraham Webb Hill [1]	Thomas York
Thomas O. Berry	John Litton	
Garrett E. Boom *	John Long [2]	[1] Substitute for Middleton
George W. Brazeal	Edward Manton	M. Hill on July 12, 1836.
Aaron Burleson *	Samuel McClelland *	[2] Substitute for Jacob Long
John Caldwell	Robert Mitchell	on July 20, 1836.
Hugh M. Childress	Dempsey C. Pace *	*Source:* Partial roster based
William Connell	George Self *	on author's research of audited
James A. Craft *	John Stewart	military claims, Republic of
John G. Craft	Robert Townsley	Texas.

Note: There is no complete roster available for Captain Jesse Billingsley's ranger company of Burleson's battalion. Many of his men (*) continued in service under Captain McGehee after Billingsley entered service with Congress on October 1, 1836. Azariah G. Moore and Nicholas H. Eastland joined Billingsley's rangers on July 1 but were later transferred. Moore joined Colonel Coleman's battalion.

Captain York's Rangers: July 1 - November 20, 1836		
Captain:	Wm Thomas Dunlavy	William Kuykendall
John York	Frederick Ernst	Benjamin McDaniel
Rank and File:	James Foster	A. G. McNeil
Clement Allen	William Frels	John Freeman Pettus
Andrew Jackson Bell	Francis Henece	Noah Scott
James Bell	Alexander Isbell	Isaac Welden
E. W. Best	John H. Isbell	Christian G. Wertzner

Source: Partial roster based on author's research of audited military claims of the Republic of Texas.

Captain Lockhart's Spy Company: July 4 - August 16, 1836		
Captain:	Adam Coble	Elisha Moss
Byrd Lockhart Sr.	Almond Cottle	Claiborne Rector
Privates:	George W. Davis	Pendleton Rector
Young Perry Alsbury [1]	Travis Davis [2]	William J. Russell
John D. Basdale	William Gibson [2]	John Sweeney
Josiah H. Bell	John Kaiser [2]	Joseph Tumlinson
T. T. Bell	Byrd B. Lockhart Jr.	
William Bell	William A. Matthews	
John P. Carson	Barthol D. McClure	
Joshua Clella	Joseph M. McCormick	

Source: *Muster Rolls of the Texas Revolution*, 70-71.
[1] General Land Office records.
[2] Per audited military claims of Texas.

major contributor of frontiersmen for Colonel Burleson. Bastrop's townsmen were by now well accustomed to turning out when duty called. Captain Robert Coleman had first commanded the Mina Volunteers from November 17 to December 17, 1835, during the capture of San Antonio. One of Coleman's men had been Jesse Billingsley, who later commanded a second Mina Volunteers company, which fought bravely at San Jacinto. During the battle, Captain Billingsley was hit by a

> shot in the right hand, ball entering the lower and back part of the right hand and passing out between the hand and wrist, breaking nearly all the bones in same.[24]

The Mina Volunteers were largely disbanded by June 1, but the renewed violence would not allow these men to work their fields for long. General Rusk persuaded Captain Billingsley in late June to reassume command of his company for a few more months to protect Bastrop and the other Colorado River area settlers. Audited military claims show that Billingsley had taken command of his rangers as of July 1, 1836.[25]

Three other men began organizing ranger companies on July 1. Captain John York began raising his company on this date and eventually mustered in his men on July 20 for three months of service. York, a portly man with blond hair and blue eyes, was born on July 4, 1800, in Kentucky. He moved to Texas in 1829 and settled in San Felipe. He commanded the "Brazos Guards" company from October 7 through December 13, 1835, for the Béxar siege. York was appointed by the General Council in early 1836 to help raise a mounted company to fight Indians in the Mill Creek (present Austin County) and Colorado River areas.[26]

The third man to begin organizing a new ranger company on July 1 was twenty-six-year-old Captain John Gilmore McGehee. An acquaintance of Colonel Burleson, McGehee had brought his wife and children to Texas from Alabama and settled in the Bastrop area before being forced to help escort families from the area during the Runaway Scrape.[27]

Like York's, McGehee's company continued to expand over the next few weeks. For example, Private John Litton served with Captain Billingsley's Bastrop ranger company through July 15, on which date Billingsley and Colonel Burleson honorably discharged him. On the same date, Litton "entered the ranging corps" under the command of Captain McGehee. McGehee signed military documents pertaining to his company as Captain of "M. R. Corps." This designation is further clarified on some of his rangers' discharge papers that his company was part of the "Ranging Corps of Mounted Riflemen" under Edward Burleson.[28]

A fourth company, that of Captain William Warner Hill, also began organizing on July 1 and was mustered into service on July 3. Hill had been captain of Company H under Burleson's command at San Jacinto but had been sick at the time of battle. He had previously served as lieutenant of Captain George Washington Barnett's volunteer ranger company on Colonel Moore's 1835 Indian expedition. Captain Hill's first lieutenant was Richard Hope, a Béxar veteran who had served with Hill in Barnett's 1835 company. Ironically, the new company's second lieutenant was George Barnett, who had been Hill's commander on Moore's campaign in 1835.

Some of those joining Hill's rangers, such as George Erath, had been recruited by Sterling Robertson in June. The company would remain in service for three months, operating between the Brazos and Colorado Rivers. Hill's rangers were organized at Asa Mitchell's place according to Cicero Rufus Perry, a young private from the Bastrop area, who would not turn fourteen until August 23. One of his buddies later described Perry as a tall, muscular young man with dark eyes "bright with the fires of intelligence and enthusiasm" which gleamed out from "waving masses of black hair." Energetic young Rufus Perry was making his start with

Colonel Edward Burleson (1789-1851), an ever-present leader in the Texas Indian wars, commanded a six-company ranger battalion following the Texas Revolution.
Archives & Information Services Division, Texas State Library.

Captain Jesse Billingsley (1810-1880), wounded at San Jacinto, commanded one of Burleson's ranger companies until being called to serve in the First Congress.
Prints and Photographs Collection, Center for American History, University of Texas at Austin, CN Number 03725.

the fabled Texas Rangers, and his career would be colorful. He would serve in various Indian campaigns until being critically wounded by three arrows in an 1844 encounter with Comanches while serving under Captain Jack Hays.[29]

In addition to these first four companies, Colonel Burleson also organized a small spy company for his battalion under Captain Byrd Lockhart Sr., who had been a ranger recruiter prior to San Jacinto. On July 4, 1836, he mustered in his company of Mounted Riflemen. Among his recruits was George W. Davis, one of the four ranger superintendents authorized in 1835.

Lockhart and his men passed through San Antonio on one of their ranging circuits during the summer of 1836. Halting at the battered remnants of the Alamo, his rangers searched for the ashes of the fort's brave defenders. One source states that Lockhart's men gathered these remains into a coffin and buried them with full military honors in a peach orchard near the scene of the battle. Most other sources, however, place the time of the burial of these fallen soldiers to have been in February 1837.[30]

Burleson's new ranger battalion would operate in addition to the three-company battalion under Major Isaac Burton. In the months following San Jacinto, there were other units that could conceivably be viewed as ranger companies. Captain William Scurlock formed a mounted volunteer company under General Rusk's supervision on July 4, 1836. In discharge papers issued to Privates Elijah Gossett and John Goyette on August 12, Captain Scurlock wrote that they were part of "my ranging company."[31]

Another seventy-five-man unit formed in Cincinnati on June 5 under Captain James C. Allen called itself the Buckeye Rangers. They arrived in Texas on June 29, 1836, via boat from New Orleans and were assigned to General Thomas Jefferson Green's First Regiment of Permanent Volunteers as of September 1836. The company was revamped in October, with Captain William C. Hart taking charge. Among the men transferred into the Buckeye Rangers after San Jacinto was James Edmundson, who had previously served in Captain Tumlinson's ranger unit.[32]

Neither Scurlock's company nor the Buckeye Rangers were properly attached to either of the two ranger battalions in service during July 1836. These and other companies, particularly some of the cavalry companies, operated in fashions very much like the true ranger units. Some of the cavalry companies, such as that of Captain Thomas Robbins, included a number of men who had previously served in ranger units.

Captain William H. Smith was promoted to major of cavalry on July 17, 1836, and served until December 3, 1836, after which time he continued service with a ranger battalion. Smith, who had immigrated to Texas in 1829, had originally served as second lieutenant of infantry from December 2, 1835, through March 16, 1836, and participated in the Béxar siege. He became captain of cavalry on March 16, 1836, and had served as such at San Jacinto. His company was alternately viewed as a cavalry or ranger unit following San Jacinto. For example, military papers of Private John W. Williamson show that he served as a "ranger in Captain William H. Smith's company from March 16 - June 23, 1836."[33]

These other companies having been mentioned, it should be stated that the ranger companies under the direction of Major Burton and Colonel Burleson were the only ones designated to operate specifically as frontier battalions unattached to the movements of the Texas army.

★　★　★　★　★

Shortly after Burleson's frontier corps was organized, a sixth company was added. General Rusk sent a note to ranger recruiter Sterling Robertson on July 12 ordering him to enroll men for the purpose of protecting the frontier from Indian depredations. You are expressly forbidden from enrolling any men now in the Army or on his way to the Army, and you will not enroll any man for a less time than four months.[34]

Robertson was further directed that he would subject himself directly to the orders of Colonel Burleson.

Rusk also authorized Robertson to take John Marlin with him to the frontier and to enroll the company of eleven men, which he already had with him on the Colorado River. One of these men was John A. F. Gravis, who was on furlough from the army at this time. Gravis had served in Captain Joseph Chance's company of the Second Regiment of Texas Volunteers as a private from April 19 until the company broke up on June 1.[35]

In a follow-up to Rusk's orders, new colonel of rangers Edward Burleson wrote to Robertson on July 14 to order him out on his recruiting. It is interesting to note that Burleson refers to him as "Major Robertson." Burleson stated that, "The Indians has committed repeated depredations on the frontier of Colorado and Brazos and has caused the settlements to be broken up and has went unmolested." Robertson was to "order out all able bodied men and cause them to go against the Indians that has not been in the service of the country."

Robertson had authority to enroll men into the ranger service. If men refused to serve, Robertson was to press their property and hire men in their places. He was ordered to enroll up to fifty-six men for the period of four months' time.

Finally, Burleson ordered Robertson to communicate with him and the regular army frequently. He was also to unite with Captain Jesse Billingsley at Taylor's on the Little River within three weeks of this time. Burleson expected by that time to be personally in command of the frontier troops.[36]

At the same time Robertson was receiving new orders for the ranger service, another military leader was acting on one of his requests. General Edmund Gaines, who had received Robertson's letter of June 16 concerning Indian depredations, was investigating such attacks being committed in Robertson's Colony by United States Indians who lived outside the Texas borders. Gaines' chief intelligence officer of Indian activities along the Texas-Louisiana border was First Lieutenant Joseph Bonnell of the U.S. Army. Bonnell was in Nacogdoches on July 19 and there met with Spy Buck of the Shawnees before the Nacogdoches Committee of Vigilance and Safety.[37]

Spy Buck, one of the principal men of his tribe and brother to the head chief, brought information of an Indian pact against the whites of Texas. His uncle had knowledge that the Comanches, Wacos, Tawakonis, Towash, and Kichais had all made a pact to combine against the whites. They had since killed nine men, eight in one raid and one in another attack on the Sulphur Fork near Red River. Spy Buck also informed those in Nacogdoches that the Mexican army had supplied a number of arms to the Texas Indians after the fall of the Alamo earlier in the year.

Michel B. Menard and Indian agent Isodore Pantallion were sent to verify this report, while General Gaines maintained a strong presence of U.S. Army troops near the eastern and northern borders of Texas. Menard returned to Nacogdoches to report no activity among the Indians, while Pantallion reported Chief Bowles and the Cherokees to be acting "suspiciously." U.S. troops maintained a strong showing until late in 1836 before the lack of serious Indian or Mexican difficulties compelled them to withdraw back across the Sabine River.[38]

By late July the companies of Colonel Burleson's battalion were on the move. Captain Lockhart's spies were in the vicinity of San Antonio. The companies of Captains Jesse Billingsley, John York, William Hill, and John McGehee took on supplies prior to moving out to their assigned stations. According to Private Rufus Perry, Captain Hill's company moved from its original mustering spot of Asa Mitchell's to take on supplies. "We came along the Gotier Trace to Bastrop," wrote Perry, "thence to John Caldwell's ranch, where we found plenty of corn to feed our horses."[39]

Audited military claims against Burleson's ranger battalion show that the companies were well provisioned by the locals, many of whom would not be repaid for years. The Colorado settlements furnished a great deal of supplies on July 22. David Ayers, for example, was pressed for six shirts worth $13 dollars and six pairs of pantaloons worth $18.50 on this date by Captains McGehee and Billingsley. This voucher also stated:

> We John G. McGehee and Jesse Billingsley are appointed to press horses and all other articles as the army may stand in need of.[40]

Ample quantities of corn, potatoes, and pork were furnished to the rangers on July 22, as evidenced by vouchers signed by Captain McGehee for many frontier settlers, including Micah Andrews, Edward

Blakely, Jacob S. Burleson, Joseph Burleson, John Y. Criswell, Samuel Craft, Moses Gage, James Rogers, Joseph Rogers, and Josiah Wilbarger. McGehee and Billingsley pressed Frederick W. Grasmeyer for twenty-three pounds of tobacco, at 62.5 cents per pound, for the rangers' use.[41]

By July 22 Sterling Robertson had departed Victoria for the northern frontier of his colony. Pursuant to General Rusk's orders, he already had a small group of men with which to form his new frontier ranging company. John Gravis was serving as the company's first lieutenant by this date. Other Colorado area residents had joined him prior to his arrival in his colony, such as Jack Hobson, whose service records reflect that he enlisted in Robertson's company on July 18.[42]

He proceeded to Tenoxtitlan and there began enrolling men for four-month enlistments. His men were to range the upper country of the

---

Captain Robertson's Rangers: July 25 - September 11, 1836

Captain:	Henry Fullerton	John Needham
Sterling Clack Robertson*	Robert Furgeson	Elijah B. Reed *
First Lieutenant:	Thomas A. Graves *	Joseph Reed *
Calvin Boales *	John A. F. Gravis *	Thomas Reed *
Second Lieutenant:	Moses Griffin *	Thomas J. Reed
Enoch M. Jones *	John Hobson *	Elijah S. C. Robertson *
Privates:	James A. Hudson *	Montgomery B. Shackleford*
Samuel Tabor Allen *	James Lane *	John David Smith
Thomas Hudson Barron	Thomas Mackey *	William Crain Sparks
Matthew Boren *	John Marlin *	Levi Taylor
Peyton Burnes	Harry Matthews *	John Teal *
David Wilson Campbell	(J?) A. McCullough	Jasper N. M. Thompson
Nathan Campbell	Jeremiah McDaniel	John Walker
Michael Castleman	George W. McGrew *	Philip Walker
Francis Childers *	Hardin McGrew	Skeaugh Walker
Robert Childers	John McLennan	Ezra Webb
James Robertson Childress*	Edward D. McMillan	John B. Webb *
Henry Cook *	James M. McMillan	Thomas R. Webb
Josiah Cook	Robert Moffitt *	James A. Wilkinson *
James Coryell *	William Moffitt *	John Wilkinson *
John Robert Craddock	Daniel Monroe *	
David Dorson	A. W. Moore *	* Present for original
James Dunn	Andrew J. Morgan *	company muster on
Stephen Eaton	Claibourn Morgan	July 25, 1836.
Benjamin Franklin Fitch	George Washington Morgan*	Sources: *Muster Rolls of*
Louis B. Franks *	John C. Morgan *	*the Texas Revolution*, 128-
Stephen Frazier	William J. Morgan *	29; McLean, *Papers*, XV:
John Fulcher *	Jesse Munford *	34-37, 108-11, 137-39.

Colorado area, remaining subject to the orders of Rusk's main army. Including himself, Captain Robertson's new ranger company numbered thirty-nine men when mustered into service on July 25, 1836. Those enrolled in his company as of July 25 signed the muster roll with the following agreements:

> We whose names are hereto annexed do agree to volunteer under Sterling C. Robertson to range against the Indians for the protection of the frontiers of the upper country for the term of [four] months under the rules and regulations of the army . . . . we hold ourselves subject to the orders of the comma[nder in chief] of the army.[43]

Captain Robertson's new unit was composed largely of veteran Texas Rangers. In addition to those men who had previously served in Robertson's first ranger company back in January, others had served duty under Captains Daniel Friar, Eli Hillhouse, and Eli Seale during the Texas Revolution. Sterling Robertson continued to recruit rangers from within his old colony, and by August 14 his company had grown to seventy-two men.

★　★　★　★　★

Captain Robbins' Scrape

About the time that Robertson was organizing rangers in his old colony, President Burnet and his government were warned of a new threat. Arms supplier Thomas Toby & Brother of New Orleans wrote a letter to the Texas president on July 23. They had read an anonymous letter in the *New Orleans Bulletin* describing how a delegation of six or seven Indian chiefs representing tribes including the Cherokees had held meetings with Mexican officials in Matamoros, Mexico, on July 1. The reported plan of General José Urrea, now the commander in chief of Mexican army forces, was to help arm and employ the Indians of Texas against the white settlers. In return for cooperating with Mexico, the Indians were promised land and cattle.[44]

A deadly clash with Indian forces during early July also served to support the continued presence of frontier ranger companies in the wake of the Texas Revolution. The first appears to have occurred in early July near a Texian camp in the vicinity of Gonzales. The two companies involved were portions of Captain John J. Robinson's volunteer company and Captain Thomas Robbins' cavalry unit.

Robinson had been second lieutenant of a company of Louisiana

Captain Robbins' Cavalry Company: April 25 - August 13, 1836		
Captain:	James Douthit	Joseph H. Moore [2]
Thomas Robbins	William H. Ewing [2]	John Robbins [2]
First Lieutenant:	Daniel B. Friar	Enoch Robinett
James Shaw	Joshua Fulcher [2]	James Robinett
John H. Dyer [1]	Richard Garrett	John Robinett
Second Lieutenant:	Albert G. Gholson [3]	William Sherrod
James Hopkins	Simon Gonzales	John Teal [2]
Privates:	James S. Hunter	Alexander Whitaker
George W. Anderson	Samuel Hunter	Benjamin F. Wright [2]
John Barton	William Johnson [2]	Key Source: *Muster Rolls*
William W. Bell	John Landrum	*of the Texas Revolution*, 72.
Charles Burkham	John Lindley	
Elijah Burkham	Benjamin McCullough	[1] Dyer promoted to first
George W. Chapman	George W. McGrew [2]	lieutenant and later to
Hiram Chapman	William A. McGrew [2]	captain.
Joseph A. Clayton [2]	Collin McKinney [2]	[2] Per audited claims and
Isaac Clover	Daniel McKinney [2]	Texas pension papers.
Ansel Darniell	James McKinney [2]	[3] Joined July 30 per his
Richard Davis	John Moore	audited claims.

Independent Volunteers at the time his unit had been mustered into Texas service on May 1, 1836. Robbins had served as an officer in Captain Burton's rangers and Captain William Smith's cavalry before taking command of his own company on April 25. Among his men were former ranger superintendent Daniel Friar and one of his original rangers, Ansel Darniell, both of whom had also served under Smith at San Jacinto.

According to early Texas Indian wars writer J. W. Wilbarger, a small force of about twenty-four men under Robinson and Robbins were ordered out from General Rusk's main Texas army camp. They were to "reconnoiter the position of some Indians who were encamped on a little stream called Sandy." Wilbarger says that this was in August 1836, but late June appears more likely. While carrying out their scouting mission, the Texan force was boldly attacked by a large band of Indians at night, who had surrounded them under the cover of darkness.[45]

The Texans stood their ground and defended themselves bravely. Wilbarger's account of this battle claims that the Texans suffered a high casualty rate, but there is little documentation of this fight to verify the claim. The Indians captured all of the Texans' horses and camp equipment. The defeat was sorely felt, because it came at a time when Texas was battling for its liberty from Mexico, who was being aided by its Indian friends.

Pinpointing the exact date of this defeat is difficult, but best guess would place the time as approximately July 1, 1836. The men of Captain Robbins' company had made their way into the Texas army camp above Victoria by July 4, on which date some of his cavalrymen were issued notes for the loss of their horses. For example, Private Ansel Darniell was issued a note on this date by camp commander William H. Smith and General Rusk certifying that Darniell had lost his horse while in service of Texas "when camped on the Guadalupe." Fellow company mates Daniel Friar and James McLaughlin were called upon to place a value on this horse lost by Darniell.[46]

Many of the other members of Captain Robbins' company were not issued notes for their losses until later dates. Robbins resigned from his company on August 13, 1836, and discharged a number of the men. He signed their discharges as "Captain of Cavalry" at a camp west of San Patricio. John H. Dyer had been promoted to the company's first lieutenant by that date, and Dyer became acting captain of Robbins' company as of August 13. Dyer and Lieutenant Colonel David M. Fulton of the cavalry issued notes to other members of Robbins' former company on August 24 at the headquarters of the Texas army on the Coleto on August 24. These promissory notes, for men such as Private James McKinney and Daniel McKinney, were issued for the value of the horses they had previously "lost in the service of Texas."[47]

★   ★   ★   ★   ★

Cowboys and Cavalry

Captain Ripley Wheelock of Major Burton's ranger battalion found his duties split in providing for the army. His military papers state that he "was ordered on extra duty at Cole's Settlement in June" and was forced to be away from his ranger company most of that time. By late July Wheelock was an honorary colonel attached to the quartermaster department under Quartermaster General Almanzon Huston and would continue in this service after his company was later disbanded.[48]

Huston had been impressed enough with Captain Wheelock's "enterprising spirit and energetic manner of doing business" that he sent a letter to General Rusk on July 24 asking to add him to his own department. During the latter days of July, Wheelock and his men had been involved in rounding up cattle for the army's use and forwarding them to Quartermaster Theodore S. Lee at Velasco.[49]

The herds of loose cattle and horses on the plains of the Nueces and about San Antonio had become so numerous, in fact, that the Texas government took steps to put them to use. Deciding that these cattle without real owners would make good supplies for the army in the field, President Burnet authorized Richardson R. Royall to raise a company of one hundred "independent rangers" to collect and drive such cattle for the use of the government. This order was issued by Burnet from Velasco on August 8, 1836.[50]

These cowboys would collect and drive the herds of cattle, which were said to be owned by Mexican citizens beyond the Rio Grande, between the Nueces and the Rio Grande. This would increase the stock and supplies of the Texas army and would make things difficult for Mexican troops advancing from Matamoros.

Under the direction of General Rusk, the army erected its first cattle pens at Goliad of cedar posts and rawhide. The first sweep by these cowboys resulted in 327 head of cattle driven to Goliad headquarters. Colonel Henry Karnes later in 1836 formed two companies to range west of San Antonio with authorization "to rob and steal everything that they meet with in their progress." These men were offered seven cents per pound "for the beeves they may drive in."

As the army dwindled in 1837, the task of rounding up loose cattle on the southwest frontiers fell to discharged soldiers, adventurers, and other enterprising Texans who sought to increase their own ownerships in return for the losses they had sustained during the revolution. These "cowboys" raided into areas west of the Nueces, driving cattle from Mexican ranches and those that were abandoned.

The ranger battalion previously under Lieutenant Colonel Griffin Bayne saw a decline in size during the summer of 1836. This battalion ultimately reported to General Rusk, but Captain Wheelock's final muster roll of August 8 shows that the senior army commander was directing the rangers. His company was shown to be a part of the "Regiment ordered to be raised by the Convention of Texas Rangers, under the Command of Lieut. Col. Bayne, but now under the immediate command of Brigadier General Felix Huston." Huston was the acting commander in charge of the army's cavalry at this time.

Wheelock's rangers were disbanded on August 8 at the headquarters of the Texas cavalry at a fort on the San Antonio River between Goliad and San Patricio. Wheelock and Lieutenant Francis Doyle signed the discharge papers of their men. The main army had moved from Victoria during the end of July to a point about ten miles west of town on Coleto Creek, where a new camp was set up. Rusk's army maintained its headquarters at Coleto throughout August.[51]

The disbanding of Wheelock's company left only three companies still active in Lieutenant Colonel Bayne and Major Burton's battalion. One of these companies was that of Captain Dickinson Putnam, who had been promoted to his command in June after Burton became a major. In military records for Private Felix Goff, Putnam noted that his company was part of "the 2nd Division of Texas Rangers" through November 1836. The ranger division under Colonel Burleson's battalion was referred to as the "1st Division."[52]

There is evidence that Major Burton had difficulties in his new billet. A group of rangers that included Humphrey Porter, William Dempsey, P. W. Gilman, and Sam Hawes drafted a protest of their own continued service in Burton's ranger corps. Dated July 21, 1836, from White Hill Camp, this letter was addressed to President David Burnet in Velasco. These men felt that they were improperly provisioned in their efforts to defend the country's frontiers.[53]

They cited Burton's promises to provide provisions, and in light of his being unable to do so, they demanded to detach themselves from the ranger service or elect new leaders. Burnet replied to these petitioners that

> Major Burton has the reputation of a brave man, an enterprising officer and a gentleman, and his inability to equip you according to his alleged promise, is probably to be attributed to the general destitution of the country.

Burnet then absolved these men's commitments to the ranger service under Burton and let them complete their enlistments with "such other portions of the Army as you may prefer."

Aside from Putnam's company, Burton had only the remnants of Captain John Tumlinson's company comprising his battalion by the second week of August. Another of his former rangers, Samuel Smith, had been promoted on June 25. During the first week of August, he was put in charge of organizing a third company of rangers, to bring the battalion back to strength. Since this company never reached full strength, Smith was only able to command the men as a second lieutenant instead of being commissioned a captain.

A muster roll from August 1836 shows Lieutenant Smith to be in command of the "3rd Company of Rangers," a unit that remained in service through October 25, 1836. Some of the men under his charge had originally enrolled in March under Captain Burton for a twelve-month enlistment.

Lt. Smith's Third Company of Rangers: Aug. 21 - Oct. 25, 1836			
	Date Enrolled:	Simon Gonzales*	June 1
Second Lieutenant:		James Hunter*	March 12
Samuel Smith	March 10	W. Levin	August 21
First Sergeant:		Henry F. Maillard	August 23
Alexander Bell	August 21	William Pigmassey	March 12
Privates:		Humphrey Porter	August 16
William H. Bishop	March 12	N. C. Rogers	March 12
Peter Castle	August 20	George Ross	August 6
James Clifford	August 12	William Scattleburg	August 23
Eliza J. Dale	August 23	W. J. Usher	August 21
F. D. Davis	August 21	Claiborne A. West	August 6
James Douthit*	August 8	* Joined from Capt. Robbins.	
Richard Eggleston	August 21	Source: *Muster Rolls of the Texas*	
James George	August 23	*Revolution*, 144-45.	

Smith began organizing his company on August 6 and was in command by late August. By August 21 he had enough men to appoint Alexander Bell as his first sergeant. Captain Thomas Robbins' cavalry company was largely disbanded on August 13, and Captain Tumlinson ended his ranger service on August 16. Several of Lieutenant Smith's men served under Captain Robbins through August 13.

A payment voucher issued at camp to Private Daniel Elam on August 25 was endorsed by "Samuel Smith, 2nd Lt. of the 3rd Corps of Rangers" and Alexander Bell, "1st Sgt. of said Corps."[54] During the month of August, Smith's company took on new recruits. Pay records show that Smith was paid $189 for service as a ranger lieutenant for four months for the period ending October 25, 1836.[55]

Several of Smith's men—Henry Maillard, Alexander Bell, Richard Eggliston, and James George—had served briefly in Captain Joseph Soverein's volunteer company, which had been formed August 1. Another of the men in Lieutenant Smith's company was Humphrey Porter, one of those who had petitioned to be transferred away from Captain Burton in July.

Lieutenant Smith's company and that of Captain Putnam would continue in service at reduced strengths for another few months. Their companies and the battalion under Edward Burleson would soon be joined by two new ranger battalions, one of which would become the main fighting force on the Texas frontiers during the next year.

Texas Ranger Units in Service
May - December 1836

First Division of Rangers under Colonel Edward Burleson

Sterling Clack Robertson, Capt.	July 25 - September 11, 1836
Calvin Boales, Capt.	Sept. 11 - November 14, 1836
William Warner Hill, Capt.	July 3 - October 3, 1836
Byrd B. Lockhart Sr., Capt.	July 4 - August 16, 1836
John Gilmore McGehee, Capt.	July 1 - November 20, 1836
John York, Capt.	July 1 - November 20, 1836
Jesse Billingsley, Capt.	July 1 - October 1, 1836

Second Division of Rangers under Colonel Jesse Benton

Griffin Bayne, Lt. Colonel	Acting commander
Isaac Watts Burton, Major	Served through Sept. 24, 1836
William C. Wilson, Capt.	March 1 - June 1, 1836
E. Louis Ripley Wheelock, Capt.	May 8 - August 8, 1836
Isaac Watts Burton, Major	December 17, 1835 - June 24, 1836
Dickinson Putnam, Capt.	June 24 - November 1, 1836
Samuel Smith, Lieut.	August 6 - October 25, 1836
John Jackson Tumlinson Jr., Capt.	January 17 - August 16, 1836

Colonel Robert Morris Coleman's Battalion

Company A:	
Alfred P. Walden, Capt.	August 15 - October 5, 1836
Alexander Robless, Lieut.	October 5 - December 31, 1836
Company B:	
Thomas Hudson Barron, Capt.	August - December 31, 1836
Company C:	
Benjamin R. Thomas, Lieut.	September 6 - December 31, 1836

Major James Smith's Battalion

Elisha Clapp, Capt.	Sept. 10 - December 10, 1836
Michael Costley, Capt.	Sept. 11 - December 11, 1836
George Washington Jewell, Capt.	Sept. 19 - November 1836 *
Squire Haggard, Capt.	Nov. 1936 - March 19, 1836

* Promoted to major of rangers. Captain Haggard took over company.

Superintendent Silas Mercer Parker's District

James Wilson Parker, Capt.	January 1 - May 19, 1836

CHAPTER 9

A Chain of Frontier Forts

August 10 - December 1836

By the fall of 1836, the corps of Texas Rangers was at an all-time high in terms of number of men enrolled and number of companies. Colonel Edward Burleson had at his disposal the companies of Captains Billingsley, Hill, Lockhart, McGehee, York, and Robertson. The original corps, now under Major Isaac Burton, included the companies of Captain Putnam and Lieutenant Smith by late August.

During August authorization was given for Colonel Robert Coleman to create three additional companies. In September Major James Smith in the East Texas area became supervisor of yet another three ranging companies. Although Captain Lockhart's company disbanded in August, by mid-September there were thirteen ranger companies on the frontiers comprising approximately 450 men in four battalions.[1] Not counting later expeditions by the Texas militia, this strong showing of ranger companies would not be equaled until 1839.

★ ★ ★ ★ ★

Captain Robertson's Senate Race
During the early days of August, preparations were made for the next election of governmental officers for Texas. Extra copies of the August 2 issue of the *Telegraph and Texas Register* were distributed to make Texans aware of the upcoming election.[2]

As of August 11 Captain Sterling Robertson's company was near the home of pioneer Jesse Webb, from whom the rangers received four and a half bushels of corn at one dollar per bushel and 221 pounds of pork at five dollars per hundredweight. Paymasters Samuel T. Allen and Thomas Graves certified that these goods were for "the use of S. C. Robertson's Ranging Company."[3]

Captain Robertson kept a small notebook created of legal size sheets of paper, which he folded into quarter sheets and crudely stitched together along the left-hand margin. The resulting pages were 4.5" x 7" on which Robertson kept records of his rangers. He began this notebook on August 14. Beside each man's name was recorded all items provided to his company. The men were charged with pantaloons, shoes (ranging in size from 6 to size 10), gunlocks, guns, shirts, plugs of tobacco, a coffee boiler, and a thin fabric called lawn. This notebook also listed entries of the men receiving "strouding" from Colonel John Darrington, a former U.S. Army officer who had recently been out among the Caddo Indians. This strouding was a coarse woolen blanket or garment issued to the rangers in two to two and a half yard lengths in either red or blue color.[4]

By about August 20 Captain Robertson's ranger company was on the northern frontier of the old Robertson Colony. During this time he received a letter from Judge Joseph Hood in Washington announcing the impending election just a couple weeks away. Robertson's nemesis, Stephen F. Austin, was one of the serious candidates for president. Robertson himself became a candidate for senator covering the new precinct of Milam.

Captain Robertson, upon deciding to make a serious run for the Texas Senate, furloughed twelve of his sixty-three-man ranger company for fifteen days beginning on August 21, 1836. This would give his men enough time to return home briefly to see their families and help campaign in the Milam precinct for Robertson among their friends. Robertson's ranger notebook shows these men to be Levi Taylor, Daniel Monroe, Moses Griffin, David Dorson, James Wilkinson, Calvin Boales, John Fulcher, Thomas Graves, George Morgan, Enoch Jones, Jesse Munford, and John David Smith.

Hood's letter to Robertson had invited "you all" to come in to Tenoxtitlan for the election on September 5. Captain Robertson was elected senator for Milam, and one of his rangers, Private Samuel Allen, was elected as the representative for Milam. After this election, it became necessary for Robertson to relinquish command of his ranger company. He did so on September 11, 1836, turning it over to Captain Calvin Boales, who had been his first lieutenant. The men who had enrolled for a four-month period completed their remaining two months under Boales from that date.

Private Thomas Ross, who had joined Robertson's rangers on July 15, stated that at the time Boales took command, Ross was out "performing a specific duty in conformity" with Captain Robertson's orders. While so doing, Ross became ill from "excessive fatigue and exposure in discharging his duties as soldier." Ross was left entirely destitute at or near the Falls of Brazos River and in this situation not being able from illness to join the company encampment and not being able to see a member of the company, he procured John Chalmers Esq. a member of Captain Barron's company to report him his situation and ask for him relief as his situation demanded from Captain Boales, which he did.[5]

Captain Boales' Texas Rangers: September 11 - November 14, 1836

Captain:	Henry Cook	Elijah B. Reed
Calvin Boales	John Robert Craddock	Elijah S. C. Robertson
First Lieutenant:	Britton Dorson	Neill K. Robinson
Enoch M. Jones	David Dorson	John David Smith
Second Lieutenant:	James Dunn	William Crain Sparks
Thomas R. Webb	Stephen Frazier	John Teal
First Sergeant:	John Fulcher	Jasper N. M. Thompson
Warren Lyman	Henry Fullerton	James Walker
Privates:	James A. Hudson	John B. Webb
Michael Borin	Thomas Marren	
Nathan Campbell	Edward D. McMillan	Source: *Muster Rolls of the*
Walter Campbell	James M. McMillan	*Texas Revolution*, 128-29.
Francis Childers	Jesse Munford	

The discharge papers of Private Stephen Eaton show that Robertson had departed for Congress by September 14. Eaton's papers were signed by Orderly Sergeant Thomas H. Barron, under the command of Captain Robertson, Capt. Rangers, and Edward Burleson, Colonel of Detachment of Rangers.[6]

Captain Hill's Battle on the Yegua: August 1836

Edward Burleson made every attempt to keep his new ranger battalion properly provisioned. He did not hesitate to call upon the army to supply his men, as evidenced by a supply note of August 10, 1836, from Quartermaster General Almanzon Huston in Quintana. The provisions shipped on this date included sugar, coffee, soap, salt, shoes, powder, lead, and three boxes of percussion caps. This was all from Burleson's order, excepting flints, which Huston's department did not have. Burleson's men were also denied clothing, which Huston stated "has not yet arrived but is expected soon."[7]

Sometime in late August there was a battle involving many of Colonel Burleson's rangers. The *Telegraph and Texas Register* on September 13, 1836, reported that "companies under Billingsley, Yorke and Hill...pursued and thrashed the marauding Indians." Together, these companies reportedly accounted for about thirty-five Indians killed, without the loss of a single Texan. The editors of the *Telegraph* concluded that this success helped persuade some Colorado River families to return to their homes.[8]

Captain William Hill's company is known to have been in the settlement of Tenoxtitlan for a short time during August. Located in Robertson's Colony on the west bank of the Brazos River in present northeastern Burleson County, Tenoxtitlan was the site of a Mexican fort from 1830 to 1832. Only a handful of settlers had returned by this time, after having abandoned the town during the Runaway Scrape.[9]

According to young ranger Rufus Perry, Captain Hill's company had ranged the areas north of Bastrop during its early existence in July. In Bastrop they found during the Runaway Scrape that "part of the town had been burned by Indians." They had then proceeded to the San Gabriel River, "finding bee trees and lots of fish" to enjoy.[10]

Captain Hill's battle occurred in late August, but the exact date remains unknown. A search of some of the audited claims submitted by Hill's men reveals little more. Horatio Chriesman, who enlisted in the company as a private on July 3, was promoted to orderly sergeant on August 18. His records, however, do not indicate whether he was replacing someone who had been wounded in battle or had left the company. It is also unknown whether any of the other companies under Colonel Burleson participated in this battle.[11]

While out scouting with his rangers on the San Gabriel River, Captain Hill discovered the trail of foot Indians near a high bluff at the mouth of Brushy Creek. Their trail led toward the lower country where Cole's Settlement, the present town of Independence, was located.[12]

Captain Hill's rangers immediately took up the pursuit and followed the relatively fresh Indian trail without taking a rest. They overtook their enemy, twenty or more Caddos, in thick post oak country in the Yegua River bottomlands. Rufus Perry later gave an account of the subsequent battle to friend John Jenkins.

> After sundown we discovered the smoke of their campfire not very far off. Dismounting, we prepared to attack them in camp, but a straggling warrior hastened the issue by coming out and meeting us accidentally and unexpectedly. Of course, we

killed him immediately but not before he had raised a war whoop, rousing his comrades to action.

We continued to advance, notwithstanding the fact of their being aroused and ready to meet us. We killed three and wounded several whom we did not get. Andy Houston was the only man in our company who was wounded, he being struck in the wrist with an unspiked arrow. This occurred on a prong of the Yegua, twelve miles from the settlements.

We were somewhat surprised and puzzled just after the fight to see a member of our company, an old backwoodsman named Dave Lawrence, step up and cut off the thigh of one of the slain Indians. I asked him what he intended to do with it.

"Why," he answered, "I am going to take it along to eat. If you don't get some game before noon tomorrow we'll need it!"[13]

Private Aaron Colvin was said by one of his fellow rangers to wish to be known as a desperado. Approaching the body of the first dead Indian, he jumped upon it and began stabbing it. "I think if the Indian had been alive," Perry reflected, "Colvin would have gone the other way."[14]

Captain Hill's men managed to drive their opponents from the thicket they had occupied during the battle fought in the post oaks between the Yegua and Little Rivers in present Burleson County. In their panic, the Indians left the bodies of their dead and their entire camp equipage. In their camp was found a large number of human scalps, taken from white people of both sexes and all ages.[15]

At sundown the rangers camped about a mile below the battleground on a little unnamed creek. Many of the small creeks flowing through Texas in the early days were named after the man who eventually claimed the land through which it ran. This particular creek received the humorous sobriquet "Cannonsnap Creek" by Hill's men. Cannonsnap Creek is located in present Milam County, north and slightly west of Milano. Rufus Perry later related the naming of this body of water.

Thus it occurred on this very night in the summer of 1836 that a Portuguese, a dark, very dark man [Abedingo Bedy], so black that we called him "Nigger Biddy," was placed on guard.

During the night he rushed in on our crowd exclaiming, "Oh! I heard a cannon snap!" Poor fellow, he was so much frightened that he magnified a twig's snapping or an owl's laughing into threatened danger. Then and there the little creek received its present name of "Cannon Snap."[16]

Captain Hill's company moved on the next morning to Yellow Prairie, located on the waters of the Brazos River. They stopped at the home of Jesse Thompson, an original Old Three Hundred colonist, in present Fort Bend County. Thompson ran a ferry on the Brazos, and he helped provision the men. "The hospitable old gentleman furnished us beef and corn, a sumptuous dinner," recalled Perry, "so old Dave Lawrence did not have to eat his Indian meat."

Fresh from their fight and now recharged with proper food, Captain Hill's company soon set out to scout further for hostile Indians. They proceeded up the Little River and spent more weeks searching for Indian trails but did not have any further battles with Indians. He and his men returned to the settlements and were discharged on October 3, 1836, at the conclusion of their three-month commitment.

★ ★ ★ ★ ★

Colonel Coleman's Ranger Battalion Forms

By mid-August 1836, a third ranger battalion began formation to supplement those already in the field under Colonel Burleson and Major Burton.

Almanzon Huston, Quartermaster General of the Texas army, sent authorization on August 10 to Colonel Robert Coleman to prepare himself for a campaign to the northern Texas frontiers. Coleman had served as an aide-de-camp under General Houston from April 1 to July 15, 1836. He had previously served as a ranger captain during Colonel John Moore's 1835 Indian campaign of summer 1835 and had commanded a volunteer company during the storming of Béxar. Coleman's prompting to Texas leaders had also helped to formally create the Texas Rangers during 1835.

Quartermaster Huston's August 10 note authorized Colonel Coleman to purchase seventy-five horses, saddles, and bridles for a campaign authorized by the acting secretary of war. Coleman was cautioned to keep duplicate copies of all of his receipts for the army. Should he be unable to purchase enough horses for the men in his battalion, Coleman was authorized to round up all "the cattle in or between the Brazos and Colorado rivers" to exchange for horses.[17]

On August 11 General Edmund Gaines wrote from Camp Sabine to report to the U.S. secretary of war of a serious Indian threat. He had received a report from a Frenchman named Michael Sacco that the Cherokees, Alabamas, Shawnees, Biloxis, Kickapoos, and several other Indian tribes had joined against the whites. It was understood that there

Colonel Robert Morris Coleman (1799-1837) organized the first company of Texas Rangers to be legally recognized by the Texas government in 1835. Following his service at San Jacinto, Coleman was commissioned to command a three-company ranger battalion in August 1836. (From DeShields' *Border Wars of Texas*.)

were runners operating constantly between the Indians and the Mexican army. An attack on Texan settlers was imminent. The only decision, according to Sacco's intelligence, was whether the Indians should wait for support from the Mexican army or not.[18]

Further support of this disturbing report was received from Texas Indian agent Michel B. Menard. He reported that all of the wild prairie Indians had gathered above the three forks of the Trinity, near present Dallas, in preparation for hostilities against the settlers. Other Indian tribes said to have joined this group were the Comanches, Wacos, Tawakonis, Caddos, and Pawnees. The entire group, according to Menard, was waiting on the Cherokees to remove their cattle and provisions to safer grounds and for Cherokees sent to the Mexican army to return. Menard called for an attack to be made at the forks of the Trinity against these tribes.

Such increasing threats of Indian hostilities forced Texas leaders to provide for the more exposed frontier settlements. Acting Secretary of War Frederick A. Sawyer issued orders from Velasco on August 12 for Colonel Coleman to organize two or three companies of rangers. Sawyer informed General Thomas Rusk that these companies of "mounted men" would be organized "principally from among the citizens of the disturbed settlements" that had been visited by Indian attacks during the summer. Sawyer reminded Coleman that his specific mission was to ensure "the complete protection of the inhabitants" within his ranging circuit.[19]

You are hereby ordered to raise for the term of one year three companies of mounted men for the special purpose of protecting the frontier inhabitants of upper Brazos—Colorado—Little River—and Guadalupe;—You will make your headquarters at some suitable point above the settlement, and take such other measures as you may deem best calculated to protect the persons and property of the citizens aforesaid. So soon as a company shall be complete, you will report an election for officers, the result of which you will report to this office that the persons elected may be commissioned to the Secretary of War.

Colonel Coleman was also to furnish the necessary arms and provisions as required by his troops. His battalion was "raised under the provisions of the ordinance and decree of the Council" in the same format as the Texas Revolution rangers previously under Major Williamson. His three companies were under direct orders from the brigadier general of the army. Private soldiers were to be paid $1.25 per day for furnishing all of their own necessities except ammunition.[20]

The first two companies of his battalion began organization during mid-August. Command of the first company was given to Captain Alfred P. Walden, an officer of the regular Texas army. He had been elected captain of a First Regiment of Texas Artillery company, which had been mustered into service on July 25, 1836. Walden's company was reorganized about August 15 as Company A of Colonel Coleman's Regiment of Rangers.

At least fifteen men from his previous artillery company were transferred into the new ranger Company A. Most of Walden's new officers were among these transferees. Almost all of the men of Company A were newer arrivals from the United States who had joined the Texas army after the battle of San Jacinto. One exception was Private Dennis Mahoney, an Ireland native who had come to Texas with the New Orleans Greys and had participated in the siege of Béxar.

Company B was formed under Captain Tommy Barron, who was a veteran of the ranger service. He had first served under Captain Daniel Friar in 1835 and briefly commanded his own company during March 1836. Unlike Walden's company, Barron's company was made up almost exclusively of men who were already Texas residents, most of them from Robertson's Colony. His son John Barron was among his new recruits. Many of Barron's rangers were pulled from Captain Sterling Robertson's company when it reformed on September 11. At least seventeen men, including former Orderly Sergeant Barron, were used to help fill the ranks of Coleman's Company B. The balance of Robertson's men continued their service under Captain Calvin Boales.

Colonel Coleman was able to draw from other existing ranger companies over the fall months to help bolster his own regiment. The men of the Colorado River area who had originally enlisted under Captain John Tumlinson in January were ordered to report to Colonel Coleman, as their one-year term of enlistment had not yet expired. Noah Smithwick, for one, was allowed to work in the settlements for most of his term, as his services as a blacksmith were under heavy need.[21]

While the one-year rangers who enlisted during the revolution were required to complete their service, some of the companies formed after the revolution were not. Captain Byrd Lockhart's small spy company, formed on July 4 in Colonel Burleson's battalion, was dissolved on August 16, 1836. General Rusk signed discharge paper of privates Byrd B. Lockhart Jr. and George W. Davis on this date at the Texas army headquarters on the Coleto. Captain Lockhart affirmed that each man had served in "my company of Mounted Riflemen."[22]

Lockhart's company had recently returned from a scouting mission to San Antonio before disbanding. A note in the *Telegraph and Texas Register* in Columbia on August 23 stated:

> Col. R. M. Coleman has left this place with his men, to go and protect the inhabitants of the Colorado from incursions of marauding Indians and to enable the farmers to attend their crops and gather them . . .
>
> Our indefatigable ranger, Capt. Byrd Lockhart, has returned to camp and reports the corn in the neighborhood of Béxar to be remarkably fine and abundant, and that several thousand bushels will be the result.[23]

Coleman's battalion was organized and provisioned during August and early September. The third company of the battalion was commanded by Colonel Coleman during its early formation. The military papers of Private Henry Wilson state that he joined Company C under Robert Coleman on August 12, 1836.[24]

By September 21 Company C had raised enough men to warrant a proper acting commander. Colonel Coleman promoted Benjamin R. Thomas to second lieutenant in charge of the first seventeen men. James Pratt, who had joined the rangers on August 24, was promoted to orderly sergeant and Samuel Marshall became Company C's corporal.

The three-company ranger regiment set out from the upper settlements to erect their first fort to protect the farmers from the marauding Indians. According to Coleman, he and his men reached the Colorado River area on September 23 and started "Camp Colorado" on Walnut Creek.

It was at this location that his battalion was ordered to build their first blockhouse for defense of the vulnerable Colorado River settlers who lived near and above Bastrop. Coleman's men and their new fortification would significantly aid the companies under Colonel Burleson who were still in service.

The rangers then commenced building Fort Colorado on September 24. It was located about six miles below present Austin and became alternately known over the next two years as Fort Colorado, Coleman's Fort, and Fort Houston.[25]

It consisted of a pair of two-story blockhouses and was enclosed by a high stockade fence pierced for rifles. Within the defensive stockade

---

Colonel Robert Morris Coleman's Ranger Battalion
Muster Rolls of Original Companies

Captain Walden's Company A: August 15 - December 31, 1836

Alfred P. Walden [1]	Capt	Dennis Mahoney	July 25
Alexander Robless [2]	1st Lt	Francis Malone	Sept. 5
Charles H. Leeds	2nd Lt	John Malone	October 23
Richard Collard	1st Sgt	Philip Martin	July 25
Van R. Palmer	2nd Sgt	Felix McCluskey	July 25
Alanson T. Miles	3rd Sgt	John H. Peoples	October 23
Thomas McKernon [3]	1st Corp	William H. Perry	August 15
Samuel K. Blisk	2nd Corp	John Pierson	July 25
Ferdinand C. Booker	3rd Corp	Evan Reed	October
Privates:	*Enrolled:*	Jefferson Richards	October 7
Henry Alderson	Nov. 3	Henry Rogers	July 25
John Angel	Dec. 10	John Seekill	October 25
Charles Bender [4]	August 26	John W. Seymour	October 25
Fee C. Booker [5]	Oct. 22	Levi H. Smith [10]	October 19
James Benny	Oct. 28	Jonathon Taylor	October 25
James O. Butler	Dec. 10	Gasper Whisler	October 25
James Christian	October 25	Henry Wilson [11]	July 25
Archabald G. Denson	October 22	[1] Absent on special duty as of Nov. 1.	
Richard Eggleston	October 25	[2] Became company commander.	
William T. Evans [6]	October 25	[3] Discharged by Col. Coleman in Dec.	
Samuel Fowler	October 27	[4] Deserted August 27.	
Andrew Galicia [7]	Sept. 17	[5] Committed suicide November 8.	
Jose Gasceo	Sept. 17	[6] Deserted November 13.	
William Goodman	October 20	[7] Died December 29.	
Hugh Hammond	Oct. 22	[8] Deserted November 8.	
Jacob Herald [8]	Oct. 19	[9] Enlisted for two years.	
John Henry [9]	January 5	[10] Absent sick as of Nov. 30.	
William Lupton	October 21	[11] Absent waggoning as of Dec. 31.	
		Source: *Muster Rolls of the Texas Revolution*, 160-64.	

Captain Barron's Company B: September 11 - December 31, 1836

Captain:
Thomas H. Barron [1]
First Lieutenant:
David W. Campbell [1]
Second Lieutenant:
Charles Curtis [2]
First Sergeant:
James McLaughlin
Second Sergeant:
Joseph P. Jones [8]
Third Sergeant:
Lee R. Davis [3]
Corporal:
Ezra Webb [1]
Privates:
John M. Barron
Silas H. Bates
Alfred Berry [3]
Samuel Burton
Patrick T. Carnell [1]
Michael Castleman [1]
John Chalmers
David Clark [3]
John R. Cockrill
James Coryell [1]
William R. Cox
Aaron Cullins

Daniel Cullins
Ansel Darniell [6]
Charles Duncan
Green B. Duncan
James Duncan
Alfred Eaton [4]
Thomas H. Eaton [5]
Tilford C. Edwards
Calvin B. Emmons [7]
George B. Erath [3]
Benjamin F. Fitch [1]
John Fokes
James Frasier
Robert Furgeson [1]
Jacob Gross
John H. Hobson [1]
William Isaacs
Thomas D. James
John Joseph Long
Thomas Matthews
Green McCoy
Jeremiah McDaniel [1]
William McLaughlin
Robert Moffitt [1]
William Moffitt [1]
Lewis Moore
Morris Moore

Andrew J. Morgan [1]
George W. Morgan [1]
John C. Morgan [1]
William C. Neill
Hardin Nevill
Abel Parsons
Ezekiel Robertson
Neill Robertson
G. B. Smith
John S. Stump
Empson Thompson
Jasper N. Thompson
John Tucker
John Wilkinson [1]
William Woodford [3]

[1] Joined from Robertson's.
[2] Promoted 1st Lt. in Nov.
[3] Joined from Capt. Hill's.
[4] Enlisted on September 5.
[5] Joined on September 18.
[6] Joined Sept. 23 from Capt. Robbins'.
[7] Joined Oct. 6 from Capt. Putnam's.
[8] Joined on Sept. 11.

Source: *Muster Rolls of the Texas Revolution*, 151-52, 164-65.

Lieut. Thomas's Company C: September 21 - December 31, 1836

Benjamin R. Thomas	2nd Lieut.	Isaac Lowry	August 11
James Pratt	Ord. Sgt.	John McDougald [3]	August 15
Samuel R. Marshall	Corp.	William H. Monroe	Sept. 20
Privates:	*Enrolled:*	Azariah G. Moore [4]	August 24
George W. Barnett [1]	August 24	James Moore [2]	Nov. 29
Spirus Bennett	Nov. 15	Robert W. Nabors	August 24
Isaac Castner	Oct. 17	John B. Robinson	Dec. 30
Thomas Eldridge	August 14	William C. Stiffey	Dec. 21
John Fowler	August 14	Samuel Wolfenberger [5]	Sept. 1
Thomas M. Fowler	August 24	Nicholas Wren	Nov. 1
William Friedlander	Dec. 30		
Francisco Garcia	Sept. 20	[1] Died September 6. Joined from Hill's.	
James Hamilton	August 24	[2] Joined from Capt. Hill's.	
John Husbands	Sept. 6	[3] Died on September 28.	
Elijah Ingram	Dec. 30	[4] Promoted to Sgt. Major August 24.	
William Johnston	Sept. 19	[5] Promoted to Commissary August 29.	
James Leech	August 11	Source: *Muster Rolls of the Texas Revolution*, 159-60.	

were also a number of log cabins, which served as barracks, storerooms, and service buildings, plus a corral for livestock. Coleman's Fort stood on the high ground overlooking the Colorado River to the south and Walnut Creek to the east, situated about a mile from the settlements of Hornsby's and Mitchell's forts.[26]

Coleman wrote to Senator Sterling Robertson on October 16, describing Fort Colorado and the deployment of his new ranger battalion.

> I have selected the most beautiful site I ever saw for the purpose. It is immediately under the foot of the mountains. The eminence is never the less commanding, and in every way suited to the object in view.
>
> I have ordered Capt. Barron to build a block house at or near Milam, where he will station one half of his company. The other half of the company under the 1st Lieut. is also ordered to build a block house at, or near, the three forks of the Little River. I shall in a short time commence a block house at the head of San Marcos, and one at the crossing of the Guadalupe, by which means I hope to be able to give protection to the whole frontier west of the Brazos.[27]

Coleman's letter shows that Company B had been stationed at Fort Milam near the Falls of the Brazos by early October. Fort Milam, constructed originally in 1834 at Sarahville de Viesca in Robertson's Colony, was located on the Brazos River's west bank near the falls in present central Falls County. A Texas marker now stands four miles southwest of Marlin to mark the site.[28] Barron's company's muster roll shows "Company B of the 1st Regiment of Texas Rangers" to still be stationed there as of December 31, 1836. This roll is signed by "T. H. Barron, Capt. Commanding Fort Milam."

The other two companies were stationed at the new Fort Colorado, which was originally known by many as Coleman's Fort since it served as his ranger headquarters. During the early construction on Coleman's Fort, more rangers continued to join his battalion as their companies were disbanded. Some had signed agreements to serve for one year, so they just transferred their service to other frontier companies of Texas.

For example, Captain William Hill's three-month ranger company was disbanded on October 3, 1836, at Hickory Point, as evidenced by discharge papers signed by Captain Hill and General Rusk. Two of Hill's men, George Erath and Lee Davis, joined Captain Barron's Company B and became officers.[29]

Fort Coleman viewed from the northwest with the Colorado River to the right and Walnut Creek to the left. This sketch by N. Donaldson is from Noah Smithwick's *The Evolution of a State*. Fort Coleman was used extensively from 1836 into 1838 by the ranger battalion organized by Colonel Coleman. It was more often referred to as Fort Colorado and briefly as Fort Houston. *UT Institute of Texan Cultures at San Antonio, No. 73-883.*

Erath had already been in almost constant service to Texas for more than a year when he joined Colonel Coleman's rangers.

> In the fall of 1836 a battalion of rangers for the defense of the frontier was raised of which I became a member. We were promised twenty-five dollars a month and 1280 acres of land for every twelve month's service; the government furnished ammunition and rations, but we furnished our own horses and arms; we lived for the most part on game out of the woods. I have known more than one man enlisting to give his whole claim for land and money in advance for a horse, saddle and bridle, with which to serve for it. Ammunition was the only thing furnished us, and some beef now and then.[30]

Colonel Coleman's ranger companies continued to grow during the fall months. These men would protect the Colorado River frontiers from the summer of 1836 through early 1838, a tenure surpassing any previous Texas Ranger battalion.

★ ★ ★ ★ ★

Major James Smith's East Texas Rangers

Coleman's ranger companies were a significant showing of force in the western settlements of Texas. Eastern Texas was heavily populated with Indian villages, and the white settlements were especially vulnerable to Indian hostilities in the wake of the Texas Revolution.

President Houston took steps to organize mounted men in this area to maintain order. On September 1 he issued orders to Major James

Smith of the Texas army concerning the rising flow of volunteers arriving to serve in Texas. Smith, who had also helped Sterling Robertson recruit rangers during June, was to organize men into companies of fifty-six, require a muster roll, and then press them into service.[31] Within two weeks Smith would oversee three companies of rangers in eastern Texas.

According to available records, one small company of men had already been in service in Nacogdoches County for some time. Michael Costley, twenty-seven, had enlisted in the Texas army on June 22 for three months, and from his Nacogdoches home, he served in a mounted group under Hugh McLeod.

Despite the fact that he had graduated last in his thirty-five-man class from West Point Military Academy on September 18,

Major James Smith (1792-1855) moved to Nacogdoches County in 1835 and he commanded a cavalry company during the Texas Revolution. He was involved with recruiting rangers after San Jacinto and commanded an East Texas ranger battalion during the fall of 1836. He later served as a lieutenant colonel during the Cherokee War in 1839 and as a brigadier general of the Texas army during the 1840s. *Archives & Information Services Division, Texas State Archives.*

1835, McLeod would rise to great prominence in Texas history. He had been duly commissioned into the U.S. Army as a second lieutenant and was posted at Fort Jesup in Company B, Third Infantry. McLeod headed to Texas on March 7 with others to join the Texas Revolution. In Nacogdoches, he established a volunteer guard company consisting of some locals and some men previously serving at Fort Jesup. Michael Costley joined McLeod's guard company, which served from April through July 1836, patrolling the Béxar Road between the Angelina and Neches Rivers.[32]

Sam Houston issued orders to Costley on September 1 to go into Cherokee Nation with several men to monitor the local Cherokee Indians' activities. Captain Costley was to "watch well, and keep the men with you in good order. By no means do I want you to begin hostilities" with the Indians. As Houston noted, there were several men and women of the Cherokees trading in Nacogdoches at the time.[33]

Upon receiving Houston's orders, Michael Costley and two others proceeded into Cherokee Nation, where the Indians appeared "to express all friendship toward us." Upon departing their lands, Costley found the chief of the Caddos with three others from his tribe. They appeared alarmed and had come in for the purpose of talking out matters. Costley reported to Houston on September 2 that he and his men stood ready for further orders. His men were furnished provisions and ammunition to brace themselves for future deployment against Indian hostilities. Sam Houston on September 6 ordered Colonel Henry Raguet, chairman of the Committee of Vigilance and Safety in Nacogdoches, to deliver to Captain Costley "one keg of powder and a sufficient quantity of lead to go with it."

True to his orders, Major Smith formally organized ranger companies in his area into companies of fifty-six men each. The first to completely organize itself and call a muster was that of Captain Elisha Clapp in Nacogdoches County on September 10, 1836. Clapp had served in Captain William H. Smith's cavalry company at San Jacinto. Prior to the Texas Revolution, his fortified home in present Houston County had become known as Clapp's Blockhouse.

Located slightly north of the Old San Antonio Road, this blockhouse served as a mustering point and as a refuge during times of Indian hostilities. The muster roll of his new company states:

> Pursuant to an order from the Commander in Chief, the following men assembled themselves at the house of Elisha Clapp in Mustang Prairie, on Saturday the 10th of September and proceeded to the Election of Officers.

It is signed by Clapp as "Captain Mounted Rangers." Each man joining was to furnish his own horse, arms, ammunition, and provisions.[34] His company included some men from cavalry companies whose service had expired during September, including former ranger superintendent Daniel Friar.

Clapp submitted his muster roll and officer election returns to Sam Houston in Nacogdoches, who acknowledged their receipt on September 16 and sent orders to Captain Clapp.

> You will range from any point on the Brazos to Mr. Hall's Trading House on the Trinity. For your orders, I refer you to copies of those given to Captain Michael Costley of the N.W. Frontier, therewith enclosed for your information. The general principles of them you will find applicable to your command as

well as to all officers employed on the frontier. You will detail eight men from your command for the service and place at the disposition of Dan Parker Esq., as the local situation of the frontier may require.[35]

Daniel Parker Sr. had attracted the attention of Sam Houston in the wake of the tragic Parker's Fort massacre. The report he, Armstead Bennett, and Thomas Lagow had penned on June 18 demanded attention be focused on this area.[36] Parker received orders from Sam Houston that he should oversee the construction of a blockhouse and ferry on the Trinity River above Comanche Crossing and near Fort Houston. Parker was to use twenty of Major Smith's rangers to complete this task.

The second ranger company under Major Smith was formed on September 11 and placed under Captain Michael Costley, who was already in service observing Indian activities. In pursuance to Houston's new orders, Costley enlisted a new company of men at his home. Three of his new recruits, Daniel Crist, Henry Jeffrey, and Robert Williams, had been present on Mustang Prairie the day before when Elisha Clapp's rangers

---

Captain Clapp's Rangers: September 10 - December 12, 1836

Captain:	Chandler Johnson	Stephen Crist [3]
Elisha Clapp	W. H. Kennedy	Richard Duty [3]
First Lieutenant:	William G. Kennedy	Robert Earls [3]
George Aldrich	Samuel Maas	Henry Jeffery [3]
Second Lieutenant:	Burrill Morris	Reason Jones [3]
Henry G. Hudson	Isaac Parker	Samuel Lawrence [3]
Privates:	William H. Pate	Samuel Long [3]
Thomas Anander	Anthony Rivers	James Madden [3]
Abram Anglin [1]	Joshua Robbins	J. Marsh [3]
Dolors Ariola	Nathaniel Robbins	Henry Masters [3]
Francisco Ariola	Isaac Roberts	Daniel Milligan [3]
Juan Ariola	Finis G. Robertson	William R. Powell [3]
Marsimo Ariola	George W. Robinson	Robert Rogers Jr. [3]
Alfred Benge	Marmaduke G. Sandefer	Stephen Rogers [3]
Thomas Boatwright	Robert Stanley	Ira Short [3]
John F. Chairs	Thomas R. Townsend	Robert Williams [3]
Martin Copeland	Levi W. White	[1] Transferred to Costley's
Richard Dixon	Stephen White	company 9/28/36.
Andrew E. Gossett	George W. Browning [3]	[2] Substitute for George W.
Elijah Gossett	Barton Clark [3]	Browning.
James Lockridge Gossett	Daniel LaMora Crist [3]	[3] Present at formation, but
James S. Hunter	John Crist [3]	did not serve.
Thomas James [2]	Reason Crist [3]	Source: *Muster Rolls of the Texas Revolution*, 199-201.

were formed. They did no service for Clapp but instead joined Costley's rangers.

A few other men joined the company after its initial mustering. One such man was Abram Anglin, a survivor of the Parker's Fort massacre, who enlisted with Costley's rangers on September 28 to complete two months of service that he still owed another company.[37] Costley signed his roll as a correct return of

> a company of mounted rangers, mustered into service by me, under the orders of Genl. Sam Houston on the 11th day of September 1836, for a term of three months, which expired on the 11th day of December 1836, at which time they were discharged.[38]

George Washington Browning, a native of Scotland who had immigrated to Texas in 1835, was originally present for the mustering of Captain Clapp's company. Prior to joining the rangers, he had served for a year in the Texas army and had fought at San Jacinto. His enlistment with Clapp was substituted by another man so that Browning, under

Captain Elisha Clapp (1792-1856) served at San Jacinto and later commanded rangers in 1836 from his fortified home at Mustang Prairie in Houston County. A tavern owner in the county, Clapp would also serve as a major in the Texas militia during Indian hostilities in 1838 and in 1839. In 1847 he acquired Robbins' Ferry at the Old San Antonio Road crossing of the Trinity River from his father-in-law, Nathaniel Robbins. Wilfred Clapp, a great-granddaughter, painted this rendering of Captain Clapp and his Trinity River ferry. *Courtesy of Wilfred Clapp.*

orders from Sam Houston, could become the commissary for Major Smith's ranger battalion. He carried the original muster rolls of Captain Clapp's company to Sam Houston in Nacogdoches. From Nacogdoches, Browning was ordered by Houston on September 13 to carry a message to the Ioni Indians near Fort Houston, with an escort from the rangers under Captain Costley.[39]

Upon reaching the Neches crossing on the San Antonio Road, Browning was prevented from crossing that evening by the absence of ferryman Leonard Williams. Reaching Costley's men on September 14, he then set out to meet with the Ioni chief.

> I went on the 15th to the Ioni village to see if I could find Chickasaw Jim or some Ioni Indian that I could send for the chief to meet me, but found the village entirely evacuated. I desired that Capt. Costley should send a file of six, 8 or 10 men as a lifeguard to go with me to the neighborhood where the Indians were encamped and I would send an Indian to the chief, which guard was refused me. Consequently, yours to the chief is yet in my hands.

Browning wrote to Houston from the home of Martin Murchison on September 17. Murchison's Prairie, located in present Houston County, is listed on many early republic military documents as a stopping point for troops. Browning noted that Costley's company was split between several places. Ten rangers were at Murchison's, and thirteen men were near the Neches Saline just outside of Cherokee Nation. The rest of Costley's men had not been sent out yet but "the Capt. says they will be out probably by next Sunday."

Browning considered this "a loose way of doing business" with Costley's men being so spread out. Costley, however, informed him that the men who had gone to the saline were all on foot and were working on trading for horses from the Indians.

Browning also informed Houston that "the Indians have been committing some depredations in the horse-stealing way" since he had left Nacogdoches on September 13. They had stolen six horses from Daniel McLean, and Finis G. Robertson had had some of his horses stolen but was fast enough to overtake the Indians. He succeeded in regaining his horses and shot at one of the Indians. It was unknown whether he had wounded the Indian or not.

Browning received orders from Captain Elisha Clapp on September 17 to report to his house together with as many men who would volunteer their services for an Indian expedition. It was expected to be a ten-day expedition in which each man would need at least one hundred rounds of ammunition. Clapp planned to go against the Ioni Indians, who were suspected of being involved in the latest horse-stealing offenses.

"The people generally believe that the Ioni Indians intend war," wrote Browning. Concerning the state of commissary duties, Browning informed Sam Houston, "The people who have provisions plenty to spare demand just double the common selling prices." Browning stated that for the time being he would "furnish the company out of my own private fund, believing it not right to pay such enormous prices." The common price for beef was 2.5 cents, and Browning proposed to pay people three cents per pound. Corn was valued in the area at between seventy-five cents and one dollar per bushel, although "double those prices are demanded of the government."

In response to Browning's report of the loose state of Captain Costley's company, Sam Houston wrote to Costley on September 17. He warned him about taking on "private interests" at public expense. "I regret to hear that a part of your command has been detached for the

---

Captain Costley's Rangers: September 11 - December 11, 1836

Captain:	Mark W. Dikes	Alfred S. Thurmond
Michael Costley	Austin Ferguson	William Tipton
First Lieutenant:	Joseph Ferguson	Benjamin A. Vansickle
Beverly Pool	Simeon Gashman	Elias S. Vansickle
Second Lieutenant:	Absolom Gibson	Hiram C. Vansickle
William T. Jackson	Joseph B. Hughes	John C. Wallen
Orderly Sergeant:	Henry Jeffrey [2]	Thomas D. Walpool
John N. King	Jesse Jones	William S. Walpool
Privates:	John Jordan	Wade Hampton Walters
Ezekiel Abel	Martin Lacy	James Jefferson Ware
Harrison Abel	Henry McGee	John West
John Abel	Hamilton McNutt	Joseph West
Joseph S. Abel	Isaac Midcalf	Joseph E. White
Abram Anglin [1]	George W. Miller	Robert Williams [2]
John Batey	John T. Murrell	William Williams
Seth M. Blair	Henry Myers	Tobias Wolf
Neriah Chamberlain	John D. Pierson	
Joseph Thomas Cook	Jonathan C. Pool	[1] Transferred from Capt.
Thomas Cook	Walter Pool	Clapp's on Sept. 28.
Daniel LaMora Crist [2]	John Sheridan	[2] Initially enrolled under
Elisha J. DeBard	James Sillman	Captain Clapp.
Levi Dikes	William Sims	Source: *Muster Rolls of the*
Lovick P. Dikes	William Smith	*Texas Revolution*, 165-66.

purpose of making salt for individual advantage," Houston wrote, "when our country might require the assistance of these men in the field."[40]

He therefore directed Costley to unite his company and keep them "in constant vigilance." Costley's rangers were to range strictly between the Trinity and Neches Rivers. He further advised Costley that twenty-five Cherokees would "range from the Sabine to the Comanche crossing above the Saline of the Trinity." His further orders were for Costley to follow the advice of Daniel Parker in constructing fortifications that were deemed necessary "to give protection to the inhabitants." If the Cherokee scouts were pressed hard by wild Indian tribes, Costley's rangers were to give them assistance. To distinguish them from other Indians, these Cherokee scouts were to wear a white feather in their cap or headdress.

To alleviate the problem of whites working the Neches Saline for their own gain, Houston sent orders on September 17 that directed Martin Lacy to "take possession of the Neches Saline, which is under the control of the government." Lacy, a member of Costley's rangers, was to use it to the best advantage, selling the salt he produced at the lowest price he could afford "to those who buy it for consumption." In payment for the use of this saline, Chief Bowles of the Cherokees was to be paid six bushels per month.[41]

Lacy was further cautioned by Houston not to engage in the importation of liquors. If caught so doing, he could be fined $500 for each offense. He was free, however, "to trade with the Indians in all things, except liquors and lead." Lacy was directed to maintain government control of this saline for two years.

A third company of rangers was soon added under the superintendence of Major James Smith in East Texas. A volunteer company under Captain George Washington Jewell, a successful businessman and landowner, had formed in McMinnville, Tennessee, on August 16 and left for Texas after hearing of the tragedies at the Alamo and Goliad earlier in the year. Known as the Tennessee Volunteers, Jewell's company arrived in San Augustine and announced themselves ready for duty. Sam Houston sent orders from Nacogdoches on September 18 for Jewell "to advance to this place with your command" for special employment.[42]

Jewell's company was mustered into service of the Republic of Texas on September 19, 1836, for a six-month period. His original company muster roll was filed in San Augustine County on September 19, 1836, before militia registrar John Love. Houston assigned Captain Jewell's company to operate from Fort Houston in present Anderson

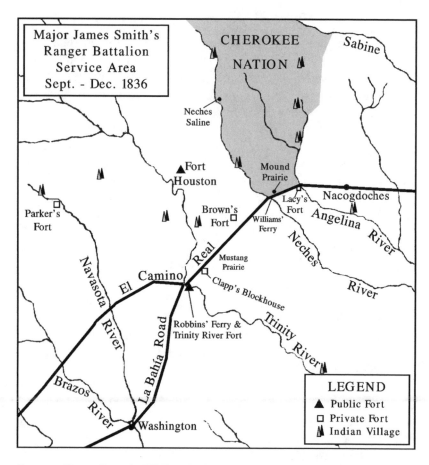

County. Since Captain William T. Sadler's men had helped build and man the initial blockhouse during early 1836, it had been abandoned during the Runaway Scrape. The area settlers did return, and the fortification served as their refuge once farming resumed.

Jewell's men were to complete the construction on Fort Houston, including the addition of a proper stockade. His men were supplied by local residents such as James Madden, who provided twenty-four bushels of corn for thirty dollars on September 26. Madden's promissory note was signed at Camp Murchison by George Browning, "Commissary for Rangers."[43] The ranging company of Captain Costley was soon added to the Fort Houston project.

Captain Clapp's rangers, in the meantime, were ordered to secure the upper crossing of the Trinity River with a new blockhouse. The fort was advantageously located on Texas's main east-west road, El Camino

Captain Jewell's Rangers: Muster Roll of September 19, 1836		
Captain:	Joseph T. Green	Anthony B. Patton
George W. Jewell	Henry H. Greer	Berry Payne
First Lieutenant:	J. B. Hardin	Jabediah Payne
Thomas Barton	E. E. Harrell	William Phillips
Second Lieutenant:	James B. Harris	John D. Raines
Squire Haggard	George Hider	John Raines
Third Lieutenant:	James Higgins	Joseph S. Shanks
John Graham	William B. Hill	Lee C. Smith
Privates:	Solomon Hopkins	William Spier
M. Adair	George W. Humphreys	A. J. Stephens
William C. Allen	William Ishmore	Isaac Stout
C. Columbus Anderson	William M. Jackson	George Tonnage
Eli Baily	Samuel Jones	Davenport Wiseman
John B. Baker	Elisha McDonald	Harrison York
Landan F. Carter	William McGuire	James Allison York
Benjamin Clark	Jesse A. Oakley	
J. P. Cummins	Washington Oakley	Key Source: *Muster Rolls of*
Jonas A. Duty	Hardin Pace	*the Texas Revolution*, 151.

Real, at the Robbins' Ferry crossing of the Trinity (at present State Highway 21 on the western border of Houston County). This fort became known as the Trinity River Fort.[44]

Houston County settler Joel David Leathers came to Texas in the summer of 1836 looking for a place to settle. According to his daughter, Leathers followed the San Antonio Road "until his ox train had reached the stockade on the Trinity River where Elisha Clapp and a number of other settlers were making their homes at the time."

★　★　★　★　★

Erath's Rangers Build Little River Fort

Indian depredations continued in the more remote areas of central Texas. On September 21 three men from Columbia-on-the-Brazos, Leander and Collin Beason and Maxwell Steel, were attacked while searching for runaway slaves belonging to the Beasons. The ambush took place as they were crossing the Guadalupe River just below Gonzales. Collin Beason was shot and killed, and his companion Steel was mortally wounded. Leander Beason, whose horse was shot out from under him, survived by swimming the river and fleeing.[45]

Wounded and exhausted, Leander Beason managed to make his way back to the settlements, where he rounded up help. A company of ten men was made up, including William B. DeWees. They started out after the Indians and spotted them through a spyglass fifteen miles from Gonzales. DeWees and his posse approached the Indians from an unexpected quarter and charged them with complete surprise. Confused and routed, the Indians fled. The possee pursued for a time but gave up. On arriving at the river, they found and buried the body of Collin Beason but did not find the body of Maxwell Steel. According to DeWees, it was learned that the head of Steel had been seen in the Indian camp, about three quarters of a mile above Gonzales.

Such occasional killings helped reinforce the need for the various ranger battalions in the field. Colonel Coleman's ranger battalion had settled into the newly built Fort Colorado and Fort Milam by early October. The Executive Department in Columbia issued paperwork to help provision these frontier troops on October 5, 1836. Instructions were sent by David Burnet to Captain Alfred P. Walden of Coleman's battalion to procure provisions from Thomas Toby & Brother in New Orleans for "a detachment of the army stationed on the northern frontier."[46]

Walden was to secure clothing, blankets, forty patent-breached Yagers, thirty good rifles, 150 brace of good horseman's pistols, 150 cavalry swords, and ammunition. His instructions note that

The powder should be of a very good rifle quality. The lead in small bars is more convenient than in large masses for the peculiar service in which Capt. W. is engaged.

Captain Walden was to hurry, as his return was deemed "very important to the protection of our frontier from Indian depredations." Despite best intentions for a hurried return, it would be quite some time before Walden returned. When he left his Company A of rangers in October, he turned command over to his first lieutenant, Alexander Robless. Securing the needed armament must have been no easy task, for Walden did not return to Texas that year.

Company A's muster roll for November 30 shows Captain Walden as "on furlough." On the year-end 1836 muster roll, Walden is shown as "absent without leave." This was signed by Colonel Coleman and Lieutenant Robless, commanding Company A. It is likely Robless added that note. Walden's trip was not without effect, for in early 1837 new clothing did arrive for Coleman's rangers.

By mid-October Colonel Coleman was well into his aggressive plan to construct a string of frontier forts. His report to Senator Sterling Robertson on October 16 shows that half of Captain Tommy Barron's company was building the blockhouse at Milam. The other half of

Company B had been ordered to build another blockhouse at or near the three forks of the Little River. Coleman planned to soon build a fourth blockhouse at the head of the San Marcos River and a fifth at the crossing of the Guadalupe River. In this manner, Coleman hoped to protect the whole Colorado area frontier west of the Brazos. He had previously written to the secretary of war requesting permission to raise two more companies so that he could extend the chain of frontier forts from Fort Houston to Béxar.[47]

Coleman boldly stated his objectives to Robertson:

> My highest ambition is to give protection to this frontier and I hope you will sustain me. There are many who oppose me, and some of my county men particularly, but by the 1st of Decr. I will show to the govt. as well as all others what a Kentuckian can do. Give me men, ammunition, provisions and arms, and I pledge my honor with all that is sacred to check immediately all Indian depredations.

Coleman's string of forts, as planned, would extend from south to north, beginning with his Fort Coleman on the Colorado. This would then extend north to Little River Fort, and from there to Fort Milam on the Brazos. His request for five ranger companies in service would eventually be honored as Fort Fisher at present Waco and Fort Henderson along the Navasota were later constructed.

Goldsby Childers wrote to Senator Robertson on October 21 from Nashville and informed him of the progress of Captain Barron's company working on their blockhouse, Fort Milam, at the Falls of the Brazos. Childers did not feel confident that this fort would deter the Indians. He sent his wishes and those of other area residents that Congress would allow them "to have a garrison stationed at the three forks of the Little River."[48]

Colonel Coleman, of course, already shared the same goal as Childers. One of the early Robertson Colony settlers, Newton C. Duncan, later wrote a description of Captain Barron's ranger company, of which his brothers Charles and thirteen-year-old Green B. Duncan were members. According to Duncan, Barron's company was generally based out of Viesca at most times from late 1836 through early 1837.

Captain Barron remained at Viesca in charge of Fort Milam, while a detachment of approximately twenty men from his Company B was ordered out in November to construct the Little River fort. It is interesting to note that Coleman mentions this detachment in his letter of

October 16 as being headed by Barron's "first lieutenant."

The man who was placed in charge of this group was George Erath. In his memoirs, Erath wrote that he was considered a "lieutenant" in charge of half of Captain Barron's company. Erath's own military papers, however, show that he enlisted in Company B as a private and was promoted to orderly sergeant on November 15, 1836.[49] It is likely that Erath was serving as the company's acting first lieutenant during his November assignment.

Sergeant Erath departed Fort Milam in early November with about twenty men to assist in building the fort on the Little River. The others known to have accompanied him were Sergeants Lee Davis and James McLaughlin and Privates Jesse Bailey, David Clark, Aaron Cullins, Daniel Cullins, David M. Farmer, John Fokes, Jacob Gross, Jack Hobson, Green McCoy, Lewis Moore, his brother Morris Moore, Claiborne Neal, Sterrett Smith, and Empson Thompson. The families of Goldsby Childers and others also accompanied this detachment to help with construction.[50]

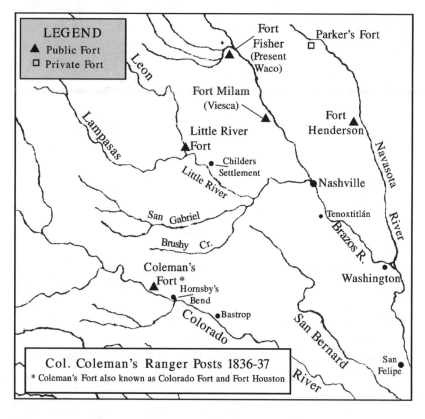

LEGEND
▲ Public Fort
□ Private Fort

Leon

Lampasas

Fort Fisher (Present Waco) ▲

Parker's Fort □

Fort Milam (Viesca) ▲

Little River ▲Fort

● Childers Settlement

Little River

Fort Henderson ▲

● Nashville

Navasota River

San Gabriel

Brushy Cr.

● Tenoxtitlán

Brazos R.

Coleman's Fort ▲ *
Hornsby's Bend

Washington ●

● Bastrop

Colorado

San Bernard

River

San ● Felipe

Col. Coleman's Ranger Posts 1836-37
* Coleman's Fort also known as Colorado Fort and Fort Houston

Colonel Coleman and a few other men accompanied Erath's detachment to the point designated. After the men had traveled, marked, cut out, and measured a road from the Falls of the Brazos to the location of the Little River Fort, Coleman left this group. He proceeded on, measuring a road to his own fort on Walnut Creek about six or eight miles above Hornsby's, then the highest settlement on the Colorado River.[51]

Erath's men found that attempts had been made to settle this area before the Runaway Scrape had chased all the settlers away. Occasional patches of corn planted in the spring had reached maturity during the favorable season. Several bags of nubbins were procured from the remaining crops, and Erath issued the rangers an ear of corn per day. They used this to grind on a steel mill to make bread. Meat was from the plentiful wild game in the area. Honey was kept in rawhide or deerskin sacks with the hair outside.

Coleman left this little detachment with basic tools, including several axes, a wagon, two yoke of steers, and the steel mill for making bread. The rangers were able to find pots and cooking utensils around the evacuated country in or near deserted cabins where settlers had hidden them in thickets before running away. A small amount of coffee had been brought up with the group, and it was "used with great economy."

Erath's men were quick about the business of building Little River Fort.

> I am at a loss how to account for the amount of work done that winter by men who had to guard, cook, dress deerskin, and make clothes of it, particularly moccasins, and in all ways provide everything, and yet in six weeks time, by Christmas, I had up seven or eight houses with wooden chimneys, well covered, and with buffalo hide carpets down. I can say, however, that I had the honor to command a set of men unexcelled in capacity and industry, all of whom became good citizens of Texas.

The fort and its compound were smaller than Coleman's Fort, covering only about a half-acre. The little cabins Erath's men built were ranged along the north row of post oak pickets, which comprised the outer stockade. A good spring ran past the fort at about one hundred yards distance and became the local water source.[52]

Another early Texan, Wilson T. Davidson, later wrote of the construction of Little River Fort. He remembered that is was located at a place one mile north of the Three Forks, three or four hundred yards east of the Leon River on the high ground, about one and a half miles west from the present railway station of Little River on the M.K. & T. Railway. During the months of November and December 1836, Sergeant Erath and his men built there a fort consisting of a blockhouse, a stockade and seven or eight log cabins inside the stockade. The fort was first known as Little River Fort, sometimes as Smith's Fort and the Block House, but was afterwards known as Fort Griffin, as it was situated on the headright league of Moses Griffin, one of the early pioneers of Bell County...

The block-house was about sixteen feet square, the four walls built of logs to the height of about eight or ten feet and the gable ran up with a continuation of the logs and the roof was made of bur oak boards held down by weight poles in the usual mode of construction [of] the pioneer's cabin. The block-house and cabins were protected by a stockade or picket fence surrounding it and enclosing about half an acre of land. There were portholes cut through the logs of the block-house through which to shoot the enemy in case of attack or siege.

By Christmas the men had several hundred pounds of honey collected in sacks made from animal skins about the camp. The men lived in their little cabins inside the fort. One soldier, Dan Cullins, had his family with him, and they occupied a cabin by themselves. The family of Goldsby Childers also made their home in one of the cabins of the new fort. The oldest son, Frank Childers, served with the rangers while the younger son, Robert Childers, was a volunteer not officially enlisted with Coleman's battalion.[53]

Commonly known as Little River Fort, Sergeant Erath's new compound was consistently referred to as Fort Smith by the rangers during late 1836 and into 1837. It was named for Major William H. Smith, who made the fort his headquarters during part of 1837.

★ ★ ★ ★ ★

Controversial Death at Coleman's Fort

While Erath's detachment was building Little River Fort, a huge controversy developed at Coleman's Fort in early November. Colonel Coleman was in the field at the time helping to lay out the new road, and Captain Walden had been sent on his supply mission, leaving his

Company A under the command of First Lieutenant Alexander Robless. The men at Fort Colorado, or Coleman's Fort, would remain under Robless's charge until early January 1837.

A soldier from Company A died while being disciplined by Lieutenant Robless. A muster roll entry for this company states that Private Fee C. Booker committed suicide on November 8, 1836.[54]

The men of the company, however, did not see Booker's death as a suicide. Their acting commander, Lieutenant Robless, was not respected by his men. Frontiersman Noah Smithwick, who joined the ranger battalion at this post shortly after this episode, paints a different picture of the events regarding the accidental death of Booker.

There was in Coleman's company a man who had been a United States regular; some said a deserter. However that may be, he was, by virtue of his military knowledge, raised to the rank of lieutenant, upon which he proceeded to visit upon his subordinates the abuses which he may have undergone at the hands of some upstart cadet. Among the men was one poor fellow who had a weakness for intoxicants, which he would indulge whenever an opportunity offered. Having imbibed too freely, Lieutenant R[obless] ordered him tied up to a post all night to sober off. The man was so completely under the influence as to be unable to maintain an upright position; his limbs gave way, and he sank so that the cord around his neck literally hung him. The outburst of indignation frightened [Robless] and he skipped out, leaving Colonel Coleman to bear the odium of the inhuman deed.[55]

Robless apparently stayed with his company until the wave of controversy became overwhelming. Such discipline was certainly not typical of the early Texas Rangers. In fairness to Colonel Coleman, he was not present at the time to prevent this tragedy. He was an organizer and leader of the early rangers during 1835 and 1836, but the negligent death at the frontier outpost bearing his name would end up costing Coleman his command in short time.

★   ★   ★   ★   ★

Burton and Burleson's Battalions Disband
The Texas Rangers had had their strongest showing during the early fall of 1836. With the approach of winter, service terms for two of the ranger battalions were nearing completion. Neither of these two

battalions saw any major skirmishes during the fall months, but their presence obviously helped to keep Indian hostilities in check.

Among those companies completing their service were the remnants of the Second Division of Rangers under Major Isaac Burton, who had completed his own service on September 24. The ranger company of Captain William Hill was disbanded several weeks later in mid-October. The third company of the Second Division, under Lieutenant Samuel Smith, served through October 25. According to the military papers of Private Felix W. Goff, Captain Dickinson Putnam's company was disbanded in Columbia on November 1, 1836.[56]

Edward Burleson was occupied during November, disbanding the companies of his First Division of Rangers as their service periods ended. Captain Jesse Billingsley had entered service as a representative to the First Congress of Texas in Columbia on October 2, leaving his ranger command behind. Bounty Land Certificate No. 3056 was issued to Billingsley for his service in the ranging service from July 1 through October 1, 1836.[57]

Many of Billingsley's men were taken under command of Captain John McGehee for the balance of their enlistments. McGehee's own company had been mustered in on July 1 for a four-month period. At the end of this time frame, Burleson was busy issuing payment notes to the men who had provided services to his companies.

Samuel Gochier was issued a promissory note on November 15 for forty dollars for eight days of hauling supplies for Burleson's rangers. The service papers of Private John Litton show that he was discharged on November 18 "on the Colorado" by Captain McGehee and Edward Burleson, "Col. Commanding Rangers," after honorably fulfilling his four-month service. The balance of McGehee's rangers were discharged from service on November 20 at the Colorado.[58]

Captain John York's ranger company was also disbanded on the Colorado on November 20, 1836, at the completion of four months' service. Discharges of men such as William Frels, Alexander Isbell, John H. Isbell, and William Kuykendall were signed by York and Colonel Burleson.[59]

The last of Burleson's First Division to disband was the company of Captain Calvin Boales, originally commanded by Captain Robertson. His men completed their four-month enlistments on November 25, 1836, and were discharged at the three forks of the Little River at Nashville Colony. The honorable discharges of Second Lieutenant Thomas Webb and Private Elijah Robertson were signed by Captain Boales and Edward

Burleson, "Colonel Commanding Rangers."[60]

A small detachment of men continued to serve through at least December 1 under Burleson's command after their formal companies had been disbanded. Burleson himself was discharged from military service on December 22, 1836, on which date he collected his pay in Columbia.[61]

With the passing of these two ranger regiments, defense of the frontiers of Texas was left to Colonel Robert Coleman's battalion in the west and to Major James Smith's three companies in the east.

★ ★ ★ ★ ★

The New Mounted Rifleman Battalion

The First Congress of Texas convened in October 1836. The men of this congress were charged with moving Texas from its revolutionary state to that of a strong independent nation.

The issue of properly providing for the frontier settlements was a key concern. The senate had formed a Standing Committee on Indian Affairs on October 11, of which Sterling Robertson, Robert Anderson Irion, and James Seaton Lester were members. Robertson, of course, had left his commission as a captain of rangers once he was elected into the Texas government. He was instrumental in seeing that these frontier forces were not ignored. After receiving the October 16 letter of Colonel Coleman, which described the need for additional companies in the field, Robertson on October 21 had introduced a bill "for the further protection of the Indian frontier."[62]

When President Houston finally signed this bill on December 5, 1836, it was entitled "An Act to Protect the Frontier." It called for a battalion of mounted riflemen, consisting of five companies of fifty-six men each, totaling 280 men. They would protect the frontier, furnishing themselves with suitable horses, a good rifle, and a brace of pistols. Pay was the same as the army, although they were given an extra fifteen dollars per month for the rifleman furnishing his own horse and arms. Over this battalion of riflemen, the president was authorized to order them to build "such block houses, forts and trading houses as in his judgement may be necessary to prevent Indian depredations."[63]

This act further stated that the president held the power to call these men to service with the army or at points other than the frontiers if such emergencies existed. The president was also authorized to appoint "agents to reside with the Indians" and could distribute gifts to them where deemed necessary, providing that these did not exceed the amount of $20,000.

This act also gave the president the power to enlarge the ranger battalion to a full regiment of 560 men in ten companies, "should a larger force be necessary."

Congress passed another military act that provided for the "National Defense by Organizing the Militia." This was approved by President Houston on December 6 and was the first attempt to further define the Texas militia since its organization by the General Council of the provisional government on November 27, 1835. This act provided full instructions on the men to be enrolled, how they were to be armed, and how the service was to organize itself.

Although well defined, this act was not yet destined to be fulfilled, owing largely to the strong showing of the army in Texas.

On December 10 the First Congress passed an act adopting a national seal and standard for the Republic of Texas. The national flag would be called the "National Standard of Texas," and it would feature "an azure ground, with a large golden star central." This lone star would become synonymous with Texas in the decades to follow.

In another act passed on December 10, 1836, Congress further refined the role of the frontier battalion that would take the field for the coming year. Both houses passed an act "defining the pay of Mounted Riflemen, now and hereafter in the ranging service on the frontier." Each mounted rifleman entering the ranging service was entitled to twenty-five dollars per month in pay, plus the same bounty of land as other volunteers in the field. A captain would receive seventy-five dollars per month, a first lieutenant sixty dollars per month, a second lieutenant fifty dollars per month, and the orderly sergeant forty dollars per month.[64]

Section Three of this act makes a very important note

> That all officers and soldiers who have been actually engaged in
> the ranging service since July 1835, shall be included in this act,
> and shall receive pay for the time he is in service.

Most accounts on the Texas Rangers have this service being legally created by the act of October 17, 1835. The fact that Congress recognized the ranger service as being created in July gives credence to Robert Coleman being the driving force behind this service's true organization. Less formalized ranger companies had, of course, served Texas since the 1820s.

Once the new mounted rifleman battalion was authorized, Congress nominated and appointed the new leaders of the ranger service. President Houston appointed William H. Smith as major of the battalion of rangers on December 14, 1836. Smith had served as major of Texas cavalry from July 18 and now would continue as the number two man under Colonel Robert Coleman.[65]

In short time Smith would actually replace Coleman in the fallout of the controversial death of the Company A soldier. "Colonel Coleman was deposed by General Houston, and Major Smith appointed to take his place," wrote ranger George Erath.[66] Although Smith was appointed in mid-December, it would be several weeks before he actually replaced his predecessor.

Several of the newly appointed officers—Tommy Barron, Charles Curtis, and David Campbell—were men who were already in service with Colonel Coleman's battalion. The other men were all veterans of either various Texas Revolution companies or ranger type units. Stephen McLaughlin, named as one of the new second lieutenants, had previously served in Captain William Smith's cavalry company from April 12 to July 12, 1836. Robert Lusk had recently completed service as orderly sergeant of Captain John M. Bradley's San Augustine Volunteers, a company formed after San Jacinto. Lusk and John Applegate had also fought in Captain John Bradley's volunteer company during the Béxar siege. Nathan Mitchell had served in Captain William Hill's

---

Mounted Rifleman Battalion
New Officer Appointments: December 14, 1836

Major Commanding:	SECOND COMPANY	FOURTH COMPANY
William H. Smith	Mina (Bastrop) County	(County unspecified)
Battalion Surgeon:	*Captain:*	*Captain:*
Alexander Ramsey	Micah Andrews	Thomas Hudson Barron
Assistant Surgeon:	*First Lieutenant:*	*First Lieutenant:*
Robert Montgomery	John H. Wade	Charles Curtis
	Second Lieutenant:	*Second Lieutenant:*
	Nicholas Wren	David Wilson Campbell
FIRST COMPANY	THIRD COMPANY	FIFTH COMPANY
(Gonzales County)	(Shelby County)	(County unspecified)
Captain:	*Captain:*	*Captain:*
William M. Eastland	Robert O. Lusk	Daniel Monroe
First Lieutenant:	*First Lieutenant:*	*First Lieutenant:*
Joel Walter Robison	John P. Applegate	William H. Moore
Second Lieutenant:	*Second Lieutenant:*	*Second Lieutenant:*
Nathan Mitchell	David Strickland	Stephen McLaughlin

rangers, while William H. Moore had recently completed a six-month stint as first lieutenant of a mounted unit in General Thomas Green's brigade.

Three other new appointees, Micah Andrews, William Eastland, and Nicholas Wren, had recently served in Captain McGehee's ranger company of Colonel Burleson's division. Coleman likely suggested some of these nominations, as Eastland, Wren, and Robison had served with him on the 1835 ranger campaign under Colonel John Moore.

The First Congress specified that three of these new rifleman companies were to patrol the counties of Mina (later Bastrop), Gonzales, and Shelby.[67] The newly approved mounted rifleman battalion would actually replace the three-company battalion under Coleman's command.

★   ★   ★   ★   ★

Downsizing of Major James Smith's Battalion

This revamped frontier ranging service act on December 5 would also replace the need for the three short-term East Texas ranging companies still in the field in Nacogdoches County. By the time the new officers of the mounted rifleman battalion were named on December 14, two of these three had already completed their service.

Captain Elisha Clapp's company had completed work on the Trinity River Fort during its three months. He disbanded his rangers at "Headquarters Mustang Prairie" on December 12, 1836. The discharge papers of Private Isaac Parker state that the men were discharged on this date "by the limitation of an order from General Sam Houston," which caused the company's end. Parker's discharge was signed by Elisha Clapp, Captain, Company of Rangers.[68]

Also disbanding by orders of President Houston was the ranger company of Captain Michael Costley. With Captain George Jewell's men, they had been assigned to complete the work on Fort Houston in present Anderson County. The secretary of war had also required the companies under Costley and Captain Jewell to construct two additional blockhouses and a ferryboat at the upper crossing of the Trinity River.

Jewell's men refused this additional labor on the west bank of the Trinity, although the two companies did complete Fort Houston. Major James Smith was only involved with the companies he organized for a brief period of time. Under orders from Sam Houston, he left his post to attend to other business, for which some of the men accused him of deserting them. Houston later wrote that he had granted the leave and that "Smith has [not], therefore abandoned his post!"[69]

In Smith's absence, the Fort Houston troops promptly promoted Major Jewell into command of the two companies. He made a verbal report to the war department in Columbia that his men had no intentions of completing the Trinity River Fort. Houston was bitterly disappointed in the belligerence of Jewell's men, who failed to submit regular reports and muster rolls. He wrote that Jewell

> disobeyed the very orders he had received—but reported that when those detailed were ordered to perform the duty for which they were stationed at that point—their reply was, that *by God they had come to fight, and they would be damned if they were going to work for anybody, or obey any such orders.* The consequence of this determination, on their part was, that the country derived no benefit from them, but sustained an injury.

Jewell was named major about October 26, at which time Squire Haggard was promoted to captain of the company at Fort Houston. Second Corporal Washington Oakley was promoted to second lieutenant of the company on this date.[70]

Sam Houston refused to acknowledge Major Jewell's new promotion, sending word that these men would not receive pay or land bounties if they did not behave. He wrote that with the exception of completing Fort Houston, Jewell's rangers "disobeyed every order given to them." Despite commissary George Browning's efforts in provisioning these troops, Houston claimed that the rangers "made spoil of the citizen stock, and other property" vital to the subsistence of the community.

Captain Costley's three-month company completed its required service period, and his men were discharged from duty on December 11, 1836. This left Major Jewell in charge of the forty-odd men of Captain Haggard's six-month company, the only rangers left on duty in East Texas. Haggard's men spent their time patrolling the area about Fort Houston.

The fort these rebellious volunteers had completed was a solid fortification. A stockade measuring about 150 by 80 feet surrounded the main blockhouse and two rows of cabins inside Fort Houston's walls. The original blockhouse, started in 1835, was modified.

Anderson County historian Mary Kate Hunter later had occasion to view Fort Houston. She wrote that the main blockhouse was "a building made of heavy hewn logs, about 25 feet square, 10 feet high, with but one entrance, strongly barred from within." A second story was added on top of this structure. It stood "about eight feet high, jutting over the first about two feet all round, with portholes for directing fire laterally." There were also openings between the upper and lower story through which rifles could be fired perpendicularly against "any daring savage who might approach the wall."[71]

Captain Haggard's rangers remained on duty at Fort Houston into early 1837, and battalion commissary Browning continued to supply these men. Haggard did take in several new recruits toward year's end, including George Kimbro and John Sheridan, the latter having previously served under Captain Costley.

★　★　★　★　★

Harvey Massacre and Karnes' Cavalry

Although less frequent, there were still occasional incidents with the Indians during the late months of 1836. An attack was made during late November in Robertson's Colony against the home of John B. Harvey, located twenty-five miles above Tenoxtitlan on the east side of the Brazos River.

Harvey, thirty-one, his wife, Elizabeth, twenty-six, and their two children had arrived from Alabama and been sworn in as Robertson's colonists on January 9, 1836. The attack was vicious, with the parents and their son, William, being murdered and scalped. The blood of Elizabeth Harvey was found splattered across the open pages of the family's Bible. Six-year-old daughter Ann Harvey was taken captive with a servant girl. The two were later sold as slaves for the price of a few blankets and were recovered by Ann's uncle, James Talbot, after four years in Mexico.[72]

News of the attack was published in the *Telegraph and Texas Register* on Friday, December 30, spreading more fear. Captain Thomas Barron, the ranger commander at Tenoxtitlan, wrote to Senator Robertson on December 22 with details of the Harvey massacre. Barron signed his letter as "Comd at Tenoxtitlan." He urged Robertson and Congress to do something to help guard the frontier.

> Your Honorab[le] Body are well aware of the situation of the company of rangers under my command. We are without clothing, ammunition or provision and it under these circumstances is expected of us to guard a frontier of 170 miles . . .
>
> I am trying to raise volunteers to join my company and follow them Indians and if I raise none, I will follow them and find where they go. As from every circumstance, they are Norther[n] Indians.[73]

At the time Barron was urging more help on the frontiers, the First Congress of Texas was allowing for more military buildup. A joint resolution on December 22 authorized the army to receive any number of volunteers up to forty thousand men to meet any renewed invasion attempts from Mexico. "An Act to Organize and Fix the Military Establishment of the Republic of Texas," approved by Sam Houston on December 20, also helped organize the military. In addition to the new mounted riflemen, existing volunteer companies and militia, the Texas army was to consist of one regiment of cavalry, one regiment of artillery, and four regiments of infantry.[74]

General Felix Huston was passed over for senior brigadier general of the army, the senate instead selecting Albert Sidney Johnston, who had previously served as adjutant general of the army with the rank of colonel.

Veteran scout and cavalry company commander Henry Wax Karnes was given command of the Texas cavalry. Karnes had served as a captain of cavalry from March 20 to September 22, 1836, "at which time he resigned." Republic of Texas War Department records show that Karnes was appointed "Colonel of the First Regiment of Cavalry" on January 2, 1837, and served as such continually through March 14, 1838.[75]

His cavalry battalion would primarily serve the western frontiers of Texas beyond the reaches of the mounted riflemen and rangers. It appears that the first company to organize under Colonel Karnes was that of Captain Erastus "Deaf" Smith, a hero of the Texas Revolution. His company was assigned to range the area west of San Antonio on to the Texas border at the Rio Grande, a virtually treeless plain some 150 miles wide that stretched from the Gulf Coast to the western mountains.[76] From San Antonio, Smith began recruiting his company, which was alternately classified as either a ranger company or a cavalry company, while camped below town on the San Antonio River during the late days of December 1836.

During early 1837 Henry Karnes concentrated his cavalry forces in the south central and coastal areas of Texas. He placed Lysander Wells' men at San Patricio on the lower Nueces River, James W. Tinsley's men along the coastal areas near Copano Bay, and companies under Deaf Smith and Juan Seguín in the San Antonio area.[77]

At least one cavalry company, however, was stationed as far east as the Sabine River. First Lieutenant David L. Kokernot and a small detachment of cavalrymen were assigned in November 1836 to command Post Sabine, located on the Texas border. This post was likely located near the important Gaines' Ferry crossing (near the present Highway 21 bridge over the Sabine in Sabine County) which led to Natchitoches, Louisiana.[78]

The army stationed troops at such important river crossings on the Sabine River from late 1836 until at least September 1837. These troops often assisted official travelers in crossing the river, prevented soldiers without proper orders from using the more accessible crossings, and apprehended deserters.

Captain William C. Swearingen assumed command of Post Sabine on February 20, 1837, and his company remained on duty through August 31, 1837. Private George W. Davis, who had been named as one of four regional ranger superintendents during the revolution, served six months under Captain Swearingen. It is interesting to note that Davis's military papers state that he was honorably discharged from the "Company of Rangers" stationed at this post. He was discharged on May 14, 1837, by a ranger pay paper signed by Barnard E. Bee, Secretary of War and Captain Swearingen, Captain Commanding Post Sabine.[79]

The post-revolution companies designated as part of the cavalry generally served at remote posts or on the frontiers, thus making the argument for their true classification less definitive. Captain José Antonio Menchaca, for example, was captain of a company of mounted scouts that performed basic ranger duties in the San Antonio area from October 1836 until the decline of the Texas army in March 1837. A veteran of San Jacinto, Menchaca organized his nineteen-man company from Mexican-born citizens of the San Antonio municipality. His scouting company fell under the supervision of Colonel Juan Seguín's cavalry regiment.[80]

The acts of the First Congress passed during December were important in shaping the role of the frontier service. The powerful strength of the Texas army would dwindle during 1837 and elevate the importance of the Texas Rangers to a new level.

CHAPTER 10

Elm Creek and Trinity River Fights

January - February 1837

The sweeping changes to the ranger forces dictated by the First Congress took several weeks to complete. Colonel Robert Coleman remained in command of his ranger battalion during December 1836, although the process was already in progress for his own removal.

Major William H. Smith, based initially from Nashville-on-the-Brazos, would eventually command this mounted rifleman battalion during 1837. His quartermasters frequently bought supplies in Nashville, as it was the most sizable town in the Colorado River area at the time. Hauling contracts were arranged, frequently with local merchants and farmers of the Nashville area, to deliver the supplies to Smith's ranger posts.[1]

During January Coleman's battalion still consisted of three companies. Each of these was reorganized by the first of the year. Captain Tommy Barron, the former commander of Company B, took command of the new Company A. His first lieutenant was Charles Curtis, and his second lieutenant was David Campbell. The core of Barron's company was based out of Fort Milam at the Falls of the Brazos, while Orderly Sergeant George Erath and a detachment of Barron's unit was manning the Little River Fort.

The second company under Major Smith was that of Captain Daniel Monroe, a Robertson's Colony settler who had survived an Indian attack on June 4, 1836, and had served with Captain Robertson's rangers. Monroe began recruiting rangers for his Company B during January. He recorded that Private Jesse Bailey "was regularly enlisted in the company of mounted rangers under my command on the 2nd day of January 1837 for the term of twelve months."[2] Company B's first lieutenant was William H. Moore, who had previously served as a lieutenant of cavalry in Captain William E. Harrold's company of Colonel Felix Huston's regiment, which was mustered into service on May 16, 1836. Captain

Monroe's company was ordered to man the Little River Fort in early 1837.

Captain Micah Andrews became captain of Company C at Coleman's Fort during the early days of January 1837. Andrews had come to Texas with his brothers Richard and Reddin Andrews. Richard had been killed during the Texas Revolution while fighting at the Battle of Concepción. Micah Andrews fought at San Jacinto and had served in Captain McGehee's rangers prior to his new commission. The new senior officers of Company C under Andrews were First Lieutenant John H. Wade and Second Lieutenant Nicholas Wren.

Captain William Mosby Eastland became commander of Company D. His audited claims show that he was paid as a captain of rangers beginning December 14, 1836, but it appears that Eastland did not actually take over Company D until about the first of January. Military papers show that Eastland was still in Columbia at the army auditor's office on January 2, 1837.

Eastland had previously served as a first lieutenant on the 1835 Indian campaign under Colonel John Moore. Immediately thereafter, he had enlisted in Captain Thomas Alley's volunteer company on September 28, 1835, and fought with it at Béxar before being discharged on December 13. He lost a black mare in the Béxar siege that Captain Alley valued at sixty dollars. Eastland was also a San Jacinto veteran, and from July through November 1836 he had served with Micah Andrews in the ranger company of Captain McGehee.[3]

The fifth company commander named by Congress for the mounted rifleman battalion was Robert O. Lusk. It does not appear that Lusk was successful in ever raising his company, for Captain Lee C. Smith was in command of Company E of Smith's battalion by March.

★ ★ ★ ★ ★

Sergeant Erath's Elm Creek Fight: January 7, 1837

In consequence to the changes in ranger structures, Captain Barron had sent his first lieutenant, Charles Curtis, to the newly established Little River Fort around Christmas 1836, with orders to take command from Orderly Sergeant Erath. Erath was ordered to "hold myself in readiness to proceed at any moment, under additional special orders still to be sent to Colorado [Coleman's] Fort with notification to Colonel Coleman."[4]

These special orders relieving Coleman arrived at Little River Fort on January 4, 1837, via Sergeant James McLaughlin. En route, however, McLaughlin spotted the tracks of approximately a dozen Indians who were on foot in the area about twelve miles away from the fort on the waters of Elm Creek.

Erath recalled McLaughlin's arrival:

> All was bustle and confusion during the night, as we determined that these Indians should not be allowed to go down the country to do mischief.
>
> Besides mine and Lieutenant Curtis' there were but ten horses belonging to the service. Lieutenant Curtis was properly in command, but he did not intend to go, nor let his horse go, but wanted me to go and take eight or ten men on foot. I was eager to go but opposed to taking men on foot. No decision was made during the night and in the morning it was raining, and continued to rain till the middle of the afternoon. By this time or at least with the closing of day it was decided what we would do, and next morning we started, after the horses were got out of the woods, perhaps by nine o'clock.

When Sergeant Erath set out on the morning of January 6, he had ten rangers under his command on horseback. He also had with him a man named Leishley, who was scouting the country and had been in Texas only a short time. Finally, he had the two younger boys, Robert and Francis "Frank" Childers. Francis had served until November as a member of Captain Calvin Boales' rangers. Four other young men from the settlements started out with Erath's party. These men had lived in the country prior to the Runaway Scrape and had come out to look after their property. As they were now starting for home, they agreed to also accompany this patrol as far along as the settlements. Once Erath's party had proceeded about six miles, they parted company to head toward their homes in Nashville, about sixty miles away.

This left Erath with thirteen men. Ten were servicemen from his ranger detachment, and three were volunteers. According to Erath, rangers Lewis Moore, Morris Moore, and Green McCoy "were mere boys, two of them not fifteen years old, but expert with the rifle, good woodsmen, good hunters, and they had good rifles." Lee Davis was armed with two good pistols, while volunteer scout Leishley had one. Jack Hobson carried a musket, and young John Fokes, not very experienced with the frontier life, carried a shotgun.

Ranger Green McCoy was a paternal nephew of the ranger Jesse McCoy, who had perished at the Alamo. David Clark was from Lincoln County, Missouri, son of Captain Christopher Clark.[5] Erath felt that all

George Bernard Erath (1813-1891) was regularly employed as a Texas Ranger throughout the republic years of Texas. On January 7, 1837, he led a small detachment of Colonel Coleman's rangers in a fight with Indians on Elm Creek. From DeShields' *Border Wars of Texas*.

his men were proficient in handling a rifle. He carried "a very good rifle and fine pistol, and with McL[aughlin] was the best mounted."[6] Only Erath, Davis, McLaughlin, and Jack Hobson had ever been involved in an Indian encounter before. Hobson's previous Indian encounter had been during the attack on the Goldsby Childers party on June 4, 1836, in which he had fled for his life instead of fighting.

After only a few hours along their way, the ranger party struck the Indian trail and were startled to find not the tracks of a dozen-odd Indians on foot, but what appeared more like one hundred! All indications were that the Indians were proceeding through the country down toward the nearest pioneer settlements. Erath's party followed and came upon a camp the Indians had kept the previous day.

Their fires were still there; they had erected eight or ten shelters out of sticks and grass; each could shelter eight or ten men. The trail made a plain road; it was no trouble to follow. An Indian, or an old hunter, could have told by the cut of the moccasin soles to what tribe they belonged; but we did not have the art, and were perplexed on the subject. It was agreed that if they were wild Indians we could manage them; but if Caddos, or the like, we might find our hands full.

Sergeant Erath's rangers would have their hands more than full. By nightfall on January 6, they were about twenty-three miles from Little River Fort and about eight miles from where Cameron now stands. At this point they lost the trail, but they soon heard the Indians calling to each other in the bottom less than a half mile away. Erath fell back about a half mile and sent scouts James McLaughlin and Robert Childers on ahead to reconnoiter. They returned before midnight without having had any luck in finding the Indian camp.

About 4:00 a.m. on January 7, the rangers quietly saddled their horses and tied them off to trees. They proceeded ahead on foot to where they had lost the trail and found it again at dawn. It led down a ravine, which they followed. The ravine ran parallel with a creek, known as Elm Creek in present Milam County, several hundred yards to another ravine at right angles, and at that point the Indians were found to have turned square down to the creek.

Following toward this creek, Erath's men could hear the Indians coughing. Creeping up a bank across a bend in the creek, they suddenly came into full view of the Indian party. Erath recalled that all were

> dressed, a number of them with hats on, and busy breaking brush and gathering wood to make fires. We dodged back to the low ground, but advanced toward them, it not yet being broad daylight. Our sight of them revealed the fact that we had to deal with the formidable kind, about a hundred strong. There was not time to retire or consult. Everyone had been quite willing to acquiesce in my actions and orders up to this time. To apprehensions expressed I had answered that we were employed by the government to protect the citizens, and let the result of our attempt be what it might, the Indians would at least be interfered with and delayed from going farther down the country toward the settlements.

The Indian force was camped in a horseshoe bend of the creek. Erath's men took position at a point under the bank of the creek. It was still dark enough that some of the men could not even see the sights of their guns. The believed their distance to be about fifty yards away, although it later proved to be more like twenty-five yards. While waiting on the sun to provide more light, the rangers were surprised to find a large spotted dog come from camp and approach them. The Indians had still not seen the Texans, and luckily the dog merely gave them a look and quietly trotted back to the Indian camp.

At the command, the Texans took first fire and dropped some of the Indians around the fires. Most of the Indians stooped to gather their guns and then took cover behind trees. A savage yell was raised, and they returned fire on Erath's men. The Indians quickly flanked out from both sides of camp to surround the Texans and estimate their strength. Half of the Texan party had jumped up on the bank of the creek to fire. "Had we all had pistols, or the six-shooters of the present day," Erath later wrote, "we could have charged them and kept them running."

As it was, they were forced to maintain their position to reload their guns. The Indians opened a heavy fire with their rifles, but no bows and arrows were seen. Erath's men noted that the powder used by the Indians cracked louder than their own and that the report of a shotgun was heard but once or twice out of five or six hundred shots.

After several minutes of exchanging gunfire near the creek, ranger David Clark and young volunteer Frank Childers fell mortally wounded. Shouting at the wounded rangers to fall back as far as they could, Erath ordered his men to retreat in two squads to the other side of the creek. He told them to reach the top of the bank and to cover themselves behind trees, which they did. Erath himself maintained position and covered their retreat from under the creek's bank. He carefully loaded his gun and watched the Indians approach. Once his men were posted, the Indians "commenced charging with a terrible yell."

Sergeant Erath retreated to the other side of the creek but suddenly found himself under a steep bank of five or six feet height. The Indians rushed forward, jumping down the bank to the spot he had just vacated. One armed Indian took aim and fired at Erath from point-blank range but somehow missed his mark. "I couldn't miss him, and he fell right before me."

The crack of Erath's gun and the firing of his other rangers from their new cover above the creek sent the Indians again scrambling back a few feet behind the trees on the other bank. As Erath fired his lethal shot at the Indian from point-blank range, the concussion of his heavily charged rifle knocked him off balance. When one of his rangers called to ask if he was hurt, the German immigrant replied, "No, I'sh not hurt: my gun knocks down before and behind!"[7]

Erath desperately attempted to scramble backwards up the steep

Sergeant Erath's Elm Creek Battle: January 7, 1837		
Acting First Lieutenant:	John Fokes	*Volunteers:*
George Bernard Erath [1]	Jacob Gross	Francis Childers [2]
First Sergeant:	John Hobson	Robert Childers
James McLaughlin	Green McCoy	____ Leishley
Third Sergeant:	Lewis Moore	[1] Erath was officially an
Lee R. Davis	Morris Moore	orderly sergeant during
Privates:	Empson Thompson	this period.
David Clark [2]		[2] Killed in fight.

creek bank, so as to continue facing his enemy. Grasping a tree root with one hand, he swung partially up but fell back down. His men yelled to see if he was wounded. "No," he hollered back, "help me up the bank!"[8]

Rangers Lewis Moore and Empson Thompson laid down on the ground, reached their hands down, and pulled Erath up with his gun. Rallying his troops, Erath had Sergeant Davis fall back about fifty feet with one squad to a new position. The rest of the men covered their movement before also falling back about the same distance beyond them. The men continued to stand and retreat in alternate groups until they had covered several hundred yards back to an open bottom. The trees were elms of about six-inch diameter, and the balls from the Indian rifles struck them all around.

The left group of Texans reached the gully bank from which they had first descended. A big thicket lay on the opposite side. At this point the Indians charged "with great fury and yells, and we could not be blamed for seeking shelter." Seeing Indians dashing towards them on the right, McLaughlin and Erath took shelter behind a big tree. McLaughlin raised his gun to shoot but suddenly found it to be useless. In the midst of the running fight, an Indian ball had broken McLaughlin's ramrod, another had broken his gunlock, and yet another had gone through his powder horn and emptied the powder! Another shot went through the handkerchief on McLaughlin's head, cutting his hair. Still another passed through his coat without hitting him.

Erath's gun was loaded, and he took good aim at a bunch of Indians close by but did not have time to see the effect of his shot. McLaughlin and Erath ran to another thicket, while the Indians, continuing their loud yelling, managed to interpose themselves between these two men and the others.

These two ran fifteen or twenty steps more, finally reaching the ravine that went square up from the creek. At this point they found wounded ranger Clark, who said something to them about fighting to the last or that they would all be killed. McLaughlin said that his gun had been broken and he now had nothing to fight with. Clark urged him to take his, but McLaughlin did not, opting instead to run on up the gully and find the other men. Erath stayed a little longer with Clark "who was then sinking, but went on when I saw a half dozen Indians coming."

Reaching a different prong of the gully, Erath ran two or three hundred yards more before reaching open ground. He then reloaded his gun and spotted some of his men up ahead among the elm trees. He called and they waited for him. By then the Indians no longer advanced after the

Texans but instead headed back. A group of them found the dying Clark, proceeded to yell, and brutally butchered him. The Indians did not find young Frank Childers, who had sat down beside a tree mortally wounded. He leaned his gun upright against it and died there within twenty-five steps of the heaviest fighting.

Erath collected his men and found only one unaccounted for. They correctly guessed that this person (likely Leishley) had fled from the area uninjured. At this time, they heard the Indians turn

> their noise from a yell to a howl. I thought then that they would not stay long in the place, and that we might remain around and later in the day go back to look after our dead men, but I cannot blame my men for rejecting my proposition to do so. Several of them informed me that they would never have gone into the affair except for the possibility of being impeached for cowardice or disobedience to authority.

As it turned out, the Indians when attacked were within eight miles of William Henry Walker's house, where Neil McLennan's family and his son-in-law's family were living. McLennan himself, with his son and two slaves, was at work at the time on Pond Creek some twelve miles higher up. "Women and children left alone might have suffered the next day had we not then turned the Indians from going farther down the country," wrote Erath.

Erath's remaining men retreated from the area and arrived back at Little River Fort that night, Saturday, January 7. The next morning Erath and four other men set out for Colorado Fort "to carry out the orders I had received" concerning Coleman.

Lieutenant Curtis sent Sergeant McLaughlin and a party of about fifteen rangers out from Little River Fort on the day after the battle. They arrived at the scene after nightfall and concluded from signs that the Indians were still in the area. McLaughlin sent one of his men to the Falls of the Brazos via a roundabout way to inform Major Smith and returned with the rest to Little River Fort. The messenger disseminated the information along the way. News of the attack spread to Nashville on the Brazos and into Washington County, creating considerable fear of Indians.

Sergeant McLaughlin's men returned to Little River Fort on the night of January 9 with news of the fresh Indian signs. A big snowstorm came up that night, and sleet and snow delayed all movements or hopes of chasing the Indians. Once the weather cleared, a call was put out to take on the Indians again. Lieutenant Curtis sent a dozen men from the Little River Fort to meet Major Smith and another ranger party coming up from the Falls of the Brazos. With what volunteers he could muster from the settlements, Smith planned a big fight against the Indians.

The ranger company moving up was that of Captain Daniel Monroe. A promissory note issued to John Marlin on January 10 shows that he provided two blankets for the purpose of fitting out Monroe's rangers at the Falls of the Brazos.[9]

Major Smith and Captain Monroe met with Curtis's dozen men and the volunteers. This combined force went to the site of the Elm Creek battle on January 15 and there found Frank Childers untouched where he had died against the tree.

The Indians apparently had stayed in the area only long enough to gather up their own dead, which they later claimed to be ten braves to Erath's two casualties. The Indians carried their casualties about a mile from the field and threw them into a big hole of water.[10]

The joint force under Major Smith returned to the Little River Fort on January 16, feeling secure that the Indians had moved on. Sergeant Erath and his four men arrived back at Little River on the evening of January 16 and heard the details of the men just returning from the battlefield.

A brief account of his fight was noted in the Saturday, January 21, 1837 issue of the *Telegraph and Texas Register*. George Erath chose to never return to this scene.

★ ★ ★ ★ ★

Colonel Coleman Relieved of Command

When George Erath arrived at Fort Coleman on January 9, he delivered the orders from Sam Houston that ultimately relieved Colonel Robert Coleman of his command of the ranger battalion. The wrongful death from several months previous and the scorn of the settlers had left him in a bad situation. Ranger Noah Smithwick remembered that "Coleman was not popular with the settlers [and] his men were allowed too much license in the way of foraging." Although the ranger's death was a result of another officer's negligence, "the settlers and the comrades of the victim preferred charges against Colonel Coleman, on which he was relieved from command."[11]

These relief papers ordered him to report to the War Department in Columbia. Coleman was held as a prisoner under military arrest in Velasco by orders of Sam Houston. He claimed his treatment was "harsh and arbitrary." William Fairfax Gray recorded in his diary on February 22, 1837, that he met Coleman in Velasco. Coleman said that he was poor and, with no means to support himself, he offered to sell as many acres as Gray would buy for seventy-five cents per acre.[12]

The subsequent investigation was months in the process, and while it was still pending Coleman accidentally drowned in a fishing accident about July 1, 1837 when his boat capsized.[13] The *Telegraph and Texas Register* reported on Saturday, July 8, that he had drowned several days prior near Velasco.

In Coleman's absence, Company C's Captain Micah Andrews became senior commander present at the fort on Walnut Creek. Other rangers arrived during the winter to bolster the numbers of those whose commissions had expired. Fortunately, there was no shortage of men whose army terms were expiring.

Noah Smithwick, an original member of Captain Tumlinson's revolutionary rangers, had worked as a blacksmith in the frontier settlements since the summer of 1836. He reentered the ranger service on January 20, 1837, for Private John Husbands, who had originally enlisted in Coleman's Company C on September 6, 1836. Audited military claims show that "Noah Smithwick took his place as a substitute by the consent of Captain Andrews."[14]

The weather was cold and wet during the early weeks of 1837. The ill-provisioned rangers suffered from improper clothing. Buckskin was considered sufficient during warmer weather but tended to draw up uncomfortably when wet. Private Jimmy Manning, for one, found that warming himself by the fire only caused his wet buckskins to shrink to the point that he could not completely conceal himself.[15]

The Texas government did purchase United States army uniforms for the rangers early in 1837. The men, however, found that most of it was undersized. Company C's Private Isaac Castner, being a large man of about two hundred pounds, was given a suit that "would have been snug for a man of 140." Castner could not stuff himself into the uniform and went around to his fellow rangers trying to find a larger suit. None could fit his frame, and Castner's wife ended up ripping open the outseams of his pantaloons and sewing in stripes to add the necessary extra dimensions. She also added an extra stripe down each sleeve and the center of his jacket, so that "a stranger would have taken him for commanding officer on account of his stripes."

Commissary Samuel Wolfenberger received equal laughs from his compatriots after inheriting a suit whose pants legs only reached halfway down his legs. His jacket missed the top of his pantaloons by a full six inches, and his arms extended a foot beyond the sleeves. Wolfenberger "stalked up and down like an animated scarecrow, trying to negotiate a trade." Like others, he eventually pieced his uniform together with strips from a blanket to make it fit comfortably.

Another source of fun for the Fort Coleman rangers during this time was Corporal Samuel K. Blisk of Captain Andrews' company. Smithwick later wrote:

> He was a genuine down-east Yankee, with his peculiar twang scarcely more intelligible to us southerners than the Virginia dialect would have been in Connecticut. The corporal one day killed a fine fat raccoon while out on a hunt, and dressing it neatly hung it up outside his camp to freeze over night, thereby destroying the disagreeable flavor attached to an adult male raccoon. During the night, the guard stole the coon, roasted and ate it, piling the bones up before Blis[k]'s camp.
>
> The old fellow had stood the teasing of the boys quite patiently, but that was the last feather, and if he could have found the thief there would have been trouble.[16]

★ ★ ★ ★ ★

Anderson-Faulkenberry Slayings: January 28, 1837

While Coleman's rangers battled the lack of suitable uniforms, the rangers stationed at Fort Houston in present Anderson County were battling more formidable foes. Indians in East Texas were continually raiding the pioneers' settlements and stealing horses. In a letter dated January 27, 1837, Daniel McLean, the first settler of what became present Houston County, described the conditions. McLean had first come to Texas in 1812 with the Gutierrez-Magee Expedition, had been one of only ninety-three survivors of a deadly Indian battle on the Medina River on August 18, 1813, and had in 1821 become one of the "Old Three Hundred" original settlers of the Austin Colony.[17]

McLean wrote to his son James, who was in school at the time in Natchitoches, of the conditions in the area. He described George Erath's recent Elm Creek fight with the Indians and that he had lost horses recently to Indians.

> I have no prospect of getting any of my horses but a great prospect of losing the few that I have—the Indians have been in the neighbourhood a few days back and have stolen every horse

that Mr. Greenwood had. Since the[y] have stolen two from the rangers at Houston so that we may suppose that at the rise of grass the[y] will be on all sides . . . .

There is various reports about the Mexicans. It is generally believed the[y] are making every preparation to invade us in the spring. It is supposed that there is from four to six thousand troops at Matamoros and several thousands more coming on. We get no news authentic . . . Our army is said to be one thousand strong.

Ironically, the next major encounter with hostile Indians occurred against the white settlers of the newly established Fort Houston on the day after McLean's letter was penned. The rangers here were under command of Captain Squire Haggard and Major George Jewell as of this date. The incident on January 28, 1837, involved six rangers—eighteen-year-old Abram Anglin, David Faulkenberry, Evan Faulkenberry, James Douthit, James Hunter, and Columbus Anderson.

Anglin was a native of Kentucky, born December 28, 1817, who had immigrated with his parents to Illinois in 1818. He had come to Texas in 1833 with the Parker family, only then to endure their massacre in May 1836. He and fellow massacre survivors Evan and David Faulkenberry had since settled near Fort Houston.[18]

Hunter and Douthit had served in Lieutenant Samuel Smith's Third Company of Rangers through October 1836 and were under Captain Haggard's command at Fort Houston as of January. Jewell's original muster roll includes C. Columbus Anderson, who served under Haggard after Jewell's promotion.

On January 28, 1837, the six-man ranger party was dispatched from Fort Houston for the Trinity River bottom to search for stray hogs. They found some of the hogs on the east side of the river, which they sent back to the fort via Hunter and Douthit. These two promised to return from the fort the next day with a canoe with which to cross the river in search of more hogs.[19]

The other four rangers became impatient and improvised their own log raft in the meantime. They then crossed the Trinity at a point that later became known as Bonner's Ferry. After spending the late morning hours searching unsuccessfully, they returned to the river to await Hunter and Douthit with their canoe.

Upon arriving back at the river, the rangers were startled to find a large number of fresh moccasin tracks near the water but dismissed them as friendly Indian tracks. Being cold and tired from their morning's search, they sought shelter beneath the riverbank and lay down to take a nap. According to Anglin, they "were soon aroused by the war whoops and firing of a party of about thirty dastardly red skins," who had crept to within fifteen feet of them.

The Indians fired on the unsuspecting Texans with rifles and bows and arrows. The fact that all four were not immediately slaughtered is surprising. Columbus Anderson was hit by the first shot and was mortally wounded. David Faulkenberry was also mortally wounded, but he called out, "Come on, boys, it's time to go!" With that, Anderson and Faulkenberry both plunged into the Trinity and swam across in spite of their wounds.

Abram Anglin had a bullet pass through his powder horn and penetrate his thigh, carrying fragments of the horn into his flesh. Evan Faulkenberry, the fourth man, took protection behind some trees while the Indians fired from behind a bluff. Anglin, unable to assist, took to the river and swam for his life. He relates:

> As I was swimming, the Indians were discharging their arrows, and while climbing the opposite bank, I received several other slight wounds. Weak and exhausted, however, as I was, I reached the bank, where I found David Faulkenberry too badly wounded to travel. He told me to escape if I could and hasten back relief. Poor fellow, I knew he would soon be gone, but I did not know that I would survive him long.

Good fortune greeted Anglin, who after traveling only about four hundred yards, encountered James Hunter, who was returning early from Fort Houston with a canoe. Jumping onto the back of his horse, Anglin stated that they "rode as rapidly as possible for the fort."

Captain Haggard sent out a relief party from Fort Houston that night to search for survivors of the Indian attack. The rangers found the body of David Faulkenberry. He had cut some long grass near a pool of water, upon which he had laid down to die. The body of ranger Columbus Anderson was found an amazing two miles from the scene of the attack. After swimming the river, he had apparently gone as far as his body would hold out, even though he had two arrows protruding from his neck!

The body of the other ranger, Evan Faulkenberry, was not found. His footsteps were found behind the tree from which he was last seen firing. The tracks led down the bank a short distance to where they disappeared. The stream was sounded for his body, but it was never found and

Abram Anglin was nineteen years old when wounded by Indians in an attack on January 28, 1837, in which his three fellow rangers were killed. Anglin had also survived the Parker's Fort massacre eight months prior. From DeShields' *Border Wars of Texas.*

he was never heard from again. One Indian tale claimed that Faulkenberry had fought like a wild man, killing two Indians and wounding a third. When he had been wounded and scalped, Faulkenberry was said to have jerked away from the Indians, thrown himself into the river, and swam to the middle before sinking from sight.

Anglin, now a veteran of the Parker's Fort massacre and this latest slaying near Fort Houston, recovered from his wounds. After Captain Haggard's company was disbanded, he would join another ranger force in March 1837.

Two weeks after the rangers were killed, Secretary of War William Fisher issued stern orders on February 13 to Major Jewell, commander of "rangers at Post Houston." Due to the Indians' "late outrage," Jewell was asked to call on James Smith, Captain Costley, Daniel Parker, or Captain Clapp to "procure copies of orders heretofore issued by the Executive and strictly comply with the directions contained in the same."[20]

Major Jewell was chastised for the slackness of his rangers in following President Houston's prior orders.

> The first orders for the erection of a blockhouse and a ferry boat [on the Trinity] were issued five months since, and a part of this time more than one hundred men might have been employed for that purpose. The care advised by the President has been utterly disregarded and owing to that alone is to be attributed the present melancholy accounts.
>
> You will perceive the necessity of preserving the most sleepless vigilance and keep out guards under all circumstances and never allow [your] enemy the slightest opportunity to catch you off your guard.

Captain Haggard's company continued to serve at Fort Houston through early March. Evidence of their continued use of this fort is apparent from audited republic claims. "Adrin" Anglin was given a note for supplying two bushels of corn for the troops at Fort Houston on March 10. Anglin had previously provided 125 pounds of pork to the troops at this fort on February 17. These receipts were signed by ranger quartermaster George Browning.[21]

Receipts of Private John Sheridan show that he furnished bacon for the troops on the road on February 19. Sheridan had previously furnished corn and pork for the troops "on the road" and ten bushels of corn that was sent to Fort Houston on December 8, 1836. He had also provided corn and fodder to Jewell's men on October 30, 1836.[22]

A receipt of corn and bacon furnished to Haggard's company on March 13, 1837, places the company in Nacogdoches.[23] They had apparently departed Fort Houston and were discharged on March 19, perhaps in San Augustine. The rangers' discharge papers do not list a specific place. Captain Haggard signed each man's discharge paper with the statement that he

> carries with him the thanks of his commanding officer and merits the applause of his countrymen and is hereby honorably discharged by expiration of his term of enlistment.[24]

The slaying of rangers Columbus Anderson and David and Evan Faulkenberry was the closest killing to Fort Houston since the Parker's Fort massacre more than seven months prior.

President Houston later blamed the deaths of these rangers at the Trinity on the disobedience of Major Jewell's own troops in fulfilling his orders. His men died "for the want of a ferry-boat to cross in, or a block-house to protect them." Texas auditor John W. Moody was instructed by Houston not to pay the men who had served under Jewell, Haggard, and Costley because of their conduct while in the field. Houston cited that Haggard's company, "something less than 30 in number," did not even complete a muster roll of their service.[25]

Without such proof of service, Houston felt that "five hundred discharges might be made out, and land scrip and treasury notes drawn to an unlimited amount" on Texas. Captain Costley's belligerence may well have cost him his life. He was shot through the heart in November 1837 in Nacogdoches during an altercation with another man. Frontier leader Jacob Snively indicated in a letter to Sam Houston that, due to his own character, Costley "well deserved his fate."

Following the departure of Captain Haggard's company, the Fort Houston settlement petitioned Sam Houston in Nacogdoches for better defenses. Although he was unable to furnish troops, Houston sent a note for the settlers to present to Fort Jesup, the U.S. Army post near the Louisiana border.

The defenders of Fort Houston, farmers and volunteers, were given a twelve-pounder cannon that weighed 963 pounds. This was transported back to Fort Houston and was properly mounted for use against the Indians. The story of this gun's presence spread quickly, and many felt that it was what kept the Indians from ever making a direct attack on this fort.[26]

★ ★ ★ ★ ★

Fort Fisher/Colorado Area Depredations: February 1837

In the wake of Erath's fight and the removal of Colonel Coleman in early January, the new senior commander of the Colorado River area ranger battalion decided to fortify the area further. In late January Major William Smith took steps to establish new frontier outposts.

By this date he had four companies with Captains Barron, Monroe, Andrews, and Eastland under his command. Captain Daniel Monroe, another former Robertson ranger, had raised enough men to muster in Company B by this time. Fort Colorado, or Coleman's Fort, was under charge of Captain Micah Andrews' Company C. Smith intended to build an outpost at the Waco village on the Brazos River, making it the most remote frontier post. About the end of January, he ordered Captain Tommy Barron's Company A out from Fort Milam to construct this fort. Monroe's company then assumed command of Fort Milam. A receipt for beef donated to the ranger battalion by Albert Gholson shows that his men were in Milam by January 25. This receipt was signed by Monroe's Lieutenant Gabriel Long, who doubled as "Quartermaster of Rangers."[27]

Among those participating in the construction of the new ranger outpost at the Waco village was George Erath of Barron's company. He later wrote that this area had only recently been vacated by the Waco Indians.

Corn stalks were found in the fields they had cultivated, and peach trees were growing where the city now stands. We built some shanties for barracks near the big spring of the river, but only remained there for three weeks, when an order came from the Secretary of War for us to return to the falls [of the Brazos], as we were too far out to do good service. We went back, calling the place we had left Fort Fisher.[28]

This Fort Fisher was named for Secretary of War William Fisher and had been vacated by Captain Barron's rangers by March 1837. Barron's company fell back for a time to Fort Milam. At least some rangers used it during April, however, as Lieutenant Gabriel Long of Monroe's company traveled from there to Columbia and back. Long was quartermaster for Major Smith's battalion, and Smith himself later made his headquarters at Fort Fisher during June 1837 in company with Captain Daniel Monroe's rangers.

Captain Tommy Barron was buried on the grounds of old Fort Fisher in Waco, site of the Texas Ranger Hall of Fame and Museum. This is one of two markers in the cemetery adjacent to the museum that commemorate his service. *Author's photo.*

The Indians were back to their depredations during February 1837. A party of thirty to forty Comanche Indians came down into Fayette County on a horse-stealing expedition. They left behind a bloody carnage and took prisoners.

On their way out from horse stealing, the Comanches came upon the Honorable John G. Robison and his younger brother, Walter Robison. Robison's family had come to Texas in 1831 from Georgia and settled on his headright league on Cummings Creek in present Fayette County. During his session in the First Congress of the Republic of Texas, he had purchased a supply of groceries and sent them to the home of Mr. Stevens, a neighbor who lived some five miles from his home.[29]

Soon after departing Columbia when Congress broke in February, Robison and his brother had gone with a team to the home of Stevens to gather their supplies. The two made it to Stevens' and stayed the night, intending to head home the next morning. One of Judge Robison's sons was Joel Robison, a famed veteran of San Jacinto who had captured Santa Anna and a ranger of the 1835 expedition under Colonel Moore.

Joel Robison, en route from the family home toward Washington-on-the-Brazos the morning after his father had departed, learned that Comanches were in the area and had stolen all of neighbor Mr.

Breeding's horses. Feeling that the Indians would attack his father and brother with their supply of goods, he armed himself and set out about noon toward Stevens' home. Joel Robison:

> I had scarcely gone a mile, when, in the open post oak woods I found my father's cart and oxen standing in the road. The groceries were also in the cart. But neither father nor uncle were there. I had now no doubt of their fate. The conviction that they were murdered shot into my heart like a thunder bolt. Riding on a few yards further, I discovered buzzards collecting near the road. My approach scared them away and revealed to my sight the body of my father, nude, scalped and mutilated. I dismounted and sat down by the body. After recovering a little from the shock, I looked around for uncle. I found his body, also stripped, scalped and mangled, about fifty yards from my father's remains.

The grieving son covered his father and uncle with a coat and saddle blanket. He then piled brush over them to prevent the waiting vultures from devouring them. Then young Joel Robison rode back to break the horrible news to his elderly mother.

On the same day, this band of Indians attacked another family. The Gotcher house was located on Rabb's Creek, near present Giddings in Lee County. James Gotcher (spelled Gotier in some accounts) was an Alabama native who immigrated to Texas in 1835. He and his family had first cut out a trail or road from a lower Texas colony that became known as Gotcher Trace. He had settled there with his family and son-in-law, Mr. Crawford. At the time of the Indian attack, Gotcher, one of his sons, and son-in-law Crawford were away from the home, occupied with cutting and hauling wood from the river bottom.[30]

Two parties of Indians approached the house. They came upon two of the Gotcher children, capturing a little girl and killing and scalping the young boy. Inside the house were Nancy Gotcher, her daughter Jane Gotcher Crawford, and several children. Seeing no men about, the Indians immediately rushed the cabin to attack. The two women used the few guns left for them to fire at their attackers as they burst in. There was not time to reload. A number of arrows were fired into Mrs. Gotcher and one armed Indian finished her life with a blast of his rifle. Mrs. Crawford and her two children, the youngest only two months old, were overpowered and taken captive. Another little boy of Mrs. Gotcher was captured.

James Gotcher, his son, and son-in-law heard the commotion and rushed back toward the cabin to help, running so fast that they left their weapons behind. Seeing their loved ones being killed and captured, they bravely dashed for the house to try for their other guns. They fought desperately but never had a chance to make it through the spears, arrows, and gunfire of the numerous braves. The son fought valiantly, even ripping open the throat of one brave with his teeth. Another young man was mortally wounded, managing to crawl away unobserved and slowly expire with his head upon a rock.

Due to the remote location of Gotcher's home, it was several days before noted frontiersman Edward Burleson casually visited the home and found the scene of the massacre. The news then spread rapidly and put fear into the hearts of the settlers. It was considered too late to find the raiding Indians' trail by the time the news of the murders was found out.

Washington H. Secrest, a resident of the Colorado River, wrote a letter to President Houston on March 1, 1837. Secrest reported that the Indians were killing and stealing livestock in the area, but that the residents could do little to defend themselves. Like many others, he was forced to stay home to defend the women of his household from depredations.

The suffering of the survivors of the Gotcher massacre was even worse. The Indians had taken Mrs. Crawford, her two children, and the little Gotcher daughter. The Indians tried to brutally murder her youngest baby a number of times, but the valiant mother fought them so fiercely over the passing days that the Indians finally cursed her and told her to keep her child.

Crawford and the children endured two years of captivity before being ransomed at Holland Coffee's trading station by a Mr. Spaulding, a trader. Spaulding married the widow and took in the children, returning with them to Bastrop County to settle.[31]

CHAPTER 11

Spring Setbacks for Smith's Battalion

March - May 1837

By the time Abram Anglin was discharged from service with Captain Haggard's Fort Houston area rangers on March 19, he was already an old hand with the Texas Rangers. He had previously served under Captains Hillhouse, Seale, and Parker during the Texas Revolution. Anglin had survived the Parker's Fort massacre in 1836, and most recently on January 2, he had been wounded by Indians at the Trinity River, narrowly escaping with his life. Three of his fellow frontiersmen had been less fortunate.

Anglin remained undaunted by his recent brush with death. The frontier service provided adventure. More importantly, it was a paying job that also rewarded its employees with free land in Texas. Within two weeks of the breakup of Captain Haggard's company, Anglin had found a new ranger unit to join.

The battalion he joined would serve an important role in protecting the frontiers as the Texas army soon began reducing its size. Many of these ranger companies would find their fair share of interesting encounters with Indians during the spring of 1837.

★ ★ ★ ★ ★

Captain Lee Smith's Rangers and Fort Henderson

Private Abram Anglin was among the men who were formally mustered into service on April 1, 1837, under the command of Captain Lee C. Smith. The unit was the fifth company of Major William H. Smith's Colorado River area frontier battalion and was appropriately enough designated as Company E.[1]

Captain Smith and at least five of his men had just completed serving with Captain Haggard's East Texas rangers in March. Republic-era documents show that Lee C. Smith had assumed command of Fort Henderson by March 17, when he began recruiting his six-month ranger company.

This new fort was located on the Navasota River and was apparently built just after Captain Barron's men had completed building Fort Fisher. Fort Henderson was named for General James Pinckney Henderson, a recruiter of Texas army soldiers in the United States.[2]

As with the other posts of Major Smith's rangers, Fort Henderson was located in Indian country out from the nearest white settlements. It was obviously difficult to secure supplies and ammunition at such a remote post, and it appears the fort was destroyed soon after the rangers deserted it. Although the exact location of the fort is unknown, an inspector's report indicates Fort Henderson was located on the upper Navasota River near where the river forms the boundary of Robertson and Leon Counties.

In claims filed by Lee Smith, he signed as "Captain of Cavalry." During the early years of the republic, the terms *rangers, mounted riflemen, cavalry, spies,* and *mounted gunmen* were often synonymous. Service papers for his company clearly show it to have been Company E of Major Smith's ranger battalion. The unit's first lieutenant, Joseph Mather, and Major William Smith signed many discharges from Company E.

Due to Fort Henderson's remote location, Captain Smith was financially responsible for providing for Company E. He was later paid on a claim for furnishing rooms from March 17 to September 17, 1837, for six months for his men at $26 per month. His total claim came to $191.70,

---

Captain Smith's Ranger Company E: March 17 - October 1, 1837

Captain:	Josiah Culp	Alexander Parks *
Lee C. Smith *	William C. Daylrymple	Luther M. Plummer
First Lieutenant:	Brinkley Davis	James P. Rice
Joseph Mather	William C. Davis	John G. Rice
Rank and File:	Stephen Eaton	Augustus W. Slawson
William Allen *	Charles G. Fox	Willson Strickland
Mathew Anderson	John Henry	Robert M. Tyus
Abram Anglin *	Fletcher W. Hubert	John Vance
Seth H. Bates	John R. Hubert	Martin Walker
William Beard	Newton C. Killough	Simon Warwick
Warren Burgess	Artimon L. Martin	William Welch
Hiram B. Bush	W. W. Martin	James Wilson
George Calmes	John McCoy	
Hugh Carroll	Elisha McDonald *	* Previously served with
Samuel Cox	Jacob Mickler	Capt. Haggard's rangers.
Ganey Crosby	James H. Mitchell *	

Note: This incomplete roster compiled from research of Republic of Texas Audited Claims for men whose ranger service records were signed by Captain Smith or Lieutenant Mather.

including $35.70 worth of food he provided to his rangers. During April Smith supplied one twenty-five-pound keg of gunpowder, twenty-five pounds of lead for bullets, twenty bushels of corn, plus pork, beef, and salt. For these provisions and for five days of hauling with his wagon team, Lee Smith was issued a note for $271.50 by Major Smith.[3]

New recruits continued to join Captain Smith at Fort Henderson during the company's service. Seventeen-year-old James P. Rice was a native of Alabama who had freshly arrived in Texas with his older brother John G. Rice. The two brothers joined Smith's company in late May 1837. By the accounts of these two men, Lee Smith's company did not participate in any Indian battles during the next three months.[4]

The other four companies of William Smith's battalion would not escape the attention of hostile Indians during 1837. It was perhaps the lure of just such encounters that attracted men to continue joining the ranger service as the warmer weather set in. Many of the newer recruits were men freshly arriving in Texas, who needed the money and the chance to earn land by serving their new country. Twenty-five-year-old Francis Zellner, for example, immigrated to Texas from Georgia in 1837, joined ranger Company B of Captain Daniel Monroe in April, and later was transferred into Captain Tommy Barron's Company A.[5]

★ ★ ★ ★ ★

Deaf Smith's Laredo Campaign: March 1837

The Texas Congress, while revamping the army and frontier services in December 1836, legislated that a cavalry corps be stationed at designated frontier posts during the following year.

The first of Colonel Henry Karnes' new companies, that of Captain "Deaf" Smith, had formed in San Antonio in late 1836. During the early weeks of 1837, they remained on the San Antonio River below the town as they trained on frontier warfare and took on provisions. One of Smith's first recruits was John Coffee "Jack" Hays, a nineteen-year-old youth who had served in the Texas Revolution. Hays, destined to become one of the most famous Texas Rangers, was advised by President Houston to join Smith's company. Jack Hays' simple mannerisms and sense of humor quickly endeared him to his fellow privates. He passed his twentieth birthday while Smith's spies camped in early January.[6]

Smith's cavalrymen were required to furnish their own horses, rifles, pistols, and equipment, for which they were paid thirty dollars per month for a twelve-month enlistment. One of his new recruits was Francis W. White of San Antonio. White had served with the cavalry in 1836 under Captain Van Norman and Major William Cook. In company service records, Captain Smith recorded detailed facts about his men, as evidenced by White's papers.

> Know ye that private F. W. White of my company of volunteers belonging to the First Regiment of Cavalry in the service of the Republic of Texas was enrolled on the 6th day of February 1837 for the period of four months . . .
>
> Said White was born in Ireland, is thirty years of age, five feet eight inches high, light complexion, dark eyes, black hair, by occupation when enrolled a trader [at] San Antonio de Bexar.[7]

By mid-February 1837 Captain Smith was forced to move his company to the Medina River due to the scarcity of good grazing for their horses.[8]

At the Medina River, Smith's rangers somehow lost their entire stock of horses to either outlaws or Indians on February 21. The audited claims of Private Francis White include a voucher signed by Deaf Smith and Colonel Karnes that describes the loss of his horse.

> This is to certify that a certain bay mare was stolen from my encampment on the Medina on the 21st of Feby 1837 belonging to F. W. White, which was appraised by James S. Lee and Perry James to be worth seventy-five dollars.[9]

Orders arrived from Secretary of War William Fisher at this inopportune time for Smith to conduct a mission to Laredo to assert the Texas claim to that area. Laredo was in early 1837 the only town to the east of the Rio Grande. It was a major crossing point for armies, traders, and outlaws. The townspeople only questionably recognized the sovereignty of the Republic of Texas. With his mission thus assigned him, Captain Smith succeeded in securing new horses for his men for this assignment.[10]

While securing horses, his company took part in a patriotic ceremony in San Antonio on February 25. His rangers joined Lieutenant Colonel Juan Seguín, who commanded another small cavalry corps, in town for the burial of the ashes of the fallen defenders of the Alamo. The remains were collected from three ash piles where they had been burned in March 1836. These were placed in a black coffin, given a full military parade, and were buried with military honors.

Smith's men immediately returned to their Medina River camp to complete preparations for their expedition. They departed on Monday,

March 6, twenty rangers bound to plant the Texas flag on the spire of the church at Laredo.

After traveling ten days through bleak country, Smith's men arrived on the evening of March 16 at the old San Ygnacio Ranch on the Arroyo Chacón, about five miles east of Laredo. There, they discovered five Mexicans, who instantly fled toward Laredo to spread word that Texans were approaching. Captain Smith was unable to overtake the fleeing Mexicans, so his men made camp for the night.

In an official report written ten days later, Deaf Smith described his company's actions on March 17.

> Early the next morning, taking one man with me, I went out to view the road and, if possible, to take a prisoner in order to ascertain the force of the enemy station in the town. I then found the trail of the cavalry sent out to intercept us and returned to camp and prepared for their reception.[11]

The men waited until 1:00 p.m. without sight of the expected Mexican forces. Smith then ordered his unit to fall back a few miles to a spot where their horses could graze on the available grass, as they had gone without the previous night. After proceeding about two miles, Smith again discovered the enemy, this time less than a mile away and advancing on them.[12]

Smith quickly ordered a retreat to the camp he had just left, which had been situated in the dry bed of a river. Before reaching this spot, however, he discovered that a portion of his men were about to be cut off by the pursuing force of forty cavalrymen from the Laredo garrison. Therefore he and his men found it necessary to take cover in a nearby mesquite thicket, where they tied off their horses and prepared for immediate action.

Captain Smith's report describes the March 17 battle.

> We had scarcely prepared for battle when the enemy commenced firing on my right and left, at about 150 yards distant—a portion of their force advancing with great rapidity to my rear—keeping up a brisk firing on my right, left and rear.
>
> When they were about 50 yards distant, I returned their fire, giving strict orders that not a piece should be discharged until every man was sure of his aim. The engagement had continued about forty-five minutes when the enemy retreated, leaving ten killed and taking off about as many wounded.

Private Jack Hays later claimed that the attacking Mexicans shouted such insults as "cowardly Texans" and "damned rascals" as they attacked. They were probably a little surprised to find that "the rangers did not surrender," recalled Hays. He felt that the charging enemy was met with such a heavy volley from the rangers that it "threw them into confusion and completely routed them."[13]

Another of the leading men of Smith's force was Nicholas Mosby Dawson, a veteran of San Jacinto. Smith reported that Dawson's "cool and intrepid conduct afforded great encouragement to the younger soldiers" during the Laredo campaign. Two of Smith's cavalrymen, Peter Conrad and George Dolson, were slightly wounded.

Captain Erastus "Deaf" Smith (1787-1837) served as a key scout for the Texas army during the revolution. His San Antonio area mounted company fought Mexican cavalrymen near Laredo on March 17, 1837. *Archives & Information Services Division, Texas State Library.*

The small band of Texans managed to capture twenty enemy horses, but due to the condition of their own horses were unable to pursue their enemy. Captain Smith decided it more prudent for his small band to retire back to San Antonio rather than continue their Laredo mission. For his men, he wrote that all had fought in the "most gallant manner," even though less than one half "had ever witnessed a field of battle before."

Deaf Smith reported to Secretary of War William Fisher on March 27 that he and his men decided not to enter Laredo after learning from a wounded Mexican left on the battlefield that a considerable enemy force was in that town. After a fatiguing ten-day march, Smith's cavalry company returned to San Antonio on the evening of March 26 with the twenty captured horses.

Upon entering town, Smith noted that there was "no shout of exultation" to welcome them. The San Antonio townspeople obviously showed that "their sympathy was with the enemy." The day after arriving, Smith turned command of his little cavalry unit over to Captain Nicholas Dawson, whom his men elected to this position for his conduct during the Laredo campaign.

Deaf Smith remained involved with the cavalry through at least June 10, 1837, on which date he signed discharge papers for some of the men he had commanded.[14]

In a harsh twist, President Houston was very critical of old friend Deaf Smith's campaign. He wrote a strong letter to Colonel Henry Karnes on March 31, after having received Smith's report from Secretary of War Fisher. He was not pleased that Smith had allowed all of his horses to have been stolen in February and felt that "Smith and his men have acted badly" in their fight with the Laredo Mexicans. Houston added that Smith and his men had made their campaign without his orders and were to draw no more provisions from the merchants of San Antonio.[15]

At least one account offers that Houston may have been angered that Captain Smith's expedition was an action that could have potentially stirred new controversy with Mexico. Others, such as the editors of the *Telegraph and Texas Register*, were much more supportive of the Laredo fight. They bragged of these brave rangers that the Mexican military did not stand a chance "against even half their number of the sturdy backwoodsmen of the west."[16]

After turning over the company to Captain Dawson, Deaf Smith soon retired from military service to settle at Richmond in Fort Bend County, where he died on November 30, 1837. The intrepid scout and hero of the Texas Revolution was honored in 1876 when Deaf Smith County was created from Béxar Territory.[17]

Captain "Deaf" Smith's Laredo Fight: March 17, 1837

Captain:	Abraham Goshay	Francis W. White
Erastus Smith	Owen P. Hardeman	William F. Williams
First Lieutenant:	John Coffee Hays [3]	Daniel Winchell
Nicholas Mosby Dawson [1]	Logan B. Henderson	
Orderly Sergeant:	Perry James	[1] Elected captain of
Dudley W. Babcock	James Matthew Jett	company March 27.
Privates:	Stephen Jett	[2] Slightly wounded.
James C. Boyd	James F. Johnson	[3] Per James K. Greer's
John L. Bray	James S. Lee [4]	*Texas Ranger: Jack Hays in*
Peter Conrad [2]	Mark B. Lewis	*the Frontier Southwest*, 24.
George Dolson [2]	Antonio Lockmar	[4] Detained at San Antonio.
Cyrus Washburn Egery	John C. Morgan	

Today a monument stands at the Lake Casa Blanca golf course club-house near Laredo that describes Captain Smith's battle of March 17. For the Texas Rangers, this battle marked their first encounter west of the Nueces River and an important step in asserting the claim of the Republic of Texas on its territory between San Antonio and the Rio Grande.[18]

★ ★ ★ ★ ★

The Decline of the Texas Army

During the early months of 1837, the Texas army was not nearly as taxed with the threat of Mexican invasion as it had been in the post San Jacinto months.

One of the slated changes in command for the army almost ended in a death. Colonel Albert Sidney Johnston, the adjutant general, had been appointed by the First Congress in December to become the senior brigadier general. President Houston sent word of his promotion to Johnston in New Orleans, where he was conducting business on behalf of the Republic of Texas.[19]

General Johnston arrived at Camp Independence, on the east side of the Lavaca River about five miles from Texana, on February 4, 1837. There Brigadier General Felix Huston, who had been commanding the army during Johnston's absence, challenged him to a duel. Johnston accepted the challenge as his public duty and in order to prove his courage to the somewhat unruly volunteers of the Texan army.

Generals Huston and Johnston faced each other at 7:00 a.m. on February 5 with long horse pistols and began firing upon signal. Incredibly, the two leaders fired, reloaded, and fired their inaccurate dueling pistols at each other five to six times before blood was drawn! Johnston was severely wounded in the right hip, leaving Huston in acting command of the army for the next few weeks while Johnston was bedridden.

By early spring the army's strength had grown with new recruits from New Orleans to more than two thousand men. The lack of battle or even a true campaign caused the discipline of the troops to deteriorate during the early months of 1837. The soldiers rebelled against General Johnston's command at times and often turned to illegal whiskey to relieve their boredom and frustrations.

The main camp for the Texas army from April 22 into mid-June 1837 was Camp Bowie, located on the Navidad River at a point known as Red Bluff, a mile below the little settlement of Texana. In this camp, Colonel Henry Teal was murdered in his sleep on May 5 by another soldier named John G. Schultz. This event and the number of mutinies that had begun occurring in several other army camps compelled President Houston to begin furloughing soldiers during May.

General Johnston, still suffering from his dueling wound, requested that Secretary of War William Fisher relieve him of his command. Fisher delayed replacing him, but Johnston left the army on May 7, delegating his command to his next senior officer, Colonel Samuel C. A. Rogers.

Rogers allowed all discipline to break down over the ensuing two weeks, even abolishing the guard system. President Houston dispatched Secretary of War Fisher on May 18 with sealed orders for the army to furlough three of its four regiments. Once accomplished, this left only about six hundred armed men in Texas. This number trickled down over the coming months with additional furloughs, desertions, and the expiration of enlistment terms.[20]

Fisher arrived at Camp Bowie in the latter part of May and issued furloughs to a large number of the soldiers in this camp. The camp was under command of Colonel Henry R. A. Wigginton, commander of the Second Regiment of Permanent Volunteers, during June. The remaining servicemen of Wigginton's command abandoned Camp Bowie during the middle of June and transferred to Camp Crockett by the third week of that month.[21]

Although the army was mustered out, several companies of cavalry remained in service under Colonel Karnes on the southwestern frontier. Captain Dawson's cavalry spy company remained on duty in the San Antonio area. Jack Hays was promoted to sergeant, and as such he often commanded a patrol party of several men who ranged out distances up to fifty miles from their base camp.

On one occasion Sergeant Hays reportedly led his men to capture Mexican bandits in a sundown surprise roundup. In the ensuing fight, one Texan was wounded and three Mexicans were killed. Taking up the chase of five fleeing bandits, Hays used his pistol to shoot one Mexican from his horse. In the end another bandit was thrown from his horse, while Hays and a fellow ranger reportedly trailed and captured the remaining three outlaws.[22]

★ ★ ★ ★ ★

Lieutenant Wren's Ambush Near Fort Houston

After Sergeant George Erath's battle in January, the rangers under Major Smith saw no significant action with the Indians for several months. Erath was promoted quickly through the ranger ranks. From orderly sergeant, he was promoted to quartermaster sergeant on

February 3, and on April 15, 1837, he was again promoted to acting judge advocate for the battalion.[23]

By mid-March Major William Smith was making his headquarters at his namesake fort, the Little River Fort now called Fort Smith. Captain Monroe's Company B, which had recently taken over command of Fort Smith from Lieutenant Charles Curtis's detachment, was stationed with the Texas Ranger commander. Smith's forces were spread between the other posts. Fort Milam was manned by Captain Barron's Company A, and Captain Lee Smith's Company E had taken station at the new Fort Henderson during March. The other two outfits, Captain Eastland's Company D and Captain Andrews' Company C, were posted at the old Colorado River Fort.

Known originally as Coleman's Fort and Fort Colorado, this post was redesignated as "Fort Houston" during the spring of 1837. The original Fort Houston, of course, was located in present Anderson County but had ceased to be manned by rangers after Captain Haggard's company departed in early March. The original Fort Houston would not be regularly manned again by rangers or militiamen for more than a full year. By April 1837 the name Fort Houston had thus been passed on to the old Coleman's Fort. This move was perhaps made to honor President Houston instead of Colonel Coleman, who was still being held pending his court-martial hearings. Audited military claims for Private John Angel show that the Colorado post was being called "Fort Houston" by at least April 25, 1837. Angel was issued a note for forty-two dollars on this date for hauling provisions with his oxen team for Andrews' company.[24]

During the early spring of 1837, likely in late March, Captain Andrews' rangers had a chance encounter with a band of Comanche Indians near their fort. It was a clear night with a bright moon that lit the hills and prairies. In the "new" Fort Houston, Noah Smithwick and his fellow frontiersmen were enjoying a quiet evening.

> The older men were smoking and spinning yarns, the younger ones dancing, while I tortured the catgut. The festivities were brought to a sudden close by a bright flame that suddenly shot up on a high knoll overlooking the present site of Austin from the opposite side of the river. Fixing our eyes steadily on the flame, we distinctly saw dark objects passing and repassing in front of it. Our scouts had seen no sign of Indians, still, we knew no white men would so recklessly expose themselves in an Indian country, and at once decided they were Indians.[25]

Captain Andrews was quickly summoned, and the company made plans for moving against the Indians. They decided that the braves must have just struck camp or they would have otherwise realized that their fires could be seen from the ranger fort. Since the Indians were camped on the other side of the river near a regular crossing spot, Andrews suggested that his men start out early and intercept them at this ford. Smithwick argued that his "easy-going" captain should call for an immediate attack before the opportunity was lost.

"Well," Andrews said, "I hate to order the boys out after night."

"No need to order them," Smithwick countered. "Just call for volunteers."

To this suggestion, Captain Andrews agreed. Almost everyone in camp was eager to be in on the attack, with Second Lieutenant Nicholas Wren offering to lead the volunteers. Wren was a veteran ranger. He had served under Willie Williamson as first corporal on Colonel Moore's 1835 campaign. Following the Texas Revolution, he had served in Captain John McGehee's rangers through October 31. He enlisted in Colonel Coleman's ranger battalion on November 1 as a private and was promoted to second lieutenant on December 17, 1836.[26] Now in command of a raiding party, Wren selected fifteen of the best mounted men and hastened off with them. The moon was beginning to set as they started for the river crossing. As they moved slowly forward, cloudy skies further darkened their surroundings.

Lieutenant Wren with Joe Weeks and Smithwick formed the advance party. They crept forward slowly, being deliberately careful not to make any noises that would alert their enemy. A good portion of the night was consumed in slowly slipping up on the Indian camp. As morning approached, the rangers had the misfortune of emerging directly into a *caballado* of stolen horses and mules, which had been tied up not far from the camp. As the horses stamped their feet and the mules brayed loudly, Wren's men fully expected the Indians to be alerted.

"We kept perfectly still till the horses and mules, having recovered from their fright, began to feed," wrote Smithwick. He felt that the Indians must have been very exhausted to not be awakened by the commotion. Wren, Smithwick, and Weeks dismounted and left their horses with the other dozen rangers.

The trio crept up near the Indian camp, where their fire had died out. Moving near a small clump of cedars, they nearly walked right over several sleeping Comanches! Satisfied that the Indians were fully asleep, Wren and company quietly moved back to alert the others. A plan of attack was made, and the Texans tied their horses behind a clump of trees.

Lieutenant Wren divided his forces, leading one of the small divisions himself to the right of the trees where the Indians slept. Smithwick led the other division, including Joe Weeks and Tom McKernon, to the front of the camp. Smithwick recalled:

> In making the detour, Wren mistook the tree under which our game was sleeping, getting away beyond. I could hear the boys stumbling over obstructions, and momentarily expected the sleeping savages would be awakened thereby.
>
> By this time, the twittering of birds announced the approaching day; still the Indians lay wrapped in slumber, unconscious of the enemy only waiting for the signal to pour a deadly fire upon them.
>
> I had just raised my gun to see if I could draw a bead on the Indian nearest me, when he raised himself to a sitting posture, and began to sing his matin lay, "ha ah hah."
>
> Upon hearing the song, Wren perceived his mistake and, hastily retracing their steps, the boys made enough noise to wake the dead.

The Indian near Smithwick heard this crashing and sprang to his feet, turning in the direction of the ruckus. Joe Weeks could not resist the temptation of this easy target presenting his backside to him. Without waiting for orders, he raised his rifle and dropped his target with one shot. The other Indians were instantly on their feet and running for cover as other Texans fired a volley at them.

The braves managed to take cover in a ravine, from which they began returning fire on the rangers. One of their rifle balls struck Private Philip Martin in the head through his mouth, killing him instantly. The remainder of the Indians escaped into the cedar brakes, but the Texans managed to capture all of their horses and camp equipage. Noah Smithwick noted that he had stepped right over the Indian Weeks had shot while charging. Upon returning to this scene later to look for him, the Indian was gone. It was later learned that these Comanches had suffered one killed and three wounded.[27]

The rangers returned to Fort Houston that morning, confident that they had scored a victory over the Indians this time, although it came at the loss of one of their own. Genial, warm-hearted Philip Martin had been considered "one of the best men in camp." His body was carried back and buried with the honors of war outside the fort on the north side, alongside the body of the young private who had died the previous November due to a senior officer's negligence.[28]

$$\star \quad \star \quad \star \quad \star \quad \star$$

Seguin's Cavalry Fights for its Horses

On orders from General Johnston, Lieutenant Colonel Juan Seguín withdrew from San Antonio de Béxar in early March. His three-company cavalry corps performed special scouting duties and collected and herded cattle from the San Antonio River area for the main body of the Texas army. He left Captain Thomas A. S. Pratt and ten men in Béxar "to keep a look-out and communicate with me."

Seguin's one-hundred-odd men operated briefly from Camp Vigilance, about thirty-two miles below San Antonio in present Wilson County. With the balance of Captain Pratt's men and those of Captains Antonio Menchaca and Salvador Flores, he next established Camp Houston. The new camp was located on Cibolo Creek at a crossing known as El Paso del Nogal (later Rocky Ford) a few miles south-southwest of present Stockdale in Wilson County.[29]

From Camp Houston, Seguín sent Adjutant Juan A. Zambrano on March 13 to the main army with a supply requisition for General Johnston. Seguín wrote that many of his cavalrymen were "chiefly on foot, naked and barefoot" for lack of supplies and horses.[30]

Juan Seguín set out from camp with six of his men on March 19 "for the purpose of exploring the country around and ascertaining the resort of the best droves of wild horses." On the morning of March 21, Seguin's men had a run-in with seven Tonkawa Indians near Cibolo Creek.

> In the encounter we killed two of them, took two of their horses and wounded another Indian, who escaped with the balance, without any loss on our side. From appearances I have good reason to believe that they had been in among the American settlements and have no doubt committed depredations there as they had American horses with them, no arrows left in the quivers, and from other certain signs on those whom we killed I drew this conclusion.

On March 26, Lieutenant Colonel Seguín sent orders for captains Pratt and Menchaca to "collect and press for the public service and use of this Regt. all the horses and mules you can find." The cavalrymen proceeded to round up every horse and mule in the Béxar area, some even being taken at gunpoint from owners who were less than willing. San Antonio alcalde Nicolas Flores implored Captain Pratt to halt while a petition was sent to Seguín at the cavalry's Camp Houston. Flores wrote of "the anguished state of these residents," who could not survive without the animals they used for their livelihoods and their safety.

Although he had proper orders from the army's commanding general to press every single horse and mule, Seguín allowed the San Antonio residents to keep twenty-five animals to protect themselves. Seguín received orders on April 10 from General Johnston to return to San Antonio with his cavalry corps. With Lieutenant John W. Keating, he sent a report of his corps' actions and their current strength, which showed:

Company	A	Aggregate	48	Horses and mules	28
	B		55		49
	C		_28_		_13_
			131		90

Lieutenant Colonel Seguín sent Major Thomas Western to Columbia to report to the secretary of war as his men prepared to return to Mission San Jose on the banks of the San Antonio River. Prior to making this return, the cavalry had another encounter with Indians. Around 3:00 a.m. on April 17, a party of Tonkawas raided the cavalry camp and made off with thirty-two horses. Lieutenant Leandro Arreolo and sixteen men were immediately ordered to pursue them. Seguín wrote:

> They did so and overtook them at a place called las Cuevas, about 36 miles from our camp. They had a small skirmish with them without either party being injured, retook the horses and arrived in camp with them about 12 o'clock the same day. There were about one hundred Indians.

Indians Rob the Rangers: April 1837

Things were quieter for the rangers in the ensuing weeks. This relative peace, in fact, led to a laxness of the part of these remote frontiersman that caused Lieutenant Nicholas Wren, who had so recently led the Indian fight, to be reprimanded by President Houston for his conduct.

Taking half a dozen men with him, Wren had taken the company's horses out to graze one morning late in the month of April. The men were carefree, feeling no apprehensions of experiencing a raid against them. The horses were feeding towards the creek. As they neared the timber, a number of Indians suddenly appeared, rushing forward while blowing whistles and yelling. "The horses snorted and started to run," wrote Noah Smithwick, "when an Indian mounted on a quick horse rushed in ahead of them, leading off up the creek, the other Indians following, still yelling and whistling."[31]

The surprise stampede was made so quickly that the guard had only the chance to fire one errant shot at the Indians. A number of the horses fortunately broke for the fort. Smithwick's horse headed straight for the fort, and he managed to open the gate and herd it right to safety. Wild-hearted Irishman Felix McCluskey, having just saddled his horse to go out and round up the other horses, was ready to go. Smithwick mounted his own horse, and the pair galloped out of the fort in pursuit of the horses that had escaped from the Indians. A large group of these horses were running madly towards Hornsby's Station, located a short distance downriver from Fort Houston.

In his memoirs, Smithwick left a humorous account of the rangers' misfortune.

> Old Isaac Castner, who had left the service and was then living at Hornsby's, had been up to the fort and was jogging along leisurely on his return. He had crossed the creek and gained the open prairie when he heard the clattering of hoofs coming in his rear. He turned in his saddle and took one look behind. The frightened animals pursued by McCluskey and myself were bearing right down on him. We had lost our hats in the wild race, and our hair flying in the wind gave us much the appearance of Indians. Uncle Isaac, who, as previously stated, weighed about 200 pounds, laid whip to his horse, which was a good animal, and led off across the prairie to Hornsby's Station, about a mile distant, the horses following in his wake and we trying to get in ahead of them. McCluskey's sense of fun took in the situation. "Be Jasus," said he, "look at him run!" and the reckless creature could not refrain from giving a war whoop to help the old man along.
>
> Hearing the racket, the men at Hornsby's fort ran out, and seeing the chase, threw the gate open. Breathless from fright and exhaustion, Castner ran in, gasping, "Injuns."

McCluskey and Smithwick managed to get ahead of the fleeing horses and stop them. Smithwick chastised McCluskey for scaring poor Castner, but the witty Irishman only explained, "Be Jasus, I was thryin' to stop him." The exhausted horses were driven back to the fort, where the rangers were forced to rest their badly winded animals until the next morning before going in pursuit of the Indians who had stampeded them. The pursuit party tailed the Indians for three days to the San Gabriel River. They found the remains of one horse the Indians had butchered and apparently eaten pieces of raw flesh from. Near the head of the San Gabriel, they found a great many wild mustangs, whose tracks obliterated the trail of the Indians. The dejected rangers were forced to return to camp empty-handed. Smithwick noted, "The rascals were doubtless gratified to find some of the very same animals among their haul that we took from them a short time before."

He was not alone in his criticism of his fellow rangers' carelessness in allowing the Indians to steal a number of their horses. President Houston suspended Lieutenant Wren for this mishap. He was well respected by his fellow company men, and they felt that "no power on earth could have held those terror stricken animals after the Indians made their dash." The company made a unanimous petition to Houston to reinstate Wren, which the president granted. Having learned a tough lesson, the rangers never went out on foot again while herding the horses.

The Fort Houston rangers were fortunate in saving many of their stampeded horses. The Indians made a similar stampede on the horses of Captain Daniel Monroe's rangers at Fort Smith with far greater success. In a letter written several weeks later, Monroe stated that the Indians "took my horses from me on Little River on the morning" of April 28, 1837.[32]

Another of Major Smith's rangers, George Erath, wrote several years later that the stampeding occurred "in the prairie in sight of Fort Smith." He also noted that, "The Indians made their escape, the whites being too weak to follow."[33]

★　★　★　★　★

Post Oak Springs Ranger Massacre: May 6, 1837

Shortly after the Indians began showing their increasing boldness to steal the rangers' horses, Major Smith moved his headquarters from his namesake post on the Little River back to Fort Fisher. He felt it more important to guard the citizens of the major settlements from depredations, and the remote Fort Smith was thus soon abandoned.[34]

Two weeks after losing his horses, Captain Monroe decided it was time for Company B to pull out of Fort Smith. In a letter written soon thereafter to Major Sterling Robertson in the senate, Monroe described the latest news from the frontier. He declared that the Indians "are committing depredations on the frontier daily" and had on April 28 relieved his rangers of their horses.[35]

Due to this situation, rangers in this most remote area of Texas without horses, Monroe wisely decided "I could do nothing for myself or the citizens." He therefore prepared to abandon Fort Smith for the time being and to fall back to Fort Fisher (present Waco). There were several families living at Fort Smith at this time. The families of Goldsby Childers and ranger Dan Cullins had resided there since first helping George Erath to construct the fort in late 1836. The wagons, which these families had brought to Texas years earlier, were worn out and broken up, and their teams had since been stolen by Indians.

Prior to Fort Smith being abandoned, five men were sent to Nashville by Captain Monroe to fetch wagons and teams to move the belongings of the two or three families residing at the fort.

According to Monroe, he sent out three of his rangers: Jesse Bailey, David McCandless Farmer, and Aaron Cullins. They went to Nashville with "volunteers" Claiborne Neal and John Hughes. In many early ranger companies, other men served with the companies as volunteers and guides, although their names were not officially entered on muster rolls. In this sense, these men were truly serving as rangers but were not hindered by the legal requirement of fulfilling a service enlistment should they choose to move on to other endeavors. Many early Texas pioneers served the Texas Rangers without ever having their names scribed to a roll for history's sake.

The rangers and volunteers went into Nashville on May 5, 1837, and obtained wagons and teams. The teams were then driven back toward Fort Smith on the Little River, where their largely horseless company and the few families remaining there would be ushered back to the safety of a large community.

The recent run of bad luck for the Texas Rangers would not be broken this day, however. A large band of mounted Indians was seen in the vicinity of Nashville. A smaller group of them approached the settlement close enough in the prairie during broad daylight to overtake and kill an older man named Mr. Neal. His body was found only about three hundred yards from the home of former ranger captain Calvin Boales. This man's son, Claiborne Neal, was one of the five helping to guide the oxen teams back to Fort Smith.

The large band of Comanches then followed the wagon tracks along their northwesterly route toward the Little River Fort. They caught the five-man ranger party on May 6, well shy of its destination. The Indians attacked this wagon train just as it approached an island or grove of post oaks in the prairie at a place known as Post Oak Springs in present Milam County. This spot later became the residence of Ad Hall, for whom a small station of the Gulf, Colorado and Santa Fe Railway was named.

The five Texans fought valiantly, but the Comanches soon killed them all. Ironically, the spot of the so-called "Post Oak massacre" was only about five miles from the scene of Erath's Elm Creek Fight four months previous.

At this point it is fair to point out that previous accounts on the Post Oak massacre disagree on the date of the attack and on the names of the men killed. Area resident James Dunn of Dunn's Fort wrote to Senator Robertson on May 15 to provide details of the recent attacks in the area. By his account, the men killed were Claiborne Neal, Jesse Bailey, David Farmer, and "the two Cullinses." Dunn was correct in that both Daniel and Aaron Cullins were active with the Texas Rangers, but Daniel Cullins was still very much alive in the Nashville Colony after May 1837.

Dunn also clearly states that the elder Mr. Neal was brazenly killed just outside of town on May 5. Neal's son and the other rangers were killed at Post Oak Springs "about the same time."

According to Captain Monroe, his rangers were killed on May 6. In the military papers of Private Jesse Bailey, Monroe and Major Smith both recorded on June 14 at the new ranger headquarters of Fort Fisher that Bailey had "faithfully performed his duties of a soldier up to the sixth day of May following, at which time he was killed by the Indians."[36]

Other sources have listed the fifth man killed in the Post Oak massacre to be Sterrett Smith instead of volunteer John Hughes. The memoirs of ranger officer George Erath and the account of Captain Monroe, written nine days after the attack, both clearly list Hughes as the fifth victim.[37]

Once the wagon team was believed overdue, Captain Monroe sent out a scout patrol to look for them, and they soon came upon the grisly scene. There was evidence of a desperate fight. The bodies of two of the men were found in one of the wagons, while the other three were scattered between the wagons and the timber. The Indians had apparently set up an ambush and waited for the unsuspecting Texans to ride into their trap. The Comanches made off with all the teams, guns, pistols, and other goods being hauled by the rangers.

Captain Monroe and the remainder of his Company B moved the families from the Little River and abandoned Fort Smith. They proceeded to Fort Fisher and joined Major William Smith at his new command post. "All the news I have for you is of the worst sort," Monroe wrote to Senator Robertson on May 15. Freshly arrived at Fort Fisher, he was bitter from his losses.

> I was ordered to this place and was two days coming and has seed no sign going up the country sufficient for the number of Indians that was down. Without more assistance, we are nothing but a drug to the government and no assistance to the people. It is useless to write any more, for you know our situations.

News of the killing of Mr. Neal and the five rangers on May 5 made it to Houston, where the publishers of the *Telegraph and Texas Register* recorded the panic in their May 23 issue.

> A body of Indians (supposed to be 200) had appeared within 15 miles of Nashville, Milam County—a small detachment of them even came to the immediate vicinity of that place. They killed one man in sight of the town. The main body went on the track of a wagon train bound to the fort on Little River, overtook the wagons, and killed every one of the men (five in number) attached to them, together with the oxen. Some alarm seems to prevade the remote settlements in consequence of the incursion.
>
> A force will probably be marched against the villages of these savages, in order to drive them to their houses.

The Indians continued on their warpath in the days following the Post Oak massacre. James Dunn's note to Sterling Robertson of May 15 described various other citizens who had been attacked. He wrote that "they attacked Mr. Robinett's house in daylight" on May 8, wounding one man and driving away all the horses. Mr. Webb was attacked on May 9 "while at work in his field." Dunn stated that the locals were "waiting hourly to be attacked" and implored of Senator Robertson that the "Government will not hesitate to assist us in our distress."[38]

★ ★ ★ ★ ★

McLean-Sheridan-Barnes Slayings: May 10, 1837

Within days of the Post Oak massacre, a large group of Indians carried the recent wave of depredations into more eastern settlements of Texas. It is possible that this band was the same as those who had killed Captain Monroe's rangers several days previously.

Hostile Indians moved through present Houston County and stole as many as one hundred cattle from the settlements near San Pedro Bayou. Since the last ranger company on duty in this area had disbanded two months previously, the settlers organized their own volunteer pursuit party.

John Sheridan and his brother-in-law Dan McLean, two of the area's earliest residents, helped organize the posse. Sheridan, a veteran of the Béxar siege, had served in the ranger company of Captain Costley during late 1836 and as one of Captain Haggard's Fort Houston rangers during the early months of 1837. Both he and McLean were considered expert Indian fighters and were employed at times by area settlers as guides and protectors.

One other known member of this posse was James Barnes, one of the earliest residents of the area that soon became Houston County. He was one of the signers of a petition in April 1837 that helped to create the new county. Census records show that Clark Barten later became administrator for 1,280 acres of land in Houston County, which had been owned by James Barnes until his death.

In preparation for the battle he expected, John Sheridan paused long enough to take care of papers pertaining to previous military service. His audited claims include one dated May 10, 1837, in Nacogdoches County, from which Houston County was carved within weeks. Sheridan appeared before Justice of the Peace William H. McDonald to present service documents for authentication for payment.[39]

The number of men turning out to pursue the Indians is unknown. What is known is that this small party was ambushed by the Indians soon after heading northward in pursuit. During the main charge, Sheridan, McLean, and James Barnes were killed. Due to overwhelming numbers, the few surviving men of the posse were forced to retreat.[40]

According to what little information is available on this skirmish, McLean and Sheridan sacrificed their own lives holding the Indians in check while other settlers escaped.

Neither the historical marker erected by the state of Texas nor published accounts of this one-sided battle mention the death of Barnes. The *Telegraph and Texas Register*, however, made a brief mention in its May 23 issue.

> The Indians killed three men near the Mustang Prairie. Their names are McLean, Sheridan and Barnes. They stole upwards of 100 horses in the neighborhood of the same settlement.[41]

Near the present community of Slocum on FM 2022 now stands a Texas state historical marker that identifies the site of what came to be called the McLean-Sheridan massacre. Lucinda C. Nugent Sheridan took a Mexican boy with her to the scene of the massacre in present Anderson County. They loaded the bodies of her husband and brother-in-law McLean onto an oxcart and carried them back to their respective properties several miles south. Sheridan's body was buried under a black walnut tree near his home on Silver Creek. McLean was buried on San Pedro Creek on the land he settled in 1824 east of present Augusta.[42]

Another Texas historical marker, erected in 1971, stands in the community of Augusta in Hayes Park. It describes the massacre that occurred twelve miles northwest and commemorates this area's first permanent residents.

★ ★ ★ ★ ★

Slaying of Ranger James Coryell

Following the massacre of Captain Monroe's rangers, the First Congress took steps to protect the frontiers. On May 12, 1837, Senator Robertson submitted a joint resolution for an expedition against the hostile Indians on the frontier. On May 15 the House sent over a resolution requesting that a special joint House-Senate committee meet to draft a bill to properly provide for better frontier protection. By May 23 a bill had been approved by both the House and Senate for more frontier forces on the northern frontiers, but it would not be signed by President Houston until June 12.[43]

While the Senate worked on legislation to provide for more rangers in response to these killings, the violence continued. After Captain Monroe's losses in the Post Oak massacre, Major Smith had consolidated his rangers in May at three key posts, Forts Houston, Henderson, and Milam.

The companies of Monroe and Tommy Barron were stationed at Fort Milam at the Falls of the Brazos, while those of Micah Andrews and William Eastland remained at Fort Houston on the Colorado. Captain Lee Smith's Company E remained at the new Fort Henderson on the Navasota River.

The Indians remained on the warpath and became increasingly bold. During May, George Erath was among a large party of Major Smith's rangers out on a scout west of the Little River. In their absence, another Indian attack occurred against some of the rangers left behind. Erath wrote that "a skirmish took place in three hundred yards of the station at the Falls of the Brazos."[44] Pioneer Newton C. Duncan remembered that "The Indians had troubled us so much that we had all gone into Robertson's headquarters at Viesca." Other families congregated at the community of Wheelock, "they having come back here on account of the Indians being so bad further west." Among the displaced families gathered about Fort Milam, there were a number of boys who had no way to be educated due to the current crisis. Therefore, Captain Barron detailed Benjamin Fitch of his ranger company to teach some of these kids.

"He had a small school house and a very few pupils who were advanced far enough to 'cipher,' as we called it then," wrote Duncan. Fitch was later killed in a hunting accident. While creeping along below the edge of the riverbank with a turkey call, fellow ranger Alf Johnson spotted the black cap he wore moving along the top of the bank and fired, killing Fitch by mistake.[45]

While Company A was stationed at Fort Milam, Private James Coryell and some companions from Captain Barron's command went about a half mile down the road to Perry Creek, near the home of Judge Albert G. Perry. Coryell had come to Texas about 1828 from Ohio and settled on land in present Coryell County, the county later taking his name.[46]

Indians attacked Coryell's party on this date. According to the letter of Nashville Colony resident James Dunn of May 15, the event occurred on May 11. A war department draft from January 16, 1838, however, shows that Coryell was paid for service as a private in Captain Barron's company from September 11, 1836, to May 27, 1837.[47]

Coryell's little party on this date also included fellow rangers Alfred Berry, Sam Burton, Michael Castleman, and Ezra Webb, all members of Barron's Ranger Company A. Near Perry's Creek, they found and cut a bee tree. They took seats and sat around talking, eating the honey. Coryell, who had been sick, told his friends that he would not be able to run if Indians should show up. A short time later the men heard the sound of twigs snapping and looked up to see a dozen Caddo Indians creeping up on them.

Coryell quickly rose to his feet and grabbed one of the three guns available. By the time he could fire at the Indians, three of them had fired at him. Of the other two guns in the party, one was not loaded and the other failed to fire. Coryell fell wounded, grasping at some bushes as he fell and pulling the tops off them. The other rangers ran for their lives as the Indians moved in.

Alfred Berry, one of Coryell's friends, stood and unsuccessfully snapped the faulty rifle until the Caddos began scalping Coryell. Berry then beat a hasty retreat while they were occupied. Back at the ranger headquarters in Viesca, Newton Duncan recalled the site of the first ranger to make it back.

Ezra Webb was the first one of the party to reach the settlement. Coming to the house of Capt. Barron, he found a crowd of ladies gathered awaiting the orders of Capt. Barron, as they were expecting to be ordered to the block-house for protection. When Webb ran in with great haste and fright, and breathless from his run, he fell on the bed, past speaking. The ladies gathered around, anxious to know what had happened. After a little time, he was able to whisper, "Indians! Poor Coryell!"[48]

Coryell was the only ranger killed, and from the blood found at the scene later, he was credited with having fatally wounded one of his assailants with his own shot. He was forty years old at the time of his death and was respected as an "excellent woodsman" and a "brave soldier."

"During May and June, there was perpetual skirmishing of a slight nature without much damage on either side," wrote ranger George Erath. He noted that Coryell's killers "were pursued by men from the garrison, but not overtaken. This was in the month of May 1837."[49]

CHAPTER 12

Stone Houses Fight

June - November 1837

New Mounted Rifleman Battalion: June 12, 1837

The killings near Nashville in May and the recent furloughing of the regular army required action on the part of the Texas Congress. President Sam Houston officially excused himself from government business for thirty days on June 7, 1837. By means of a joint resolution, he provided himself a month to help organize the new corps of mounted gunmen, which would protect the northern frontier in the absence of a regular army.

On June 9 Senator Sterling Robertson published an announcement in the *Telegraph and Texas Register* stating that the ranging corps needed thirty or forty good horses. Robertson set aside a league (4,428.4 acres) of his own premium land to pay for these horses, at a rate of one dollar per acre. Those interested were to contact Captain John Bowyer or Niles F. Smith, who supplied goods to ranger companies during 1837, at Houston.[1]

The Second Congress on June 12 officially approved the battalion of mounted riflemen, a corps to consist of six hundred mounted men, rank and file included. The act was entitled "An act for the better protection of the northern frontier."

This corps would include ten companies divided into three divisions. This act declared that, if practicable, one company of Indian spies should be attached to each division. This company should be composed of Shawnees, Delawares, Cherokees, or other friendly Indians who would be supplied with provisions and were to be paid in goods for their services.

Officers and privates were required to provide themselves with a good horse, a good gun, and two hundred rounds of ammunition, plus all other necessary equipment. The government's appointed corps quartermaster would supply beef. Officers would be paid in the same fashion as those of the ranging service, while privates were to be paid twenty-five dollars per month. A bounty of 640 acres of land was to be given to each officer and private.[2]

The act stated that the corps

> shall be raised by voluntary enlistment, for a term of six months, dating from the time of rendezvous, and officered in the following manner, viz: one colonel, one lieutenant colonel, one major, ten captains, ten first and second lieutenants; all of whom shall be appointed by the president, by and with the advice and consent of the senate.

These volunteers were only required to enlist for six months instead of the customary one-year period. Every group of six men was to furnish themselves with a packhorse. Any spoils from an enemy engagement would be split equally among the officers and men. The act also established guidelines to handle officers and enlisted men who disobeyed orders. The president maintained the option of discharging this corps of mounted gunmen at a period earlier than six months, "if he should deem it expedient."

The new riflemen corps would station ten new ranger companies in nine different frontier counties. President Houston appointed the original officers with the advice and consent of the Texas Senate. Joseph L. Bennett, who had previously served as lieutenant colonel of the Second Regiment of Texas Volunteers at San Jacinto, was appointed colonel commanding the new ranger battalion. His lieutenant colonel was Alexander Horton, an aide-de-camp of Sam Houston at San Jacinto. Major John McGehee had commanded a ranger company under Colonel Burleson through November 1836.

The designated company commanders and their lieutenants were all Texans well seasoned in frontier and military service. Elisha Clapp, John Pierson, Ben Fitch, John Walker, and James Wilkinson were veterans of revolutionary ranger companies. San Jacinto veteran John Robert Craddock had served in the 1836 companies of William Hill, John Hart, Sterling Robertson, and Calvin Boales before being appointed as captain of mounted gunmen in Red River County. The others were considered equally well qualified by the senate for frontier command.

First Lieutenant A. B. Vanbenthuysen had been an officer in a volunteer company during the early months of 1836. Hannibal Good was a Béxar siege veteran, and George English had already commanded a volunteer company during 1836. Dr. Robert Kemp Goodloe, born in 1813 in Virginia, was a medical student in 1835 before coming to Texas with

Sidney Sherman's Kentucky volunteer company. Goodloe served in Henry Karnes' cavalry company at San Jacinto and was appointed first lieutenant of Captain John Clark's San Augustine Mounted Gunmen.[3]

Recruiting began at once for the new ranging companies. In Houston, Captain John Bowyer formed his Harrisburg County company immediately. One man who struck out from his home near San Felipe to join was John Denton. He never made it to Houston. His wife, Susannah Denton, penned a listing that ran in the Saturday, August 26, 1837 issue of the *Telegraph and Texas Register* "seeking info on her husband John, who left her home on June 12 to join a company of Rangers forming at Houston. He may have been murdered."[4]

Captain Bowyer's mounted gunmen would be the first of Colonel Bennett's battalion to form. This was perhaps due to the fact that the First Congress had moved from Columbia to Houston between its two called sessions. Under the eye of the president and congress, Bowyer's

Nominations for New Regiment of Rangers: June 12, 1837			
Joseph L. Bennett	Colonel	Robert Ragsdale	2nd Lt.
Alexander Horton	Lt. Col.	John H. Dyer	Captain
John Gilmore McGehee	Major	Richard Peters	1st Lt.
		James E. Hopkins	2nd Lt.
Galveston County			
James Perry	Captain	*Milam County*	
Hiram Thompson	1st Lt.	James A. Wilkinson	Captain
Edward Pettus	2nd Lt.	John Walker	1st Lt.
		Benjamin F. Fitch	2nd Lt.
Harrisburg County			
John M. Bowyer	Captain	*Washington County*	
A. B. Vanbenthuysen	1st Lt.	John G. W. Pierson	Captain
Michael Dick	2nd Lt.	John Milton Swisher	1st Lt.
		George W. Robinson	2nd Lt.
Nacogdoches County			
Elisha Clapp	Captain	*Jasper County*	
James L. Gossett	1st Lt.	Hannibal Good	Captain
Thomas J. Anthony	2nd Lt.	William Thomaston	1st Lt.
		John N. Taylor	2nd Lt.
San Augustine County			
John Clark	Captain	*Shelby County*	
Robert Kemp Goodloe	1st Lt.	George English	Captain
James Burrus	2nd Lt.	Claiborne Walker	1st Lt.
		James Strickland	2nd Lt.
Red River County (2 companies)			
John Robert Craddock	Captain	Source: *Muster Rolls of the Texas*	
Thomas Jouett	1st Lt.	*Revolution*, 247-48.	

rangers may have been the only new company to fully organize. There is little evidence to suggest that most of the other designated county ranging companies ever formed at all. Captain Bowyer's company would later operate in cooperation with the companies of Major William Smith's ranger battalion.

★ ★ ★ ★ ★

A Truce with the Comanches

While Colonel Bennett's new mounted rifleman battalion was attempting to organize, Major Smith's existing frontier battalion was enjoying peaceful conditions during the summer of 1837.

At Fort Houston on the Colorado River, Noah Smithwick of Captain Andrews' Company C recalled that the Indians "gave us a respite and we had an easy time of it at the fort, hunting being now our principal occupation." Smithwick managed to kill an old buffalo bull that had charged his hunting dog in the brush. Two other rangers, Reuben Hornsby and Jacob Harrell, shot another buffalo, which charged them after being wounded. Hornsby, an older man of large size, scaled a nearby tree with great agility. Harrell managed to bring down the charging bull with another shot before being run down.[5]

On another occasion, Smithwick and several others were scouting near the head of Gilleland's Creek, an area full of prickly pears and dense evergreen dwarf oak trees known as chaparral. In one thicket of cactus and brush, they managed to corner a panther and wound it. The large cat quickly turned to the offensive to protect itself.

Some of the older rangers decided it would be fun to break in one of their green recruits, James O. Butler, by letting him bring down the angry panther. Arming young Butler with a musket, the men sent him forward into the brush to finish off their prey. As he advanced, the enraged cat suddenly sprang from its den with glaring eyes and its tail erect, as Smithwick recorded.

> Dropping his musket, he crashed through the brush and prickly pears, regaining the open just as the infuriated animal made a spring for him. Fortunately the panther was so crippled that his spring was rendered ineffectual, and before he could collect himself for another, I shot him dead. It took Butler some time to get rid of the cactus needles, and he never got rid of the joke while he remained in the service.

Smithwick states that some of the rangers who had joined the service after the Texas Revolution were not well suited for their new occupation. Many were without a horse or had little skill in the use of firearms. A couple of men came in from the Little River Fort during the summer to obtain ammunition from Captain Andrews at Fort Houston. Fearful of an attack being made on these two men, Andrews thus dispatched an armed escort to return with these two men to their fort. Smithwick and another mounted ranger rode along with them, and Andrews sent a number of his green recruits on foot as mounted infantrymen in order for them to gain some needed frontier experience.

Upon reaching the San Gabriel River, Smithwick and his companion accompanied the other two back to the Little River Fort. He left the infantry detachment camped at the river with word that he would be back the next day to lead them back to Fort Houston. When he returned, he found these men hungry. Even with abundant buffalo and other game all about them, they had been unable to successfully kill anything to eat. Smithwick managed to kill a fat buffalo cow and brought it back into camp that evening.

"The ravenous crew couldn't wait for the meat to cook," he wrote. "They snatched it off the fire before it got warm through, bolting it like hungry dogs."

Company C did secure food from sources other than wild game during the summer months. The papers of ranger John Litton, who had previously served under Captain John McGehee in 1836, show that he was issued a note on June 15, 1837, for supplying "784 pounds of pork for which the government will pay $5 per hundred." Litton's promissory note was signed by "M. Andrews, Capt. Rangers at Fort Houston." Another payment voucher from June 28, 1837, at Fort Houston on the Colorado shows that Joseph Duty supplied 19.75 pounds of pork at five dollars per hundredweight and thirty pounds of bacon at fifteen cents per pound.[6]

Republic papers show that Captain Tommy Barron's Company A was still stationed at Fort Milam during June 1837. The audited claims of Private Thomas H. Eaton show that he donated fifty dollars' worth of beef on June 14 for the use of the frontiersmen at the Milam Post of the battalion of rangers. This note was signed by Quartermaster General William G. Cooke and First Lieutenant Charles Curtis, the assistant quartermaster and second in command of Company A.[7]

Captain Daniel Monroe's rangers operated at times from Fort Milam under the supervision of Major Smith. On July 15 Smith allowed

Monroe's fourth sergeant, John D. Brown, to leave the service to attend to family matters. Brown had enlisted in Company B on January 15, 1837, and served as a private through April 11, at which time he was promoted to fourth sergeant. He served six months of his service period before Major Smith allowed him to be honorably discharged from the ranger service "in consequence of his having a large and helpless family entirely dependent on him for support."[8]

During the early summer of 1837, a band of eight Comanche Indians rode into Fort Houston waving a white flag. There were six warriors and two chiefs, named Quinaseico and Puestia. They were unable to speak English, but several rangers sent forward to meet them were able to communicate with them in broken Spanish. These Comanches desired to enter into a treaty with the rangers, and they requested a commissioner to be sent out to their camp to talk over the matters.[9]

Captain Andrews allowed the Comanches into his fort. The Colorado River settlers were so weary of the fear of Indian attacks that any possibility to make peace was welcomed. Despite their good intentions, ranger Noah Smithwick wrote that "the Indians were so treacherous that the office of commissioner was not one to be coveted." Due to his grasp of the Spanish language, Smithwick was selected by the chiefs to make the treaty with them. "Knowing that there is a degree of honor even among Indians touching those who voluntarily become their guests," he recalled, "I yielded to the stress of the circumstances and agreed to accompany them back to their camp, only about thirty miles distant, on Brushy Creek."

Smithwick bid his farewells to his company, most of whom figured they would never see him alive again. He went with them back to their camp and greeted their old chief Muguara. He found about one hundred Indians in camp and six prisoners, one white woman, two white boys, one Mexican woman, and two Mexican boys. Smithwick gained the confidence of these Comanches and stayed with them for some time during the summer. When he was able to speak privately with the captives, he found that the women had both become wives to Indian braves. He found that the Mexican woman desired badly to escape but that the white woman, who had been captured while a child, remembered nothing of her previous life. She now had an Indian husband and children and appeared content with her new life.

The Comanches gave Smithwick the Indian name he called "Juaqua." He found six chiefs among this tribe, recording their names as best he could translate them—Muguara ("eagle"), Quinaseico, Potesenaquahip ("buffalo hump"), Cataniapa, Pahauco, and Esanap. Among many interesting observations he made of this tribe, he noted that there were not any severely wounded braves from previous battles. Those with minor battle wounds, such as bullet scars, proudly enhanced the scars by tattooing lines around them.

While learning of their customs and forms of entertainment, Smithwick happened to hear a story of one particular raid against some of these Comanches who were returning to their camp with horses they had "collected." They stated that one of their braves had been killed and three others wounded. This was, of course, the fight under Lieutenant Nicholas Wren in which Smithwick had participated earlier in the year near Fort Houston.

After spending much of the summer living with and holding talks with these Comanches, Smithwick induced five of their chiefs to go with him to Houston. President Sam Houston by this time had made his namesake town the seat of Texas government. Ranger sergeant Van Palmer accompanied them, hoping to receive payment for goods he had furnished to the Indians.

In meetings with President Houston, a peace treaty was worked out with Chief Muguara and his chiefs. Among the stipulations was that a trading post be established on Brushy Creek at the site of the old Tumlinson blockhouse, where the Indians could come to get supplies. Palmer agreed to take command of this post once built. In Smithwick's place, the Comanches agreed to take on ranger Alanson Miles as a resident commissioner. With their gifts from Texas collected, the Indians proceeded back to their camp. The provisions of the treaty were not important, according to Smithwick, because "they were never complied with by either party."[10]

During his stay with the Comanches and in the immediate wake of the treaty, hostilities were noticed by Smithwick to have declined dramatically for the Colorado River settlers.

> Open hostilities ceased for a time, however, and gave the settlers a chance to quarrel among themselves. Dissensions arose, and, lulled by the fancied security, the more venturesome spirits pushed further out, exciting anew the distrust of the Indians. Then, when the time in which the trading post was to have been established passed, and they came in with their skins to trade and found no trading house, they came to call on me why the treaty had not been complied with.

He soon found that the disillusioned Comanches had no intention of staying in the area where the whites would not honor their contract. They soon made announcements that they were heading toward Mexico for an expedition to round up more horses for their tribe. Smithwick says that the Comanches held elaborate councils and war dances for several nights before packing up their camp and moving out.

Their departure for Mexico would later prove to not be a permanent move. The Houston treaty had brought some respite from Comanche attacks in 1837, but many of these Indians would later be involved in hostile attacks against Texan forces.

During Noah Smithwick's absence with the Comanches during the summer of 1837, the Texas Rangers had begun a slow dwindling of forces that would become more dramatic by year's end. Many of the men employed in Major William Smith's battalion had, of course, originally enlisted under Colonel Robert Coleman in August 1836 for one-year enlistments.

Some chose to re-enlist for another term of service, but a large number decided to take their liberty and return to more civilized life. Among those who retired from the ranging service during August 1837 was Captain Micah Andrews. He had been well respected by his rangers, who considered him to be possessed of a genial disposition that rarely compelled him to have to issue direct orders. His men were pleased to follow his directions at a mere suggestion.

Command of Company C fell upon Lieutenant Nicholas Wren. The discharge papers of Private Henry Wilson, who had completed his full year's service with Coleman and Smith's battalion, are dated August 8, 1837. They are signed at Fort Houston on the Colorado River by Wren as Lieutenant, Commanding Company C.[11]

Captain Andrews' departure from Major Smith's battalion is curious. His audited claims to the Republic of Texas show that he continued to receive payments as a ranger captain through January 5, 1838. His actions and in what capacity he acted after leaving Fort Houston are unknown. It is known, however, that he proceeded to settle in La Grange, where he engaged in the hotel business.[12]

Upon the departure of Captain Andrews, command of Fort Houston soon fell upon Company D's Captain William Eastland. The men of the fort, accustomed to Andrews' casual command style, were not pleased when Eastland tried to assume a more militant approach to running the fort. As one of these rangers wrote, "Captain Eastland was disgusted with the want of military discipline among the men and the easy familiarity with which they treated their commander."

Eastland then determined to put a strong control on his troops. The result was a near mutiny. The troops one morning marched on the parade, stacked their weapons, and declared to Eastland that he could "go to hell and they would go home." With no other choice, Eastland gave in gracefully to their request and thereafter treated his men with more respect. Perhaps he realized that on the Indian frontiers in the absence of a regular army, these were the best men he had with which to wage his expeditions.

Eastland's first lieutenant by this time had become veteran frontiersman John L. Lynch. The man designated by Congress as Eastland's first lieutenant, Joel Robison, had apparently left the service by this time. Records of John L. Lynch show that he was "appointed a 1st Lieutenant in the Ranging Corps on the 17th May 1837" and served as such through November 18, 1837. Service papers of Samuel Blisk show that Lieutenant Lynch and some of his men were stationed at Fort Houston on the Colorado during August. Eastland promoted one of his subordinates, George W. Chapman, from private to second lieutenant on August 14, 1837. Lieutenant Chapman was paid through March 1838 as an officer of the battalion of rangers.[13]

Private Noah Smithwick took a break from the frontier service at the close of summer. Lieutenant Nicholas Wren and Major Smith discharged him from service at Fort Houston on September 6. Papers filed in Mina County show that Smithwick, who had substituted back into ranger service in January 1837, fulfilled the other man's obligations. During his service, he had been issued $8.70 worth of clothing. He was eligible for land due him and payment of $300 for twelve months service. Smithwick then proceeded to Bastrop, opened a blacksmith shop, and assisted in the early organization of Bastrop County.[14]

Other veteran rangers were discharged during September as their one-year enlistments expired. From Captain Barron's Company A, Alfred Eaton was discharged on September 3 and Ansel Darniell was discharged on September 23. Both men's papers were also signed by Major Smith at the "Headquarters, Battalion of Rangers" located at "mouth of Brushy" near Nashville-on-the-Brazos.[15]

Goldsby Childers, a settler who had lived at Fort Smith prior to its being abandoned in May 1837, had been kept busy hauling supplies for Smith's rangers. According to a note from Assistant Quartermaster

Charles Curtis issued on July 9, 1837, in Nashville, Milam County, Childers lent out his wagon and team for twenty-seven days at two dollars per day for the rangers. Curtis signed another note in Nashville on September 14 stating that Childers had additionally supplied the ranger battalion one yoke of oxen for thirty days at fifty cents per day.[16]

During the late summer of 1837, there were a few Indian encounters by the settlers. Traveling in small numbers between towns was still a dangerous routine. Reports from the *Telegraph and Texas Register* describe attacks in both August and September 1837. The Saturday, August 19 issue states that: "Two men, named Ross and Stevens, have been found murdered and scalped near Goliad." These murders were believed to have been committed by Lipan Apaches. Another Indian depredation was reported in the next issue on Tuesday, August 22:

> A man named Jackson M. Parker [was] killed recently near the Nueces by Tonkawa Indians. While gathering cattle for the army, Parker and a companion went after 3 or 4 oxen that strayed from the drove and entered a mesquite thicket. One of the Indians was in hiding and instantly killed the young man.[17]

The *Telegraph*'s September 2, 1837 issue further reveals that former Texas army general Thomas Green was shot and scalped by Indians in an encounter near Béxar. Green survived and was reported to have "been taken to Béxar and is recovering slowly."

★ ★ ★ ★ ★

Second Congress Addresses Indian Issues

President Sam Houston issued a proclamation on August 10 for the Second Congress to assemble in Houston on September 25. He was deeply concerned over "a serious impediment, growing out of the circumstances of our unsettled boundary on the east" which had presented itself in the execution of recently passed land laws of Texas.[18]

An election was held on the first Monday of September 1837, with the members of the House of Representatives and one-third of the senators for the Second Congress of Texas being elected. The senate race for Bastrop was tight, with Leander Calvin Cunningham receiving sixty-four votes to former ranger captain Jesse Billingsley's sixty. Cunningham was a veteran of Captain Billingsley's Mina Volunteers and both men had fought together at San Jacinto.

Sparks flew between the two shortly after this election, however. Cunningham was seated when the Second Congress began. Billingsley

List of Citizens and Rangers Voting in Milam: September 4, 1837

John Bailey *	Samuel Gholson	John T. Porter
Silas H. Bates *	Thomas A. Graves	Neill K. Robinson
John Beal	Jonathan R. Hardin	A. W. Sillaven
William W. Bell	Thomas Harvell	William H. Smith *
Calvin Boales	John A. Hill	Josiah Taylor
Leroy Boggus	Gabriel Long *	William H. Taylor
George Bond	Lucien Hopson	William D. Thomson
John D. Brown *	Joseph P. Jones *	Andrew J. Webb
John Chalmers *	James Lewis	Jesse Webb *
Goldsby Childers	David McCanless	John B. Webb
Daniel Cullins *	George W. McGrew	Joseph Webb
Thomas Dillard	James T. McGrew	Thomas R. Webb
James Dunn	William A. McGrew	John Welch
Thomas Eaton *	John McLennan	Joseph Welch
Massillon Farley	Neill McLennan	Thomas Welch
Benjamin F. Fitch *	Daniel Monroe *	James A. Wilkinson *
Stephen Frazier *	Hardin Neville *	E. M. Wood

* Served in Major Smith's ranger battalion per military records.

Voter record source: McLean, *Papers Concerning Robertson's Colony*, XVI: 160-61.

protested that the election was illegal because thirteen of Cunningham's votes came from Texas Ranger Company C under Lieutenant Wren. Billingsley stated that these rangers did not have the right to vote in such an election.[19]

Cunningham then pointed out that ten of those voting for him from Company C were merely volunteer rangers who had never taken any kind of formal oath as soldiers. This left him with a one-vote majority over Billingsley, who then produced a muster roll of Company C for argument. He showed that all thirteen voters were listed on the company's muster roll and were therefore technically members of the company. The House of Representatives took a vote on the issue and Jesse Billingsley won, thirteen to eleven. He took his seat the following day. Cunningham was elected county judge of Bastrop that same year.

Voter records of September 4, 1837, show that ranger Company B of Captain Daniel Monroe was stationed in Milam County at Nashville. In this election, the House representative receiving the most votes was Gabriel Long, who was currently serving in Milam as quartermaster of the ranger battalion. The list of voters on this date is significant (see chart) in that a large portion of these men were members of Monroe's company, for which no muster roll is known to have survived.

On September 5 Senator Sterling Robertson went to the firm of

Hamilton and Henderson to acquire goods for Major Smith's ranger battalion stationed on the frontier. Robertson purchased ninety-one pounds of powder, eighty-four bars of lead, forty-eight gun flints, and one hundred pounds of rice and delivered these that day to Charles Curtis, assistant quartermaster in Columbia.[20]

On September 14 Secretary of War Thomas Rusk and General Kelsey Douglass issued written instructions to Tennessee native Jesse Watkins to conduct peace talks with the Indians. Watkins was to proceed with Lewis Sanchez of Nacogdoches, who would serve as an interpreter. They were to head to the prairies and talk with the chiefs and head men of the Kichais, Caddos, Tonkawas, and Ionis. The hope was to open commerce between the Indians and the white settlers, and to "bury our tomahawks with them." Watkins and Sanchez were to distribute presents as they felt appropriate. The Indians were to give up any prisoners they held, return all stolen property, refrain from murdering and stealing, and warn other Indians from conducting depredations. "If they will agree," instructed Rusk and Douglass, "you may promise them that we will make a treaty of peace with them which shall last forever."[21]

The hope was that the pair could convince the Indian chiefs to come to the Texas seat of government to iron out such a treaty. Two Indian commissioners were to be designated by President Houston to enact treaties should the Indians choose not to come to the government.

Per Sam Houston's proclamation, the first called session of the Second Congress began in the city of Houston of September 25, 1837. Chairman of the Military Committee Tom Rusk helped pass a bill to formally organize the militia of the Republic of Texas. President Houston vetoed the bill, which would also provide payment to volunteer outfits that had served their respective colonies. Rusk rallied the Second Congress to override the president's veto, and a joint session of the two houses thereafter nominated Rusk for the position of major general of the Texas militia.[22]

Once Rusk assumed his new command, he and Sam Houston would continue to clash in their views on how to run the militia throughout Houston's term of office.

The Second Congress also made special effort to study the Indians of Texas. Senator Issac Burton, former Texas Ranger captain, was now chairman of the senate's standing committee on Indian Affairs. In secret sessions held on October 12, 1837, Burton's committee reviewed intelligence that recognized twenty-seven different bands of Indians living in Texas.[23]

They were the Abadaches, Alabamas, Anadarkos, Ayish, Biloxis, Caddos, Cherokees, Chickasaws, Comanches, Coushattas, Delawares, Huawanies, Ionis, Karankawas, Kichais, Kickapoos, Lipans, Menominis, Muscogees, Nacogdoches, Skidi Pawnees, Potawatomis, Shawnees, Tonkawas, Towash, Tawakonis, and the Wacos.

As for locations of these tribes, the Abadaches, Anadarkos, Ais (Ayish), Caddos, Comanches, Ionis, Kichais, Nacogdoches, Pawnees, Towash, Tawakonis, and Wacos were described as living on the prairies, many concentrated on the headwaters of the Trinity, Brazos, and Colorado Rivers. The Alabamas, Biloxis, Coushattas, and Muscogees were described as living "south of the San Antonio Road," in the counties of Nacogdoches and Liberty. The Karankawas, Lipans, and Tonkawas were concentrated in West Texas, while the vast county of Nacogdoches largely harbored the tribes of the Cherokees, Chickasaws, Delawares, Huawanies, Kickapoos, Menominis, Potawatomis, and Shawnees.

★ ★ ★ ★ ★

The Eastland Campaign: October 1837

During October Major Smith maintained his ranger headquarters near Nashville-on-the-Brazos. Each passing month in the fall of 1837 saw large numbers of his men fulfilling their service enlistments and fewer new recruits joining the service to keep up with those leaving.

Captain Lee Smith's Company E served through September 17 at Fort Henderson near the Navasota River. After this time Captain Smith retired from the Texas Rangers, having been active a full year since entering Texas service with Captain Jewell's rangers in September 1836. The balance of Company E's men were discharged on October 1, 1837, by Major William Smith and Joseph Mather, "1st Lt. Commanding Company." The majority of Lieutenant Mather's men, who had enlisted on April 1 for six months, had also fulfilled their commitments to the ranger service.[24]

Captain Barron's Company A lost many key personnel in October. Fourth Sergeant Lee Davis, a veteran of Sergeant Erath's Elm Creek battle, completed his enlistment on October 3 and was discharged at headquarters. Barron on October 6 also lost Calvin Emmons, perhaps the ranger with the longest service tenure in the battalion. Emmons had originally enlisted in November 1835 under Captain Daniel Friar and had since served under Captains Burton, Putnam, and Barron. Acting Judge Advocate George Erath was also discharged on October 6 at ranger headquarters.[25]

Although Erath had completed his enlistment, he quickly volunteered again on October 8 upon learning that Major Smith was organizing an expedition into Indian territory. A large group of men departed Fort Colorado about October 8 for the previously abandoned Fort Smith on the Little River, where they would rendezvous with another frontier force.

A detachment of Captain John Bowyer's mounted gunmen from Houston arrived at Fort Smith to join this expedition. The senior officers from Major Smith's battalion were Captain William Eastland, who would take command of the men, and First Lieutenant John Lynch. The pension papers of Private George Green of Company D show that this expedition was referred to by some of the rangers as the "Eastland campaign."

The mounted gunmen of Captain Bowyer's company were commanded by First Lieutenant A. B. Vanbenthuysen and Second Lieutenant Alfred Miles. Vanbenthuysen later wrote a detailed report on this campaign, which states the purpose of their offensive.

> October 13, 1837, left Fort Smith situated on the waters of Little River, in company with Captain Eastland of Colorado [Fort], in pursuit of horses stolen from the Colorado by the Indians.[26]

Various accounts give the number of rangers participating in Captain Eastland's campaign to be between sixty-three and sixty-eight. Expedition member George Erath said the total party comprised sixty-six men under Captain Eastland and that they "made a campaign of nearly two months time." Erath stated that the men "penetrated the Indian country between the Brazos and Colorado, further than the same number of men had done before or since." Eastland's men subsisted entirely on the game they killed, without even salt to use.[27]

The expedition did not find any Indians by the end of the month. At this time some sort of disagreement arose near the Colorado River on November 1 between the officers in command of the party. This conflict occurred when the expedition was near the head of Pecan Bayou, a tributary to the Colorado River. This site would have been in present Callahan County, just southeast of present Abilene.

Captain Eastland and Lieutenant Lynch led the majority of their men back down Pecan Bayou for the Colorado River and ultimately back to Fort Colorado on Walnut Creek. In his report, First Lieutenant Vanbenthuysen of Captain Bowyer's company simply stated that he "parted company with Captain Eastland."

Eastland's rangers headed back for the Colorado River. Somewhere along the way, Eastland and twenty-four of his men fought a battle with what was estimated to be two hundred Indians. The site of the battle was on Ruan Bayou, and the fight continued for two hours. None of the Texans was killed. Another party of the returning rangers from Eastland's campaign was "closely chased" but escaped without casualties. One of the small parties, of which volunteer George Erath was a member, included eight men from the Brazos. Erath wrote that he and his fellow men "succeeded in taking seven horses and mules from another party of Indians on our way homeward and arrived safely at home."[28]

Captain Eastland's rangers were back at Fort Houston on the Colorado by mid-November. He signed the discharge papers of Addison Litton on November 20 at this post.[29]

★   ★   ★   ★   ★

The Stone Houses Fight: November 10, 1837

While all of these small bands of rangers succeeded in making it back without loss to their posts, one eighteen-man group under Lieutenant Vanbenthuysen was far less lucky. After parting ways with Captain Eastland, he and Second Lieutenant Alfred Miles continued on with sixteen rangers. Most of these men were originally from Vanbenthuysen's detachment, but his remaining party did include some of Captain Eastland's men who had decided not to end the expedition.

They pursued the trail of stolen horses in an east-northeast direction toward the Brazos River until meeting a party of Cherokees on November 3 near the forks of the Brazos. The site was likely in present Stonewall County. Vanbenthuysen wrote of his party's encounter with the Cherokees.

> They were a going to the Comanche Indians with powder and lead for the purpose of exchanging it for horses and mules. A party of seven Keechi [Kichai] Indians piloted this party of Cherokees. When first discovered, one of the Keechis was [a] half mile in advance of his party. Our men surrounded him and tried to make him surrender, but he would not be friendly with us.

This Kichai raised his rifle to shoot Lieutenant Miles but was shot dead by one of the rangers. Felix McCluskey, a wild-natured Irishman, was the ranger credited with this killing. Afterwards he is said to have scalped the Indian and rifled his pockets. Some of the riflemen were critical of him for this harsh act. McCluskey, however, ruthlessly displayed a chunk of tobacco he had lifted from the dead Indian's pocket and swore that he "would kill any Injun for that much tobacco."[30]

By this time the Cherokees came up and informed Vanbenthuysen that the Kichais were acting as their guides. They also explained that Jesse Watkins, who had been appointed an Indian agent by President Houston in September, had made a partial treaty with them. Watkins would not live long in his appointment. He and his interpreter Lewis Sanchez worked largely with the Kichai, Caddo, and Tawakoni Indians near present Dallas County. According to Sanchez, Watkins was captured by the Cherokee Indians of Chief Bowles and killed. It is possible that the very Indians Vanbenthuysen's rangers encountered were those who killed Watkins.[31]

"I immediately called off my men from the pursuit," wrote Vanbenthuysen, "but told the Cherokees that they could not furnish the hostile Indians with powder and lead to murder the inhabitants on the frontier."

The Indians were informed that if they attempted to go onward, the rangers would take their goods away from them. The Cherokees promised that they would return home and apparently did so. Lieutenant Vanbenthuysen's rangers crossed the forks of the Brazos River on November 4. They were troubled to continue finding horseshoe tracks going in a northeasterly direction. Shod tracks indicated horses stolen from the white men, as the Indians did not shoe their horses.

By November 10 the eighteen-man ranger party had reached a rock formation in the hills near the headwaters of the West Fork of the Trinity River that was known to the Indians as the "Stone Houses." This stone formation, standing out above the surrounding scrub brush and cactus, was thought to resemble early houses or tepees from a distance. The Stone Houses formation is located about ten miles south of Windthorst on Highway 61 in present Archer County. A historical marker is located just south of the West Fork of the Trinity River. The formation is actually 1.5 miles south of U.S. 61 down Prideaux Road, a gravel country lane.

Vanbenthuysen's report continues:

> I fell in with a large body of Indians in a moving position towards the southwest. I first supposed them to be Keechis, but was afterwards informed that they were Toweash, Wacos and a few Keechis and Caddos. I got this information from the Shawnees and Delawares. I judged the Indians to be about one hundred and fifty strong. About fifty or sixty of them were armed with rifles and the balance had bows and arrows.

When they first spotted the Indians, the Texans noticed that they had a large *caballado* of horses with them "and were accompanied by many women and children." Vanbenthuysen climbed atop the high Stone Houses rock mound "until I saw about one hundred and fifty mount their horses and come towards us." He immediately rushed down and stationed his men in a point of timber with a deep ravine for protection.

About three o'clock, the Indians made a charge upon us and completely surrounded our position. When they commenced firing from their rifles upon us, they had fired eight or ten shots before we returned their fire. There was a continual firing kept up on both sides until about half past four.

The Texans made their defensive stand in a deep ravine, and the Indians took position about seventy yards in front of the ravine. At one point Nicholson, who understood some of the Indian language, was sent out to try and make peace talks with them. He climbed a tree and opened conversation with the enemy.

The Indians reportedly first demanded the surrender of Felix McCluskey, who had killed the Kichai Indian one week prior.[32] When this was refused, the battle as described by Vanbenthuysen ensued. He recorded that the battle, later known as the "Stone Houses fight," was fought on November 10 at 33.5 degrees North latitude.

The Indians remained on horseback and fired at the Texans. The leading chief of this band rode his horse rapidly up and down the ravine in order to cause the Texans to waste their ammunition firing at him. He boldly held his shield up between him and his men. This shield did not faze one of the veteran Indian fighters among the Texan group. He took good aim, fired, and killed the chief.

In his battle report, Vanbenthuysen stated that his men were no more than a pistol's shot apart from their enemies during this exchange. He also noted that his men had "the good fortune to kill their principal chief" during this exchange.

When the chief fell from his horse, the other Indians rushed forward to retrieve his body. The Texans poured a volley into their midst as the Indians tied a rope around the chief's body and galloped off out of range. They returned on foot within fifteen minutes and took position within sixty yards of the ravine occupied by the rangers.

The gun battle now became intense as the Indians tried to avenge their fallen leader. The Indians had the better position in thick timber, which was adorned with underbrush and tall grass. The Texans were

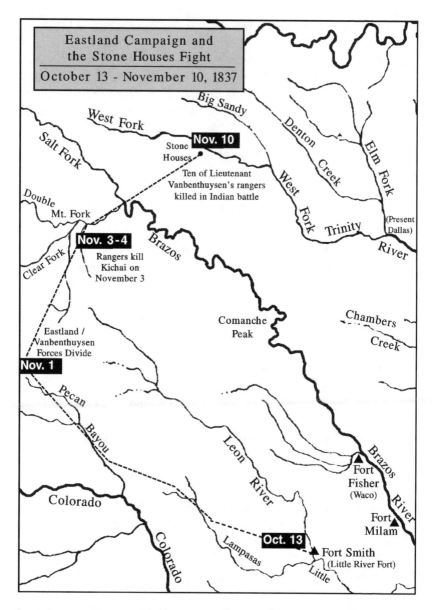

Eastland Campaign and
the Stone Houses Fight
October 13 - November 10, 1837

Nov. 10

Stone Houses

Ten of Lieutenant
Vanbenthuysen's rangers
killed in Indian battle

Nov. 3-4

Rangers kill
Kichai on
November 3

Eastland /
Vanbenthuysen
Forces Divide

Nov. 1

Comanche
Peak

Oct. 13

Fort Smith
(Little River Fort)

Fort Fisher
(Waco)

Fort
Milam

(Present
Dallas)

forced to sneak a peek over the top of the ravine to spot an Indian and
then quickly fire. Each of their shots drew a volley from the enemy.

During the fight the rangers would pull off their hats, place them on
the end of their ramrods, and raise them above the walls of the ravine.
The Indians, mistaking the empty hats for hats with heads in them, would
fire at them, sometimes putting as many as half a dozen balls through one

hat. The rangers would then immediately rise, take aim, and fire at the Indians.

After an hour and a half, the firing died off about 4:30 p.m. The Indians withdrew, having suffered a number of casualties in the heated firing. Lieutenant Vanbenthuysen's men had done surprisingly well against their numerically superior foe. They had, however, lost four rangers and six horses killed.

Those killed had been Joseph Cooper, Alexander Bostwick, Dr. William Sanders, and William Nicholson. Dr. Sanders had enrolled in Captain James Price's Kentucky Volunteers on June 1, 1836, for six months and had subsequently joined the ranger battalion under Major Smith. Bostwick, an atheist, had argued to his fellow soldier James Ogden Rice on several occasions that he did not believe in the existence of God. Rice had prophetically chastised the man with, "I may yet see you die on this trip."[33]

Vanbenthuysen gave praise to his men for fighting valiantly during the early gun battle.

> Too much praise cannot be bestowed upon those brave men who fell. All of them received their death shots and died in a few minutes after being shot. Their cry was, "Fight on! Fight on! You can whip the Indians!" Mr. Bostwick, after being shot through the body, loaded and fired his rifle three times and had the fourth load in his gun when he expired in the act of drawing his ramrod from his rifle. Young Cooper insisted that we should help him up and let him fight after securing a death shot.

After a fifteen-minute hiatus, the Indians again advanced on the fourteen surviving Texans. The tall, dry grass and brush of the woods on three sides of them were set ablaze. A strong wind blew thick, blinding smoke over the rangers. The Indians took defensive positions at either end of the ravine to prevent the Texans from escaping. "We discovered a smoke rising around us," wrote Vanbenthuysen. "The Indians had made a ring [of] fire completely around our position, [and] the fire was advancing rapidly."[34]

As the flames rose, Vanbenthuysen realized that the only escape for his men lay on the fourth side, an open prairie where horsemen with bows and arrows were stationed!

The only other option left for the hapless rangers was to brave a charge on foot through the rifle-armed Indians. This was considered preferable to those armed with bows and arrows, who could reload

This rock formation in present Archer County near the West Fork of the Trinity River came to be known as the Stone Houses. From a great distance, early Indians thought the stones resembled tepees or houses. A seventeen-man party of Texas Rangers fought for their lives against superior Indian forces at Stone Houses on November 10, 1837. *Author's collection.*

quicker and discharge more shots at them. When the horses would not move through the flames, the men were forced to leave them. According to Oliver Buckman, the dense smoke helped hide the Texans until they made their final charge from it.[35]

The surviving rangers now charged approximately fifty armed Indians and drove them ahead of them. Finding the ravine heavily populated with Indians on horseback, the men ultimately decided to race up the hill and across the open prairie for the thicket beyond.

Leading the charge was Private James Rice, a young man of about twenty-two years who had served in one of the early Texas Ranger companies under Captain Tumlinson during the Texas Revolution. Rice was nearly killed when he met an Indian with a raised gun. As he sprinted, he raised his own gun, leaped to a stop, and fired a chance shot at his adversary. Good aim or pure luck was with Rice this day, for his shot hit the brave squarely and dropped him dead on his face.[36]

While making this most desperate charge from the ring of fire, six of Lieutenant Vanbenthuysen's men were not as lucky as Rice. Lieutenant Alfred Miles, Lewis F. Sheuster, James Joslen, James Christian, Jesse Blair, and Westley Nicholson were shot and killed while trying to escape the burning field.

James Christian was one of the original enlistees into Colonel

Lieut. Vanbenthuysen's Stone Houses Fight: November 10, 1837		
First Lieutenant:	Oliver Buckman	William Nicholson [1]
A. B. Vanbenthuysen	James Christian [1]	James O. Rice
Second Lieutenant:	Joseph Cooper [1]	Dr. William Sanders [1]
Alfred H. Miles [1]	Robert Fletcher [2]	Lewis P. Scheuster [1]
Privates:	John Hobson	John Zekel [2]
Jesse Blair [1]	James Joslen [1]	
Samuel K. Blisk [2]	Felix McCluskey	[1] Killed by Indians.
Alexander Bostwick [1]	Westley Nicholson [1]	[2] Wounded in battle.

Coleman's ranger battalion, having previously served in Captain Walden's infantry company. Lieutenant Miles was a San Jacinto veteran who had been involved in the capture of Santa Anna. The *Telegraph and Texas Register* on Saturday, December 16, 1837, announced that Miles was originally from Richmond, Virginia, and that he left behind a sister and mother in Texas.[37]

In the end, only eight of eighteen rangers escaped the deadly Indian encounter at Stone Houses. Three of these men, John Zekel, Robert Fletcher, and Samuel Blisk, were wounded in the process. Five men escaped without bullet or arrow wounds—Vanbenthuysen, James Rice, Felix McCluskey, Oliver Buckman, and John Hobson.

The survivors broke through the Indians and commenced their retreat on foot. They had just crossed the skirt of timber when they again came in sight of the Indians. This time the braves did not pursue the Texans but merely stood and watched. "They had enough of the fight," thought Vanbenthuysen, "for we had killed about fifty of their warriors."

Unfortunately for the ragged survivors of the ill-fated ranger expedition, escaping from the Indians would not end their ordeals in returning to safety.

★ ★ ★ ★ ★

Lynch's Rangers and Karnes' Treaty

Other Indian encounters were experienced in the settlements during November. On November 12, 1837, Indians came into Bastrop and stole ten horses. Local residents pursued them and recaptured twelve horses, several mules, and other property.[38]

These Indians also attacked two men who were working on the farm of James Rogers, a man who would later command a company of volunteers in an 1839 Indian fight. His son Joseph Rogers and a Captain McCullom, a recent arrival in Texas from Alabama, were cutting timber to build a wolf trap in the forest when they were fired on by Comanches. The Texans fled through the woods toward Wilbarger Creek. McCullom was shot in the back and killed, while Rogers escaped.[39]

Two days after the Indians first swept through Bastrop, Joe Rogers, Jim Craft, and another man named Floyd went to Hornsby's on November 14 to secure ammunition for the Colorado River settlers. They departed and were about a mile from the Joe Duty home when they spotted a band of Comanches charging at them full speed across the open prairie. A race for life ensued. One party came at them from the rear while a second charged from the right. Craft and Floyd escaped on their good horses to the Duty house, but Rogers was on an inferior horse and was overtaken by the Indians. He was speared to death in sight of the house and then scalped.

Joe Rogers, son of James and Rachael Rogers, had come to Texas in 1831. A brother-in-law to Colonel Edward Burleson, Rogers had also served as first lieutenant of Captain John Tumlinson's rangers during the Texas Revolution.

The Indians continued on to the home of Reuben Hornsby and tried to cut him off from his house. His son saw what was happening and raced to the farm on his horse to rescue his father. They rushed into the home and barred the doors, presented their rifles, and bluffed the Indians into moving on. After circling the place, yelling, and making a scene for a time, they eventually moved on. Mrs. Harrell, who lived near the Hornsbys, took several children to the river bottom and hid there until the Indians had departed.

Some of the rangers from Fort Houston on the Colorado River were sent out by Major Smith. They pursued these Indians but were unable to overtake them.[40]

Shortly after the killings near Hornsby's settlement, Major Smith authorized another ranger company to take up station in this area. Captain Lee Smith's Company E had completed its six-month service at Fort Henderson by this time. Smith issued a promissory note of fifty dollars on November 4 to two of his rangers, Privates Elisha Anglin and Seth H. Bates, for beef and pork provisions they left after departing from Fort Henderson.[41]

★ ★ ★ ★ ★

Captain Daniel Monroe's Company B, Captain Tommy Barron's Company A, and Lieutenant Nicholas Wren's Company C had dwindled significantly in number. There are very few detailed records of these companies, but it appears likely that Barron's and Wren's units had been disbanded by November due to numerous men fulfilling their enlistment requirements.

Major William Smith promoted another of his junior officers, First Lieutenant John L. Lynch of Captain Eastland's company, into a new command that month. Pay records show that Lynch had served as a first lieutenant in the ranger corps for the six-month period of May 17 through November 17, 1837. Another payroll voucher shows that Lynch was paid from November 10-20, 1837, as "Lieutenant Rangers" and from November 28, 1837, to March 3, 1838, as "Captain Rangers."[42]

Captain Lynch immediately began enlisting men into his new company, many from the Hornsby settlement along the Colorado River. Brothers Joseph and Malcolm Hornsby enlisted for three months' service on December 7, 1837. Their father, Reuben, provided twenty-six bushels of corn to Lynch on December 10 "for the use of my company of rangers."

Reuben Hornsby had long been involved with and acted in support of frontier ranger companies. He had furnished corn to Captain Eastland's company at Fort Houston on October 6 and was paid $240 for work hauling provisions for Major Smith's rangers. The elder Hornsby eventually joined his sons in Captain Lynch's company, enlisting on January 26, 1838.[43]

As Lynch struggled to find willing volunteers to add another company to Smith's battalion, another frontier force was treating with the Indians. Colonel Henry Karnes and Major James W. Tinsley commanded a small First Cavalry Regiment at Camp Sherman, which was located in the San Antonio area in the fall of 1837.[44]

A Texas War Department document dated June 6, 1838, certified that "Col. H. W. Karnes was appointed with full power to enter into a treaty of peace with the Comanche Indians Nov. 16, 1837." He held meetings with Indian leaders in San Antonio and concluded a peace treaty with the Tonkawa Indians on November 22.

The treaty was signed at the "Texas Post of Bexar" by Colonel Karnes and three Tonkawa chiefs, Ouchala, Hosata, and Harshokena. In this document, the Tonkawas promised to "bury the Tomahawk and live upon terms of peace and amity" with the government of Texas. Under the terms of this treaty, merchant Nathaniel C. Lewis was to be a trading agent among these Indians and they were to buy articles from him and make sales to no other person.[45]

An audited claim approved by Texas auditors for payment to Karnes

Frontier Ranger Companies of 1837 Major William H. Smith Commanding	
Company A	
Capt. Thomas H. Barron	January 1 - November 1837 *
Capt. John L. Lynch	November 28, 1837 - February 20, 1838
Company B	
Capt. Daniel Monroe	January 1 - December 14, 1837 *
Company C	
Capt. Micah Andrews	January 1 - August 1837
Lieutenant Nicholas Wren	August - October 1837 *
Company D	
Capt. William M. Eastland	January 1 - March 2, 1838
Company E	
Capt. Lee C. Smith	March 17 - September 17, 1837
Lieutenant Joseph Mather	September 17 - October 1, 1837
Harrisburg Mounted Gunmen	
Capt. John C. Bowyer	June 18 - December 18, 1837
* Approximate ending date based on author's research of Texas audited military claims.	

shows some of the items the cavalry colonel exchanged with the Indian leaders.

Republic of Texas to Col. H. W. Karnes

For cash paid for 1 dozen butcher knives $6.00
1 shotgun for the Toncaway Chief   20.00
2 hatchets at $1.00 each
1 horse given in exchange for a stolen one   15.00
15 hdkfs [handkerchiefs] at 37.5 each   5.625
1 so[?]   3.00
Tavern bill paid for self and men to the post of
    San Antonio   42.50
Total   94.125[46]

The costs for such a goodwill effort with the local Indians were small. The lack of a regular army and the small number of men enrolled in the frontier forces made peacekeeping efforts all the more important. The Texas Senate ratified Karnes' Tonkawa treaty on December 19, 1837.

Lieutenant Vanbenthuysen and the other survivors of the Stone Houses fight of November 10 were still fighting to survive at the time Karnes was penning his treaty with the Tonkawas.

Although they had killed as many as fifty of their attackers, ten rangers had died in the battle. Zekel, Fletcher, and Blisk were painfully wounded. Vanbenthuysen, Rice, Hobson, McCluskey, and Buckman were the only five to escape being wounded. All of the men, however, had lost their horses and their provisions in escaping the battleground.

In the ten days following the fight, Vanbenthuysen's men roughed it on foot through the wilderness as they cautiously followed the West Fork of the Trinity River in an east-southeasterly fashion through present Fort Worth. They had nothing to eat for the first four days until the men managed to kill some buffalo and save themselves from starvation. The wounds of the three injured rangers were bound up and greased with buffalo tallow.[47]

By November 20 Vanbenthuysen's men were fortunate enough to find a friendly Indian camp in present northwest Dallas. The camp was located near the junction of the West and Elm Forks of the Trinity River. Lieutenant Vanbenthuysen wrote:

> We first discovered an Indian on the prairie. We followed him to his village. When we arrived there, we found the warriors drawn up to receive us in a hostile manner. They were all armed with rifles and the squaws had bows and arrows. I expected nothing else but we should have to fight them, but after a good deal of parleying they said that our little party might stay there that night. We then dressed the wounds of the men and camped in the midst of the hostile camp.[48]

On November 21 the rangers crossed the Trinity River at the three forks. That evening they arrived at a Kickapoo village, where the Indians were friendly and treated them with "the utmost hospitality." The Kickapoos gave them food to eat, and the next morning two of their young men led the Texans to a trail. They were told that it would lead them to the Neches Saline near the Neches River.

Vanbenthuysen's report noted the beauty of the North Texas area.

> The country on the waters of the Trinity is handsomely situated, well watered, plenty of timber of large growth consisting of hickory, oak and cedar. The prairies abound in game of every kind: the game is chiefly bear, deer antelopes and buffalo. I have seen the prairies black with immense herds of buffalo, as far as the eye could extend. I think that this country is the garden of America, and will in time be the most valuable part of Texas.

They reached the saline in Cherokee Nation and proceeded on to Martin Lacy's trading post on the Old San Antonio Road. On November 27 Vanbenthuysen's men reached their first white settlement since the battle, making seventeen days and one night that they had retreated through hostile Indian territory—on foot without horses or blankets or provisions!

Lieutenant Vanbenthuysen left the wounded men in the white settlement, and on November 28 he started for Houston in company with rangers Rice and McCluskey. They eventually arrived on December 8, 1837, after an absence from that town of six months.

A Texas historical marker for the Stone Houses fight can be seen on FM 61 ten miles south of Windthorst.

The actual rock formation is located just off a gravel road approximately 1.5 miles west of the marker. *Author's collection.*

Today a Texas historical marker marks the site of "The Stone Houses" and mentions the battle these riflemen had survived. It is located in Archer County on FM 61 ten miles south of Windthorst.

Stone Houses was a tough loss in the early history of the Texas Rangers. Of the survivors, John Hobson settled in Harris County and Oliver Buckman near Bastrop. Vanbenthuysen never held a significant command again in Texas. James Rice continued in the frontier service, and his name would become well known for commanding rangers in a fight on the San Gabriel in 1839.

Felix McCluskey, who had killed the Indian in early November, which ultimately led to the attack at Stone Houses, was later killed in a drunken brawl.

Epilogue

The Stone Houses conflict was just one of many tough lessons for the rangers and riflemen in 1837. They had also been overwhelmed at Erath's fight in January, at the Trinity River the same month, at the Post Oak Springs massacre in May, and twice in April had their horses stampeded by Indians near their own frontier outposts.

Without army or militia support, the rangers were simply too few to mount an effective campaign against the hostile Indians. During the Texas Revolution, ranging forces had been more plentiful to protect settlers from Indian hostilities, while the army repelled the Mexican invasion. At the height of ranger enlistment during the actual revolution, there were about two hundred men enrolled in ranger companies.

After the Mexican army had been driven from the San Jacinto battlefields, Indian depredations had increased. Ranger enrollment also increased. By mid-September 1836, approximately 450 men were serving in four battalions. Beginning with Captain Eli Hillhouse's first recruits on October 23, 1835, men were continually employed in the ranging service until April 1838, when the remnants of the battalion that had endured the Stone Houses fight were disbanded.

Volume 2 of *Savage Frontier* examines the state of the Texas military in early 1838. Not only was the ranging system allowed to lapse, but the entire Texas army had been furloughed by Sam Houston in 1837. Only small cavalry forces under Colonel Henry Karnes had been left in operation. Fortunately, the Texas militia developed rapidly as the new offensive arm of the republic in lieu of an organized army.

Backed by the new commander in chief of the Texas militia, Major General Thomas Rusk, Texan settlers became united in their efforts to drive out marauders and raiders. Rusk personally led three major expeditions during 1838 and authorized the raising of ranging companies within his militia brigades.

Rusk, Edward Burleson, John Henry Moore, Henry Karnes, John Dyer, Kelsey Douglass, John Bird, Juan Seguín, and John Neill stood out as leaders of the move to quell Indian violence during 1838 and 1839.

In early 1839 a new army known as the Frontier Regiment was recruited. Its mission was to build and man blockhouses along the front lines of savage opposition. The Republic of Texas also passed legislation to support a new mounted gunman battalion and ranging companies within specified counties.

There was also a general move from the defensive to the offensive. Conflicts were more frequent and generally more violent. During the "surveyors' fight" and "Bryant's defeat," the Texans again suffered heavy losses. When the rangers and militia teamed up to quell Cordova's rebellion in East Texas, they were able to overcome their opponents during the Kickapoo War. Aided also by the new Frontier Regiment during the Cherokee War, the Texans would prevail in a deadly showdown with many hundreds of hostile Indians along the Neches River.

Through the expeditions, retaliations, and battles of 1838 and 1839, the frontiersmen would learn new tactics for taking the fight to their opponents. Legendary ranger names such as Jack Hays, Ben McCullough, and Rip Ford participated in their first Indian expeditions during this time. Countless other men served and fought with little or no acclaim. Volume 2 seeks to call attention to hundreds of such long-neglected men, who did their part to keep the peace on Texas's savage frontier.

Appendix

Roster of Texas Rangers Coleman/Smith Battalion

August 1836 - April 1838

A new ranger battalion under Coleman Robert Morris Coleman was authorized in August 1836 with three companies under his command. Command of this battalion passed in January 1837 to Major William Henry Smith. During peak enlistment, Smith commanded five different ranger companies on the Texas frontiers.

The surviving muster rolls for Companies A, B, and C have been published in the Daughter of the Republic of Texas's *Muster Rolls of the Texas Revolution* for the August - December 1836 period. No other muster rolls for this ranger battalion are known to remain. The balance of the information contained in this appendix is therefore based on my research of Republic of Texas audited military claims and pension papers filed by these rangers and their commanders.

For each company, the key below indicates the unit commander and the period of time he commanded this company. For each ranger, the letter following his name indicates the companies in which he served, in the chronological order of service dates. For example, the entry "B, A" would indicate that the ranger served under Captain Barron's original Company B and then continued in service in Company A under Barron in 1837.

KEY TO COMPANY DESIGNATIONS:

Company A: *Captain Alfred P. Walden,* August 15 - October 5, 1836; *First Lieutenant Alexander Robless,* October 5 - December 31, 1836; *Captain Thomas Hudson Barron,* January 1 - November 1837; and *Captain John L. Lynch,* November 28, 1837 - February 20, 1838.

Company B: *Captain Thomas Hudson Barron,* September 11 - December 31, 1836; *Captain Daniel Monroe,* January 1 - December 14, 1837; and *First Lieutenant William H. Moore,* December 1837 - April 30, 1838.

Company C: *Second Lieutenant Benjamin R. Thomas*, September 21 - December 31, 1836; *Captain Micah Andrews*, January 1 - early August 1837; *First Lieutenant Nicholas Wren*, August - October 1837; Andrews paid as ranger captain through January 5, 1838.

Company D: *Captain William Mosby Eastland*, January 1, 1837 - March 2, 1838.

Company E: *Captain Lee C. Smith*, March 17 - September 17, 1837; and *First Lieutenant Joseph Mather*, September 17 - October 1, 1837.

Name:	Company:
Adkisson, Allen J.	A
Alderson, Henry	A
Allen, William	E
Ambrose, Marquis	A
Anderson, B. H.	B
Anderson, Matthew	E, B
Andrews, Micah	C
Angel, John	A, C, D
Anglin, Abraham	E
Atkinson, George	D
Avery, Willis	C
Bailey, Jesse	B
Bailey, John	B
Barker, Calvin	D
Barker, Leman	C, D
Barnes, Robert S.	A, D
Barnett, George W.	C
Barrier, A. B.	B
Barron, John M.	B, A
Barron, Thomas Hudson	B, A
Bates, Seth H.	B, A
Beard, William	E
Bell, Thomas W.	D
Bender, Charles	A
Bennett, Spirus	C
Benny, James	A
Berry, Alfred	B, A
Berry, John Bate	A
Biggs, Wilson H.	A
Blair, Thomas	D
Blisk, Samuel K.	A, C
Booker, Fee C.	A
Booker, Ferdinand C.	A
Booth, Isham M.	D

Name:	Company:
Bradley, Charles H.	B
Brown, John D.	B
Brown, Richard	D
Bryson, Thomas	C
Bugg, William	B
Burgess, Warren	E
Burton, Samuel	B, A
Bush, Hiram B.	E
Butler, James O.	A, C
Caldwell, William B.	D
Calmes, George	E
Cameron, William H.	B
Campbell, David W.	B, A
Carnell, Patrick T.	B, A
Carrol, Hugh	E
Caruthers, William	B
Castleberry, B. B.	B
Castleman, Michael	B, A
Castner, Isaac	C
Chalmers, John	B, A, D
Chapman, George W.	D
Childers, Robert	B, A
Christian, James	A, C
Clark, David	B, A
Cockrill, John R.	B, A
Coleman, Robert Morris, Colonel	
Collard, Richard	A
Collins, Thomas C.	D
Colvin, Aaron	A
Cook, Miles J.	A
Cooper, Alfred M.	D
Coryell, James	B, A
Cox, Samuel	E
Cox, William R.	D

Name:	Company:	Name:	Company:
Craft, Samuel	D	Galicia, Andrew	A
Crosby, Ganey	E	Garcia, Francisco	C
Cullins, Aaron	B	Gasceo, Jose	A
Cullins, Daniel	B	Gilleland, James	D
Culp, Josiah	E	Gilman, Elijah	E, D
Curtis, Charles	B, A	Goodwin, William	A
Dalrymple, William C.	E	Gray, Daniel	C
Darneill, Ansel	B, A	Green, George	B
Davis, Allen J.	D	Gross, Jacob	B, A
Davis, Brinkley	E	Halfpenny, James	B
Davis, Lee R.	B, A	Hamilton, Frederick	D
Davis, William C.	E	Hamilton, James	C, A
Dawson, Dread	B	Hammond, Hugh	A
Denson, Archibald C.	A	Harness, Abel	B
Dickerson, L. W.	D	Harrell, Jacob M.	A, C, D
Duncan, Charles	B, A	Henderson, James	C, D
Duncan, Green	B, B, A	Henry, John	A, C, E
Duncan, James	B	Hill, John Christopher C.	D
Duty, Joseph	C, D	Hill, Isaac Lafayette	D
Eastland, William Mosby	D	Hobson, John H.	B, A
Eaton, Alfred P.	B, A	Holmes, Martin	D
Eaton, Stephen	E	Hopson, B. W.	B
Eaton, Thomas H.	B	Hornsby, Joseph	A
Edwards, Tilford C.	B	Hornsby, Malcolm M.	A
Eggleston, Richard	A, C	Hornsby, Reuben	A, D
Eldridge, Thomas	C	Hornsby, William W.	D
Emmons, Calvin B.	B, A	Horton, Hilliard T.	D
England, Harvey P.	D	Hoskins, Thomas	B
Ensor, Luke	B	Hubert, Fletcher W.	E
Erath, George Bernard	B, A	Hubert, John R.	E
Etheridge, Daniel O.	A	Husbands, John	C
Evans, William T.	A, D	Ingram, Elijah	C
Farmer, David M.	B	Isaacs, William	B, A
Ferguson, M. M.	B	Isham, Lucas D.	B
Ferguson, Robert	B, A	James, Thomas D.	B, D
Fisk, Greenlief	D	Johnson, Alfred	B
Fitch, Benjamin F.	B, A	Johnson, Samuel	B
Fokes, John	B, A	Johnson, William	C
Foley, James R.	D	Jones, Galand	A
Fowler, John W.	C	Jones, Johnson	A
Fowler, Samuel	A, C	Jones, Joseph P.	B, D
Fowler, Thomas M.	C	Kennedy, William H.	D
Fox, Charles G.	E	Killough, Newton C.	E
Frasier, James	B, A, D	Leash, James	C
Friedlander, William	C	Lee, George M.	D

Name:	*Company:*	*Name:*	*Company:*
Lee, Pertilla	D	Moffitt, William	B
Leeds, Charles H.	A, C	Monroe, Daniel	B
Litton, Addison	D	Monroe, William H.	C
Litton, John	C	Moor, Thomas A.	C, D
Lloyd, Richard J.	D	Moore, Azariah G.	C
Long, Gabriel	B	Moore, James W.	C
Long, John Joseph	B	Moore, Lewis	B, A
Lowry, Isaac	C	Moore, Morris	B, A
Lupton, William	A, C	Moore, Nathaniel	C, D
Luther, Samuel	A	Moore, William H.	B
Lynch, John L.	D, A	Morgan, Andrew J.	B, A
Mahoney, Dennis	A	Morgan, George W.	B, A
Malone, Francis	A	Morgan, John C.	B, A
Malone, John	A	Nabors, Robert W.	C
Manning, James H.	C	Neill, George	A
Manor, James	B	Neill, William C.	B, A, D
Marshall, Samuel R.	C, D	Nevill, Hardin	B, A
Martin, Artimon L.	E	Oatts, Harbert H.	D
Martin, Philip C.	A, C	Owen, J. J.	B
Martin, W. W.	E	Owen, Robert	C
Mather, Joseph	E	Owen, William	D
Matthews, Robert H.	A	Palmer, Van R.	A, C
Matthews, Thomas	B	Parks, Alexander	E
Matthews, William	A	Parsons, Abel	B
McClarney, R. H.	D	Peoples, John H.	A
McCluskey, Felix	A, C, D	Perry, William H.	A
McCoy, Green	B, A	Pierson, John G. W.	A
McCoy, John C.	E	Plummer, Luther T. M.	E
McCutchen, William	C, D	Prater, Philip	B
McDonald, Elisha	E	Pratt, James	C
McDonald, Jeremiah	B, A	Proctor, Joseph	A
McDougald, John	C	Puckett, R. R.	D
McKay, Fielding	A	Raglin, Henry Walton	B
McKernon, Thomas	A, C, D	Ragsdale, James C.	B
McLaughlin, James	B, A	Raper, Marcus D.	B
McLaughlin, William	C, D	Reed, Evan	A
Mercer, Levi	B	Rice, James P.	E
Mickler, Jacob	E	Rice, John G.	E
Middleton, William B.	D	Rice, Spencer	B
Miles, Alenson T.	A, C	Richards, Jefferson	A
Mitchell, George W.	D	Roberts, Joseph W.	D
Mitchell, James H.	E	Roberts, William W.	B
Mitchell, M. A.	E	Robertson, Daniel	D
Mitchell, Robert	B	Robertson, Ezekiel	B
Moffitt, Robert	B	Robertson, Neil	B, A

Name:	Company:	Name:	Company:
Robertson, William	A	Thompson, Jasper N.	B
Robinson, John B.	C, D	Tucker, John	B, A
Robison, Ezekiel	A	Tyus, Robert M.	E
Robless, Alexander	A	Vance, John	E
Rogers, Henry	A	Velasco, Edward	D
Rogers, James	C	Wade, Peter F.	C.
Seekill, John	A, C, D	Walden, Alfred P.	A
Seymour, John W.	A	Walker, Martin A.	E
Slawson, Augustus W.	E	Walker, Richard H.	D
Smith, G. B.	B	Wallace, James P.	C
Smith, John M.	B	Walters, John B.	C
Smith, Lee C.	E	Warwick, Simon	E
Smith, Levi H.	A	Webb, Ezra	B, A
Smith, Sterrett	B	Webb, Jesse	B
Smith, William H., Major		Webber, John F.	B
Smithwick, Noah	C, D	Weekes, Joseph	C
Speir, Abner B.	D	Welch, James	D
Stiffey, William C.	C	Welch, William	E
Strickland, Willson	E	Whisler, Gasper	A
Stump, John S.	B	Wilkinson, John	B, A
Sullivan, Patrick	A	Williams, Francis	B
Swan, William	A	Willson, Charles	B
Tally, William D.	D	Wilson, Henry	A, C, D
Taylor, Jonathan	A	Wilson, James	E
Templin, William	B	Wolfenberger, Samuel	C
Thomas, Benjamin R.	C	Woodford, William	B
Thomas L. J.	D	Wren, Nicholas	C
Thompson, Empson	B	Zellner, Francis	D

Chapter Notes

Volume 1

Abbreviations to the Republic Claims Papers, 1835-1846.
Texas State Library and Archives Commission, Austin.

AC   Audited Claims are those military-related claims submitted to the comptroller or treasurer of the Republic of Texas that were audited, approved, and paid by the republic government.

PD   Public Debt Claims are claims for services provided between 1835 and 1846 that could not be paid until after Texas's annexation in 1846. These were largely paid between 1848 and the early 1860s, mainly from the 1850 Boundary Compromise money Texas was paid for its lost territory.

PP   Republic Pension Papers were generally filed from the 1870s to the early 1900s by veterans who served in the Texas Revolution and other republic-era military units.

UC   Unpaid Claims are those documents which do not fit in one of the above categories or those whose final payment disposition is unknown.

Chapter 1
Attack and Counterattack

1. Brown, John Henry. *Indian Wars and Pioneers of Texas* (1880. Reprint, Austin: State House Press, 1988), 15-16. Hereafter cited as Brown, *Indian Wars*. See also McLean, Malcolm D. *Papers Concerning Robertson's Colony in Texas* (Fort Worth: Texas Christian University Press, 1993), Vol. X: 41. This multi-volume set is hereafter referenced as McLean, *Papers*.

2. DeShields, James T. *Border Wars of Texas* (1912. Reprint, Austin: State House Press, 1993), 106-109. Hereafter referenced as DeShields, *Border Wars*.

3. White, Gifford. *1830 Citizens of Texas: A Census of 6,500 Pre-Revolutionary Texians* (Austin: Eakin Press, 1983), viii, 239. Knowles, Thomas W. *They Rode for the Lone Star. The Saga of the Texas Rangers: The Birth of Texas - The Civil War* (Dallas,: Taylor Publishing Company, 1999), 17-18, 51-52.

4. Sowell, A. J. *Rangers and Pioneers of Texas* (1884. Reprint, Austin: State House Press, 1991), 109-11. Hereafter referenced as Sowell, *Rangers*. See also Brown, *Indian Wars*, 16, and DeShields, *Border Wars*, 109-10.

5. Sowell, A. J. *Texas Indian Fighters. Early Settlers and Indian Fighters of Southwest Texas* (1900. Reprint, Austin: State House Press, 1986), 436-38. Hereafter referenced as Sowell, *Texas Indian Fighters*. Sowell, *Rangers*, 112-13.

6. DeShields, *Border Wars*, 110-11; Sowell, *Rangers*, 113.
7. Brown, *Indian Wars*, 16.
8. DeShields, *Border Wars*, 111-12.
9. Sowell, *Texas Indian Fighters*, 439.
10. Wilkins, Frederick. *The Legend Begins. The Texas Rangers, 1823-1845* (Austin: State House Press, 1996), 59-67. Hereafter referenced as Wilkins, *The Legend Begins*.
11. Knowles, *They Rode for the Lone Star*, 17-19.
12. Brown, *Indian Wars*, 16; DeShields, *Border Wars*, 112; Sowell, *Texas Indian Fighters*, 439.
13. McLean, *Papers*, X: 41.
14. Wilbarger, John Wesley. *Indian Depredations in Texas* (1889. Reprint, Austin: State House Press, 1985), 198-200. Hereafter referenced as Wilbarger, *Indian Depredations*.
15. Wilkins, *The Legend Begins*, 5-6.
16. Webb, Walter Prescott (Editor-in-Chief). *The Handbook of Texas* (Austin: Texas State Historical Association, 1952), II: 106.
17. Wilkins, *The Legend Begins*, 5-6.
18. Hatley, Allen G. *The Indian Wars in Stephen F. Austin's Texas Colony, 1822-1835* (Austin: Eakin Press, 2001), 15-25. Knowles, *They Rode for the Lone Star*, 16-21.
19. Wilbarger, *Indian Depredations*, 204-205; Wilkins, *The Legend Begins*, 6. Captain Tumlinson has also been listed as John James (versus "Jackson") Tumlinson in some early sources.
20. McLean, *Papers*, X: 47; Webb, Walter Prescott, *The Texas Rangers; A Century of Frontier Defense* (Austin: University of Texas Press, 1991), 20; Hatley, *The Indian Wars*, 42-45.
21. Wilbarger, *Indian Depredations*, 201-202.
22. Brown, *Indian Wars*, 15.
23. Sowell, *Rangers*, 25; Webb, *The Texas Rangers*, 21.
24. Hatley, *The Indian Wars*, 49-52.
25. Ibid., 54.
26. Wilbarger, *Indian Depredations*, 206-10.
27. Wilkins, *The Legend Begins*, 10.

Chapter 2
The Original Ranger Battalion

1. Lamar, Mirabeau B. *The Papers of Mirabeau Buonaparte Lamar* (Charles A. Gulick Jr., Winnie Allen, Katherine Elliott, and Harriet Smither, Ed. 6 Vol., 1922. Reprint, Austin: Pemberton Press, 1968), Erath to Lamar, "Sketches on Milam and Robertson County," IV: # 2164, 31. Hereafter cited as *Lamar Papers*.
2. McLean, *Papers*, X: 41.
3. DeShields, *Border Wars*, 112-13.

4. Jenkins, John H. and Kenneth Kesselus. *Edward Burleson: Texas Frontier Leader* (Austin: Jenkins Publishing Co., 1990), 29. Hereafter referenced as Jenkins, *Burleson*.

5. McLean, *Papers*, X: 43.

6. Pierce, Gerald Swetnam. *Texas Under Arms. The Camps, Posts, Forts, and Military Towns of the Republic of Texas 1836-1846* (Austin: Encino Press, 1969), 14. Hereafter referenced as Pierce, *Texas Under Arms*.

7. Brown, *Indian Wars*, 26; McLean, *Papers*, X: 43-44.

8. Jenkins, John Holland. *Recollections of Early Texas. The Memoirs of John Holland Jenkins*, John Holmes Jenkins III, Ed. (1958. Reprint, Austin: University of Texas Press, 1995), 239-40. Hereafter referenced as Jenkins, *Recollections*.

9. Webb (ed.), *The Handbook of Texas*, II: 229-30.

10. McLean, *Papers*, X: 43.

11. Jenkins, *Burleson*, 29-30; "Reminiscences of Joel W. Robison," 1872 *Texas Almanac*; DeShields, *Border Wars*, 99-100.

12. Jenkins, *Burleson*, 30; Jenkins, *Recollections*, 21-22; McLean, *Papers*, X: 43.

13. Jenkins, *Burleson*, 30-31; McLean, *Papers*, X: 44.

14. Brown, *Indian Wars*, 26.

15. McLean, *Papers*, X: 44-45.

16. DeShields, *Border Wars*, 116; McLean, *Papers*, X: 45.

17. McLean, *Papers*, X: 47; Jenkins, *Recollections*, 23.

18. Coleman to Rueg of July 20, 1835 in McLean, *Papers*, X: 465.

19. Jenkins, *Recollections*, 23 and 250.

20. Brown, *Indian Wars*, 26; *Lamar Papers*, George B. Erath to Lamar, "Sketches on Milam and Robertson County," IV: # 2164, 31.

21. McLean, *Papers*, XIII: 385 and X: 465.

22. Ibid., X: 47.

23. Webb (ed.), *The Handbook of Texas*, I: 369 and II: 787.

24. *Muster Rolls of the Texas Revolution* (Austin: Daughters of the Republic of Texas, 1986), 134-35.

25. Jenkins, *Burleson*, 31-32. Yoakum, Henderson. *History of Texas From its First Settlement in 1685 to its Annexation to the United States in 1846* (New York: Redfield Publishers, 1856. Reprint, Austin: Steck Company, 1935). Volume I: 352 lists only four company commanders who assembled their men at Tenoxtitlan: Captains Barnett, Coe, Moore, and Williamson. The service of Captain Goheen's rangers, however, is confirmed by republic documents.

26. Dixon, Sam Houston and Louis Wiltz Kemp. *The Heroes of San Jacinto* (Houston: The Anson Jones Press, 1932), 333.

27. McLean, *Papers*, X: 509.

28. M. R. Goheen AC, R 36, F 251.

29. Yoakum, *History of Texas*, I: 352 and McLean, *Papers*, X: 504.

30. Day, James M. (Compiler). *The Texas Almanac 1857-1873. A Compendium of Texas History* (Waco: Texian Press, 1967). William Isbell recollections

from original 1872 *Texas Almanac*.

31. McLean, *Papers*, X: 503.
32. Ibid., XIII: 385.
33. McLean, *Papers*, X: 48; Erath, George Bernard as dictated to Lucy A. Erath. *The Memoirs of Major George B. Erath, 1813-1891* (Austin: Texas State Historical Society, 1923. Reprint by the Heritage Society of Waco, 1956), 1-22. Hereafter referenced as Erath, *Memoirs*.
34. Erath, *Memoirs*, 23.
35. Ibid., 23-24.
36. Jenkins, *Recollections*, 24.
37. *Lamar Papers*, Erath to Lamar, "Sketches on Milam and Robertson County," IV: # 2164, 31-32.
38. William M. Eastland AC, R 28, F 251; George W. Lyons AC, R 63, F 387; William Connell AC, R 20, F 49.
39. Brown, *Indian Wars*, 26.
40. Jenkins, *Recollections*, 24-26.
41. Moses S. Hornsby AC, R 47, F 51.
42. Jenkins, *Recollections*, 25-26.
43. McLean, *Papers*, X: 507-509.
44. Yoakum, *History of Texas*, I: 352; also in McLean, *Papers*, X: 49.
45. Erath, *Memoirs*, 24-25.

Chapter 3
Frontiersmen of the Texas Revolution

1. Groneman, Bill. *Battlefields of Texas* (Plano: Republic of Texas Press, 1998), 28-32.
2. Jenkins, John Holland. *Papers of the Texas Revolution 1835-1836* 10 Vol. (Austin: Presidial Press, 1973). "Martin et al to Public," I: # 703. Hereafter cited as Jenkins, *Papers*.
3. Sowell, *Rangers*, 130.
4. Erath, *Memoirs*, 25.
5. *The New Handbook of Texas* (Austin: Texas State Historical Association, 1996, Six Volumes). "Goliad Campaign of 1835," 3: 209-14.
6. McLean, *Papers*, X: 47.
7. Ibid., XII: 31-32.
8. Ibid., XII: 32 and 103-104.
9. Jenkins, *Papers*, II: 159.
10. Ibid., II: 155-57, 161.
11. *New Handbook of Texas*, 3: 1; McLean, *Papers*, XIII: 103-104.
12. Moore, Stephen L. *Taming Texas: Captain William T. Sadler's Lone Star Service* (Austin: State House Press, 2000), 23.
13. Greenwood, Hulen M. *Garrison Greenwood: Ancestors and Descendants* (Privately published by author in Houston: 1986), 57-60.
14. Moore, *Taming Texas*, 27-32.

15. McLean, *Papers*, X: 47.
16. Wilbarger, *Indian Depredations*, 190-92.
17. Joseph A. Parker AC, R 80, F 529-30.
18. McLean, *Papers*, XII: 31.
19. Evan W. Faulkenberry PP, R 214, F 604-605.
20. Silas Parker to Council of November 2, 1835 in Jenkins, *Papers*, II: 303.
21. Silas H. Bates AC, R 202, F 316-20.
22. Silas M. Parker AC, R 80, F 566.
23. Webb (ed.), *The Handbook of Texas*, II: 842.
24. Daniel B. Friar AC, R 33, F 487-88 shows Wilkinson's 1835 service. For Hardin's account see Daniel B. Friar AC, R 33, F 491.
25. DeShields, *Border Wars*, 118-23.
26. Ibid., 122-23.
27. Ibid., 124.
28. Daniel B. Friar AC, R 33, F 491. Hardin's account was included with papers supplied to the Council on January 1, 1836 by Captain Friar, showing that this Indian encounter happened between November 19 and December 31, 1835. See also Stephen Jett PD, R 164, F 536-40.
29. Calvin B. Emmons AC, R 29, F 440-45.
30. *The New Handbook of Texas*, "Siege of Bexar," 1: 510.
31. Ibid., "Battle of Concepcion," 2: 255.
32. Ira Ingram to R. R. Royall in Jenkins, *Papers*, II: #1040.
33. *The New Handbook of Texas*, "Goliad Campaign of 1835," 3: 209-14.
34. Ibid., "Siege of Bexar," 1: 510.
35. Silas Parker to Council of November 2, 1835 in Jenkins, *Papers*, II: 303.
36. Gammel, (Karl) Hans Peter Marius Nielsen. *The Laws of Texas, 1822 - 1897* (Ten volumes. Austin: The Gammel Book Company, 1898), I: 50.
37. Ibid., I: 521.
38. See McLean, *Papers*, XII: 32; Gammel, *The Laws of Texas*, I: 525-27.
39. Gammel, *The Laws of Texas*, I: 525-27.
40. Jenkins, *Papers*, II: 360.
41. Gammel, *The Laws of Texas*, I: 928-34.
42. Ibid., I: 538-39.
43. Ibid., I: 924-25.
44. Ibid., I: 925-26.
45. Ibid., I: 954.
46. Ibid., II: 601.
47. Robinson, Duncan W. *Judge Robert McAlpin Williamson, Texas' Three-Legged Willie* (Austin: Texas State Historical Assn., 1948), 129.
48. McLean, *Papers*, XII: 35.
49. Ibid., XII: 385.
50. Ibid., XII: 35 and 388-89.
51. Robinson, *Judge Robert McAlpin Williamson*, 132-33.
52. *The New Handbook of Texas*, "Siege of Bexar," 1: 510.

53. Yoakum, *History of Texas*, II: 198-201.

Chapter 4
"Loathsome Trophy"

1. Jenkins, *Papers*, III: 230.
2. McLean, *Papers*, XII: 478.
3. Silas M. Parker AC, R 80, F 566.
4. Joseph A. Parker AC, R 80, F 529-30. Minor spelling corrections have been made.
5. Ibid., F 532-33.
6. L. D. Nixon AC, R 78, F 127.
7. McLean, *Papers*, XIII: 367.
8. James W. Parker AC, R 80, F 510. Due to the death of Captain Hillhouse and "owing to the massacre of Silas M. Parker he has been unable to procure the necessary vouchers" to show that he was duly elected as captain. Silas Parker was killed by Indians in 1836 during the Parker's Fort massacre.
9. McLean, *Papers*, XII: 35, 464, 476.
10. Jenkins, *Papers*, III: 258-60.
11. McLean, *Papers*, XII: 35-36.
12. Moore, *Taming Texas*, 5-20.
13. Pension papers of Daniel Crist and Samuel Wells; Moore, *Taming Texas*, 39-41.
14. Wells, Crist pension papers; see also John Robbins AC, R 88, F 269. See also "Statement of Mr. R. R. Sadler - Taken Down by Kate Hunter, June 20, 1923." Mary Kate Hunter Notebooks, Palestine, Texas. Robert Roach "Tab" Sadler, first grandchild of W. T. Sadler, was born in 1872, making him old enough to have heard his grandfather's stories firsthand. Tab Sadler stated that at the time his grandfather later heard of the Alamo's plight, he and a party of men "were working on the house."
15. Binkley, William C. *Official Correspondence of the Texan Revolution* 2 Vol. (New York: Appleton-Century, 1936). Greenwood to President of the Convention, I: 485.
16. Ennes Hardin from Daniel B. Friar AC, R 33, F 491.
17. Peterson Lloyd AC, R 61, F 513.
18. Daniel B. Friar AC, R 33, F 447-48; see also McLean, *Papers*, XII: 548-49.
19. Ennes Hardin account from Daniel B. Friar AC, R 33, F 491.
20. McLean, *Papers*, XII: 36; XIII: 60.
21. A study of William W. Arrington AC, R 3, F 614-35 shows no references to his involvement with the ranger service during the 1830s. For Mathew Caldwell's letter, see McLean, *Papers*, XII: 572.
22. McLean, *Papers*, XIII: 38.
23. DeShields, *Border Wars*, 126.
24. McLean, *Papers*, XIII: 38-39.
25. McLean, *Papers*, XIII: 40 and *Muster Rolls of the Texas Revolution*, 128-29.

26. McLean, *Papers*, XIII: 509 states that Captain Robertson's company was disbanded before March 1, 1836. See also XIII: 292.

27. McLean, *Papers*, XIII: 61 and 293-94.

28. Jenkins, *Papers*, IV: 50; Jenkins, *Burleson*, 95; McLean, *Papers*, XIII: 60.

29. James Edmundson PP, R 213, F 568. Smithwick, Noah. *The Evolution of a State; or, Recollections of Old Texas Days* (Austin: University of Texas Press, 1983), 82. Hereafter cited as Smithwick, *Evolution of a State*. In his memoirs, Noah Smithwick wrote that Tumlinson returned from recruiting and reported for duty "early in January, 1836." The company was then formally mustered into service on January 17 after rendezvousing at Hornsby's.

30. Hugh M. Childress AC, R 17, F 551.

31. McLean, *Papers*, XIII: 40-41.

32. Smithwick, *Evolution of a State*, 82.

33. Brown, *Indian Wars*, 89. Brown took his account of this action from "the exact language of Capt. Tumlinson, written for me" during the early 1840s. By Tumlinson's account, he only had eighteen rangers when the company was first organized at Hornsby's. Noah Smithwick wrote in his memoirs decades later that he was among this company of "sixty mounted men." Tumlinson's company was slated by the General Council to include up to fifty-six men. The struggle Major Williamson had with raising his regiment and the small number of audited claims filed for service with Captain Tumlinson cast heavy doubt that the company ever came close to reaching capacity enrollment.

34. DeShields, *Border Wars*, 167-68; Brown, *Indian Wars*, 89.

35. Brown, *Indian Wars*, 89-90. Tumlinson's account and that of Noah Smithwick are the two primary sources for this battle and each differs on certain details of this fight. Smithwick wrote that the rangers engaged the Indians at 10:00 a.m. versus 9:00 a.m. Tumlinson's letter to John Henry Brown was written in the early 1840s. Smithwick's memoirs were composed in California from his recollections in the late 1890s without the benefit of historical documents to help him fill in key dates and details.

36. Smithwick, *Evolution of a State*, 85-86. Smithwick writes that only one Indian was killed in this battle, while Tumlinson wrote that his men killed four. Smithwick also wrote that the Indian he had wounded was the one who fired the shot that nearly killed Captain Tumlinson. Tumlinson claims to have killed his own attacker, so Smithwick and Rohrer may likely have finished off a different Indian.

37. Brown, *Indian Wars*, 90; DeShields, *Border Wars*, 171; Jenkins, *Recollections*, 33, 241.

38. Smithwick, *Evolution of a State*, 86-87. Smithwick writes that the man attempting to kill the brave in the buffalo skin had his gun misfire twice. On the third attempt, another ranger realized that it was the young Hibbons boy in the buffalo skin and "knocked the gun up" at the last instant. The shot narrowly missed the boy and struck the mule.

39. Brown, *Indian Wars*, 90.

40. Clara Stearns Scarbrough account in McLean, *Papers*, XIII: 41-46.

41. Wilkins, *The Legend Begins*, 18.
42. James W. Parker AC, R 80, F 512.
43. L. D. Nixon AC, R 78, F 128.
44. Joseph A. Parker AC, R 80, F 530.
45. Silas M. Parker AC, R 80, F 566-68.
46. McLean, *Papers*, XIII: 335.
47. Ibid., XIII: 53-54, 338. For background of Captain Franks, see *New Handbook of Texas*, 2: 1156.
48. *New Handbook of Texas*, 2: 1156. DeShields, *Border Wars*, 144-45 quotes an early account by DeCordova that does not specifically name the commander of this company.
49. Jenkins, *Papers*, IV: 249-50.
50. Binkley, *Official Correspondence of the Texas Revolution*, I: 409.
51. Jenkins, *Papers*, IV: 250-51.
52. Binkley, *Official Correspondence of the Texas Revolution*, "Advisory Committee to J. W. Robinson," I: 426-27.
53. Robinson, *Judge Robert McAlpin Williamson*, 132.
54. Everett, Dianna. *The Texas Cherokees: A People Between Two Fires, 1819-1840* (Norman: University of Oklahoma Press, 1990), 67-69.
55. Woldert, Albert, M.D. "The Last of the Cherokees in Texas, and the Life and Death of Chief Bowles." *Chronicles of Oklahoma*, Issued by the Oklahoma Historical Society in Oklahoma City, Okla., Vol. I, No. 3, (June 1923): 179-226. Copy provided by Donaly E. Brice of the Texas State Archives, which included supplemental notes made by Woldert after the original publication of this article.
56. Everett, *The Texas Cherokees*, 71-73, 142.

Chapter 5
The Alamo's "Immortal Thirty-Two"

1. Lord, Walter. *A Time To Stand* (New York: Bonanza Books, 1961), 92-97.
2. "A Critical Study of the Siege of the Alamo," *Southwestern Historical Quarterly*, Vol. 37, No. 4 (April 1934), 305. Hereafter cited as "A Critical Study."
3. Lord, *A Time to Stand*, 100-107.
4. "A Critical Study," 306-307; Lord, *A Time to Stand*, 14-15, 107.
5. Byrd Lockhart AC, R 61, F 560-66.
6. *New Handbook of Texas*, 3: 1097.
7. "A Critical Study," 307; Lord, *A Time to Stand*, 125-27.
8. *New Handbook of Texas*, 3: 1097; Lord, *A Time to Stand*, 126-27.
9. Binkley, *Official Correspondence of the Texas Revolution*. "Williamson to Tomlinson," II: 453-54.
10. Smithwick, *Evolution of a State*, 87.
11. McLean, *Papers*, XIII: 75.
12. *New Handbook of Texas*, 1: 395; 3: 147.
13. Recollections of Albert Gholson's son Benjamin Franklin Gholson as

excerpted in McLean, *Papers*, IX: 378-81; *New Handbook of Texas*, 1: 395.

14. McLean, *Papers*, XIII: 516-17; XIV: 39. See also XII: 576-80 for information on the men of Graves' party.

15. Jenkins, *Papers*, X.

16. McLean, *Papers*, XII: 60-61, 93-96; XIII: 735.

17. Ibid., XIII: 487-89.

18. William C. Weatherred AC, R 111, F 217.

19. Lord, *A Time to Stand*, 108-117.

20. "A Critical Study," 307.

21. McLean, *Papers*, XIII: 558.

22. Williamson to Travis letter, March 1, 1836. This letter was apparently found on the body of Travis and was later published in Mexico. William N. Bonham research, courtesy of Ed Timms.

23. Sowell, *Rangers*, 136-44.

24. Groneman, Bill. *Alamo Defenders: A Genealogy, The People and Their Words* (Austin: Eakin Press, 1990). Captain Seguín was sent out on February 25 as a messenger and thus survived the slaughter at the Alamo.

25. Nevin, David. *The Texans* (The Old West Series) (1975. Reprint, Alexandria, Va: Editors of Time-Life Books, 1980). Isaac Millsaps letter printed on 96-97. It should be noted that Alamo historians have argued over the authenticity of this letter. Chariton, Wallace O. *Exploring the Alamo Legends* (Plano, Tex: Wordware Publishing, Inc., 1992). On pages 185-88, Chariton explores the Millsaps letter and the possibility of it being a skillful forgery.

26. Lord, *A Time to Stand*, 161-79, 205-206.

27. *New Handbook of Texas*, 3: 1097.

28. For the names of those on the centennial marker in Gonzales County, see *Gonzales County History*, published by the Gonzales County Historical Commission and Curtis Media Corp., 1986, 33-34. It does not, however, show Andrew Duvalt and Marcus L. Sewell. Both Duvalt and Sewell died in the Alamo and appear on the original February 23 muster roll of the Gonzales Mounted Rangers. John King was replaced by his son William Philip King before entering the Alamo. Robert White was already in the Alamo during February. It is possible that White went home to Gonzales during February and later returned to the Alamo with Kimbell's force. For biographical sketches and ages of the Gonzales men, see Bill Groneman, *Defenders of the Alamo*.

    See also "A Critical Study," 161-62, for a list of the Gonzales volunteers who entered the Alamo on March 1. The author of this piece studied records from the General Land Office, a March 24, 1836 entry of eighteen Gonzales men who died in the Alamo that was published in the *Telegraph & Texas Register*, and other various muster lists concerning the Alamo to make his deductions.

Chapter 6
The Road to San Jacinto

1. McLean, *Papers*, XIII: 54-55, 598. See also Thomas Pliney Plaster biographical sketch in L. W. Kemp Papers, San Jacinto Museum of History.

2. McLean, *Papers*, XIII: 600-604.

3. Ibid., XIV: 170.

4. *History of Houston County: 1687-1979* (Compiled and edited by the History Book Committee of Houston County Historical Commission of Crockett, Texas. Tulsa: Heritage Publishing Company, 1979), 618.

5. McLean, *Papers*, XIV: 151; XIV: 170-72.

6. Jenkins, *Recollections*, 45.

7. Tolbert, Frank X. *The Day of San Jacinto* (New York: McGraw-Hill Book Co., 1959), 45-46.

8. Webb (ed.), *The Handbook of Texas*, II: 456. Boyd, Bob. *The Texas Revolution: A Day-by-Day Account* (San Angelo: Standard-Times, 1986), 104-105.

9. Smithwick, *Evolution of a State*, 87-88.

10. McLean, *Papers*, XIII: 311.

11. Smithwick, *Evolution of a State*, 88-89.

12. McLean, *Papers*, XIII: 95-96.

13. Zuber, William Physick. *My Eighty Years in Texas* (Austin: University of Texas Press, 1971), 57-59. See also Dixon and Kemp's *The Heroes of San Jacinto*. Although this book mistakenly lists Spencer Townsend as captain of rangers, Kemp's biographical sketches on file at the San Jacinto Museum of History show that Kemp later realized that Spencer's brother Stephen Townsend was the actual company commander.

14. "Statement of Mr. R. R. Sadler - Taken Down by Kate Hunter, June 20, 1923." Mary Kate Hunter Notebooks, Palestine Library, Palestine, Texas.

15. Daniel Crist PP, R 211, F 19-23; Samuel Wells PP, R 244, F 650-54.

16. Records at Robbins' Crossing of the Trinity River show Sadler and seven of his men crossing on this date. Nathaniel Robbins AC, R 88, F 269. This was six days behind the Nacogdoches Volunteers company, which Sadler's men would soon enlist with.

17. Binkley, *Official Correspondence of the Texas Revolution*, Greenwood to President of the Convention, I: 485.

18. McLean, *Papers*, XIII: 707.

19. Nathaniel Robbins AC, R 88, F 269.

20. DeShields, James T. *Tall Men With Long Rifles* (San Antonio: Naylor Company, 1935), 102-10. DeShields quotes the Runaway Scrape account of Creed Taylor.

21. E. L. R. Wheelock AC, R 113, F 273. Wheelock's military papers do not specify which ranger company he became an officer in. Burton and his first lieutenant, however, are known to have moved ahead to join the fighting at San Jacinto. Most of the men under Burton's command prior to San Jacinto did not fight in the battle. This raises speculation that the larger part of his company was left under charge of Lieutenant Wheelock and Lieutenant

Colonel Bayne.

22. McLean, *Papers*, XIV: 31.

23. *New Handbook of Texas*, 1: 395; Recollections of Albert Gholson's son Benjamin Franklin Gholson as excerpted in McLean, *Papers*, IX: 378-81.

24. DeShields, *Border Wars*, 142; Brown, *Indian Wars*, 46.

25. Jenkins, *Papers*, "Rusk to Briscoe," V: # 2353.

26. Ibid., "Gates to Rusk," VI: # 3194.

27. Boyd, *The Texas Revolution*, 107-109.

28. Smithwick, *Evolution of a State*, 90-91.

29. William T. Sadler PP, R 237, F 95; Daniel Parker Jr. PP, R 232, F 300. The exact date that Sadler's rangers joined the army is believed to be March 20 or March 21, based on the recollections of William Zuber. In his memoirs, he recalled a group from Nacogdoches joining Sherman's other companies on the Colorado at DeWees Crossing on March 20. Sadler mentions several times in his pension papers having soon thereafter enlisted under Captain Leander Smith, which would have only been possible prior to April 1, 1836. Smith, whose company arrived at Sherman's post on March 25, was soon promoted to major of artillery on April 1.

Thus it appears that Sadler and his men joined up with Captain Smith about March 26 (the day that Smith's company arrived) and then were officially enrolled into Captain Hayden Arnold's Nacogdoches Volunteers on or about April 1. Many men serving under Hayden Arnold were later listed in military documents as having served with this company since its inception on March 6. Some of these men, such as Sadler, very clearly did not. His pension papers variously report his having joined Arnold or Smith's company anywhere from March 6 to April 8. One must note that many pension papers were filed in the 1870s, often without full military records available to verify precise dates of enlistment.

Daniel Parker Jr., for example, related in his pension papers that he was enrolled in Captain Arnold's company on the Colorado River, but stated that this was "on the sixth of March AD 1836." Clearly he took the date that the Nacogdoches Volunteers were originally mustered into service, not the date on which he joined them on the Colorado River.

Dixon and Kemp in *Heroes of San Jacinto* (344) report that Crawford Grigsby joined the Texas army about April 1, which fits with Captain Arnold's new command of the Nacogdoches Volunteers.

30. William C. Hallmark PP, R 218, F 640. Leander Smith served as "Major Artillery" from April 1 to April 17, 1836 (Leander Smith AC, R 130, F 218-20). He had previously been paid as captain of volunteers from March 13 to March 31, 1836. In studying the Nacogdoches Volunteers company more closely, I found new information I had not reported in *Taming Texas*, 45-53.

The Nacogdoches Volunteers were organized in their namesake town on March 6 and soon departed to join the Texas army. "The first captain elected to command our company was Leander Smith on the Trinity River near Robbins' Ferry," wrote Madison G. Whitaker in his pension papers (

Madison G. Whitaker PP, R 245, F 207). This date was March 13. Captain Smith's company then "joined the main army commanded by Gen. Houston on the Colorado River in the latter part of same month."

By March 23, the Nacogdoches Volunteers were at Cole's Settlement at the Asa Hoxey Plantation. There, Smith's men took on corn, fodder, and bacon, the receipt being signed by Hayden Arnold. (Asa Hoxey AC, R 48, F 158). Leander Smith was promoted on April 1. According to Whitaker, "In the Brazos bottom, Hayden Arnold was made Capt. and continued in service as such until our discharge."

As major of artillery, Smith mustered in Captain Alfred Henderson Wyly's thirty-five-man volunteer company on April 6 at Groce's Plantation on the Brazos River. (Kemp, Dixon, *Heroes of San Jacinto*, 447.) Many of these men were transferred into other companies prior to San Jacinto. Henry M. Brewer, Thomas Bailey, and Henry Chapman were shifted from Captain Wyly's to Captain Arnold's company.

31. Robinson, *Judge Robert McAlpin Williamson*, 144-45.
32. Ibid., 146.
33. Joseph Cottle AC, R 20, F 684. Ganey Crosby AC, R 21, F 744.
34. William Sherrod AC, R 95, F 405-406.
35. Daniel T. Dunham AC, R 27, F 382; Francis M. Weatherred AC, R 111, F 207-209.
36. Recollections of Albert Gholson's son Benjamin Franklin Gholson as excerpted in McLean, *Papers*, IX: 378-81. In his memoirs, Noah Smithwick states that Lieutenant Colonel Bayne's main party was close enough to hear the battle, so it is conceivable that Gholson's men might have arrived late in the day after the conflict had ensued. Albert G. Gholson AC, R 33, F 299-305.
37. John Dix AC, R 26, F 244.
38. Smithwick, *Evolution of a State*, 91.
39. Sylvanus Cottle AC, R 20, F 694.
40. Smithwick, *Evolution of a State*, 92.
41. Moses Townsend PD, R 191, F 460-63.

Chapter 7
Parker's Fort and Little River Depredations
1. Smithwick, *Evolution of a State*, 92.
2. Tolbert, *The Day of San Jacinto*, 192-93.
3. McLean, *Papers*, XIV: 277-78.
4. William C. Weatherred AC, R 111, F 217.
5. James P. Gorman AC, R 36, F 612; Felix W. Goff AC, R 36, F 237.
6. Pierce, Gerald Swetnam. *The Army of the Republic of Texas, 1836-1845*. Dissertation from the University of Mississippi, copyright 1964, on file in the Texas Room of the Houston Public Library, 47-51. Hereafter cited as Pierce, *Army*.
7. Binkley, *Official Correspondence of the Texas Revolution*, II: 879.

8. Francis M. Doyle AC, R 26, F 780.
9. Hugh M. Childress AC, R 17, F 551.
10. McLean, *Papers*, XIV: 34.
11. Smithwick, *Evolution of a State*, 100.
12. McLean, *Papers*, XIII: 302-303.
13. Jenkins, *Burleson*, 128 and Jenkins, *Papers*, "Rusk to Lamar," Vol VI: # 3039.
14. Wilbarger, *Indian Depredations*, 255-56.
15. Jenkins, *Recollections*, 45-46.
16. Wilbarger, *Indian Depredations*, 255-57.
17. "The Records of an Early Texas Baptist Church." *The Quarterly of the Texas State Historical Association*. Volume I (1833-1847) was published in Vol. XI, No. 2 issue of October 1907. See page 100.
18. McLean, *Papers*, XIV: 72.
19. For details of the Parker's Fort massacre, see DeShields, *Border Wars*, 155-58; also McLean, *Papers*, XIV: 75.
20. Plummer, Rachel (Parker). *Narrative of the Capture and Subsequent Sufferings of Mrs. Rachel Plummer* (Houston: 1839), 5-7.
21. McLean, *Papers*, XIV: 81-82.
22. DeShields, *Border Wars*, 158-59.
23. Brown, *Indian Wars*, 40 and DeShields, *Border Wars*, 159.
24. Wilbarger, *Indian Depredations*, 308-10.
25. McLean, *Papers*, XIV: 80-83 and 357-58.
26. Brown, *Indian Wars*, 40-43.
27. McLean, *Papers*, XV: 76.
28. James W. Parker AC, R 80, F 510-13.
29. James W. Parker AC, R 80, F 509. Silas Parker AC, R 80, F 571.
30. Pierce, *Army*, 53.
31. Captain Wilson and Lieutenant Colonel Bayne both signed the discharge papers of Private Joseph Clayton in Goliad on June 1 after he completed his three-month ranger service. See Joseph A. Clayton AC, R 18, F 245.
32. Jenkins, *Papers*, VI: 392 and McLean, *Papers*, XIV: 423.
33. McLean, *Papers*, XV: 148-49.
34. Pierce, *Texas Under Arms*, 110.
35. McLean, *Papers*, XIV: 239; XV: 188.
36. Ibid., XIV: 400; XIV: 118.
37. Jenkins, *Papers*, VII: 156.
38. McLean, *Papers*, XIV: 121.
39. Jenkins, *Papers*, VII: 155-56.
40. DeShields, *Border Wars*, 180-81.

Chapter 8
Burleson's Battalion

1. Cox, Mike. *Texas Ranger Tales II* (Plano: Republic of Texas Press, 1999), 2-3. For Rusk's orders to Burton, see Jenkins, *Papers*, VI: 410. Isaac Burton referred to his command as "3rd Co. Rangers" in the audited claims of Samuel M. Rayner, R 181, F 83-84.
2. Fehrenbach, T.R. *Lone Star: A History of Texas and the Texans* (Reprint, New York, NY: American Legacy Press, 1983), 242-43.
3. Samuel M. Rayner AC, R 181, F 83-84.
4. Yoakum, *History of Texas*, II: 300.
5. Jenkins, *Papers*, VI: 513-14.
6. Ibid., VII: 135-36.
7. Cox, *Texas Ranger Tales II*, 4-12.
8. Ibid., 8-9. Henderson Yoakum's 1855 *History of Texas* also contains a narrative of Isaac Burton's "horse marines" in Vol. II, 181-82.
9. Isaac W. Burton AC, R 14, F 36.
10. Audited military claims of Isaac W. Burton show that he was paid as "Captain of Rangers" from December 19, 1835, to June 24, 1836, and that he was then promoted to "Major of Rangers" and served as such up to September 24, 1836. Isaac W. Burton AC, R 14, F 40. For information on the split of the schooners' cargo, see Burton AC, R 14, F 11-14. For Captain Putnam, see Dickinson Putnam AC, R 85, F 135-42. See also Sylvanus Cottle AC, R 20, F 694.
11. Pierce, *Texas Under Arms*, 168.
12. Nance, Joseph M. *After San Jacinto: The Texas-Mexican Frontier, 1836-1841* (Austin: University of Texas Press, 1963), 10-13. Hereafter referenced as Nance, *After San Jacinto*.
13. Henry W. Karnes AC, R 55, F 501.
14. Pierce, *Army*, 59-61.
15. Nance, *After San Jacinto*, 17-18.
16. Jenkins, *Papers*, VII: 197-99.
17. Erath, *Memoirs*, 44-45. Erath states that he joined Robertson in May, although the actually date was more likely early June.
18. Jenkins, *Recollections*, 46-47.
19. DeShields, *Border Wars*, 178; Wilbarger, *Indian Depredations*, 231.
20. Wilbarger, *Indian Depredations*, 223, 232-33, 259; DeShields, *Border Wars*, 176-80.
21. Pierce, *Texas Under Arms*, 178.
22. Jenkins, *Burleson*, 131.
23. Ibid. Audited claims of Edward J. Blakey, Garett Boon, and Joseph Burleson of Captain McGehee's company place them at Colonel Burleson's farm.
24. Jesse Billingsley PP, R 247, F 476; also Jesse Billingsley AC, R 8, F 254.
25. Pierce, *Texas Under Arms*, 15; Jesse Billingsley AC, R 8, F 260.
26. "York, John," "Pettus, John Freeman," "Wertnzer, Christian Gotthelf," The

New Handbook of Texas Online.

27. Jenkins, *Recollections*, 43, 224.

28. John Litton AC, R 61, F 437. For an example discharge, see Hugh M. Childress AC, R 17, F 553.

29. Jenkins, *Recollections*, 192-96.

30. "A Critical Study," 174-75.

31. Elijah Gossett AC, R 36, F 643.

32. *New Handbook of Texas*, 1: 110.

33. William H. Smith AC, R 98, F 370-87. John W. Williamson AC, R 116, F 204-205.

34. Jenkins, *Papers*, VII: 432.

35. McLean, *Papers*, XIV: 129, 387-402, 557.

36. Jenkins, *Burleson*, 131-32. Spellman, Paul N. *Forgotten Texas Leader: Hugh McLeod and the Texan Santa Fe Expedition* (College Station: Texas A&M University Press, 1999), 22-23.

37. McLean, *Papers*, XIV: 130-31.

38. Spellman, *Forgotten Texas Leader*, 23.

39. Jenkins, *Recollections*, 192-96.

40. David Ayers AC, R 4, F 164.

41. Micah Andrews AC, R 3, F 72; Jacob S. Burleson AC, R 13, F 446; Joseph Burleson AC, R 13, F 469; John Y. Criswell AC, R 21, F 606; Edward Blakely AC, R 8, F 647; Samuel Craft AC, R 21, F 326; Moses Gage AC, R 34, F 41; F. W. Grasmeyer AC, R 37, F 70; James Rogers AC, R 89, F 494; Joseph Rogers AC, R 89, F 521-25; and Josiah Wilbarger AC, R 115, F 199.

42. McLean, *Papers*, XIV: 129, 240, 387-402.

43. Ibid., XV: 34-37, 108-109.

44. Ibid., XV: 39.

45. Wilbarger, *Indian Depredations*, 226-27. He states that only sixteen Texans escaped the fight with their lives and that many were wounded. Eight men were reportedly killed.

46. Ansel Darneill AC, R 24, F 83.

47. George W. Chapman AC, R 17, F 294; William A. McGrew AC, R 68, F 159; James McKinney AC, R 68, F 505-15; Daniel McKinney AC, R 68, F 500-505.

48. E. L. R. Wheelock AC, R 113, F 271.

49. Binkley, *Official Correspondence of the Texas Revolution*, II: 883, 887, 892-93.

50. Nance, *After San Jacinto*, 20-21, 46-47.

51. DeWitt C. Lyons AC, R 63, F 367 and George W. Davis AC, R 24, F 336. Pierce, *Texas Under Arms*, 169.

52. Felix W. Goff AC, R 36, F 235.

53. Burnet to Porter et al, Jenkins, *Papers*, VII: 511.

54. Daniel Elam AC, R 28, F 675.

55. Samuel Smith AC, R 98, F 194. Payment note is dated October 31, 1836.

Chapter 9
A Chain of Frontier Forts

1. This figure derived from adding known muster roll quantities and low-end estimates of company quantities for those companies that have no surviving muster roll. Numbers supporting these figures Smith (21), Putnam (20), Hill (50), McGehee (36), Boales (30), Barron (62), Walden (21), Thomas (18), Costley (57), Clapp (38), Jewell (45), York (20), and Billingsley (25).
2. McLean, *Papers*, XV: 35.
3. Jesse Webb AC, R 111, F 380.
4. McLean, *Papers*, XV: 36-38, 137-39.
5. Ibid., XIV: 560-61.
6. Stephen Eaton AC, R 28, F 294.
7. Binkley, *Official Correspondence of the Texas Revolution*, "Huston to Burleson," II: 917.
8. Jenkins, *Burleson*, 135.
9. Pierce, *Texas Under Arms*, 159.
10. "Biography of Cicero Rufus Perry, 1822-1898, Captain, Texas Rangers." From special collections of the Daughters of the Republic of Texas Museum, 5. See also Jenkins, *Recollections*, 193.
11. Horatio Chriseman AC, R 17, F 627.
12. DeShields, *Border Wars*, 149.
13. Jenkins, *Recollections*, 193-94.
14. "Biography of Cicero Rufus Perry," 5.
15. DeShields, *Border Wars*, 149.
16. Jenkins, *Recollections*, 194.
17. Binkley, *Official Correspondence of the Texas Revolution*, "Huston to Coleman," II: 919.
18. McLean, *Papers*, XV: 40.
19. Jenkins, *Papers*, IIX: 214-16; McLean, *Papers*, XV: 133-35.
20. McLean, *Papers*, XV: 40, 134; Noah Smithwick AC, R 98, F 476.
21. Smithwick, *Evolution of a State*, 108.
22. George W. Davis AC, R 24, F 341; Byrd B. Lockhart Jr. AC, R 61, F 567.
23. McLean, *Papers*, XV: 147.
24. Henry Wilson AC, R 116, F 553.
25. Smithwick, *Evolution of a State*, 108.
26. Pierce, *Texas Under Arms*, 33.
27. McLean, *Papers*, XV: 42, 147, 231.
28. Pierce, *Texas Under Arms*, 103.
29. George B. Erath AC, R 29, F 604. See also Lee R. Davis AC, R 24, F 528.
30. Erath, *Memoirs*, 46.
31. Jenkins, *Papers*, "Houston to Smith," IX: # 4119, 361.
32. *New Handbook of Texas*, 2: 348. Spellman, *Forgotten Texas Leader*, 14-23.
33. Jenkins, *Papers*, "Houston to Costley," IX: # 4118, 360; "Costley to Houston," IX: # 4127, 370-71; and "Houston to Raguet," IX: # 4158, 403.

34. Daniel B. Friar AC, R 33, F 499 and Isaac Parker AC, R 90, F 446.

35. Jenkins, *Papers*, "Houston to Clapp," IX: # 4211, 483.

36. Wimberly, Dan B. "Daniel Parker: Pioneer Preacher and Political Leader." A dissertation in history submitted to the Graduate Faculty of Texas Tech University; May 1995, pp. 239, 274-75. Although this report is signed "Daniel Parker Jr.," it was actually the elder Parker who compiled this document. In his dissertation on Daniel Parker, Dr. Dan B. Wimberly points out that in his early years in Tennessee Daniel Parker had been known as Daniel Parker Jr. and that this handwritten document "is plainly in the hand of Daniel Parker." Daniel Parker Sr., a pioneer preacher, political leader, and proponent of the frontier ranging system, was the father of Daniel Parker Jr., who had served as both a ranger and a soldier at San Jacinto.

37. Abram Anglin AC, R 3, F 133.

38. *Muster Rolls of the Texas Revolution*, 165-66. Roll signed by Costley in Nacogdoches on April 20, 1837.

39. Jenkins, *Papers*, "Browning to Houston," IX: # 4212, 483-84; *Writings of Sam Houston*, I: 497-98.

40. Ibid., Houston to Costley, IX: # 4215, 486.

41. Ibid., Houston to Lacy, IX: # 4216, 487.

42. Ibid., Houston to Jewel, IX: # 4223, 493.

43. James Madden AC, R 63, F 648.

44. Pierce, *Texas Under Arms*, 162-63.

45. Ladd, Kevin. *Gone to Texas: Genealogical Abstracts from "The Telegraph and Texas Register," 1835-1841* (Bowie, MD: Heritage Books, 1994), 12 (hereafter refered to as Ladd, *Gone to Texas*); DeShields, *Border Wars*, 209-10. DeShields lists this event as having occurred in 1837.

46. Jenkins, *Papers*, IX: "Burnet to Toby," # 4286, 62.

47. McLean, *Papers*, XV: 42, 51-52, 231.

48. Ibid., XV: 257. For Newton Duncan's account on Coleman's rangers see XIV: 552-53.

49. George B. Erath AC, R 29, F 617.

50. McLean, *Papers*, XV: 275.

51. Erath, *Memoirs*, 47-48.

52. Wilson T. Davidson's account contained in McLean, *Papers*, XV: 276-77. See also Pierce, *Texas Under Arms*, 94.

53. Erath, *Memoirs*, 48; McLean, *Papers*, XV: 276-77.

54. *Muster Rolls of the Texas Revolution*, 160; McLean, *Papers*, XV: 58.

55. Smithwick, *Evolution of a State*, 113.

56. Felix W. Goff AC, R 36, F 235.

57. Jesse Billingsley AC, R 8, F 257-60. Dixon and Kemp, *Heroes of San Jacinto*, 157.

58. Samuel Gochier AC, R 36, F 215-21; Jenkins, *Burleson*, 134-35; John Litton AC, R 61, F 437; Thomas O. Berry AC, R 8, F 17; James Crawford AC, R 21, F 439-41.

59. William Frels AC, R 33, F 421; Alexander Isbell AC, R 50, F 532; John H.

Isbell AC, R 50, F 552; and William Kuykendall AC, R 58, F 328.
60. Thomas R. Webb AC, R 111, F 407 and McLean, *Papers*, XV: 318-19.
61. William Connell AC, R 20, F 51; Jenkins, *Burleson*, 136.
62. McLean, *Papers*, XV: 65.
63. Gammel, *The Laws of Texas*, I: 1113-16.
64. Ibid., 1134.
65. William H. Smith AC, R 98, F 387.
66. Erath, *Memoirs*, 48.
67. Nance, *After San Jacinto*, 41-42.
68. Isaac Parker AC, R 80, F 438.
69. *Writings of Sam Houston*, I: 497; Pierce, *Texas Under Arms*, 72-73.
70. Washington Oakley AC, R 36, F 721.
71. Mary Kate Hunter Notebooks, Palestine Library, Palestine, Texas.
72. McLean, *Papers*, XII: 606; Ladd, *Gone to Texas*, 18.
73. McLean, *Papers*, XV: 80, 437.
74. Nance, *After San Jacinto*, 29-31.
75. Henry W. Karnes AC, R 55, F 505-509.
76. Huston, Cleburne. *Deaf Smith: Incredible Texas Spy* (Waco: Texian Press, 1973), 112-13. Hereafter referenced as Huston, *Deaf Smith*.
77. Roland, Charles P. *Albert Sidney Johnston, Soldier of Three Republics* (Austin: University of Texas Press, 1964), 66.
78. Pierce, *Texas Under Arms*, 123.
79. George W. Davis AC, R 24, F 341.
80. Wilkins, *The Legend Begins*, 46; Knowles, *They Rode for the Lone Star*, 64.

Chapter 10
Elm Creek and Trinity River Fights

1. Pierce, *Texas Under Arms*, 103-104.
2. Jesse Bailey AC, R 4, F 484.
3. William M. Eastland AC, R 28, F 244-62.
4. Erath, *Memoirs*, 48-49.
5. Brown, *Indian Wars*, 47.
6. Erath, *Memoirs*, 49-51.
7. DeShields, *Border Wars*, 200.
8. Erath, *Memoirs*, 51-53.
9. John Marlin AC, R 64, F 472.
10. DeShields, *Border Wars*, 201.
11. Smithwick, *Evolution of a State*, 113.
12. McLean, *Papers*, XV: 468.
13. Smithwick, *Evolution of a State*, 113.
14. Noah Smithwick AC, R 98, F 475.
15. Smithwick, *Evolution of a State*, 112-13.
16. Ibid., 149.

17. *History of Houston County: 1687-1979*. See pages 505 and 511. Letter of Daniel McLean to his son James McLean, who was attending school in Natchitoches, Louisiana. Due to the quality of such early grammar, the author has included minor editing.

18. DeShields, *Border Wars*, 204.

19. Primary sources for this Indian battle are Brown, *Indian Wars*, 56, and DeShields, *Border Wars*, 202-204. Quotes of Abram Anglin are taken from his account in the *Groesbeck Argus*, which DeShields also quotes.

20. William S. Fisher in Columbia to Major Jewell, February 13, 1837. Army Correspondence, Box 1214-16, Texas State Library and Archives Commission.

21. Adrin Anglin AC, R 3, F 128-30. It is unclear whether Adrin Anglin was an alternate spelling for Abram Anglin.

22. John Sheridan AC, R 95, F 254, 258 and 266.

23. John Sheridan AC, R 95, F 256.

24. See John Wilson AC, R 116, F 595 as an example.

25. *Writings of Sam Houston*, II: 232-35.

26. Wylie, Edna McDonald. "The Fort Houston Settlement." A thesis from August 1958 in the collections of the Houston Public Library's Clayton Genealogy Branch, 36.

27. Pierce, *Texas Under Arms*, 102. Albert Gholson PD, R 35, F 306.

28. Erath, *Memoirs*, 46.

29. DeShields, *Border Wars*, 194-95.

30. Ibid., 185, 191-92.

31. Wilbarger, *Indian Depredations*, 15-19; DeShields, *Border Wars*, 193.

Chapter 11
Spring Setbacks for Smith's Battalion

1. Abram Anglin AC, R 3, F 125.

2. Pierce, *Texas Under Arms*, 64-66.

3. Lee C. Smith AC, R 98, F 59-63.

4. Rice autobiographies in McLean, *Papers*, XV: 446, 475.

5. Ibid., XV: 448.

6. Huston, *Deaf Smith*, 113.

7. Francis W. White AC, R 113, F 480.

8. Huston. *Deaf Smith*, 113.

9. Francis W. White AC, R 113, F 476.

10. Huston, *Deaf Smith*, 112-14.

11. Official report of Capt. Erastus Smith to Secretary of War W. S. Fisher of March 27, 1837; published in the *Telegraph and Texas Register* on April 11, 1837. Other Smith quotes given in this account from this source.

12. Nance, *After San Jacinto*, 34.

13. Huston, *Deaf Smith*, 115-16.

14. Francis W. White AC, R 113, F 476-80.

15. Huston, *Deaf Smith*, 116-17.

16. See *Telegraph and Texas Register* of April 11, 1837.

17. Webb (ed.), *The Handbook of Texas*, II: 622.

18. Huston, *Deaf Smith*, 117-18.

19. Roland, *Albert Sidney Johnston*, 59-70.

20. The killing of Colonel Teal is discussed in the biography of James Matthew Jett, Kemp Papers, San Jacinto Museum of History, Houston, Texas. Jett was also killed in his sleep by John Schultz years later. For state of the army, see Nance, *After San Jacinto*, 37.

21. Pierce, *Texas Under Arms*, 21.

22. Greer, James Kimmins. *Texas Ranger: Jack Hays in the Frontier Southwest* (College Station: Texas A&M University Press, 1993), 24-25. This book was originally published as *Colonel Jack Hays: Texas Frontier Leader and California Builder* in 1952.

23. George B. Erath AC, R 29, F 617.

24. John Angel AC, R 3, F 93.

25. For the account of this battle, see Smithwick, *Evolution of a State*, 113-14.

26. Nicolas Wren AC, R 118, F 313-23.

27. Smithwick, *Evolution of a State*, 132; DeShields, *Border Wars*, 194.

28. Smithwick, *Evolution of a State*, 115.

29. Pierce, *Texas Under Arms*, 71-72, 175.

30. Seguín, Juan N. *A Revolution Remembered. The Memoirs and Selected Correspondence of Juan N. Seguin.* Jesus F. de la Teja, Ed. (Austin: State House Press, 1991), 159-69.

31. Smithwick, *Evolution of a State*, 116-17.

32. McLean, *Papers*, XV: 517.

33. *Lamar Papers*, Erath to Lamar, "Sketches on Milam and Robertson County," IV: # 2164, 32.

34. Tyler, George W. *The History of Bell County* (San Antonio: The Naylor Company, 1936), 52-53. Tyler is also quoted in McLean, *Papers*, XV: 511-12.

35. McLean, *Papers*, XV: 516-17.

36. Jesse Bailey AC, R 4, F 484.

37. Sowell, *Texas Indian Fighters*, 299, lists Smith as one of the casualties. His account was written many years later, however. DeShields, *Border Wars*, 215, uses Sowell's version.

38. McLean, *Papers*, XV: 90.

39. John Sheridan AC, R 95, F 248.

40. DeShields, *Border Wars*, 131.

41. McLean, *Papers*, XV: 522.

42. *History of Houston County*, 223A-C; 504-505; 564-65.

43. McLean, *Papers*, XV: 89-90.

44. *Lamar Papers*, Erath to Lamar, "Sketches on Milam and Robertson County," IV: # 2164, 32.

45. McLean, *Papers*, XIV: 553.

46. DeShields, *Border Wars*, 204.
47. Scott, Zelma. *A History of Coryell County, Texas* (Austin: Texas State Historical Association, 1965), 24-25.
48. DeShields, *Border Wars*, 205.
49. *Lamar Papers*, Erath to Lamar, "Sketches on Milam and Robertson County," IV: # 2164, 32-33.

Chapter 12
Stone Houses Fight

1. McLean, *Papers*, XV: 94-95, 553, 561-62.
2. Nance, *After San Jacinto*, 41-42; Gammel, *The Laws of Texas*, I: 1334-35.
3. Dixon and Kemp, *Heroes of San Jacinto*, 312.
4. Ladd, *Gone to Texas*, 35.
5. Smithwick, *Evolution of a State*, 117-19.
6. John Litton AC, R 61, F 440; Joseph Duty AC, R 28, F 63.
7. Thomas H. Eaton AC, R 28, F 299.
8. John D. Brown AC, R 12, F 89.
9. Smithwick, *Evolution of a State*, 123-32.
10. Ibid., 138-41.
11. Henry Wilson AC, R 116, F 553.
12. Micah Andrews AC, R 3, F 68; Smithwick, *Evolution of a State*, 141.
13. John L. Lynch AC, R 63, F 283. Samuel K. Blisk AC, R 8, F 741 shows that on August 19, 1837 Lieutenant Lynch was "Commanding" at least a detachment of men at Fort Houston. These papers were also signed by Major William Smith. For service of Lieutenant Chapman, see George W. Chapman AC, R 17, F 290-91.
14. Noah Smithwick AC, R 98, F 474-76; Smithwick, *Evolution of a State*, 140-42.
15. Alfred Eaton AC, R 28, F 286; Ansel Darneill AC, R 24, F 80.
16. Goldsby Childers AC, R 17, F 527-28.
17. Ladd, *Gone to Texas*, 34-35.
18. McLean, *Papers*, XVI: 147.
19. Jenkins, *Recollections*, 243.
20. McLean, *Papers*, XV: 96, 577.
21. DeShields, *Border Wars*, 188; McLean, *Papers*, XVI: 191-92.
22. Blount, Lois, "A Brief Study of Thomas J. Rusk Based on His Letters to His Brother, David, 1835-1856," *Southwestern Historical Quarterly* XXXIV (April 1931): 278-79.
23. McLean, *Papers*, XVI: 44-45.
24. Martin Walker AC, R 108, F 586; Abram Anglin AC, R 3, F 125.
25. Lee R. Davis AC, R 24, F 525; Calvin B. Emmons AC, R 29, F 446 and 452; George B. Erath AC, R 29, F 617.
26. Lieutenant Vanbenthuysen's report published in *Telegraph and Texas Register*, December 23, 1837, and in *Lamar Papers*, I: 592-95. See also McLean,

Papers, XVI: 195-97. His report is the key source for this campaign, except as otherwise noted.

27. *Lamar Papers*, Erath to Lamar, "Sketches on Milam and Robertson County," IV: # 2164, 32; Sowell, *Ranger*, 40-41; Wilbarger, *Indian Depredations*, 192-95.

28. *Lamar Papers*, Erath to Lamar, "Sketches on Milam and Robertson County," IV: # 2164, 33.

29. Addison Litton AC, R 61, F 427-31.

30. Smithwick, *Evolution of a State*, 143.

31. McLean, *Papers*, XVI: 198.

32. DeShields, *Border Wars*, 211.

33. Wilbarger, *Indian Depredations*, 195.

34. Vanbenthuysen's *Telegraph and Texas Register* Report; see also McLean, *Papers*, XVI: 196. In his report, Vanbenthuysen lists one of the wounded men as simply "Bliss." The only man in service with Major Smith's battalion with a name that matches was Samuel K. Blisk. Formerly a corporal of Captain Walden's Company A, he served as a private in Captain Andrew's Company C during 1837. Blisk was stationed at Fort Houston on the Colorado as of August 19, 1837, and served in Smith's ranger battalion through March 8, 1838. Samuel K. Blisk AC, R 8, F 738-41. Noah Smithwick recorded Corporal Blisk's name as "Blish" in his memoirs (Smithwick, *Evolution of a State*, 149).

35. Jenkins, *Recollections*, 181.

36. Mann, William L. "James O. Rice, Hero of the Battle on the San Gabriels." *SWHQ*, Vol. 55 (July 1951) 32.

37. Ladd, *Gone to Texas*, 48.

38. Jenkins, *Burleson*, 149; Ladd, *Gone to Texas*, 45.

39. DeShields, *Border Wars*, 214-15 and Wilbarger, *Indian Depredations*, 238, 261-62. Jenkins, *Recollections*, 46, 263-64.

40. Wilbarger, *Indian Depredations*, 262.

41. Elisha Anglin AC, R 3, F 139.

42. John L. Lynch AC, R 63, F 283-87.

43. Reuben Hornsby AC, R 47, F 66-74.

44. Pierce, *Texas Under Arms*, 157.

45. DeShields, *Border Wars*, 189; McLean, *Papers*, XVI: 75-76, 306-308.

46. Henry W. Karnes AC, R 55, F 496.

47. Wilbarger, *Indian Depredations*, 195.

48. Vanbenthuysen report previously cited.

Bibliography

Documents, Manuscripts, and Collections

Aldrich, Armistead Albert. Papers. Center for American History, University of Texas, Austin.

Appendix to the Journals of the House of Representatives: Fifth Congress. Printed at the Gazette Office for the Republic of Texas, Austin, 1841.

Army Papers, Republic of Texas. Archives and Library Division, Texas State Library in Austin, Texas.

"Biography of Cicero Rufus Perry, 1822-1898. Captain, Texas Rangers." Special collections of Daughters of the Republic of Texas Library, San Antonio, Texas.

Bishop, Eliza H. John Wortham Biographical Sketch.

Edens, Dr. Frank N. Unpublished research on Daniel Parker family.

General Land Office of Texas: records and papers collection.

Hunter, Mary Kate. Unpublished Papers of, located in Carnegie Library in Palestine, Texas. Miss Hunter was a schoolteacher who collected statements in the early 1900s from many of the county's earliest citizens. Some of her collected works are referenced, including, "Statement of Mr. R. R. Sadler - Taken Down by Kate Hunter, June 20, 1923"; "Some Early History of Palestine" by Bonner Frizzell; and Judge A. J. Fowler's "The Edens' Massacre" and "Historic Sketches of Anderson County."

Journals of the Fourth Congress of the Republic of Texas. Austin, Tex: Von Boeckmann-Jones Co. Printers, 1930.

Muster Rolls of the Texas Army and the Texas Militia, courtesy of the Texas State Archives. See individual chapter footnotes and appendices for those referenced.

Nicholson, James. Papers. Center for American History, University of Texas, Austin.

Pierce, Gerald Swetnam. *The Army of the Republic of Texas, 1836-1845.* Dissertation from the University of Mississippi, copyright 1964, on file in the Texas Room of the Houston Public Library.

"Report of K. H. Douglass of the Campaign Against the Cherokees," August 1839. Courtesy of Donaly E. Brice, Texas State Library and Archives Commission.

Republic Claims Papers, 1835-1846 (microfilmed). Texas State Library and Archives Commission, Austin.

Rusk, Thomas Jefferson. Original Papers of. East Texas Research Center in Stephen F. Austin State University Library, Nacogdoches.

Sadler, Robert H. "Notes Relative to the Edens Massacre." Written on January 1, 1971. "Facts related to Robert H. Sadler by Lula Sadler Davis of Grapeland, Texas, widow of John A. Davis." Courtesy of Howard C. Sadler collection.

Sadler, William Turner. Texas Pension Papers and Audited Military Claims. Provided courtesy of Howard C. Sadler.

Starr, James Harper. Papers. Center for American History, University of Texas, Austin. Includes papers of Brigadier General Kelsey H. Douglass.

Uniform of the Army of the Republic of Texas. Prescribed and published by order of the President.

Wimberly, Dan B. "Daniel Parker: Pioneer Preacher and Political Leader." History dissertation submitted to the Graduate Faculty of Texas Tech University in May 1995. Courtesy of Dr. Frank N. Edens.

Wylie, Edna McDonald. "The Fort Houston Settlement." A thesis from August 1958 in the collections of the Houston Public Library's Clayton Genealogy Branch.

Articles

Barker, Eugene C. (editor). "Journal of the Permanent Council." *The Quarterly of the Texas State Historical Association*. Vol. 7 (1904).

Benedict, J. W. "Diary of a Campaign against the Comanches." *Southwestern Historical Quarterly*. Vol. 32 (April 1929): 300-10.

Blount, Lois. "A Brief Study of Thomas J. Rusk Based on His Letters to His Brother, David, 1835-1856." *Southwestern Historical Quarterly*, XXXIV (April 1931).

Brown, Jennifer. "Their Spirits Still Live On Battleground: Indian Group Buys East Texas Site of Famed Battle of Neches." *Tyler Morning Telegraph*, (December 14, 1997).

Chriesman, Horatio. "Reminiscences of Horatio Chriesman." *The Quarterly of the Texas State Historical Association.* Vol. 6 (1903).

"A Critical Study of the Siege of the Alamo," *Southwestern Historical Quarterly*, Vol. 37, No. 4 (April 1934).

Crosby, David F. "Texas Rangers in The Battle of Brushy Creek." *Wild West*, Vol. 10, No. 2, (August 1997): 60-64, 89-90.

Fuquay, John W. "The Smith Family." *Tyler Today* (Summer 1996), 24-26. Courtesy of the Smith County Historical Society.

Henderson, Harry McCorry. "The Surveyors' Fight." *Southwestern Historical Quarterly*, Vol. 56 (July 1952), 25-35.

Hiatt, James. "James Parker's Quest." *Wild West*, Vol. 3, No. 3 (October 1990): 10, 16, 62-63.

Johnson, Norman K. "Chief Bowl's Last Charge." *Wild West*, Vol. 2, No. 2 (August 1989): 12-16, 62-66.

Jones, Ernest. "Captain W. T. Sadler Helped Create County."*Palestine Herald-Press*, (February 5, 1969): 10.

Looscan, Adele B. "Capt. Joseph Daniels." *Texas Historical Association Quarterly*, Vol. V, No. 1 (1901-1902): 19-21.

Mann, William L. "James O. Rice, Hero of the Battle on the San Gabriels." *Southwestern Historical Quarterly*, Vol. 55 (July 1951): 30-42.

Pierce, Gerald S. "Burleson's Northwestern Campaign." *Texas Military Monthly*. Fall 1967, Vol. 6, No. 3: 191-201.

Reagan, John Hunter. "Expulsion of the Cherokees from East Texas." *Quarterly of the Texas State Historical Association*, Vol. I (1897): 38-46.

"The Records of an Early Texas Baptist Church." *The Quarterly of the Texas State Historical Association*. Volume I (1833-1847) of the church's history is published in the Vol. XI, No. 2 issue of October 1907 and Volume II (1847-1869) is published in Vol. XII, No. 1 of July 1908.

"Recollections of S. F. Sparks." *Quarterly of the Texas State Historical Association*. XII: No. 1 (July 1908).

"Sadler Descendant of County Pioneer." *Palestine Herald-Press*, (January 10, 1975).

Telegraph and Texas Register. See source notes from individual chapters for dates between 1836 and 1839 copied from microfilm in the Texas Room of the Houston Public Library.

Timms, Ed. "Remembering More of the Alamo Defenders." *The Dallas Morning News*, Friday, March 1, 2002.

Wilcox, S. S. "Laredo During the Texas Republic." *Southwestern Historical Quarterly*, Vol. 42, No. 2 (1939): 83-107.

Winfrey, Dorman. "Chief Bowles of the Texas Cherokee." *Chronicles of Oklahoma* 32 (Spring 1954): 29-41.

Woldert, Albert, M.D. "The Last of the Cherokees in Texas, and the Life and Death of Chief Bowles." *Chronicles of Oklahoma*, Issued by the Oklahoma Historical Society in Oklahoma City, Okla., Volume I, Number 3 (June 1923): 179-226. Copy provided by the Texas State Archives, which included supplemental notes made by Woldert after the original publication of this article.

Yates, Becky. "Historical Date Line: Edens-Madden Massacre." The East Texas Roundup, Crockett, Texas (December 17, 1970): 6. Courtesy of Howard C. Sadler.

Books

Aldrich, Armistead Albert. *History of Houston County, Texas, Together with Biographical Sketches of Many Pioneers*. San Antonio: The Naylor Co., 1943.

Avera, Carl. *Centennial Notebook: A Collage of Reminenece of Palestine's First Century*. Palestine: Royall National Bank, 1976.

Barker, Eugene C. *The Life of Stephen F. Austin, Founder of Texas, 1793-1836*. Austin: University of Texas Press, 1985.

Bate, W. N. *General Sidney Sherman: Texas Soldier, Statesman and Builder*. Waco: Texian Press, 1974.

Binkley, William C. *Official Correspondence of the Texan Revolution 1835-1836*. 2 Vols. New York: Appleton-Century, 1936.

Biographical Directory of the Texan Conventions and Congresses, 1832-1845. Austin: Book Exchange, 1941.

Biographical Gazetteer of Texas. Austin: W. M. Morrison Books, 1987.

Boyd, Bob. *The Texas Revolution: A Day-by-Day Account*. San Angelo: Standard-Times, 1986.

Brice, Donaly E. *The Great Comanche Raid: Boldest Indian Attack of the Texas Republic*. Austin: Eakin Press, 1987.

Brown, Gary. *Volunteers in the Texas Revolution: The New Orleans Greys*. Plano: Republic of Texas Press, 1999.

Brown, John Henry. *Indian Wars and Pioneers of Texas*. 1880. Reprint, Austin: State House Press, 1988.

Carter, W. A. *History of Fannin County, Texas*. Bonham: Bonham News, 1885. Reprint, Honey Grove, Texas: Fannin County Historical Society, 1975.

Chariton, Wallace O. *Exploring the Alamo Legends*. Plano: Republic of Texas Press, 1992.

Cherokee County History. Jacksonville, Texas: Cherokee County Historical Commission and the Publications Development Co. of Texas, 1986.

Clark, Sara. *The Capitols of Texas: A Visual History*. Austin: Encino Press, 1975.

Clarke, Mary Whatley. *Chief Bowles and the Texas Cherokees*. Civilization of the American Indian Series, No. 113. Norman: University of Oklahoma Press, 1971.

_____. *Thomas J. Rusk: Soldier, Statesman, Jurist*. Austin: Jenkins Publishing Company, 1971.

Connor, Seymour V. *Battles of Texas*. Waco: Texian Press, 1987.

_____, et. al. *Capitols of Texas*. Waco: Texian Press, 1970.

Cox, Mike. *Texas Ranger Tales II*. Plano: Republic of Texas Press, 1999.

Day, James M. *Post Office Papers of the Republic of Texas, 1836-1839*. Austin: Texas State Library, 1966.

_____ (Compiler). *The Texas Almanac 1857-1873. A Compendium of Texas History*. Waco: Texian Press, 1967.

De Bruhl, Marshall. *Sword of San Jacinto: A Life of Sam Houston*. New York: Random House, 1993.

DeShields, James T. *Border Wars of Texas*. 1912. Reprint, Austin: State House Press, 1993.

_____. *Tall Men with Long Rifles*. San Antonio: Naylor Company, 1935.

Dixon, Sam Houston and Louis Wiltz Kemp. *The Heroes of San Jacinto*. Houston: Anson Jones Press, 1932.

Dooley-Aubrey, Betty and Claude Dooley. *Why Stop? A Guide to Texas Historical Roadside Markers*, 4th Ed. Houston: Lone Star Books, 1999.

The Edens Adventure: A Brief History of the Edens Family in America. Addison: Edens Family Association, 1992.

Erath, George Bernard as dictated to Lucy A. Erath. *The Memoirs of Major George B. Erath, 1813-1891*. Austin: Texas State Historical Society, 1923. Reprint, Waco: The Heritage Society of Waco, 1956.

Ericson, Carolyn Reeves. *Nacogdoches—Gateway to Texas: A Biographical Directory*, Vol. I. Nacogdoches: Ericson Books, 1991.

Everett, Dianna. *The Texas Cherokees: A People Between Two Fires, 1819-1840*. Norman: University of Oklahoma Press, 1990.

Exley, Jo Ella Powell. *Frontier Blood. The Saga of the Parker Family*. College Station: Texas A&M University Press, 2001.

Fehrenbach, T. R. *Lone Star: A History of Texas and the Texans*. New York: American Legacy Press, 1983.

Ford, John Salmon. *Rip Ford's Texas*. Stephen B. Oates, Ed. Austin: University of Texas Press, 1994.

Gambrell, Herbert. *Anson Jones: The Last President of Texas*. 10 Vol. 1947. Reprint, Austin: University of Texas Press, 1988.

Gammel, (Karl) Hans Peter Marius Nielsen. *The Laws of Texas, 1822 - 1897*. Ten volumes. Austin: The Gammel Book Company, 1898.

Greenwood, Hulen M. *Garrison Greenwood: Ancestors and Descendants*. Houston: privately published, 1986.

Greer, James Kimmins. *Texas Ranger: Jack Hays in the Frontier Southwest*. College Station: Texas A&M University Press, 1993. This book was originally published by E.P. Dutton and Company, Inc. as *Colonel Jack Hays: Texas Frontier Leader and California Builder* in 1952.

Groneman, Bill. *Alamo Defenders: A Genealogy, The People and Their Words*. Austin: Eakin Press, 1990.

_____ . *Battlefields of Texas*. Plano: Republic of Texas Press, 1998.

Hatley, Allen G. *The Indian Wars in Stephen F. Austin's Texas Colony, 1822-1835*. Austin: Eakin Press, 2001.

History of Gonzales County, Texas. Published by Gonzales County Historical Commission and Curtis Media Corp., 1986.

History of Houston County: 1687-1979. Compiled and edited by the History Book Committee of Houston County Historical Commission of Crockett, Texas. Tulsa: Heritage Publishing Company, 1979.

Hohes, Pauline Buck. *A Centennial History of Anderson County, Texas*. San Antonio: Naylor, 1936.

Houston, Samuel. *The Personal Correspondence of Sam Houston. Volume I: 1839-1845*. Madge Thornall Roberts, Ed. Denton: University of North Texas Press, 1996.

_____ . *Writings of Sam Houston, 1813-1863*. Amelia W. Williams and Eugene C. Barker, Ed. Austin: University of Texas Press, 1938-43.

Huston, Cleburne. *Deaf Smith: Incredible Texas Spy*. Waco: Texian Press, 1973.

_____ . *Towering Texan: A Biography of Thomas J. Rusk*. Waco: Texian Press, 1971.

Jenkins, John H. and Kenneth Kesselus. *Edward Burleson: Texas Frontier Leader*. Austin: Jenkins Publishing Co., 1990.

Jenkins, John Holland. *The Papers of the Texas Revolution 1835-1836.* 10 Vol. Austin: Presidial Press, 1973.

_____ . *Recollections of Early Texas. The Memoirs of John Holland Jenkins.* John Holmes Jenkins III, Ed. 1958. Reprint, Austin: University of Texas Press, 1995.

Knowles, Thomas W. *They Rode for the Lone Star. The Saga of the Texas Rangers: The Birth of Texas - The Civil War.* Dallas: Taylor Publishing Company, 1999.

Koury, Michael J. *Arms for Texas: A Study of the Weapons of the Republic of Texas.* Fort Collins, Colo.: Old Army Press, 1973.

Ladd, Kevin. *Gone to Texas: Genealogical Abstracts from "The Telegraph and Texas Register," 1835-1841.* Bowie, MD: Heritage Books, 1994.

Lamar, Mirabeau B. *The Papers of Mirabeau Buonaparte Lamar,* 6 Vol. Charles A. Gulick Jr., Winnie Allen, Katherine Elliott, and Harriet Smither, Ed. 1922. Reprint, Austin: Pemberton Press, 1968.

Lane, Walter Paye. *The Adventures and Recollections of General Walter P. Lane.* Austin: Pemberton Press, 1970.

Lord, Walter. *A Time To Stand.* New York: Bonanza Books, 1961.

McLean, Malcolm D. *Papers Concerning Robertson's Colony in Texas.* 18 Vol. Fort Worth: Texas Christian University Press, 1993.

Memorial and Biographical History of Navarro, Henderson, Anderson, Limestone, Freestone and Leon Counties, Texas. Chicago: Lewis, 1893.

Miller, Thomas Lloyd. *Bounty and Donation Land Grants of Texas: 1835-1888.* Austin: University of Texas Press, 1967.

Moore, Stephen L. *Taming Texas. Captain William T. Sadler's Lone Star Service.* Austin: State House Press, 2000.

Muster Rolls of the Texas Revolution. Austin: Daughters of the Republic of Texas, 1986.

Nacogdoches County Families: Texas Sesquicentennial, Vol. I. Nacogdoches County Genealogical Society. Dallas: Curtis Media Corporation, 1985.

Nance, Joseph M. *After San Jacinto: The Texas-Mexican Frontier, 1836-1841.* Austin: University of Texas Press, 1963.

Nevin, David. *The Texans* (The Old West Series). 1975. Reprint, Alexandria, Va: Editors of Time-Life Books, 1980.

The New Handbook of Texas. 6 Vol. Austin: Texas State Historical Association, 1996.

Newcomb, W. W. Jr. *The Indians of Texas: From Prehistoric to Modern Times.* Austin: University of Texas Press, 1961.

Neyland, James. *Palestine (Texas): A History.* Palestine: Empress Books.

Nichols, James W. *Now You Hear My Horn. The Journal of James Wilson Nichols, 1820-1887.* McDowell, Catherine W., Ed. Austin: University of Texas Press, 1968.

Pierce, Gerald Swetnam. *Texas Under Arms. The Camps, Posts, Forts, and Military Towns of the Republic of Texas 1836-1846.* Austin: Encino Press, 1969.

Pioneer Families of Anderson County Prior to 1900. Palestine: Anderson County Genealogical Society, 1984. *Supplement to Pioneer Families of Anderson County Prior to 1900.* Palestine: Anderson County Genealogical Society, January 1991.

Plummer, Rachel (Parker). *Narrative of the Capture and Subsequent Sufferings of Mrs. Rachel Plummer.* Houston: 1839.

Pohl, James W. *The Battle of San Jacinto.* Austin: Texas State Historical Association, 1989.

Powell, Mrs. Doris Daniel. *The Genealogy of Laban Menefee.* Compiled for Hugh Alva Menefee Jr. Cleburne: Privately published, 1972.

Procter, Ben H. *Not Without Honor: The Life of John H. Reagan.* Austin: University of Texas Press, 1962.

Purcell, Robert Allen. *The History of the Texas Militia.* Austin: University of Texas Press, 1981.

Ramsay, Jack C. Jr. *Thunder Beyond the Brazos: Mirabeau B. Lamar, a Biography.* Austin: Eakin Press, 1985.

Ray, Worth S. *Austin Colony Pioneers. Including History of Bastrop, Fayette, Grimes, Montgomery and Washington Counties, Texas.* Austin: Pemberton Press, 1970.

Reagan, John H. *The Memoirs of John H. Reagan.* John F. Jenkins, Ed. Austin: Pemberton Press, 1968.

Republic of Texas Pension Application Abstracts. John C. Barron, et.al. Ed. Austin Genealogical Society. Austin: Morgan Printing and Publishing, 1987.

Richardson, Rupert N. *Texas, The Lone Star State.* New York: Prentice-Hall, 1943.

Robinson, Charles M. III. *The Men Who Wear the Star: The Story of the Texas Rangers.* New York: Random House, 2000.

Robinson, Duncan W. *Judge Robert McAlpin Williamson, Texas' Three-Legged Willie.* Austin: Texas State Historical Association, 1948.

Roland, Charles P. *Albert Sidney Johnston, Soldier of Three Republics.* Austin: University of Texas Press, 1964.

Seguín, Juan N. *A Revolution Remembered. The Memoirs and Selected Correspondence of Juan N. Seguin.* Jesus F. de la Teja, Ed. Austin: State House Press, 1991.

Scott, Zelma. *A History of Coryell County, Texas.* Austin: Texas State Historical Association, 1965.

Smithwick, Noah. *The Evolution of a State; or, Recollections of Old Texas Days.* Austin: University of Texas Press, 1983.

Sowell, A. J. *Texas Indian Fighters. Early Settlers and Indian Fighters of Southwest Texas.* 1900. Reprint, Austin: State House Press, 1983.

_____ . *Rangers and Pioneers of Texas.* 1884. Reprint. Austin: State House Press, 1991.

Spellman, Charles E. Ed. *The Texas House of Representatives: A Pictorial Roster, 1846-1992.* Austin: The House, 1992.

Spellman, Paul N. *Forgotten Texas Leader: Hugh McLeod and the Texan Santa Fe Expedition.* College Station: Texas A&M University Press, 1999.

Stroud, Harry A. *Conquest of the Prairies.* Waco: Texian Press, 1968.

Thompson, Karen R. (Editor). *Defenders of the Republic of Texas.* Austin: Daughters of the Republic of Texas via Laurel House Press, 1989.

Tolbert, Frank X. *The Day of San Jacinto.* New York: McGraw-Hill Book Co., 1959.

Tyler, George W. *The History of Bell County.* San Antonio: The Naylor Company, 1936.

Wallace, Ernest, David M. Vigness and George B. Ward. *Documents of Texas History.* Austin: State House Press, 1994.

Webb, Walter Prescott (Editor-in-Chief). *The Handbook of Texas.* 3 Vol. Austin: Texas State Historical Association, 1952.

_____ . *The Texas Rangers; A Century of Frontier Defense.* Austin: University of Texas Press, 1991.

White, Gifford. *1830 Citizens of Texas.* Austin: Eakin Press, 1983.

_____ . *The 1840 Census of the Republic of Texas.* Austin: Pemberton Press, 1966.

_____ . *1840 Citizens of Texas.* Nacogdoches: Erickson Books, 1988.

Wilbarger, John Wesley. *Indian Depredations in Texas.* 1889. Reprint, Austin: State House Press, 1985.

Wilkins, Frederick. *The Legend Begins: The Texas Rangers, 1823-1845.* Austin: State House Press, 1996.

Winchester, Robert Glenn. *James Pinckney Henderson, Texas' First Governor.* San Antonio: The Naylor Company, 1971.

Winfrey, Dorman, and James M. Day. *The Texas Indian Papers, 1825-1843.* Four volumes. Austin: Austin Printing Co., 1911.

Yoakum, Henderson. *History of Texas From its First Settlement in 1685 to its Annexation to the United States in 1846.* Two volumes. New York: Redfield Publishers, 1856. Reprint, Austin: Steck Company, 1935.

Zuber, William Physick. *My Eighty Years in Texas.* Austin: University of Texas Press, 1971.

Index

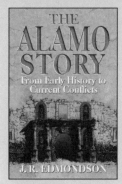

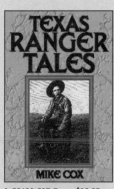

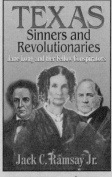
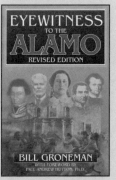